WITHDRAWN FROM STOCK

Two Paths, One Purpose: Voluntary Action in Ireland, North and South

A Report to the Royal Irish Academy's
Third Sector Research Programme

NICHOLAS ACHESON
BRIAN HARVEY
JIMMY KEARNEY
ARTHUR WILLIAMSON

D1427615

IPA

INSTITUTE OF PUBLIC
ADMINISTRATION

First published 2004
by the
Institute of Public Administration
57–61 Lansdowne Road
Dublin 4
Ireland

© The authors

Laois County Library
Leabharlann Chontae Laoise

Acc. No. ...0S/5756...

Class N. ...361.7...

Inv. No. ...7891

All rights reserved. No part of this publication may be reproduced or transmitted in any form or by any means, electronic or mechanical, including photocopy, recording or any information storage and retrieval system, without permission in writing from the publisher.

ISBN 1 904541 12 7

British Library Cataloguing-in-Publication Data
A catalogue record for this book is available from the British Library

Cover design by Slick Fish Design, Dublin
Typeset by Computertype Limited, Dublin
Printed in Ireland by ColourBooks

Contents

Introductory Notes

This is the first document to attempt, on an all-Ireland basis, to: identify the common roots of voluntary action in the two parts of the island; provide a common information base for the voluntary sector across the whole island; identify voluntary sector research; provide comparable databases; and compare and contrast the different policy environments for the voluntary sector, north and south.

Although the voluntary sector in both parts of the island has reached high levels of political influence (for example, the Community Pillar in the process of social partnership in the Republic, and the Northern Ireland Council for Voluntary Action and its role in shaping the Northern Ireland Executive's *Programme for Government* 2001), no one has yet compared these political journeys, nor their outcomes. The level of information exchange is low; critical analysis has been minimal; serious information deficits exist and there has been little engagement between voluntary action researchers and policy-makers. Furthermore, as yet there has been little comparative research into the role and work of the sectors in the two jurisdictions.

Accordingly, the research project of which this book is the report was undertaken to help to close some of the main information gaps in our knowledge of the voluntary sector, north and south, and to encourage a virtuous circle for the exchange of information, research, analysis, ideas and knowledge that would serve the voluntary sectors and the governments of both jurisdictions for the next number of years.

Despite growing co-operation in other fields between both parts of the island, the voluntary sector's experience of joint working has so far been poorly developed. The main areas of joint working thus far include exchanges between individual organisations (for example, as sponsored by Co-operation Ireland), and *ad hoc* liaison between umbrella bodies, north and south. Some cross-border partnerships have been developed in recent times, largely sponsored by the Programme for Peace and Reconciliation (e.g. Cross-Border Childcare Initiative; the Simon Community's cross-border project on homelessness) and by the Programme of Common Interest operated by the Combat Poverty Agency (e.g. Community Workers Co-operative/ Northern Ireland Council for Voluntary Action (NICVA)).

Since 1997 voluntary sector researchers have come together under the banner of AVARI (The Association for Voluntary Action Research in Ireland) to share the findings from their research and to consider how to promote and support the study of civil society in Ireland, north and south.

Specifically, this book:
- maps the voluntary sectors, north and south, setting them in the broader framework of the British Isles and the European Union

- sets the historical context for the development of the two sectors, outlining how their paths converged and diverged from 1922 to 2000
- explains the institutional architecture in which the two sectors work, such as government departments, government agencies, health boards, District Partnerships, relationships with political system, funding systems
- describes the policy, legislative and regulatory basis for the sector in each part of the island and the respective systems of governance and accountability
- compares and contrasts government policy (e.g. *Strategy for the Development of the Voluntary Sector and Community Development in Northern Ireland*, 1993, *Supporting Voluntary Activity in the Republic*, 2000)
- makes a direct comparison of the two sectors in such key areas as size, share of Gross National Product, staffing, volunteering, fields of activities, main fields of activities of the most prominent organisations, evidence of federation, networking, funding sources (government, private, European), and research done, under way or proposed
- notes and lists examples of good practice that may be of value to the other jurisdiction
- compares the respective levels of development of the two sectors and draws conclusions about how and why the paths of the two voluntary sectors diverged and converged, why different or similar models developed and why their evolution took the forms they did
- draws overall conclusions, lessons and issues arising. This returns to the key questions facing the voluntary sector in both parts of the island and how they can learn from each other to face common challenges.

Methodology

The research was carried out in the course of 2002–3 using a range of methods. We reviewed the wide literature about the history of voluntary action and on recent developments affecting the voluntary and community sector in both jurisdictions. We assembled and analysed documentation providing information about what is known at present about the sector and its constituent parts. We interviewed key people in the voluntary sector and others with special knowledge of the development of the sector and its relations with government. These included policy-makers, voluntary sector leaders and academic experts; their names are listed below.

Advisory group

An advisory group was formed to assist in the research. This was divided into a northern and a southern panel. Each of the panels was convened at the beginning of the project to advise on research sources and to propose people for interview. Each member of the advisory group was interviewed in order to gain from his or her expert knowledge. Each panel member received the draft report for comment. The help and guidance of the members of the advisory panel was invaluable.

Northern Ireland advisory panel
Mr Dave Wall, Voluntary and Community Unit, Department for Social Development
Mr Seamus McAleavey, Northern Ireland Council for Voluntary Action
Ms Avila Kilmurray, Community Foundation for Northern Ireland
Mr Niall Fitzduff, Rural Community Network
Dr Duncan Morrow, Northern Ireland Community Relations Council/University of Ulster

Republic of Ireland advisory panel
Dr Sarah Craig, National Economic and Social Forum
Dr Gemma Donnelly-Cox, Centre for Non-Profit Management, Trinity College, Dublin
Dr Fergus O'Ferrall, Adelaide Hospital Society
Professor Fred Powell, University College Cork

Note on terminology
This book covers two jurisdictions: Northern Ireland and southern counties of the island. How best to describe the latter presents problems. The term 'Republic of Ireland' has no constitutional standing, but it is a term in wide usage and has the advantage of being convenient, clear and well understood. Accordingly, it will be used here. Where the phrase 'Ireland' is used, it is employed as a geographical term to apply to the whole island of Ireland.

Acknowledgements
The authors wish to acknowledge and thank the Royal Irish Academy for its financial support for our research. They also acknowledge with thanks the assistance of the following people who contributed by personal interview or telephone interview or by the provision of documentary information and in other ways.

Mr Derek Bacon, Centre for Voluntary Action Studies, University of Ulster
Mr Jonathan Bewley, The Bewley Foundation
Prof. Derek Birrell, School of Policy Studies, University of Ulster

Ms Anne Boyle, South Eastern Health Board
Ms Dymphna Bracken, Midland Health Board
Mr David Brennan, Department of Community, Rural and Gaeltacht Affairs
Dr Rosanne Cecil, Copy Editing Consultancy
Ms Alma Clissman, The Law Society
Ms Mary Conboy, North Western Health Board
Ms Breda Crehan Roche, Midland Health Board
Ms Geraldine Donaghy, Director, Newry Confederation of Community
    Groups
Dr Freda Donoghue, Dublin University, Trinity College, Dublin
Ms Anne-Marie Donohue, East Coast Area Health Board
FÁS
Ms Therese Fitzgerald, Mid-Western Health Board
Ms Annette Fitzpatrick, Midland Health Board
Ms Catherine Fitzpatrick, Mid-Western Health Board
Ms Gillian Gallagher, Commissioners of Charitable Donations and
    Bequests, Dublin
Ms Deirdre Garvey, The Wheel
Mr David Gordon, North Eastern Health Board
Mr Edgar Graham, Lurgan Council for Voluntary Action
Mr Pat Healy, Southern Health Board
Mr Roger Healy, South Western Area Health Board
Fr Seán Healy, Conference of the Religious in Ireland
Ms Susan Hodgett, Queen's University, Belfast
Ms Louisa Hooper, Gulbenkian Foundation
Mr Tom Kelly, North Western Health Board
Ms Helen Kilbane, Western Health Board
Ms Helen Lahert, Comhairle
Ms Jane Leek, Derwent Charitable Consultancy
Ms Mary Maguire, North Eastern Health Board
Prof. John Morison, Department of Law, Queen's University, Belfast
Dr Mike Morrissey, Senior Lecturer, University of Ulster
Mr Gordon McCullough, Director of Research, Northern Ireland Council
    for Voluntary Action
Mr Paddy McDonald, Mid-Western Health Board
Mr Peter McEvoy, Midland Health Board
Ms Geralyn McGarry, Comhairle
Dr Aideen McGinley, Permanent Secretary, Department of Culture, Arts
    and Leisure, Belfast
Mr Eadoin McHugh, Irish Youth Foundation
Mr Kieran McLoughlin, Ireland Funds
Ms Liz McNeill, Centre for Voluntary Action Studies, University of Ulster

Mr David Mullins, Centre for Urban and Regional Studies, University of Birmingham

Ms Tríona Nic Giolla Choille, Galway Refugee Centre

Mr Quintin Oliver, Director, Stratagem, Belfast

Mr Bill Osborne, Director, Voluntary Services Belfast

Prof. Séamus Ó Cinnéide, National University of Ireland, Maynooth

Ms Margaret O'Donovan, Southern Health Board

Mr Liam O'Dwyer, Irish Youth Foundation

Dr Kerry O'Halloran, Centre for Voluntary Action Studies, University of Ulster

Ms Anne O'Reilly, Director, Help the Aged, Belfast

Ms Pauline O'Shaughnessy, Department of Justice, Equality and Law Reform

Dr Eoin O'Sullivan, Dublin University, Trinity College

Ms Kate O'Sullivan, Carmichael Centre

Ms Ursula O'Sullivan, Southern Health Board

Ms Mary Lee Rhodes, School of Business, Trinity College, Dublin

Mr Paul Robinson, North Eastern Health Board

Ms Tina Roche, Community Foundation of Ireland

Ms Noelle Spring, Katharine Howard Foundation

Dr Bill Smith, Department of Health, Social Services and Public Safety, Belfast

Ms Heather Swailes, Allen Lane Foundation

Mr Paul Sweeney, Department for Regional Development, Belfast

Ms Mary Upton TD

Voluntary and Community Unit, Department for Social Development, Belfast

Ms Alison Wightman, Community Change, Belfast

Nicholas Acheson
Brian Harvey
Jimmy Kearney
Arthur Williamson

Centre for Voluntary Action Studies,
University of Ulster,
Coleraine

1

Common and Diverging Histories:
the Context of Voluntary Action in Ireland
to 1922

Introduction

The first three chapters will sketch the historical development of the voluntary sector in both parts of Ireland. Our central objective is to bring together what is known about voluntary and community organisations in Ireland in a single and relatively accessible source for practitioners and policy-makers in both jurisdictions. However, behind the study lies the question of the extent to which voluntary and community action and organisations are embedded in the same political, economic and social structures as other aspects and institutions in society, in particular the state itself.

In the European context, Ireland presents a particularly interesting case study. Prior to the break up of Yugoslavia and the so-called 'velvet divorce' of the Czech Republic and Slovakia in 1994, Ireland was the only instance in Europe of the splitting of a single administration into two separate jurisdictions that nevertheless continued to adhere to a similar model of a liberal economy and state. We believe a study of the way civil society developed in the two jurisdictions since 1922 will help illuminate and contribute to a more general discussion of the ways in which civil society is itself structured and given an institutional form.

The puzzle as to why and in what ways the institutions of civil society vary from one state to another has provided us with the structure for this study. Chapter one will present an introductory discussion of the broad contemporary context for the voluntary sector – briefly what it is, how it defines itself, why it is important and how it fits in to modern notions of citizenship, human capital, social capital and governance, especially within a European context. But the main focus is to establish the baseline as to how matters stood in 1922. To what extent were differences already evident in the parts of Ireland that were to form the two new jurisdictions and to what extent were matters the same or at least similar? Information on the development of voluntary and philanthropic organisations in Ireland prior to 1922 is thus brought together – what were they and what were their features?

Chapters two and three then examine key points in the development of the voluntary sector in each jurisdiction respectively, and the principal influences and formative factors at work therein. These parallel narrative accounts take the reader up to the contemporary situation. Chapters four and five present the current formal, legislative and institutional arrangements that shape the relationships between the two state apparatuses and the voluntary sectors in both jurisdictions respectively. Contemporary public policy in respect of the voluntary sector is discussed.

A map of the contemporary voluntary sector in Northern Ireland is presented in chapter six, and in the Republic of Ireland in chapter seven. These chapters bring together what is currently known about voluntary and community organisations in Ireland, relating this to the policy and historical context where this is judged helpful and illuminating. The study is completed in chapter eight where points of comparison are analysed and discussed.

The forms of voluntary action, as with other social institutions, have unfolded within the context of the development of Irish history. It may be helpful for locating the historical accounts in chapters two and three to have an overview of where the key developments in the history of voluntary action in Ireland are located in the broader story of Irish history. A summary timeline is provided in Table 1.

Defining the voluntary sector

We have had to address from the start the tricky and unresolved issue of definition. What should and what should not be included in the class of organisations and institutions that make up the voluntary sector and comprise voluntary action? This matter is not readily resolved and there is no common set of definitions to apply to equivalent sets of organisations in both parts of Ireland and which we could use for comparisons.

Rather than devise a wholly new formula, we have adopted a pragmatic approach and relied on a reasonably satisfactory set of definitions already in existence. *State of the Sector III* (NICVA, 2002) uses a definition which is well suited to our requirements and has the double advantage that it provides a valuable map of the sector for Northern Ireland, and one that is adaptable to what is known of the sector in the Republic. The *State of the Sector III* definition is based on an amended version of the classification used by three bodies: the Charity Commission, the Office for National Statistics, and the International Classification of Non-Profit Organisations (ICNPO) developed for international comparative purposes by the Johns Hopkins University in Baltimore, Maryland. Between them, they propose that the voluntary sector is understood to comprise bodies that are:

- self-governing
- independent (excluding non-departmental public bodies, educational establishments)

- non-profit making
- benefiting from a meaningful degree of philanthropy
- for wider public benefit (excluding bodies that exist solely for their own members)
- non-sacramental (but including activities of public benefit performed by religious organisations, for example in the area of social services).

It should be noted, however, that this is a rather narrow definition and does not capture all aspects of voluntary action that may be found in civil society. The wider public benefit and non-sacramental criteria not only exclude the denominational churches and many aspects of self-help, like credit unions, but also many sports associations, a particularly important aspect of Irish voluntary action. The classification also deals rather unsatisfactorily with social movements. As a result, we admit to an element of inconsistency, particularly in relating the historical material where we have tended to take cognisance of a wider range of forms of voluntary action than the definition strictly allows. Despite these reservations, the ICNPO and *State of the Sector III* frameworks are those used in this report.

The European context and the rediscovery of civil society
Developments in the voluntary sector in both parts of Ireland should now be seen in a European political and philosophical context. Traditionally, the European Communities took a limited view of their roles and competencies, restricting them to a broad range of economic affairs and a narrower range of social issues. This began to change in the 1990s. Under the presidency of Jacques Delors, the European Union pitched for a broader range of policy-making, with the white paper *Growth, Competitiveness and Work* (1993) and its companion in social policy *European Social Policy – A Way Forward for the Union* (1994). A successful implementation of these social policies necessarily involved an engagement with civil society in general and the world of associations in particular. This was formalised when the Treaty of Maastricht (1992) adopted, in declaration 23, a phrase recognising the importance of 'charitable associations and foundations as institutions responsible for welfare establishments and services'.

The Maastricht declaration 23, combined with the white paper on social policy, paved the way for a growing European Union interest in questions of citizenship. This was a perilous area for European policy-making, for it necessitated the defining of concepts of European citizenship and civil society, demarcating them from traditional and exclusive areas of national competence. The Commission established a Comité des Sages which issued a report, *For a Europe of Civic, Social and Political Rights* (1996). This proposed

Table 1. Summary chronology of historical context of the development of voluntary action in Ireland

Main events in Irish history	Main events in the development of Irish voluntary action
1603: End of the Irish Elizabethan wars and the 'flight of the earls', followed by the plantation of Ulster	1634: First charities legislation by the Irish Parliament
1650s: Oliver Cromwell in Ireland	
1798: Rebellion of the United Irishmen	
1800: Abolition of the Irish parliament and the Act of Union between Great Britain and Ireland	1838: Irish Poor Law
	1844: Charitable Donations and Bequests Act (Ireland)
	1898: Local Government (Ireland) Act established country councils
1920: Government of Ireland Act. Establishing two jurisdictions in Ireland	
1921: Treaty between Britain and Ireland, establishing the Irish Free State and Northern Ireland	
1922/23: Civil War in Ireland	
1937: New constitution in Irish Free State	
1939/45: Second World War. The south of Ireland remains neutral, Northern Ireland a full participant in United Kingdom war effort	1948: Health Services Act (Northern Ireland National Assistance Act (Northern Ireland)
1949: Irish Free State becomes a republic	1949: Welfare Services Act (Northern Ireland)
1968/72: Outbreak of the 'Troubles' in Northern Ireland	1993: Publication by government in Northern Ireland of the *Strategy for Support of the Voluntary Sector and for Community Development*
1972: Proroguing of Northern Ireland parliament and the introduction of 'direct rule' from London	
1972: Both the United Kingdom and the Republic of Ireland join the European Economic Community (EEC)	1998: Publication of the *Compact between Government and the Voluntary and Community Sector in Northern Ireland*
1998: The signing of the 'Good Friday' agreement	2000: Publication by the Irish government of the white paper *Supporting Voluntary Activity*

the intensifying of social partnership with non-governmental organisations.

Coinciding with the completion of the single market, the European Commission announced in 1992 that it would prepare a policy paper on the role of the voluntary sector in the Union. It was eventually published as the Commission Communication, *On Promoting the Role of Voluntary Organisations and Foundations in Europe* (1997). This acknowledged the role that voluntary organisations played in employment creation, active citizenship, democracy, social inclusion, representing civic interests to the public authorities, and promoting human rights and global development. The Commission also published a draft common statute for European associations, which was designed to ensure that a voluntary organisation registered in one state could legally function automatically in another, matching legislation for co-operatives and mutual societies.

A landmark in the process of European engagement with civic society was the European white paper on governance (European Commission, 2001). The European network of voluntary organisations concerned with community development pressed the European Union to use the opportunity of the white paper as a means of redefining the relationship between the Union and the citizen in terms of civic engagement, the right of people to participate in decisions affecting them from the lowest to the highest level and to take a bottom-up approach to decision-making (Combined European Bureau, 2000). Preparatory documents for the white paper visualised a role for mass social movements in European politics in the future. The white paper endorsed and put forward the principle that Europe should be governed on common lines of openness, participation and subsidiarity. Civil society organisations (which the Commission defined to include the social partners, non-governmental organisations (NGOs), professional associations, charities, grass-roots organisations, and organisations that involved citizens in local and municipal life (including churches and religious communities)) must have platforms to change policy and society, with structured channels for feedback, criticism and protest. Overall, though, the Union has been unadventurous in its involvement of NGOs until the present time, eschewing formal structures and consulting unevenly with them.

The European Union, as noted earlier, pursued economic lines of development as its principal means of social integration. Social policy took a secondary role, at least until the 1990s. As a result, the interface between the Union and the voluntary sector tended to reflect the latter's role in the economy more than in social policy. The role of social economy organisations was recognised, the Commission even at one stage forming a social economy unit. The Essen guidelines, drawn up by the member states at their summit in Germany in 1993, referred to the importance of local initiatives in the social, economic and environmental sphere and the importance of the social economy. The subsequent annual economic guidelines, drawn up following the Luxembourg jobs summit in 1997, valued local economic development including the social economy. The European Commission has articulated, in a series of reports, the ways in which social economy organisations build local social capital, promote social inclusion, develop citizenship and spur economic development (Committee of the Regions, 2002). In 1997, the Commission launched a 'third sector and employment initiative', funding 81 social economy projects to develop the potential of voluntary organisations in promoting European economic and social objectives at local level. The subsequent evaluation found that these projects played an important role both in job creation and in promoting social inclusion (ECOTEC, 2001).

The value of non-governmental action has achieved a certain level of recognition among European Union funding programmes. Of the many budget lines funded by the Commission for internal operations, several are dedicated to and ring-fenced for NGOs, by far the largest being in the area of Third World development. The programmes against poverty initiated in 1975 were predicated on the ability of the Commission to enlist the involvement of NGOs. With the reform of the structural funds, some of the Community Initiative Programmes were built around non-governmental participation (e.g. HORIZON, NOW, EQUAL). In some national programmes, there was provision for funding to go to 'community infrastructure' (e.g. the Physical and Social Environment Programme in Northern Ireland 1994-9). The Commission also introduced the concept of the global grant in the mainstream structural funds and this was used, through Area Development Management in the Republic of Ireland, to stream additional resources into the non-governmental sector and area-based partnerships (see chapter three). With the Programme for Peace and Reconciliation (1995-9), the Commission used intermediary funding bodies for the delivery of the programme, some being closely associated with or linked to NGOs. The Commission wished to extend its funding for the non-governmental community further, unsuccessfully proposing in 1999 that the next round of the structural funds set a minimum floor of funding to go to the sector (1 per cent). NGOs continue to press for a more active role in planning, delivery, monitoring and evaluation of the funds (Harvey, 1999a).

In both the United Kingdom and in Ireland there have been developments in government policy towards the respective national voluntary sectors that reflect this context. These will be discussed in more detail in chapters four and five. As we shall show, Northern Ireland, reflecting the United Kingdom policy context has had a much longer history of explicit government policy towards voluntary action than has the Republic of Ireland. However, it is striking how policy in both jurisdictions has been converging around an emphasis on the role of voluntary action in achieving and maintaining social inclusion in contemporary societies. This is a central theme in the Irish Government's white paper on voluntary action of 2000. It has also formed a core part of the social policy approach of the Labour Party administration that has been in power in the United Kingdom since 1997 and is fully reflected in current government policy in Northern Ireland, having been endorsed by the Northern Ireland Executive during its life.

Two particularly influential sets of ideas have underpinned these developments. First has been the influence of 'communitarianism' which has called for the remoralising of society and emphasised the necessity of community for the achievement of human dignity and self-realisation (Etzioni, 1993). At its core has been a concern to emphasise the responsibilities of citizens for civic engagement and the maintenance of community. The Communitarians' analysis and prescription for change developed in the late 1980s and early 1990s as a rejection of what were seen as the undesirable consequences of neo-liberal governments in both the USA and the United Kingdom. They represent an attempt to steer a path between neo-liberalism and a, by then discredited, Marxism and were highly influential in shaping policy of the first Labour Government in the United Kingdom after 1997. Communitarian ideas have been identified as being a key influence in the reconsideration of the British Labour Party's views on public ownership.

Second has been the popularising of the concept of social capital, a new Atlantic and European paradigm that has proved useful for the analysis of voluntary activity. The concept has been defined in a number of different ways. At its core is the idea that successful societies are able to draw on shared norms, networks and trust. These are generated and sustained through associational activity. Its most important populariser, the American academic Robert Putnam, has argued that these aspects of society are generated through voluntary associations that encourage what he called horizontal linkages between people that can be applied flexibly for collective problem solving. Putnam's arguments have had a remarkable degree of acceptance among politicians and policy-makers on both sides of the Atlantic, notwithstanding the efforts of critics who have questioned both his definition of social capital and the use to which he has put the concept in diagnosing contemporary social problems (Healy, 2001).

These controversies go to the heart of a comparative analysis of voluntary action in the two jurisdictions in Ireland and thus it may be helpful to state the issues at stake very briefly. In *Making Democracy Work: Civic Traditions in Modern Italy* (Putnam, Leonardi and Nanetti, 1993), Putnam argued that healthy democratic institutions and effective administrative arrangements were generated by, and depended upon, the richness of social capital which was in turn generated by the richness of associational life. Voluntary action, in this view thus underpins successful and responsive government. Not so, say his critics (Tarrow, 1996). They argue that he has misunderstood Italian history in his analysis and that the Italian evidence points to the opposite conclusion – that broader processes of state building and economic development generate voluntary action and associational life. In his next book, *Bowling Alone*, published in 2000, Putnam charts the decline of social capital and civic life in the USA, a decline that he views as dangerous to the health of the democratic system of government. Putnam's analysis of social trends has been questioned, but if his critics are right, then whatever trends in voluntary action are evident are themselves largely the consequences of large-scale economic change and the state's response to that change, rather than, as Putnam argues, changes in cultural practices.

The Irish case offers an interesting commentary on these arguments. Putnam's introduction of the concept of social capital as a vital ingredient in successful modern societies is based on an analysis of differences in the development of Northern and Southern Italy after the unification of the country in the 1860s. In Ireland, the opposite process has occurred. A single administrative unit was split in 1922 into two jurisdictions, each of which, for the ensuing 60 years, looked elsewhere for models of economic and social development. If Putnam is correct, then we would expect to find differences in how the two jurisdictions have developed to be grounded in differences in associational life and the extent of social capital generated by that associational life. However, if Putnam's critics are right, then any differences that are to be found in associational life in the two jurisdictions are much more likely to be the consequence of the process of state and institution building in each jurisdiction.

Given this context, the first task is to try and establish a baseline. How did voluntary action develop in Ireland prior to 1922 and, at that date, what were the similarities and differences in the extent and form of voluntary action in the areas that were to become the two separate jurisdictions? This chapter will present a common framework for the development of voluntary action in Ireland up to 1922. It will offer some tentative conclusions on the extent to which differences were already evident by that date.

Many students of voluntary action now see voluntary action in Ireland and Britain not just in a European, but in a global perspective. Salamon, the pioneer of international comparative studies of the voluntary sector, has written about what he describes as a 'massive global associational revolution in every corner of our planet' (Salamon and Anheier, 1998b). That this associational revolution has become part of the philosophical mainstream may be seen in the writing of contemporary theorists such as Hardt and Negri (2001), who foresee an important place for the non-governmental sector in the new, early twenty-first century global, post-Fordist and post-modern society.

Historians such as O'Ferrall (2001) trace the role of voluntary action in the present day to theories of active citizenship and civic republicanism. Such ideas were developed by Alexis de Tocqueville in the nineteenth century, and have been articulated by present-day democratic political theorists such as Henry Tam, Amitai Etzioni and Vaclav Havel. Powell and Guerin (1997) see the roots of present-day voluntary action as also belonging to another tradition, that of social solidarity, the welfare state and social movements, drawing their inspiration from a complementary set of philosophical sources, notably Hegel, Marx, Gramsci and Habermas. Bringing these two traditions together, Powell (2001) believes that non-governmental associations reinforce social capital and civil action and can have a humanistic, reforming influence, making what he calls a 'good society' out of fragmented political communities and Darwinist economies.

The early voluntary sector in Ireland

The antecedents of modern charity may be found in the Irish medieval church. Ireland probably matched the great period of institution building in the Christian church in England in the twelfth and thirteenth centuries (Leadbetter, 1997). Institutions for the sick and poor were run by monks either in or adjacent to monasteries, but most were closed down, without replacement, by the suppression of the monasteries by Henry VIII (1509-47). Ireland's two voluntary sectors arose within the British context, when the island was governed as a single political unit, under the College Green Parliament until 1800, thenceforth from Westminster until 1922.

Early Protestant philanthropy

Voluntary organisations as we now know them date to the late eighteenth century. Organised charitable, philanthropic and voluntary activity was first evident in medicine and education. Action to relieve poverty took the form of *ad hoc*, once-off committees and subscriptions to provide relief during famines and emergencies, or charitable sermons in normal times. Ten hospitals were founded over 1718-60. Those of Dublin are best documented. Some were set up as a result of endowments or gifts of individuals: for example, Mercer's Hospital from Mary Mercer, Dr Steevens' Hospital from Dr Steevens and his sister Grizel (1720), the Rotunda from Dr Mosse, and St Patrick's Hospital for 'fools, madmen and idiots' from the endowment of the writer and cleric Dean Jonathan Swift. Governance of these bodies was entrusted to trustees known to the bequeathers, though in the case of Dr Steevens' hospital this broke down and new trustees drawn from the great and good in the city were appointed by Act of the Irish Parliament in College Green.

Parliament established the Foundling Hospital in Dublin in 1703 to care for destitute, abandoned and orphaned children. The hospital even had a revolving cradle, where a parent could abandon a baby and ring a bell for the child to be brought in anonymously. In the eighteenth century, the hospital became a byword for corruption and maltreatment and was thankfully closed in 1831 when it was found that over three-quarters of the children taken in died within a few months.

These early voluntary organisations and charities developed separately within the Protestant community and the Catholic community. Catholic doctors formed the Charitable Infirmary, later Jervis Street Hospital, and later St Nicholas Hospital. Four surgeons established the (Earl of) Meath Hospital in 1753 to serve, among others, Protestant weavers. Outside Dublin, the North Charitable Infirmary was established in Cork by 1730 and the lying-in hospital in Belfast in 1793. By 1835, there were 36 infirmaries and hospitals in Ireland, their standards being almost universally low. These included private institutions for the mentally ill, some of which were run on reformist principles derived from best practice in Britain and France (Powell, 1992).

Early features of voluntary organisation are in evidence, for doctors gave their time voluntarily, private subscriptions were solicited, donations of bed linen were sought and other funds were raised by charity concerts (Fagan, 1986). A lottery was set up in 1730 to raise funds for the Dublin hospitals. Dublin was a majority Protestant city in the first half of the eighteenth century, confident in building institutions in its own image. The institution-building projects extended to agriculture and education (e.g. The Royal Dublin Society, 1731) and science (The Royal Irish Academy, 1785). Much of this came to an abrupt halt with the Act of Union. Despite this, however, some institution-building continued, the Adelaide Hospital Society being founded by lay Protestant people as a hospital for the sick poor in 1839. Much of what would now be considered a state responsibility was undertaken by voluntary or philanthropic action.

Education in the eighteenth century was provided by a mixture of parish primary schools and by private enterprise for secondary schools, being often named after their founder. All the Protestant parishes had primary schools and 45 Catholic primary schools were recorded in 1730 (Fagan, 1986). From 1810, the first of 200 primary and later secondary schools called English schools was established by the Erasmus Smith Trust, to be funded by the benefactor's trust, landlords and the local community.

The tradition of Protestant philanthropy was most evident through the institution-building projects in health, medicine and education, principally in Dublin. It was diverse, for it was accompanied by projects to build model industrial and rural communities in places like Portlaw, Co. Waterford; Bessbrook, Co. Armagh; Prosperous, Co. Kildare; and Ralahine, Co. Clare.

Many were associated with leading members of the Society of Friends (Quakers) and these models were by today's standards an unlikely combination of industrial development with paternal philanthropy, self-help provident societies, housing, health, and civic and social improvement (Williamson, 1992a). The Society of Friends made a large and distinctive contribution to Irish philanthropy from the provision of relief during the great famine to measures to alleviate distress in the 1920s (and later in Northern Ireland during the Troubles by providing support to the families of prisoners) (Society of Friends, Central Relief Committee (1852)).

In the second half of the eighteenth century economic hardship in the north of Ireland, largely the result of restrictions imposed on Irish trade by the English Parliament, resulted in 'a ceaseless drift of labourers into the towns in search of work, and beggars and destitute people roamed the streets of Belfast' (McNeill 1960, 1988). In response, the Belfast Charitable Society was established in 1752 to inaugurate a fund to 'build a poor House and Hospital and a new Church in or near the town of Belfast' (Strain, 1953). It was not until 1767 that the Society was in a position to proceed, and it was not until 1771 that the foundation stone of the present building in Clifton Street was laid. It was opened in 1774 (Williamson, 1995). However, in the eighteenth century, Belfast was a relatively minor provincial town compared to Dublin and, in its day, the Belfast Charitable Society was an exception. The twenty-two years that elapsed between its foundation and the opening of its facilities is perhaps a commentary on how difficult it was at the time to raise public charitable subscriptions away from the capital city.

However, there was a quickening of voluntary activity at the end of the eighteenth and beginning of the nineteenth centuries. A hospital for the 'Relief of Lying-In Women' opened in 1794 and this was followed in 1817 by the opening of the Belfast Fever Hospital and Dispensary. The latter subsequently went through various changes throughout the nineteenth century, finally emerging as the new 300-bed Royal Victoria Hospital which opened in 1903.

The beginnings of Catholic social action
There was little recorded Catholic charity before the nineteenth century. Traditionally this has been explained by the penal laws, whereby documentation could constitute a form of self-incrimination in the event of prosecution or persecution: such fears were not fully lifted until emancipation in 1829. Powell and Guerin (1997) take a different view, which is that there was little to document in the first place. Powell (1992) suggests that Catholic charity was obliged to operate in a quasi-underground manner until legitimised by the Charitable Bequest Act, 1844, which opened the way to extensive Catholic charity and social action.

The Catholic church began to challenge Protestant philanthropy during the high tide of the ascendancy. In 1750, a rival to the Foundling hospital was set up: the Patrician Orphan Society (Raftery and O'Sullivan, 1999). Partly, it was motivated by the desire to provide something better than the brutal Foundling Hospital, but the desire to supply a Catholic alternative was dominant. By the end of the century, several Catholic orphanages were in operation (e.g. St Joseph's).

The instigator of Catholic charitable action in the capital was Archbishop Thomas Troy (1786-1823) and more especially his successor, Archbishop Daniel Murray (1823-1852). In 1812, Archbishop Murray asked Mary Aikenhead to form the Sisters of Charity to minister to the poor, to establish schools and found hospitals, beginning a wave of institution-building in the Catholic church in Ireland that was to last a century and a half. In the eighteenth century there were very few religious congregations in Ireland (only five small communities of nuns in Dublin in the mid-century) and they had almost no social role (Enright, 2000). This changed out of all recognition. The population of nuns grew from 120 in six orders in 1800 to 8,000 in 35 orders and congregations by 1900 (Raftery and O'Sullivan, 1999). On the male side, the fastest-growing, largest order was the Christian Brothers (1812). They rose from 45 brothers in 1831 to 1,000 by 1900 and 4,000 by 1960.

Following the Sisters of Charity, Archbishop Murray encouraged Frances Ball to begin the Loreto Sisters' schools several years later. Where suitable people were not available, religious orders abroad were invited to come in and establish congregations and schools. Several orders were imported, as it were, from France, for example the Daughters of Charity of St Vincent de Paul, the Sisters of St Clare, the Ursulines and the Sisters of St Louis. In 1824, Murray encouraged Catherine McAuley to found the Sisters of Mercy, which eventually became the largest religious order in the English-speaking world. In the next 50 years, the order founded 168 convents. St Vincent's Hospital, the first major Catholic hospital in the city was formed in 1833, following a series of outbreaks of cholera.

Why the sudden burst of institution building? Observers explain it in terms of a rising, more prosperous, more confident Catholic bourgeoisie with the will and the wealth to endow schools, orphanages, churches and hospitals. Indeed, Archbishop Murray worked closely with the leading Catholic professional and commercial families of the city to do so. For professionally minded women, such work provided an outlet otherwise denied them in the professional and commercial world. From the early eighteenth century, the penal laws, the confiscation of land and barring from traditional professions had the ironic effect of forcing Catholics into trade, commerce and manufacturing, the new industries of their day, where they prospered and generated sufficient revenues to provide endowments for charity.

But why was it institutional? Raftery and O'Sullivan (1999) explain that there was a strong conviction at the time that institutional services were efficient, controlling, scientific and offered economies of scale not available in any other way. In the strongly sectarian environment of the nineteenth century, institutions offered a more certain means of protection (or control) than other approaches.

A striking feature of early Catholic voluntary action was the role played by female philanthropists (Enright, 2000). Teresa Mulally was a businesswoman who founded schools for poor girls as far back as 1766, later handed over to the Presentation Sisters. Nano Nagle likewise set up schools for the poor in Cork in 1751.They had a distinct focus on the poor, to the extent that some of the long-established religious orders (e.g. the Poor Clares) began to reorientate themselves around the needs of the poor. Nano Nagle exemplified many of the trends of early Catholic social action. She came from a wealthy family and was sent to Paris for her education. After some time in a convent there, she returned to Cork to set up schools and hospitals, funded both by her immediate family and by an inheritance from her uncle. She invited the Ursuline nuns into Cork in 1771, despite some opposition from local Catholic clergy and questions by Cork Corporation (the penal laws were still on the books, though enforced ever less strictly) (Coleman, 2002).

In time the various schools became quite delineated according to social class, some serving the very poor, others those with modest incomes, some pitched at the children of wealthier families. The religious motivation for these initiatives should not be overlooked, for Catholic social action went hand in hand with a rapid growth in fraternities or associations of the faithful. It is no coincidence that the Dublin branch of the Association for the Propagation of the Faith was established at the peak of this activity, in 1838.

The first of what became known as the Magdalen Asylums or Homes (also, more pejoratively, known as 'rescue homes for fallen women') was opened by Mrs Brigid Bourke and Patrick Quarterman in Townsend Street in Dublin in 1798. It was taken over and made part of an expanding national network by the Irish Sisters of Charity in 1833 who also took over the Cork services in 1844 (similar services were established for fallen Protestant women at the end of the eighteenth century). The first known service for homeless women was opened by the Sisters of Mercy in 1861. Two French congregations, the Sisters of Our Lady of Charity and Refuge and the Sisters of the Good Shepherd, were invited in to manage hitherto private services (O'Sullivan, 1999). Several religious orders became involved in services for people with disabilities such as the Christian Brothers, Vincentians, Dominicans, and the Daughters of Charity of St Vincent de Paul for the deaf and the Sisters of Charity and the Carmelite Brothers for the blind. The extent to which

French models of religious and social care were imported into Ireland has probably been underestimated for there are many other examples (e.g. the Oblates). Most of these services were institutional, seen as providing sanctuary from an unsupportive, hostile, outside world. In Ireland, they had a strong salvationist ethic, saving souls from corruption, lapse from the faith and further exposure to sexual and other risks. To this was added the Victorian idea of reform, that in an appropriate environment, a fallen individual could be rehabilitated as a productive, exemplary member of society.

By the time Archbishop Daniel Murray died in 1852, there were 28 women's communities in the Dublin archdiocese. Visitors to Dublin described the city as full of magnificent hospitals, orphanages, industrial schools, asylums, reformatories, and institutions for the poor and disabled (Enright, 2000). Catholic social action combined ecclesiastical leadership, socially concerned men and women, the emerging bourgeoisie, the post-emancipation Catholic revival and an institution-building church. Religious orders reinvented themselves from contemplative to activist roles. Several Catholic merchant families associated with the emancipation movement were generous benefactors of the new schools, orphanages and services for the poor. Three religious orders were dominant in social care: the Sisters of Mercy, the Sisters of Charity, and the Daughters of Charity. They set up numerous orphanages in the nineteenth century or, as often, took over existing services with the promise of more professional management.

The Society of St Vincent de Paul would become the leading Catholic charity in Ireland. Founded in Paris in 1833, the society was established in Ireland by Margaret Kelly in Kingstown (now Dún Laoghaire) in 1843. During the archepiscopacy of Paul Cullen (1852-78), the institution building continued apace (O'Carroll, 2000). His time saw the construction of hospitals such as the Mater and St John of God as well as many prominent schools (e.g. Blackrock College, Terenure College and St Patrick's College). No less than 39 religious foundations opened during his time.

Charity moved to more complex organisational forms in the Dublin Mendicity Society in 1818 and extended as the century progressed (Luddy, 1995). The association aimed to provide relief, work and resettlement for beggars, though an important sub-text was to get beggars off the streets and prevent them from impeding business. The society established what, for its day, was a complex committee system to fulfil these ambitious goals, which kept records and issued reports giving an account of its work. Formal institutional relief was set down by the government in 1838 when the Poor Law was applied to Ireland, in a form and application that was universally disliked and considered inappropriate.

Institutionalisation was a particular feature of voluntary activity during the Victorian period. Here, theories of institutionalisation introduced from

Britain combined with Catholic religious resurgence to provide extraordinarily high rates of institutionalised voluntary activity. Their legacy, especially for children, still remains in the twenty-first century. Over 105,000 children were committed to the industrial schools between then and 1969, with as many as 52 institutions detaining up to 8,000 children at a time. The emphasis on physical work, combined with the brutality of the staff, made them virtually indistinguishable from labour camps (Raftery and O'Sullivan, 1999).

The institutional period began on 14 April 1859 when the first boy was admitted to Glencree Reformatory in Co. Wicklow, a converted military barracks. The first such schools had been set up in Great Britain in the 1840s, starting in Scotland. Proposals to extend them to Ireland had been defeated in Parliament. Irish MPs insisted that any such schools in Ireland must be provided by bodies managed by people of the same religion as the offenders, making it a voluntary-sector, religious-order responsibility. The Oblate Fathers and Glencree paved the way for a massive programme of building of reformatories and, from 1868, industrial schools managed Glencree. Many reformatories later reclassified themselves as industrial schools. Industrial schools were entitled to capitation grants, and orphanages became part of the system. They became the residence for a broad category of children: orphans (actually a small number); homeless and abandoned children; children who had committed minor offences (these were often very minor); and children belonging to poor families deemed unable to cope (often the largest number). Later, they took in large numbers of children of single mothers, both first offenders and recidivists and children with disabilities. The Sisters of Mercy and the Christian Brothers provided 90 per cent of places.

In the northern counties there was little formal Catholic social action prior to the latter half of the nineteenth century. However, the appointment of Cardinal Cullen as Archbishop of Armagh in 1849 marked a start of a period of intense institution-building by the Catholic Church. By the close of his life in 1878, the Church had been transformed, leaving the institution at the heart of the everyday life of the Catholic community (Elliott, 2001). New religious orders were introduced: the Redemptorists, the Passionists, the Sisters of Mercy in 1854 and the Christian Brothers in 1856. By the 1920s, about 60 convents had been established in Ulster, only two or three of which dated from before 1840. The new Bishop of Down and Connor whose diocese covered Belfast, Bishop Dorrian, appointed in 1865, presided over an unprecedented expansion of Catholic institutions including the Mater Hospital, opened in 1883 and run by the Sisters of Mercy. By the time of his death in 1885, the Catholic Church had become the main provider of resources for the Catholic populace and Catholicism had forged a community.

The development of the work of the Sisters of Nazareth in Belfast is illustrative. The Order emerged in France in 1851 as part of the Little Sisters of the Poor although its early work was in London where it ran an old people's home. In 1857 the Order opened a home with 150 beds in Hammersmith, London. During the 1860s they were recognised as an independent Order, the Sisters of Nazareth, and received permission to undertake the care and protection of destitute children. In 1876 they were invited by Bishop Dorrian to establish an old people's home and to care for children in Belfast, initially in the Bishop's own house on the Ormeau Road. By 1884 a new building had been erected on an adjacent site. In 1897, a further site was purchased where an industrial school for boys was established, initially to provide accommodation for the 50 boys who up to then had lived with the old people. The first boys moved there in 1900 and the institution held its Jubilee in 1999. It has been estimated by Caul and Herron (1992) that in the succeeding years, the Order cared for nearly 5,000 old people and 4,500 boys. The old people's home, Nazareth House, continued in its 1884 building until 2001 when the site was sold for redevelopment. The now empty former boys' industrial school, Nazareth Lodge, was demolished and a new care home built on the site in the same year.

In addition to the importation of religious orders the Catholic church also laid particular emphasis on the importance of the lay apostolate. The Society for St Vincent de Paul was established in Belfast in 1850 and it subsequently played a central role in the relief of the Catholic poor, in which practical action was combined with an emphasis on the dissemination of information on Catholic social teaching (Harris, 1993). In this, the church was partly motivated by a fear of socialism. Considerable effort went into supporting the development of church-based forms of social solidarity among the working class as a counter-weight to the development of the trade union movement.

Protestant charity in nineteenth and early twentieth-century Belfast
The population of Belfast grew from 19,000 in 1801 to 350,000 in 1901. By then, it was among the foremost industrial cities in the world. Endemic poverty and disease that reached crisis proportions at times of economic slump accompanied this growth. People poured in from the surrounding countryside. The proportion of Catholics in the population increased substantially, and from the 1830s onwards relations between the Presbyterian majority and the Catholic community deteriorated rapidly. The patterns of segregated housing and periodic sectarian rioting were established by the mid-nineteenth century.

There is some evidence to suggest that philanthropy retained something of its non-sectarian origins in the first half of the century. The Day and Night Asylum, for example, although it had its origins in the Non-Subscribing

Presbyterian Church, included on its committee the Roman Catholic bishop of the time, Bishop Cornelius Denvir (Williamson, 1995). However, the Night Asylum closed in 1847 and thereafter there appears to have been little joint philanthropy between leaders of Protestant denominations and the Roman Catholic hierarchy.

In her exhaustive study of the growth of nineteenth and early twentieth-century philanthropy in Belfast, Jordan concludes that in the latter part of the nineteenth century less than 2 per cent of the members of 'non-religious' charities in Belfast were Catholics. She notes that 'by the end of the nineteenth century the division between Catholic and Protestant benevolence was almost complete' (Jordan, 1989). Thus a pattern was established that persisted through much of the twentieth century.

Accounts of nineteenth-century philanthropy make clear that much of it had a religious basis. In this respect Belfast was doubtless little different from industrial cities in England. Indeed, this pattern of charitable activity reflected the pattern in England where it has been estimated that three-quarters of the charities established in the second half of the nineteenth century were evangelical in origin (Lewis, 1995). This powerful evangelical social movement transformed charity in Britain and created organisations such as Dr Barnardo's Homes, the National Institute for the Blind and the National Institute for the Deaf, whose direct descendants remain among the biggest voluntary organisations in the United Kingdom. Jordan's study of Belfast philanthropy makes clear that many of the charities established during the latter part of the nineteenth century had an explicitly religious character (Jordan, 1989). Some, for example the Cripples Institute, founded in 1877, combined a variety of charitable activities and a religious mission. The Society for Promoting the Education of the Deaf, Dumb and Blind included a religious test of parents who were intending their children to be sent to the Society's school in Belfast, which also opened in 1877.

The influence of this religiously inspired social movement was particularly evident in Belfast. The industrial development of the city throughout the nineteenth century was accompanied by the rise of a large and powerful Protestant middle class. The growth of Protestant philanthropy in the latter part of that century was not replicated elsewhere in Ireland. In the period between 1865 and 1873 no less than seven charitable hospitals were established in Belfast.

The presence of clergy on the management committees of many of these charities doubtless played its part in discouraging Roman Catholic participation in their activities. However, the rise of a specifically Catholic form of social action in the latter part of the nineteenth century was at least as important in shaping a distinct sectarian division in the development of voluntary action at that time.

Voluntary action in rural areas

The nineteenth century was an important period for voluntary sector formation outside the cities. Rural co-operatives first developed toward the end of the nineteenth century, both as producer co-operatives and dairies and consumer co-operatives, the latter designed to circumvent profiteering by middlemen (gombeens). Fifteen producer co-ops were functioning in the rural areas by 1891 and the Irish Agricultural Wholesale Society was formed in 1894.

Particularly important were co-operative banks, also called village banks and agricultural banks. They were consciously modelled on the Raffeisen banks in Germany and introduced to Ireland by the reformer Tom Finlay SJ (Bolger, 1985). The first co-operative bank was established in Belmullet, Co. Mayo, in 1894 and a second by Paddy 'the Cope' Gallagher in Dungloe shortly thereafter. Most operated out of parish halls and school houses. The Irish Agricultural Organisation Society appointed a full-time organiser of the co-operative banks in 1897, George William Russell (the writer Æ). So rapid was their growth that there were 268 by 1908, being most successful in Connacht. Intriguingly, they received government help from the Congested Districts Board in the form of funding and the organiser's salary, the government seeing merit in underwriting voluntary activity. It is important to point out that the advocates of the co-operative movement (e.g. Horace Plunkett and George Russell) did not see co-operatives purely in economic terms or as liberating small farmers from the grip of shopkeepers or as combating the depressing and endemic rural poverty of the time. Rather they saw them as an empowering means of creating a more just and democratic rural society, a mission they pursued with messianic zeal and whose full philosophy was articulated in their weekly newspaper *The Irish Homestead* (1895-1923). By 1915 there were 344 dairy co-ops, 225 credit banks and 219 agricultural co-operatives (Harvey, 1986). Some of these small co-operative banks later evolved into today's credit unions.

Women's involvement in philanthropy and political reform

Women and Philanthropy in Nineteenth Century Ireland (Luddy, 1995) was the first of a series of publications to provide an in-depth consideration of an important but hitherto neglected topic. Luddy demonstrates that through 'voluntaryism' middle-class women were able to discharge what they saw as their religious and moral duty to society. They were also able to use their considerable influence to 'shape the provision and direction of philanthropic enterprise and to guide it into those areas which they considered to be of major importance' (Luddy, 1995: 214). She suggests that the reformist tradition in Irish philanthropy owed its existence principally to Quaker and Nonconformist women and she notes that these women worked with men in societies such as the Dublin Aid Committee (later to become the National Society for the Prevention of Cruelty to Children) and the Philanthropic Reform Association. A principal aim of these societies was to lobby the state to legislate for improvements in the conditions in workhouses and for increased protection of children.

Demonstrating that women's involvement in philanthropic societies was often a precursor to political activism, Luddy points out that 'women in reformist societies were most likely to become involved in the suffrage issue and to fight for the right to sit as poor law guardians' (Luddy, 1995: 217). She suggests that participation in philanthropic societies offered women a sense of identity and community together with a sense of purpose and achievement and an opportunity to exert considerable power. Participation in organisations such as the Philanthropic Reform Association, one of the most progressive reformist organisations of the day, offered women political influence. It is particularly notable that Quaker women had a highly developed sense of individual responsibility and benefited from the egalitarian ethos of the Quaker tradition. This led them to play a major role in philanthropy and in social reform and, later in the nineteenth century, in the suffragette movement (Luddy, 1995).

A new wave of women's organisations developed in Ireland in the years around the turn of the century. These were the Ladies Land League, the suffrage movement and the Irish Women Workers Union. Inspired by Russell, the Irish Countrywomen's Association was formed in 1910 to improve the situation of rural women. Although driven by and presenting some traditional considerations of women's role in the family, it has a strong orientation toward the effective participation of women in citizenship and public life. Some analysts have suggested that these organisations found it necessary to portray themselves in traditional terms in order to win any public space for themselves in a society otherwise hostile to the politicisation, still less the emancipation, of women (Kelleher Associates, 2001).

Voluntary action, 1900-1922

In 1902 a register of Dublin's charities listed over 400 organisations (Williams, 1902). At the same time, the Church of Ireland published a *Social Services Handbook*, a guide to its services. Williams' directory comprised evangelical groups, denominational welfare services, orphanages, religious bodies and other groups formed to relieve distress. Much the largest was the Society of St Vincent de Paul, which combined visiting, moralising and material and cash relief. The society was run by professional people and merchants, raising money from collections, donations, bequests, concerts, bazaars and sales of their bulletin (Daly, 1984). The denominational basis and religious ethos of these voluntary organisations were among their strongest features.

There was little mention of non-denominational organisations. One of the few was the Sick and Indigent Roomkeepers Society, which experienced considerable difficulties in steering a neutral path between the denominations of its patrons and supporters. The society dated back to the eighteenth century, and in the second half of the nineteenth century provided cash and other relief to between 20,000 and 30,000 people a year, sometimes more. Few groups saw beyond cash relief to question the underlying roots of poverty and deprivation. One of the exceptions was the Philanthropic Reform Association, which put forward proposals for the reform of services for children, policing and works for the unemployed – but it was outlived by many of the traditional organisations.

The development of voluntary action in Ireland was shaped both by Protestant philanthropy, particularly in the north, and by the emergence and triumph of Catholic social action throughout the island. But it was also influenced by developments in charitable activity in England. For example, Dr Barnardo's Homes established an 'Ever Open Door' in Belfast in 1875. Interestingly, no home was established in Dublin and initially children who required residential care were moved to homes in Britain. The first Barnardo's Home in Northern Ireland was not opened until the 1940s (Caul and Herron, 1992).

The Belfast Charity Organisation Society, 1906

The establishment of the Belfast Charity Organisation Society in 1906 illustrates that it was difficult to identify philanthropy that did not directly express the social action work of the clergy. Furthermore, the way it was subsumed into the Belfast Council of Social Welfare in 1919 also shows how English models of philanthropic organisation were adapted to local circumstances. Two of the key features of the Northern Ireland voluntary sector were established before the jurisdiction came into being in 1922. As with the rest of Ireland, the northern counties were characterised by sectarian and religiously defined structures. Most of the voluntary organisations in Northern Ireland were indigenous to that part of Ireland and did not operate elsewhere.

The Belfast Charity Organisation Society was established as a result of an initiative of the Belfast Christian Civic Union founded in 1903 'for the uplifting of the community by the furtherance of social reform and civic purity' (Caul and Herron, 1992). As its name perhaps implies, this was a quintessential example of Protestant social action in which the clergy played a leading role along with socially aware members of the business class. The close identification of social and moral reform was reflected in the wide scope of its activities. These included a concern for the exploitation of children in employment and the promotion of proper leisure facilities for children, but it also campaigned against 'immoral literature' and 'objectionable postcards' (Caul and Herron, 1992).

The Civic Union was instrumental in establishing the City of Belfast Charity Organisation Society. The Union called and chaired its initial meeting and subsequently provided support and back-up for the tasks of the new committee. The first Charity Organisation Society had been founded in London in 1869 and by the time of its arrival in Belfast, there were 80 local societies in England, 12 in Scotland and 170 in the United States of America. The appeal and role of the Charity Organisation Society has to be understood in relation to Victorian assumptions about the respective place of the state and voluntary social action. These were rigidly separated. The state was responsible solely for the Poor Law. As amended in England in 1834, and subsequently extended to Ireland in 1838, this was based on the twin principles of less eligibility and deterrence. Relief was only available in the general workhouse and on terms that were less than were available from possible earnings outside, although from 1898, Poor Law Guardians were empowered to give outdoor relief to able-bodied workers. Paupers in the workhouse lost their civil and legal rights; in effect, relief was only available at the cost of citizenship. The role of charity was to assist those on the verge of destitution to ensure that they did not become a charge on the state. Underlying this division was the assumption that pauperism was the result of personal moral failure. From the start the objects of the Charity Organisation Society were to 'improve the condition of the poor by co-operating with the poor law, repress mendicity, to investigate and effectively assist the deserving and to promote good habits' (Lewis, 1995: 11). Thus the Charity Organisation Society aimed to restore the deserving to self-maintenance by which was meant the personal capacity to participate in the labour market. An ethical society was one supported by the good character of those within it.

A fundamental concern of the Charity Organisation Society was with indiscriminate charity and alms-giving that paid no attention to the character of its recipients. Parts of the function of the Charity Organisation Society were thus to co-ordinate charitable activity locally and channel it into the provision of help to those seen as deserving of it on investigation. This appears to have been the motivation of those who set up the Belfast Charity Organisation Society. While there had up to this point been somewhat less debate on the proper distinction between the state and voluntary action than in England, circumstances were similar in many respects. The 1838 Irish Poor Law replicated the principles and arrangements of the 1834 English Poor Law. The assistance of those in need of help who were not in the workhouse was left to charity. Thus speakers at the founding meeting of the Belfast Charity Organisation Society expressed concern about how much of the 'great stream of charity' had gone astray and served no purpose, calling for better co-ordination between charity and the Poor Law, appropriate investigation and intelligent help (Caul and Herron, 1992).

The subsequent amalgamation of the Belfast Charity Organisation Society into the Belfast Council of Social Welfare again reflected developments in England. Councils of Social Welfare had begun to appear from the 1890s onwards. While they shared many of the assumptions of the Charity Organisation Society, they tended to be less hostile to the development of the state's role in welfare provision, especially the introduction of old age pensions and national insurance in 1906. Nevertheless amalgamations between the two did occur at local level in England, so events in Belfast were by no means unique. The reforms of the early twentieth century and the cataclysmic events of the First World War effectively put paid to the Victorian ideal of two separate spheres for the state and voluntary action. As Lewis sums up in her history of the Charity Organisation Society, the idea that the state and charities dealt with different kinds of people (the irredeemable and the redeemable) was replaced by the idea that they performed different but complementary tasks. The establishment of the Belfast Council of Social Welfare in 1919 therefore marked the end of Victorian philanthropy in Ulster and the promise of co-operation between voluntary organisations and the new state apparatus that emerged in the early 1920s.

The early housing movement

Prototypical social housing movements were in evidence in Dublin at the turn of the century, probably inspired by early English movements dating back to the 1860s. Philanthropy and the desire to improve working-class housing did not stand in the way of such schemes providing a return for their investors. Indeed, it is difficult to distinguish between those schemes that were genuinely philanthropic and profit-making projects aimed at the lower end of the housing market (Daly, 1984). Many were cheerfully able to reconcile both objectives at the same time and had no trouble describing themselves as philanthropic even though it is doubtful if they would pass modern definitions of 'non-profit'.

The Artisan Dwellings Company was formed in Dublin in 1876, following reports on the poor state of working-class homes, and attracted support from the Chamber of Commerce and the city's medical, business and legal élite. By 1914 the company had built 3,081 dwellings and housed 13,988 tenants. It also paid a dividend of up to 5 per cent, arguing that such profit-making schemes were preferable to building these homes at ratepayers' expense. The Association for the Housing of the Very Poor built 157 flats by 1914, aimed at people who could not afford the rents of the Artisans Dwellings Company. Attracting start-up capital from the great and the good of the city at the time, it gave them a return of 2 per cent. The most philanthropic of these schemes was probably the Iveagh complex, founded in 1890 with a gift of £50,000 from Viscount Iveagh. This constructed 586 flats by the time of the Great War (the Iveagh Trust continues in existence to the present time). By 1914, social housing (corporate and philanthropic) comprised 18.75 per cent of the city's housing stock. But these achievements were inadequate in the face of some of the worst slum housing in Europe. Local authorities, in their modern form, were established in Ireland in 1898 and legislation enabled them to become involved in housing for people on low incomes. The first significant local authority housing in Ireland was begun by Dublin Corporation.

Housing was not the only urban concern of the late Victorian period. In the late nineteenth century, social reformers drew attention to the treatment of children. In 1889, the Irish Society for the Prevention of Cruelty to Children (ISPCC) was formed, originally as a branch of the national society. At this stage, the number of charities formed as branches or clones of English-based organisations began to tail off. They tended to be seen as 'British' (hence earning nationalist suspicion) and 'Protestant' (most were secular but they were not overtly informed by Catholic social principles, which was enough to make them suspect). Perhaps the last one of this phase was formed ten years after the Free State came into existence: the National Council for the Blind in Ireland (1931), a lay body, modelled on the United Kingdom system with a strong work ethic (work and craft shops) (Dolan, 2000).

Nineteenth-century charity legislation
Before concluding the historical review, it should be mentioned that the nineteenth century saw a substantial body of legislation governing charities, applicable of course to the whole island:

- Charitable Donations and Bequests (Ireland) Act, 1844, the main regulatory legislation
- Trustees Act, 1893, governing the operation of trusts
- Industrial and Provident Societies Act, 1893, 1894 (Amendment Act, 1913), designed to meet the needs of the then emerging co-operatives
- Friendly Societies Acts, 1896, 1908 (these acts established three types of friendly society: the friendly society, the cattle insurance society and the benevolent societies).

This subject is comprehensively treated in O'Halloran (2000), in O'Halloran and Cormacain (2001) and in Cormacain, O'Halloran and Williamson, (2001).

These acts were the legal basis of the charitable and voluntary organisations that operated in Ireland prior to Partition and subsequently in the jurisdictions of Northern Ireland and the Free State and Republic. They are treated in more detail in chapters four and five. The history of the voluntary sector in both parts of the island will be examined separately for the period after 1922.

Comments and conclusions

Voluntary sector activity in Ireland now takes place against a background of a rising consciousness of the importance of associational activity in the modern world. Non-governmental organisations have been the focus of attention of political theorists who seek to explain a range of trends from globalisation to local social capital. Other academics have sought to classify and categorise the sector according to standardised norms.

By the end of the second decade of the twentieth century, there had been at least two hundred years of voluntary action in Ireland. Our knowledge is uneven, with Dublin's being the most documented. From what we know, the origins of voluntary action lie in the medieval church. A sustained period of building of voluntary institutions is associated with the Protestant ascendancy before the Act of Union in 1800, principally in medicine and hospitals. As the penal laws were relaxed and as the Catholic bourgeoisie expanded, there were sufficient resources and motivation to fund the beginning of a long period of Catholic social action, with the establishment of charities to help the poor. Women, either as religious sisters or as lay philanthropists, led many of these. The Victorian period was associated with a highly institutional form of voluntary action that reflected convictions both of evangelism and of reform. By the twentieth century, voluntary action was evident in the rural areas, in the women's movement, and in improved housing. A legislative environment was constructed, the most important aspect of which was the 1838 Irish Poor Law that defined the role of the state in welfare provision and gave legal force to the space occupied by voluntary organisations in relation to that role. As important, particularly for the development of institutional Catholic social action, was the Charitable Donations and Bequests (Ireland) Act, 1844. This legislation enabled the Catholic church to receive legacies and donations and hence raise funds.

Several features merit comment. First, the dividing lines of religion were very evident throughout Ireland. There was little space between them for a pillar of secular action. Each of the two communities saw voluntary action as an expression of, alternately, its ascendancy and nation-building during the eighteenth century and of evangelical Christian belief (the Protestant community) or a challenge to those doctrines and practices and a means of reaching out to and serving the urban poor and specific distressed groups (the Catholic community).

The impact of this division was most evident in the north where philanthropy inspired by the nineteenth-century evangelical movement and financed by a wealthy Protestant industrial class was very evident. The association of philanthropy with evangelical Protestantism typical of nineteenth-century industrial cities in Britain meant that 'secular' charities were often so only in name. The assumptions and values of evangelical Protestantism suffused them. Clergy tended to occupy prominent roles in their establishment and management. On the other hand, the period of intense institution-building by the Catholic Church at the latter end of the nineteenth century had put in place a parallel welfare system, run by the Church and its religious orders.

Modelling of Irish voluntary action on external inspiration is apparent. Religious orders took their cue from France. English example was frequently seen as a model, for example in the social housing movement, and in action for the prevention of cruelty to children and services for the blind.

There were many common threads in the development of voluntary action in Ireland before Partition. This is not surprising given that the island was a single legislative and administrative unit. In both parts of the island voluntary action developed in the context of the 1838 Irish Poor Law that restricted the state to a residual role in welfare. The spread of the rural co-operative movement was evident throughout Ireland.

However, clear differences were also becoming apparent by the early twentieth century. The development of Belfast into an industrial powerhouse of the British empire was accompanied by the rise of a powerful and wealthy Protestant middle class. This gave rise to a form of voluntary action that had more in common with the industrial cities of Britain where evangelical Protestantism was also a major motivator. In Belfast, voluntary hospitals, and a Council of Social Welfare along with a number of charities addressing the needs of disabled people emerged from this tradition. And, by the time of Partition, new conceptions of the relationship between voluntary organisations and the state that saw voluntary action as a form of partnership (rather than as an independent entity operating in separate spheres), were emerging around these charities. This was very different from both Victorian social thought and Catholic social teaching, both of which insisted on a residual role for the state in welfare, albeit for somewhat different reasons.

Belfast, however, presents a contradictory picture. While middle-class philanthropy modelled itself on charitable work in Britain, the development of the Labour Movement with its welfare arm in the form of friendly societies, working men's clubs and other institutions, was inhibited by the sectarian rivalry between Protestant and Catholic workers; between an élite Protestant trade-based working class and a poorer and more subservient Catholic working class that remained firmly in the ambit of the Catholic Church.

Although its effects were felt throughout Ireland, the development of the institutional Catholic Church towards the end of the nineteenth century had a somewhat different impact in the north and the south. Firstly, up until the middle of the nineteenth century, the Church had been much weaker in the north where folk practices and the lay involvement in the appointment of priests had been relatively common. Religious orders were almost unknown and their development came much later than further south. So the difference before and after Cardinal Cullen's organisational drive was much more acute in the area that became Northern Ireland. Secondly, the presence of a large Protestant population (with its own religiously driven and very different philanthropic tradition and with both the wealth and the power for serious charitable endowment) combined with the intense Catholic social action to create two separate social spheres.

The sectarian division of welfare was perhaps not very different than in Dublin, but it had the opposite effect north and south. Power lay in different hands. In the south, the growth in philanthropy was closely associated with the emergence of a powerful Catholic middle class. The achievement of national independence enshrined the Catholic Church and its social teaching at the heart of the new state. In the north the philanthropic tradition that had grown out of evangelical Protestantism emerged as part of the creed of the new rulers of the new Unionist Northern Ireland. Catholic social institutions served their own community, but tended to embody their reluctant participation in a political settlement none wanted.

By the time of Partition, a significant voluntary sector infrastructure was in place in both parts of Ireland – in terms of legislation, buildings and facilities and human investment. With the founding of an Irish Free State the new political project of an independent Irish state opened up possibilities for changes of direction. Social action had played an important part in the national struggle – be it in the form of the Land League, the Gaelic League, or the Gaelic Athletic Association. At least some of the driving force in the struggle for independence had been fuelled by notions of misgovernment, and of uncaring social policies in the urban and especially the rural, areas. Now came an opportunity for more progressive social policies – but what role would the voluntary sector play in these? Would the new Free State develop the legislative apparatus left behind by the British administration? Would the Free State, committed to the unity of different religious traditions in Ireland, confront the essential sectarianism of the voluntary sector and replace it with a less divisive, more secular model?

In the new Northern Ireland, the new policy-makers left matters more or less as they had found them. As the only part of the United Kingdom with a devolved government, the key issue would be whether social reform would match developments in Britain. Would there be in Northern Ireland the political will to tackle the sectarian division of welfare that characterised both jurisdictions? In the event, as will be described in chapter two, there was to be little new social legislation in the next twenty years, and Poor Law guardians and the existing charities were left to continue their work with little interference from the new government.

2

Voluntary Action in Northern Ireland

Introduction

Two days before Christmas in 1920 the Government of Ireland Act received royal assent. The act marked the end of the period inaugurated by the Act of Union of 1801 under which the island of Ireland was governed from Westminster as part of the United Kingdom of Great Britain and Ireland. It led to the partitioning of Ireland into Southern Ireland (which became the 'Irish Free State') with a devolved parliament in Dublin, and Northern Ireland with a devolved parliament in Belfast. Both parts of Ireland were to send some members to sit at Westminster. Unionists accepted the act but Sinn Féin repudiated the new arrangement and continued to support the IRA in its military campaign for a united Irish republic. Unionists considered that the six northern counties comprised the largest area that they could continue to control without fear that nationalists would gain a majority. They believed that a parliament in Belfast would give them some protection if a future Westminster government sought to reunite the island at some future time. Subsequently a parliament was established, first in Belfast itself, and then in an impressive purpose-built edifice at Stormont.

The northern parliament had a permanent Unionist majority. The nationalist and republican population of the new Northern Ireland was permanently disaffected from, and disillusioned with, the new constitutional arrangements which prevailed for 50 years until, in 1972, the Stormont parliament was prorogued by British prime minister Edward Heath. There followed some 26 years of Direct Rule from Westminster, apart from several short periods which saw failed attempts to devolve power to a local administration.

From the beginning the nationalist and republican population of Northern Ireland had no confidence in unionist governments. The unionist population, beset by anxiety about its security, and episodically harassed by the IRA, took comfort from the fact that its government had an unassailable majority and that Protestant communities could count on being protected and patronised by Stormont. The state would deliver. By contrast, permanently deprived of access to the levers of political power, and embittered by a deep sense of injustice and inequality and of neglect and discrimination by the government, working-class nationalist and republican communities turned to their own resources, and often to the leadership of Roman Catholic clergy, to sustain and develop their culture and to foster social and economic development (Birrell and Murie, 1980). Thus community development grew and prospered in nationalist and republican communities and was slow to develop in unionist and loyalist communities.

Virtually every aspect of the development of society and the economy in Northern Ireland has been marked and shaped by the 'Troubles' that commenced in 1968. The years that followed saw more than 3,500 deaths and a burden of injury and pain that is impossible to tally, to say nothing of other intangible costs arising from inhibited economic progress and lost opportunities (Fay, Morrissey and Smyth, 1999). The development of the voluntary and community sector was shaped by Northern Ireland's erratic pattern of political and social evolution. Direct Rule, on and off for 30 years, provided the environment for its growth and development and the backcloth against which relations between the voluntary and community sector and government have emerged. These are qualitatively different from, and in some respects more advanced than, relations elsewhere in these islands whether in the United Kingdom or in the Republic of Ireland (Oliver, 2000).

Welfare from 1922-1945 and the Welfare State Settlement

Although the new Northern Ireland Government endorsed a 'step by step' approach to the development of the state's role in social welfare, believing that workers should be no worse off than their fellow citizens in Britain, in practice matters such as medical and social insurance fell far behind. Decisions were dominated by a need to balance the budget, and the extent of UK Treasury responsibilities towards supporting expenditure on matters within the competence of the Northern Ireland administration remained a matter of political dispute (Buckland, 1979). The baseline of social need was relatively higher and state provision relatively lower than in Britain.

By contrast with the position in England, in Ireland the provisions of the Irish Poor Law of 1838 (itself modelled on the 1834 Poor Law Amendment Act) had remained substantially unreformed. Although the Poor Law Unions did administer outdoor relief, they were very reluctant to do so and, especially in Belfast, continued to apply the workhouse test right up to the 1940s. Voluntary organisations continued to play a central role in welfare. In child care the 1908 Children's Act was not repealed until the last decade of the century, and although the Poor Law Boards of Guardians were empowered to have children 'boarded out', of the 1,501 children in care in Northern Ireland in 1947, 1,000 were in voluntary sector institutions.

In the Depression years of the late 1920s a dispute about poor relief arose between the Belfast Board of Guardians, the Belfast Corporation and the new Northern Ireland Government. The Corporation believed that the Board of

Guardians should provide outdoor relief; the Guardians believed that the Corporation should start enough relief works to employ unemployed men. Both bodies believed that the relief of poverty was the responsibility of the Government, despite the fact that the Board of Guardians was the only body empowered to provide relief. The Belfast Council of Social Welfare (BCSW) undertook a survey that estimated that more than 2,000 working-class families in Belfast were utterly destitute. Begging was rife; charities and voluntary organisations were inundated by requests for help and were unable to cope. In 1929 the Council established a Distress Committee chaired by Sir James Andrews who later became Lord Chief Justice.

State support for unemployed and poor people had not developed to any significant degree at the time of the Depression. Philanthropy was the main source of relief of poverty in the 1920s and 1930s when a range of benevolent organisations developed under the umbrella of the Belfast Council for Social Welfare. These included the Personal Service League, and the Alpha Club. Rotary and the Inner Wheel organised the collection and distribution of boots, shoes, clothing and bedclothes. Farmers sent produce from the country to be distributed among people in distress. Many schemes were started in an attempt to respond to an overwhelming situation.

The early co-ordinating tradition of the Charity Organisation Society continued with the inauguration of a Mutual Register of Assistance to avoid overlapping relief efforts and to promote co-operation between different agencies providing services and/or financial help to families. The BCSW also assisted donors to recover income tax paid on their donations. Other activities included promoting after-care of patients discharged from hospital, the provision of free legal advice, and the provision and maintenance of radio sets for people confined to bed because of illness. People suffering from tuberculosis were provided with clothing and other help. A gift of £20,000 from Mrs Harold Barbour continued the Quaker tradition of experimentation with 'model' housing for working-class people. Under this scheme 65 houses were built for working-class families. Other new activities included after-care for young men discharged from borstal, and setting up a child guidance clinic. Occasional public lectures promoted new ideas and public support for the activities of the society. Close liaison was maintained with Queen's University of Belfast. The Dean of the Faculty of Law played an important part in initiating a free legal aid and advice scheme.

During the 1930s public support for the Council continued and developed. Workers in some large factories in Belfast contributed six pence (apprentices gave three pence) from their wages on a regular basis and these funds were administered by committees of employees. Most of this money went to the voluntary hospitals with some funds being used to support the Council; at its peak this support amounted to £1,000 per year. In recognition of this funding some representatives of the workers served as members of the Council's executive committee. These funds ended in 1948 with the inauguration of the National Health Service.

Other responses to the Depression years of the 1930s included the establishment of the Northern Ireland Council for Social Service (NICSS) in 1938, which later had offices in Bryson House, the headquarters of BCSW. Mirroring the model of the National Council for Social Service established in England in the 1920s, the NICSS was established as a direct consequence of government initiative. Its aims included providing a co-ordinating focus for voluntary social services across Northern Ireland but in its early years much of its energies were devoted to providing recreational and 'character improving' activities for unemployed men through activities such as summer camps. In 1938 it opened an old people's home in east Belfast and it also administered a number of small charitable trust funds.

The inadequacies of health, housing and welfare in the inter-war years were shockingly revealed in the mass evacuation of people in Belfast following the blitz in 1941. The newly installed moderator of the Presbyterian Church, the Rev. W. A. Watson, expressed his shock:

> I never saw the like of them before – wretched people, very undersized and underfed, down and out looking men and women ... Is it credible to us that there should be such people in a Christian country? (quoted in Barton, 1989).

The lifting of the lid on the extent of poverty and malnutrition provided the spur to the Northern Ireland administration to more willingly adopt the social reforms after the war that mirrored those introduced in Britain.

The UK Welfare State in Northern Ireland: 1945-1972

The Welfare State Reforms
The reforms in social security, health and welfare services introduced by the 1945 to 1950 Labour Government in Britain were 'read across' to Northern Ireland virtually without change. Under agreement with the UK Treasury, the UK Exchequer underwrote the additional costs of matching social security benefits and health-care entitlements, making up the difference between costs and Northern Ireland tax revenues. The provisions of the British National Assistance Act that defined responsibilities for meeting welfare needs were incorporated into the Welfare Services Act (Northern Ireland) of 1949. The reforms finally repealed the 1838 Irish Poor Law in Northern Ireland and introduced eight local authority Welfare Committees (Belfast,

Londonderry and the six other County Councils) to administer welfare services. As in Britain, both voluntary and Poor Law hospitals were in effect nationalised and a new administrative structure, the Northern Ireland Hospitals Authority, was created to manage both. The only exception was the Mater Infirmorum Hospital in Belfast, which continued to be run by the Sisters of Mercy. It was finally brought into the fold of the NHS in 1971. (For a discussion of the case of the Mater Hospital as it is known, see below.)

Accounts of the development of the Welfare State in Northern Ireland during the 1950s and 1960s suggest a steady improvement in services for children and old people in need, although many services remained dependent on voluntary effort. Indeed, in passing the Welfare Services Act (Northern Ireland), 1949, the Government of Northern Ireland intended that the new arrangements would recognise the place of voluntary social welfare (Kearney, 1995). In an accompanying circular, W.28, the Ministry for Health and Local Government indicated that the new County Welfare Committees should 'give to voluntary bodies the recognition which they deserve, consult closely with them and generally assist them not only to continue in being, but to develop and expand' (Ministry of Health and Local Government (NI), 1949).

This circular was thus the first formal statement of government policy towards voluntary bodies. It was based on the principle that while the new welfare committees had a primary legal responsibility, they would not be able properly to discharge their responsibilities without the support of voluntary agencies. As a consequence, welfare committees were expected to 'enter into close partnership with voluntary effort in every phase of their work' (quoted in Kearney, 1995).

The Ministry's circular letter on the implementation of the Welfare Services Act (Northern Ireland), 1949 had cited as one of the outstanding features of the act the prominence given to voluntary bodies and the flexible provisions under which the statutory authorities could employ, aid and co-operate with them. This 'represented the declared policy of Government as endorsed by Parliament'.

The central role played by voluntary agencies in welfare services continued. Organisations that were established towards the end of the nineteenth century remained the backbone of much service provision until the 1960s. In a few cases, they survived until the 1990s. Among the most notable of these survivors is the Belfast Council of Social Welfare. Another example is the Ingham Mission for the Deaf, originally a Presbyterian initiative, that continued to be the sole provider of sign language interpreting until 1994.

Belfast Council for Social Welfare
After the Second World War the Belfast Council for Social Welfare worked closely with local authorities and other public bodies. It experimented with

employing home helps to assist mothers who were ill and it lobbied for more probation officers. It encouraged Queen's University to train social workers, and the Council collaborated by providing supervised practical training. In 1948 the Council brought all its activities under one roof when, with a large grant from the Carnegie Trust and public subscriptions, it purchased and renovated a linen warehouse in Bedford Street which was subsequently renovated and named Bryson House. The Council provided accommodation for a broad spectrum of voluntary organisations including the recently established Northern Ireland Council for Social Service, the Hospitals' After-Care Committee, the Citizen's Advice Bureau, the Poor Man's Lawyer and the Soldiers' Sailors' and Airmen's Families' Association.

Almost a century after it was established as the Charity Organisation Society, Bryson House, as the charity has been renamed after its headquarters, has an annual turnover in excess of nearly £7 million and employs 270 people. Some of its activities are developments from the early priorities of the Belfast Council for Social Welfare. Continuing a link with Queen's University, Belfast, that began in 1916 the Social Work Student Unit at Bryson House continues to provide placements and supervision for social work students. The work of the charity ranges from providing training and care services (under its domiciliary and Home from Hospital services) to environmental improvement and promoting energy efficiency. It continues to respond to social need by promoting volunteering. Several departments work closely with Health and Social Services Trusts in Belfast and further afield. Other departments provide energy education services to schools and operate a kerbside recycling programme. Reflecting its philanthropic origins it administers a number of trust funds and provides financial assistance to people in extreme need.

Many of these organisations emerged from initiatives by sections of the Protestant industrial classes, often with a strong religious character (Williamson, 1995). These charities were organised and run by Protestants. The parallel Catholic welfare system continued, based on a combination of parish support and the use of religious orders to run institutions. This division persisted into the 1960s. Barritt and Carter (1962, 1972) noted that only 4 per cent of the members of the Council of the Northern Ireland Council of Social Service and of the Executive Committee of the Belfast Council of Social Welfare were Catholics. (These figures are undated but it is likely that they refer to a period shortly before the book was first published, in 1962.)

The persistence of sectarian divisions among the range of voluntary action reflected the persistence of the very different approaches to welfare in the Protestant and Catholic communities and the very different attitudes they held towards the government and its agencies. The alienation from the

Northern Ireland state felt by most Catholics both fed and was reinforced by the institutions of the Roman Catholic Church, which in effect became a para-state. Although there were instances of working-class organisation and campaigning among the Protestant population throughout this period, the perception that the institutions of the state were 'theirs' and that the state would in the end look after their interests meant that there was never an equivalent focus for the development of voluntary action. Furthermore, there was no equivalent to the Catholic Church, which both promoted voluntary action and provided its institutional base in the Catholic community. As a number of autobiographical accounts of growing up in Northern Ireland in the 1950s and 1960s attest, e.g. *War in an Irish Town* by Eamonn McCann (1974), the church and the rituals surrounding the financial support of its welfare institutions were woven into the fabric of everyday life within the Catholic community.

The self-contained nature of Catholic social action and its ambiguous relationship with the institutions of government, particularly in relation to the developing welfare state in Northern Ireland, are vividly illustrated by the Mater Hospital.

The Case of the Mater Infirmorum Hospital

The Mater Hospital on Belfast's Crumlin Road was established in 1883 in premises donated by Bishop Dorrian. The Sisters of Mercy, who had commenced their work in Belfast in 1854, were responsible for nursing services, and in 1899 the hospital became recognised as a teaching hospital by the Royal University of Ireland. At the time of its establishment the population of Belfast was growing rapidly and was to quadruple in the fifty years between 1841 and 1891. Increasingly after Partition in 1922 the hospital was seen as an icon of Catholic moral and cultural values (although it also provided health services to fiercely Protestant working-class families on the Crumlin Road). Until it was assimilated into the National Health Service in 1971 the Mater Hospital was managed by a board of trustees who were responsible for promoting and preserving the Catholic ethical basis on which the hospital had been founded.

For twenty-three years following the establishment of the National Health Service in 1948 the hospital remained outside the National Health Service without financial aid from the government. The importance of the hospital in terms of the provision of medical care in Belfast is reflected by a statistic from 1953 when the hospital treated 3,500 in-patients and 50,000 out-patients (Tanner Report, and Gray, 1993). Its running costs were liberally supported by voluntary contributions, and by income from football pools and flag days organised by young Catholic men known as the 'Young Philanthropists'. In 1965 Bishop William Philbin wrote about the voluntary effort that sustained the hospital and spoke of the 'continued voluntary efforts of a whole complex of charitable organisations and ... the support and sacrifices of the whole Catholic community of Northern Ireland as well as of many other non-Catholic sympathisers'. Thanks to this widespread support during the decade after 1948, the Mater was financially self-sufficient although that situation was to change in the 1960s as medical costs escalated rapidly, and finance was clearly an important contributory factor to the arrangement that was made in 1971.

With the onset of the National Health Service in the late 1940s, the hospital's trustees feared that incorporation into Northern Ireland's state medical system would lead to the erosion of Catholic principles particularly in the areas of gynaecology and obstetrics, and its doctors were alarmed about possible influence and interference in their work by civil servants. From 1948 until 1971, although the hospital treated patients of different religious faiths regardless of ability to pay, it received no funding from the government. The climate of church-state relations in Northern Ireland in respect to medical care would also have been influenced by the controversy in the Republic of Ireland where the government and the Catholic Church had clashed over the government's intention to introduce free medical care to certain groups coupled with compulsory measures to control the spread of infectious diseases. The bishops who were to negotiate with the Stormont government about the status of the Mater had had recent experience of successfully defending Catholic ethical principles against what they saw as a socialist invasion of Catholic moral territory.

In Northern Ireland the Ministry of Health was unwilling to follow English practice of allowing voluntary hospitals that wished to remain outside the Health Service to receive grants. Accordingly, at the beginning of the new health service in 1948 the Mater Hospital was 'deemed not to be a hospital for the purposes of any of the provisions of this Act'. It lost all claim to future funding and lost some of the funding that it had previously received in respect to nurses' salaries and some other matters.

Gray's careful study of the relations between the trustees and the Ministry of Health chronicles the various stages leading to its eventual assimilation into the NHS (Gray, 1993). From the mid-1940s the unionist government was keen that the Mater should become part of the NHS but there were obstacles to this, not the least of which was that the Government of Ireland Act (1920) prohibited the support by government of any religion. The government's position was that for the hospital to receive financial support its property must be relinquished by the Catholic Church, a proposal which the Cardinal at Armagh termed '... this confiscation of Catholic property'. The position of the Catholic Church was that the trustees of the hospital were bound by canon law to implement the trusts they had undertaken and they could not relinquish their responsibility or hand over to the unionist government the property they held in trust.

By the mid-1960s there were several powerful drivers for change although as yet no movement was discernible on either the trustees' part or the government's part. Financial realities, in the form of a large and escalating overdraft together with the need to replace outdated buildings and equipment, were pressing on the bishop and his colleagues as the trustees of the hospital. For the government, the Mater question was acquiring a wider significance as a barometer of the progress of Captain Terence O'Neill's community relations programme. This was vividly expressed by the nationalist member for Belfast, Falls, Harry Diamond, when he said at Stormont that 'The treatment of the Mater Hospital is the acid test of justice towards the minority in this community' (Hansard HC Debates, vol. 64, c. 2902 (1965)).

By the end of the 1960s, there was wide public agreement that the situation was unsatisfactory and that the government needed to do something to provide public finance to the Mater, which was a major medical resource to the population of north and west Belfast and further afield. No way had yet been found to reconcile the government's demands of public accountability and control with the demands of the original trusts of the hospital that required the principles and values of the Catholic Church to be upheld. Finally, in November 1971 the Bishop of Down and Connor and the chairman of the Northern Ireland Hospitals Authority signed a deed of agreement that leased the hospital to the Department of Health for 999 years and passed the rights and liabilities of the hospital's board to the government. The deed of agreement was enshrined in an Order (no. 387) of the Ministry of Health and Social Services thus giving it statutory effect, a provision that was to be of great importance.

The history of the Mater Hospital is an illuminating case study of the interaction of a major Catholic voluntary institution with the devolved unionist government that was established in 1922. The hospital was an icon of Catholic moral and ethical values that, paradoxically, enjoyed the support of the Catholic and Protestant working-class population of north and west Belfast. Its settlement with the Department of Health in 1971 is contained in a remarkable document preserving the values of the hospital, particularly in the area of gynaecology and obstetrics. When the Ministry of Health subsequently found it necessary to rationalise obstetric services, the deed of arrangement preserved the position of the Mater and, by virtue of the agreement, bound the Ministry not to reduce the number of obstetric beds at the hospital. It may have been fortunate for the trustees that their eventually successful negotiations took place at a time when the government was keen to find a high-profile symbol of its commitment to improving its relations with the Catholic community of Belfast (Clifford, 1991).

Voluntary child care

The passage of the Children's and Young Persons' Act in 1950 provided a statutory basis for welfare authorities to provide children's homes, and there was a slow growth in state provision for children in need. It also introduced a policy bias in favour of fostering over residential care. This legislative framework tended to undermine the core voluntary sector services in this field, which remained focused on the provision of care in large institutions, notwithstanding the emptying and closure of a number of industrial schools in Northern Ireland in the 1920s and 1930s. Fifty years of the operation of the Children's and Young Persons' Act was marked by the publication of *A Better Future: Fifty Years of Child Care in Northern Ireland* (DHSSPS, 2003).

However, voluntary organisations remained an important source of child-care up until the mid-1980s. In 1982 there were more voluntary sector children's homes than there had been in 1966 looking after 349 children rather than 298 children. In the early 1980s there were a number of scandals concerning child abuse and paramilitary involvement in homes, and following the publication of the Hughes Report into Children's Homes and Hostels in 1985 there was a rapid withdrawal of the voluntary sector from residential child care. The exceptions were homes run by Orders in the Catholic Church. By 1997 there were six homes left run by voluntary organisations, five of them by Catholic Orders. However, by 2000 all the latter had closed. The sole remaining voluntary sector provider is Belfast Central Mission, a welfare arm of the Methodist Church.

Changes in public attitudes to child care and the increasing cost of employing professionally qualified staff were major reasons for the withdrawal of the voluntary sector from this field. It may be considered significant that the homes run by Catholic Religious Orders on average survived about ten years longer than those run by secular organisations or the Protestant Churches, based as they were on religious vocations. Further scandals of abuse in these Church homes in both jurisdictions in Ireland and the demise of religious vocations have led to the final end of this chapter in the history of voluntary action in Northern Ireland.

The Voluntary Housing Association Movement in Northern Ireland pre-1976

After the Second World War, voluntary housing in Northern Ireland operated in the shadow of dominant institutional players such as the Northern Ireland Housing Trust (1945-71) and the Northern Ireland Housing Executive (1971 onward). Before the major changes to the institutional framework in the mid-1970s, there were a number of different forms of voluntary housing provision, although they made only a small contribution to the overall housing stock. By 1976, there were 58 voluntary housing bodies in Northern Ireland. Most prominent of these was Ulster Garden Villages, set up at the end of the Second World War by a philanthropic builder from Belfast, Thomas McGrath, using loan stock issues (with the intention of paying dividends) and borrowing from friendly societies and banks to build homes in garden villages for rent (McCreary, 1999). The society built about 1,500 dwellings on four main sites. However, it ran into severe financial difficulties, Thomas McGrath was forced to resign in 1952 and a receiver was appointed. While the early experience of this society may have set back the idea of limited-profit housing in Northern Ireland, the society, when subsequently reconstituted as a charitable trust, played an important role in the voluntary sector as a source of grants and loans to a wide range of charitable causes including homelessness charities, such as the Simon Community (McCreary, 1999). Other non-state funded housing institutions included Victoria Estates, founded by Fred Tughan, in the 1950s, and the Bangor Provident Trust. This trust, while it remained 'unregistered' for public subsidy, played a direct role in supporting the establishment of a housing association movement in Northern Ireland in the late 1970s (NIFHA, 1997).

Dungannon and District Housing Association (registered 1963) and Derry Housing Association (registered 1965, now known as the North and West Housing Association) used the Industrial and Provident Society framework to provide housing for Catholics in response to alleged discrimination by some local authorities. The Derry Association was founded by Father Mulvey, a dynamic priest at St Eugene's Cathedral, influenced by the pioneering housing aid work of Father (later Bishop) Eamon Casey in London. The association in Dungannon promoted self-build schemes partly funded by the Department of the Environment. They continue today as voluntary housing associations.

'The Troubles', community development and the reform of Government in the 1970s

The pattern of two parallel systems of voluntary social welfare with very little contact between the two that had been established by the start of the First World War essentially survived with very little change until the late 1960s. The onset of 'the Troubles' in 1969 destroyed the legitimacy of this social order as certainly as it destroyed the political order of which it was a mirror image.

Cochrane and Dunn (2002) argue that the collapse of the Stormont regime in 1972 was a fulcrum around which the patterns of community activism changed dramatically. Before 1972, the Catholic community had a history of community activism, looked inward for resources and leadership, but was politically fractured and had low community morale, while the Protestant community had a low history of community activism, looked to the Stormont administration for resources and leadership, was politically united and possessed high morale. There was a close identification between the Protestant community and government. The institutions of government were 'their' institutions whose objects were seen as promoting their interests. After 1972, the Catholic community gained in morale, developed its community activism and became more politically united while the Protestant community lost its sense of power and self-confidence and fractured politically (Cochrane and Dunn, 2002). In losing its sense of preferment, the Protestant community has always found it difficult to achieve a viable focus around which community activism might purposefully coalesce. Thus in this sense, for Catholics, community development has been *against the state*, while for Protestants, it has *been the state*.

During the next decade, the shape of voluntary action in Northern Ireland was substantially remodelled, laying the groundwork for institutional changes that were subsequently consolidated in the 1980s.

Reform of Public Administration in 1973

The administration of public services in Northern Ireland was fundamentally reformed in 1973 following the collapse of the Stormont administration. Radical institutional changes were introduced as a result of the review of local government (the Report of the Review Body in Northern Ireland – the Macrory Report) in 1970. Major public services such as health and social services, education and housing, became the responsibility of new administrative structures, stripping local government of many of its key functions and leaving local councils with some residual powers, including responsibility for refuse collection and disposal, sport and recreation.

The county council-led structures were abolished and replaced by 26 district councils with very limited powers. The welfare function was amalgamated with the Northern Ireland Hospitals Authority into four unitary Health and Social Services Boards whose members were appointed by the responsible Minister. The Boards were to report to a unitary Department. Each was sub-divided into a number of administrative districts. Northern Ireland remains the only part of the United Kingdom with a structure that amalgamates health and personal social services. In this, it more closely resembles the structure of regional health boards in the Republic of Ireland. At the same time a unitary housing authority, the Northern Ireland Housing Executive, was established, and education was amalgamated with the libraries service and responsibility passed to five Education and Library Boards. Since that time public administration in Northern Ireland has been dominated by a complex structure of appointed Boards with only very residual levels of accountability to the population they serve.

The reforms were motivated by a desire to rationalise services (and, in the case of housing, remove them from direct local political control) rather than by any perceived need to adjust the levels of statutory responsibility. These remained substantially as they had been defined in the 1940s legislation. Aspects were closely modelled on parallel reforms introduced in Britain that saw the introduction of unitary Social Services Departments in England and Wales, and Social Work Departments in Scotland, and the reorganisation of the health service.

The new Department of Health and Social Services in Northern Ireland issued a circular on voluntary organisations to the new Health and Social Services Boards in 1974. The perceived need for further policy clarification was influenced by debates in Britain about the need for the new amalgamated social services authorities to develop partnership arrangements with voluntary agencies and by the appearance of community development as a method of intervention in this context. This circular reiterated the view of the 1948 circular that partnerships were needed between state and voluntary agencies in order to meet social needs. But it also emphasised the independence of voluntary action and its role in promoting 'the active participation of individuals, groups and communities in the process of social development' (Kearney, 1995: 13).

The rise of community development in Northern Ireland
Community development is a collective process whereby members of a community come together to effect change and to address the needs within the community based on principles of self-help and inclusion. Community development has had a long history in Northern Ireland. Its origins can be traced to colonial and post-colonial situations in the Third World, United Nations Programmes, the Irish tradition of self-help and the United States experience of community action and anti-poverty programmes (Community Development Review Group, 1991a). McCready refers to the beginnings of community development in unemployment and rent protests in the 1930s and the lessons learned from initiatives in Ireland such as the classical community development model, Muintir na Tíre in 1931, which made a substantial contribution to both the theory and practice of community development in Ireland (McCready, 2001).

Community development continued in the post-war era, flourishing for example, in areas such as housing associations and co-operatives and the growth of credit unions and in social protest action through for example, the Tenant movement in the 1950s and the Civil Rights Movement in the 1960s (Kilmurray, 2000). In the Catholic community there was a continuing emphasis on the tradition of self-help around the development of the social economy. This drew on the traditions established by the co-operative movement. Very often it was priest led, but not church run. Towards the end of the 1960s, there was a significant growth in the number of community groups. In the statutory sector, community development found its way into the social work setting as a result of influential reports such as the Younghusband Report in 1959 (*Report of the Working Party on Social Services in the Local Authority Health and Welfare Services*) and the Seebohm Report in 1968 (*Report of the Committee on Local Authority and Allied Personal Social Services*). McCready, however, claims that there was no great expectation that the Northern Ireland Government or local authorities would give a large-scale commitment to community development.

'The Troubles' and community development
The period from 1969 onwards is widely regarded as marking the emergence of community development and the community movement in Northern Ireland. The outbreak of 'the Troubles' in 1969 and the social, economic and political situation at that time created conditions for further growth, with the emergence of a strong community movement. McCready (2001) stresses that 'since 1969 community development in Northern Ireland has been inexorably linked with, and inter-connected with the political situation'. It can also be said that community development has had an interrelationship with government priorities and initiatives in fields such as community relations, poverty, social exclusion and tackling multiple deprivation. Furthermore, the level and extent of state intervention has varied, with definable peaks in the period since 1969.

Intervention by the State
In response to 'the Troubles', a number of government initiatives were taken to heal the divisions in society and to improve community relations. A Ministry of Community Relations and a Community Relations Commission were established under the Community Relations Act (Northern Ireland), 1969. The main strategy adopted by the Commission for promoting community relations was the initiation of community-development programmes across Northern Ireland. Community-development officers appointed under the Act delivered a community-development programme, working closely with local groups and associations and encouraging the formation of new ones. Capital grants were available under the Social Need Act (Northern Ireland), 1969 for community groups wanting to build community centres in urban areas of social need.

Fitzduff (1995) notes that while community development as a philosophy and in practice was an approach then becoming popular as a method of assisting development in some Third World countries, 'the decision to use it to assist the management of a situation which appeared to be developing into a major religio/politico conflict was however both unique and relatively untested.'

The Commission was short lived, being discontinued by the power-sharing Executive in 1974. The Commission's advisory role was to be taken over by a new, more broadly based body and its executive functions would be transferred to other agencies. At central government level, responsibility for community development and community relations was transferred to the Department of Education. Maurice Hayes, the Commission's first Chairman, who resigned in the immediate aftermath of Bloody Sunday, commented on its closure in his *Minority Verdict* (1995):

> The SDLP took the view that now it was in Government there were no longer community relations problems, that it would speak for the Catholic population, and that the Commission was superfluous. This played into the hands of the civil servants in the Department of Community Relations, which had been jealous of the Commission. They quickly captured Ivan Cooper, the new minister. The Commission had few friends, the Commission staff even fewer, and so by the efforts of an SDLP minister committed to the improvement of community relations, it was closed down, although by the time this closure came into effect the Executive itself had fallen.

Although it was short lived, a legacy of the work of the Commission and of its community-development officers was the umbrella bodies that provided an infrastructure for community groups in Belfast and community and resource centres. As Kilmurray (2000) comments:

> ... the legacy of the community development strategy implemented by the Commission field workers continued in the form of sundry Community Resource Centres across the North, and an informal network of personal contacts that was to roll forward the philosophy of community action.

The vitality of the community movement continued throughout the early to mid-1970s. Hywel Griffiths, the first Director of the Commission, saw 1974 and 1975 as 'the period when traditionally strong identifiable areas such as the Bogside in Derry or the Shankill in Belfast brought to fruition schemes for a rich variety of community development projects with workers who had emerged from the community and who had learned their skills from the community's experience' (Griffiths, 1978).

There was at that time an urgent need for a government strategy to fill the vacuum created by the Commission's demise, while the announcement of the decision to wind up the Commission was, in the words of the Community Development Review Group, seen by many as marking:

> ... the beginning of the wilderness years for community development as it no longer had a legitimating focus. The premature hope expressed by the then Minister responsible – 'the slate has been wiped clean' – and the rude rebuttal of that hope a few weeks later by what might be described as a different kind of collective action – the Ulster Workers' Committee strike – were an ironic commentary on the state of community development and community relations and on the failure to create the cross community social movement envisaged in the heady days of 1968.

McGinley (1988) also noted that by 1974, 'the pressure was mounting to develop a strategy that would involve community groups more closely with existing bodies and the agencies they were dealing with regularly, while at the same time pacifying dissatisfied councillors, who were frustrated by the limited powers they now possessed as a result of reorganisation.'

Two initiatives by government sought to fill the vacuum referred to above. The Advisory Conference of Community Associations set up in 1975 and lasting till 1979, sought to give community groups a voice in the decision-making process. But the major initiative was to give district councils responsibility for the community services remit. The 1975 Moyle Report (*Report of the Joint Working Party on Sport and Recreational Provision of Districts Councils*) identified local councils as being the most appropriate bodies to discharge the community services remit. McCready (2001) notes that community groups viewed the decision with some trepidation and saw it as having a huge impact on community development. Not only did it result in the bureaucratisation and institutionalisation of community development, but it also curtailed the development of the work of the Health and Social Services Boards which had shown a willingness to embrace community development and engage productively with the emerging community group infrastructure.

The Councils' Community Services Programme, introduced in 1976, supported the provision of community centres, local advice services, resource centres, grants to community groups and the employment of staff in district councils. Responsibility for the Programme at central government level was transferred from the Department of Education to the Department of Health and Social Services in 1995, and in 1997 the Department undertook a major review of the Programme. This culminated in a revised Community Support Programme, still in operation, under which district councils are required to draw up community support plans and provide increased support for local advice centres and community groups.

Relegation by the state: growth in the community movement
Against the background of the perceived relegation of community-work responsibilities to district councils and with state intervention in community development receding, a number of community activists and community leaders came together to form a new organisation in 1974 – Community Organisations of Northern Ireland (CONI) – to act as a co-ordinating mechanism and a lobby for change. But this potentially positive development was put under pressure by the emergence of paramilitary groupings. Some groups from Protestant communities broke away and helped set up the Ulster Community Action Group (UCAG) as a loyalist alternative to CONI. This umbrella Protestant community-development organisation was set up in early 1976 on the initiative of Andy Tyrie, one of the leaders of the Ulster Workers' Strike of 1974, and was promoted by the inner council of the UDA (McCready, 2001). UCAG organised mainly in the north-east of Northern Ireland and in Belfast. It received financial support from the Joseph Rowntree Charitable Trust and from the Northern Ireland Department of Education. It employed two full-time organisers whose main purpose was to develop community work in Protestant areas. McCready indicates that the UCAG organisers were employed to encourage community groups to identify common problems and to encourage them to develop self-help schemes.

For a short period in the late 1970s UCAG received significant support in Protestant areas of Northern Ireland and articulated the needs and frustrations of working-class communities that felt disempowered and under-represented following the suspension of Stormont in 1972. The continuation of political and sectarian violence meant that it was impossible for community work to stretch across the sectarian divide. There was little opportunity or enthusiasm for joint work with CONI. Kilmurray (2000) comments that 'the establishment of UCAG was seen as deliberately divisive by some, and as a positive stage in the development of loyalist social consciousness by others.'

McCready (2001) saw the end of co-ordinating groups such as CONI and UCAG at the turn of the decade as reflecting the increasing sense of powerlessness being experienced by communities in their attempts to exert influence on the issues of poverty, debt and redevelopment: 'The Government circulars may have provided the formula for funding and support but the community groups experienced little in the way of empowerment through experiencing meaningful participation.'

The state intervenes again
The end of the 1970s saw a period of further government intervention in the community-development field led by the Direct Rule Minister, Peter Melchett, who launched the Belfast Areas of Need (BAN) Project in 1977 to

tackle the main social problems in a number of deprived wards on a multi-agency basis and in consultation with the communities involved.

A key government initiative with significant impact on community development was the setting up of the Northern Ireland Voluntary Trust (NIVT) in March 1979. With no similar initiatives elsewhere in the UK, the government supported the creation of an independent trust, providing an initial capital donation of £500,000 and an undertaking to match on a £ for £ basis any donations that the trust might receive from private sources up to a maximum of a further £250,000, a ceiling later raised to £500,000. NIVT was established less as a result of a clear strategic policy and more as a result of the personal initiative taken by a senior civil servant who had moved to the Department of Health and Social Services from the now defunct Community Relations Commission and the openness to innovation by the then Minister, Lord Peter Melchett. The Community Development Review Group (1991a) noted the Trust's significant impact on community development in Northern Ireland and in addition: 'NIVT's importance lies in being able to take a strategic view of the contribution of community and voluntary groups and providing a new focus for ideas about community development.'

The Trust continues to play a pivotal role in the funding and wider development of community development in Northern Ireland. Twenty-three years later, in 2002, the Trust changed its name to the Community Foundation for Northern Ireland, a decision which 'not only firmly located the NIVT in a growing international network of Community Foundations, but also acknowledged a shift from the earlier seeding phase of the Trust's work to a celebration of community growth and diversification' (NIVT, 2002).

The post-1976 Housing Association Movement
The modern housing association movement grew out of a conference held at Corrymeela near Ballycastle in 1974. Convened jointly by the Department of Environment and Bangor Provident Trust, it was attended by politicians and community activists from Belfast and Derry (McLachlan, 1997). The conference sought 'an alternative to the centralised housing authority which had wiped out the diversity reflected in some 65 local government housing bodies and commissions' (Holmes, 1995: 8). At the conference, a voluntary housing steering committee was elected to press for new housing legislation to give Northern Ireland housing associations support similar to that established in England and Wales, following the passing there of the Housing Act, 1974. State funding was introduced under the Housing NI Order 1976, replicating the system operating in England under the 1974 Housing Act.

The focus of the government's early programme for the voluntary housing movement was, first, on housing for the elderly, people with physical, sensory or intellectual disability or people with mental illness; and secondly on urban projects involving the rehabilitation of working-class housing in Belfast, designed to restore declining areas through compulsory acquisition. In 1976, the government gave associations in Northern Ireland a programme to complete by 1980. This involved the completion of 1,000 new units of accommodation for elderly people and the rehabilitation of 2,000 unfit houses. The Department of the Environment's programme called for 2,000 houses to be vested each year for the following five years by housing associations. Early progress was made. By the end of 1979, there were 25 new-build schemes for 750 units either completed or on site for elderly or disabled people, with a further 80 schemes for 2,500 dwellings approved in principle or under consideration.

General-needs housing was at this time the preserve of the Northern Ireland Housing Executive. Up to then, housing associations had been involved in providing general family housing and in meeting special needs. From the late 1970s, registered associations were required to discontinue general family housing and to develop housing for special needs groups. In England, housing associations had pioneered the provision of accommodation for these groups and there was early interest in initiating projects in Northern Ireland using joint funding arrangements under which partnerships were developed between a statutory or voluntary social services agency and a housing association. Joint funding was a contractual arrangement for the duration of the contract, a selection scheme for tenants, accountancy arrangements, repairs and decoration procedures and the listing of actions that would automatically terminate the agreement. Joint funding developed during the 1980s and 1990s and enabled many creative partnerships between housing associations and voluntary social service bodies, statutory health and social services agencies and voluntary bodies.

By 1980 there were 44 registered and active housing associations in Northern Ireland. The two critical factors in the rapid take-off of the sector were state funding and links with English institutions. The new associations all used the Industrial and Provident Society model and registered with the Department of the Environment to receive nearly 100 per cent public subsidy for new schemes. The housing charity Shelter worked with the National Federation of Housing Associations and the department to set up the Northern Ireland Federation of Housing Associations (NIFHA) in 1977. Support also came from a number of English associations that set up branches in Northern Ireland which subsequently became independent. Holmes described this period as one in which 'no dedicated group of individuals seeking to serve their community was ever prevented from meeting a genuine housing need' (Holmes, 1995: 6).

Several associations were already providing accommodation for elderly people: Bangor Provident and Shankill Road Mission. Now two English-based associations, James Butcher and Anchor, were encouraged to establish associations in Northern Ireland, called the James Butcher and FOLD respectively. Shortly thereafter, a number of other organisations with a special emphasis on housing for elderly people were registered: Presbyterian, Covenanter, Royal British Legion, Masonic, McGarel, North Belfast Mission, NIH and Lisnagarvey. In the field of special housing needs, other associations were established to respond to a range of needs. These were: Habinteg (disabled people); SHAC (student housing); Ulidia (single parents); Hearth (architectural heritage); Gosford (hostel in Armagh); Craigowen (Rudolph Steiner Movement) and Broadway (hospital staff). The Northern Ireland Co-Ownership Housing Association was established to promote low-cost home ownership through equity-sharing arrangements. Some of the associations just mentioned directly managed the accommodation they provided, but others entered into joint management arrangements with specialised voluntary organisations under which the voluntary organisation provided the care services and managed the project.

Community-based housing associations
Birrell (1995) has drawn attention to the creation of community-based housing associations as an important feature of the voluntary housing movement in Northern Ireland. These associations were, he suggests, 'viewed as one way of bridging the gap between local people and the "remote" Housing Executive and central government'. The following Belfast-based housing associations specialised in rehabilitation: Botanic; Ballynafeigh; Clonard; Connswater; Shankill Road Mission; Willowfield Parish; Newington; Grove; Woodvale and Shankill; St Matthew's; Belfast Community and the Family Housing Association. Community-based housing associations are often located in small tightly-knit communities and are usually representative of the affiliations of those communities. It is a particular challenge for them to bridge the sectarian divide in terms of committees or tenants. Some community-based associations played a vital part in the rehabilitation of their areas and were closely involved in the formulation of plans for Housing Action Areas. Their contribution to the sustainability of inner-city communities during the late 1970s and 1980s was vital when those communities were disintegrating because of political violence, deteriorating housing, poor environmental conditions and the migration of families to Craigavon, Antrim and Ballymena.

Various special needs groups were the focus of the concern of these new housing associations, such as people with an alcohol addiction, women victims of domestic violence and homeless persons. Triangle Women's Housing Association was established in the Coleraine, Portrush and

Portstewart area with the immediate purpose of providing a refuge for women and their children subjected to domestic violence. From 1978, Belfast Improved Houses (BIH) provided a hostel to accommodate mothers and their children who were victims of violence. In Derry, the Derry Housing Association undertook a hostel project for alcoholics, managed by the Templemore Housing Association. The Church of Ireland Housing Association provided accommodation for retired people and in particular for retired clergy.

Other developments in public policy with implications for voluntary action
A common theme running through the major public policy documents from the 1970s onwards was the need for and value of partnership between the state and the voluntary sector based on commonality of purpose and interest. This emphasis on partnership was not new.

Following the reorganisation of the Health and Personal Social Services, the Department of Health and Social Services issued guidance in 1974 to the newly created Health and Social Services Boards on their support for voluntary organisations (Circular 15 (OS) 1/74). Principles were outlined and general guidance was given on the encouragement, mobilisation and co-ordination of voluntary effort in each Board's area. The need for close liaison between Boards and appropriate voluntary bodies and community groups was also recognised in the Department's first *Regional Plan for the Development of Health and Personal Social Services in Northern Ireland* (DHSS, 1975).

Putting this into practice was another matter, however. In 1978, the Northern Ireland Council of Social Services complained that:

> ... in spite of a wealth of public statement about the need for and the importance of co-operation with voluntary services, there is little evidence of any initiative by Government or Area Boards to promote increased assistance from voluntary organisations.

Almost a decade later, in a 1987 report, the Northern Ireland Council for Voluntary Action (this organisation is discussed in more detail later) complained about the lack of contact and joint working (NICVA, 1987). In retrospect, the fault may be seen to have lain on both sides. The only study on the voluntary sector in Northern Ireland conducted at that time, *Yesterday's Heritage or Tomorrow's Resource*, found that welfare-focused voluntary organisations tended to be inward-looking and detached (Griffiths et al, 1978). The study's authors remarked on the strikingly little effect the civil conflict, which had begun in earnest in 1969, had had on such voluntary organisations. Few of the organisations they surveyed saw themselves as promoters of social change and there was a general acceptance of existing categories of social need.

Towards a cross-departmental policy
The publication in 1978 of three influential documents was to lead to government action in Northern Ireland and paved the way both for significant developments in policy and for the first steps in articulating policy on a cross-departmental basis. The report of a Committee of Enquiry funded by charitable trusts and chaired by Lord Wolfenden, *The Future of Voluntary Organisations*, made a number of specific recommendations both for voluntary organisations themselves and for government at central and local level. The Committee had taken evidence in Northern Ireland and intended that its analysis and recommendations apply throughout the United Kingdom. In response, the Home Office (1978) issued a Consultative Document, *The Government and the Voluntary Sector*, which contained a separate chapter on Northern Ireland. The New University of Ulster's *Yesterday's Heritage, Tomorrow's Resource* was the first major academic study of the voluntary sector in Northern Ireland, focusing on voluntary organisations providing social services (Griffiths et al, 1978).

The Wolfenden Report helped bring greater conceptual clarity to the nature of the relationship between voluntary action and the state. It was the first public document in the UK to use the concept of a single voluntary 'sector', an idea that rapidly entered general policy discourse and was to have a significant impact on the development of structures in Northern Ireland.

Following publication of these documents, a wide-ranging strategic review of government policy towards the voluntary organisations in the social welfare field was carried out on an inter-departmental basis by the Co-ordinating Committee on Social Problems (CCSP). This took into account the Northern Ireland responses to the Home Office Consultative Document and the questions of future policy raised in *Yesterday's Heritage, Tomorrow's Resource*. It took account also of the findings and recommendations of a review (by a sub-committee of the Central Personal Social Services Advisory Committee) of the policy in the Department of Health and Social Services' 1974 circular to Health and Social Services Boards on *Support for Voluntary Organisations*. The resulting report *Tomorrow's Resource* (CCSP, 1980), restated the principle of partnership and defined the main elements of a partnership approach. It set out general guidelines to which each department should have regard in applying its funding policy. The report set its face against the establishment in Northern Ireland of a local equivalent of the Voluntary Services Unit in the Home Office, a development, however, which was eventually to take place in 1993. Government endorsed the recommendations as indicating the general direction which government policy should take towards the voluntary sector in Northern Ireland and as the context within which departments and statutory agencies should frame their individual policies for working with voluntary bodies.

In the health and personal social services field, the Department of Health and Social Services issued a discussion paper to elicit suggestions for practical measures to realise further the principles in *Tomorrow's Resource* at field level. This resulted in the issue to Health and Social Services Boards in March 1985 of a circular *Co-operation Between the Statutory and Voluntary Sectors in the Health and Personal Social Services* (DHSS, 1985). While confirming and augmenting the guidance in the 1974 circular, it broke new ground by giving a commitment to set up for the first time inter-departmental co-ordinating machinery, subsequently the Interdepartmental Voluntary Action Group, and by asking Boards to draw up for discussion draft policy statements on their relations with voluntary organisations.

Growth, consolidation, diversification and incorporation: the 1980s and early 1990s

The concept of a single 'voluntary sector'
The idea that the myriad organisations and associations in society that were neither part of the state nor part of the private market thereby had a single shared identity delineated by the metaphor of a voluntary or third 'sector' emerged in academic sociological and business literature in the first half of the 1970s in the United States of America (Hall, 1992). It was imported into the UK and influenced the way in which voluntary action was thought of by way of the Wolfenden Committee report, the first public document in the UK to use the term.

It is hard to over-emphasise the importance of the concept of a single 'sector' for developments in Northern Ireland since then. It has provided the essential conceptual framework around which a discourse of a single sphere of voluntary, as opposed to state or private, action has developed. This discourse has reinforced the legitimacy of generalist and single-issue networking organisations and enhanced the ability of these networks to promote the idea of a sphere of action standing apart from the deep divisions in society and built on secular reformist values. It has also provided a discourse around which government has been able to structure its support for the development of voluntary action.

It is arguable that without the power of this discourse, voluntary organisations would have been much less well placed to respond positively to the broad peace process of the 1990s, or become important drivers of change.

Like almost every other aspect of social life in Northern Ireland, until the 1970s voluntary action was substantially structured along sectarian lines. Since the 1970s there has been further polarisation of the two main communities, a process that appears to have accelerated once again in the late 1990s. As has been argued, there have been persistent differences in the development of community-based voluntary action between the Protestant and Catholic communities, based on very different experiences and expectations of broader political and social changes. The apparent paradox of the growing strength and presence of a singly conceived 'sector' in Northern Ireland against continuing deep divisions in the experience of community-based voluntary action requires some analysis.

The historical record suggests that two processes worked together to produce this result. Underlying both is a consequence of Northern Ireland being a relatively very small part of the United Kingdom. Firstly, the framework underpinning the general development of public policy and the political settlement embodied in the institutions of the Welfare State have both been imported from outside, with little reference to social and political conditions in Northern Ireland. Political debate in the UK about the proper division between public and private action, between the state and voluntary action, was barely influenced by debate within Northern Ireland itself. Yet the legislative and administrative consequences of that debate created the policy context in which voluntary organisations had to operate. Although the factors that give rise to the range of voluntary action are undoubtedly complex, the British political settlement that resulted in the policies and practices of the Welfare State have had a crucial bearing on the ways in which voluntary organisations developed. In many ways, experience in Northern Ireland paralleled developments in Britain. There, after the Wolfenden Report, both voluntary organisations and government had an interest in managing relations through a discourse based on the idea of a single sector, although each side very often had rather different interpretations of its meaning. Thus the policy environment in Northern Ireland was favourable to sectoral discourse as it reflected developments in Britain. Furthermore (and very importantly) promoting the voluntary sector as a single entity was to become an important tool in managing the conflict as it gave government a way of addressing the demands of voluntary and community organisations without having to deal with institutions embedded in each of the two main communities.

The second process was the influence of the so-called 'third wave' of voluntary action in Northern Ireland. This generated a complex network of single issue, reformist organisations that identified a common set of values with much of the more indigenous forms of community-based action developing at the same time. With roots in the social revolution and radicalism of the 1960s, the 'third wave' of voluntary action emerged at the end of that decade and in the 1970s in Britain. It re-energised the sphere of voluntary action and constituted the first social movement, since that led by nineteenth-century evangelicals, that fundamentally recreated voluntary action in its own image whose earlier influence was noted in chapter one.

Kendall and Knapp (1996) note that while some of these developments had their roots in the 1950s (earlier in the case of Citizens' Advice Bureaux), in the 1960s and 1970s a range of entirely new organisations emerged carrying no philanthropic baggage from the past. Among others that they note are Shelter and the Simon Community (homelessness), Women's Aid and Gingerbread, the Child Poverty Action Group and Friends of the Earth. Many of these organisations were to spawn counterparts in Northern Ireland, sharing their secular and reformist value base and very often their names. Usually, however, they remained formally independent of their British counterparts and very often developed in different directions. To this list can be added a number of other organisations which contributed to the blossoming of single-issue work, e.g. Age Concern, the Law Centre and the independent advice sector. Such organisations were drivers of community development and continue to play a significant role in the community-development field today.

The broader international social movement that had generated these changes had earlier informed the creation of the Northern Ireland Civil Rights Association (NICRA). NICRA had fallen foul of the zero sum game of Northern Ireland politics, due in large measure to the response of the Stormont regime to the challenge it posed. However, the new voluntary organisations were able to carve out a non-sectarian public space in which to organise and make their cases as the issues at stake were organised around a perceived failure of the Welfare State to deliver on its original promises. A British import, the Welfare State (and its institutions) has never been a political point of contention in Northern Ireland.

The influence of the women's movement was an important source of the growing ideological coherence of a civic space in Northern Ireland that existed apart from sectarian divisions and the dynamic of the political conflict. Abbott and McDonough (1989) point out that women's issues became the focus around which the women who were the backbone of many community-based associations in working-class neighbourhoods were able to find common cause. Women's issues were also to become the link between professional women working in the new voluntary organisations and women who were community activists. This was particularly evident in women's issues organisations like Gingerbread and the Northern Ireland Pre-School Playgroups Association, both of which support a network of local groups of activists, but it is evident also in more generalist organisations or those concerned with other issues. Although the influence of the women's movement would merit more investigation, it is clear from the available evidence that it has had a wide-ranging influence. One of its most visible outcomes was the establishment of the Northern Ireland Women's Coalition in the 1990s – a political party that was to have a significant impact on the Good Friday Agreement.

The NICSS becomes NICVA

These developments provide the context for the establishment of the Northern Ireland Council for Voluntary Action (NICVA) in 1985. The Northern Ireland Council of Social Service (NICSS) had been established in 1938 as a government-backed initiative to replicate the Council of Social Service model that had emerged in the inter-war years in Britain. By the late 1970s, the ongoing violence, the upsurge in community-based voluntary action and a growing concern in government to formalise relations with the voluntary sector was putting the Council in crisis. While the Moyle Report saw district councils being given responsibility for community development, the Community Relations Commission's information and publishing function was given to the NICSS which established the Community Information Service with its own standing committee within the Council in 1975. This brought the ethos and assumptions of community development into the heart of an organisation that was ill-equipped to absorb them.

The Council had established a handicapped persons committee in 1949, to coincide with the passage of the Welfare Services Act. The task of the committee had been to promote the co-ordination of voluntary and statutory services. Over the years it had engaged in a wide variety of activities from running conferences and exhibitions to pioneering rehabilitation and information services (DHSS, 1993). In 1979, it was established as a standing committee within the wider NICSS, responsible for a range of functions for which it received government funding, including in 1981 servicing the Northern Ireland Committee for the International Year of Disabled People. Other standing committees were the Northern Ireland Association of Citizens' Advice Bureaux (NIACAB) and Age Concern.

The relationship between all these standing committees and the Council's Executive effectively made the Council ungovernable. Each committee had its own quasi-independent membership structure and pursued its own agenda with little reference to the rest of the organisation. Appointed by the Minister for Health and Social Services, a wide-ranging review was conducted into the affairs of NICSS, chaired by a Methodist Minister, Harold Good. As a result, the Northern Ireland Council for the Handicapped (NICH), Age Concern and NIACAB were established as independent organisations. NICH was subsequently renamed Disability Action. The Community Information

Service was integrated into a new single management structure answerable to a single Board of Directors through the Director of the organisation. The reconstituted organisation was renamed as the Northern Ireland Council for Voluntary Action (NICVA), founded in 1985.

The restructuring of the NICSS and the emergence of NICVA may be seen as a key example of the process of formalising relations between government and voluntary action that was evident at this time. The process took place in a context provided by the Wolfenden Report (1978), which had argued strongly for the place of 'intermediary' representative bodies within the voluntary sector, and the government's response to it. But it also should be noted that the changes took the shape they did as a result of government initiative and under government direction. The Good Review into the NICSS was appointed by and reported to the Minister. It was the Minister who ensured that the recommended structural changes took place by first agreeing to them and then finding the means to finance the necessary divorces.

The new NICVA had to find a balance between the conflicting demands of the new community-based associations and the older philanthropic associations. But by the time of the debate in the middle of the 1980s, the value base of the newly formalised sector was to be drawn from the agenda of the new 'third wave' organisations rather than from the older philanthropic tradition. Thus NICVA's first mission statement started with the sentence: 'NICVA is a development agency committed to social change.' The mission statement went on to state that NICVA 'works for justice, equality and dignity throughout society by promoting opportunities for genuine popular control over the essential decisions which condition the lives of people in Northern Ireland' (NICVA, 1985).

From the beginning, NICVA sought to bridge the gap between community-based and voluntary organisations. In the view of its first director, this decision enabled the development of a shared identity across the voluntary-community divide that was not achieved to the same extent by its sister councils of voluntary organisations in England or Scotland where there are much deeper divisions between voluntary organisations and community development. However, one of the results of the shift in emphasis was a marginalisation of the older organisations with their roots in Protestant philanthropy within the identity of the newly conceptualised 'sector'. This was to have little impact on their resource base; some were quite wealthy and others were able to maintain and develop their own relationships with government funding departments.

As we move into the 1980s, we can note the development and growth of issue-based work in communities, with the emergence of a number of single-issue groups, the growing influence of the women's movement and the development of self-help groups. The women's movement brought a new dimension, new viewpoints and new vibrancy into community-development principles and practice, perhaps best exemplified in the Women's Information Days (Community Development Review Group, 1991a). McCready (2001) notes that women's groups in community centres added to an emerging infrastructure, some of them continuing today. Also in this period, some of the major voluntary organisations adopted community-development policies. As we have seen, community-development principles and practices were placed at the heart of the aims and values of the new NICVA, while community-development philosophies and policies were also adopted by organisations working in specific fields, such as the Northern Ireland Council for Disability (now Disability Action), Age Concern, the Northern Ireland Association for the Care and Resettlement of Offenders (NIACRO) and Extern. Community-based welfare rights work by organisations such as Citizens' Advice Bureaux, the Independent Advice Centres and the Belfast Law Centre also played an important role in the community-development field (see chapter six for a full discussion of advice services in Northern Ireland).

The growing influence of European Community funding streams
The period from 1986 onwards saw the re-emergence or, in McCready's terms, the re-interpretation of community development. A numbers of drivers of growth can be identified. One of these is the impact of European funding. In the 1970s, poverty was high on the agenda throughout the EU. Community projects in Northern Ireland were funded by three consecutive Anti-Poverty Programmes. The Belfast Welfare Rights Project was funded under the first European Poverty Programme 1975-1980. It successfully documented poverty in Belfast, explored the problems of low uptake of cash benefits and had some influence on the pattern of public spending. The second Anti-Poverty Programme, from 1986 till 1989, supported the Rural Action Project, the Belfast Centre for the Unemployed and the Derry Unemployed Workers' Group. The Rural Action Project, which piloted a community-development approach, demonstrated the value of community development as a means by which local communities could be engaged in the regeneration of their areas and was to have a major influence on rural development policy in Northern Ireland (see later section).

The Poverty 3 Programme followed on from the Second Programme and provided funding for one project, Brownlow Community Trust in Craigavon. The Trust provided an example of successful inter-agency co-operation, and in an evaluation of the project, Gaffikin and Morrissey (1994) described it as the first working partnership that informed the development of local area partnerships in Belfast at the same time (Spence, 1995).

Further boosts to community development came from European Union sources through two specific Community Infrastructure Measures and Social Inclusion Sub-Programmes in the Northern Ireland Single Programme 1994-1999 and the EU Special Support Programme for Peace and Reconciliation in Northern Ireland and the Border Counties 1995-1999. (The impact of these measures is discussed in more detail in chapter six.)

Hodgett (1996) has skilfully untangled the web of influences, strategies and tactics that led to the engagement of the European Union with the community and voluntary sector in Northern Ireland in the early and mid-1990s. The Northern Ireland Structural Funds Plan, published in September 1993, contained a sub-programme on 'Community Infrastructure', which was a part of the Operational Programme Plan on the Physical and Social Environment. Previous Structural Fund Plans had not contained anything similar. What was the background to the development of this policy and the use of this term? Hodgett's research suggests that there are several strands to the origins of the Community Infrastructure initiative and she lays bare the origins of the term itself. The first strand is to be found in the work of the Community Development Review Group (CDRG). The second was the strategy adopted by NICVA in 1991 to promote community development and to implement the Regional Community Development Project. Other factors include the creation of a policy network that included voluntary sector leaders, European Commission officials and influential senior civil servants based in Belfast who were subsequently to join with leaders of the sector in Northern Ireland in negotiating with Commission officials.

The CDRG was established in 1989 by community workers and researchers interested in extending the use of community-development practice in disadvantaged communities in Northern Ireland. The group appointed two of its members, Ken Logue and Niall Fitzduff, to consider the use of community development in Northern Ireland since 1970 and to assist in formulating a possible strategy for the future. Between 1989 and the summer of 1990 CDRG convened eight seminars in various locations and consulted more than 500 individuals and community bodies. Two bodies were set up that were to prove to be important and influential. The first of these was a panel of 40 people to review the material that arose from the consultations; the second was a 'small group of individuals with experience of policy making', some of whom were senior civil servants who would subsequently be influential in negotiations about the forthcoming Northern Ireland Structural Funds programme.

CDRG and NICVA recognised the importance of the European Commission and the huge potential of the Structural Funds as a source of support to Northern Ireland's voluntary and community sector. The Commission welcomed the opportunity of working with representatives of the sector because it was anxious to find a non-governmental partner with which it could work to develop regional policy for Northern Ireland.

One of the seminars held by CDRG was devoted to community development and economic development. Its report drew attention to the fact that the values implicit in economic development were 'often in conflict with the ideas of community development', and it recorded the view that 'too much is being expected too quickly without sufficient thought to community infrastructure' (Hodgett, 1996: 46). Hodgett comments that 'This became extremely significant. The phrase "Community Infrastructure" would be used *to sell back to the European Commission the values/dilemmas it was so familiar with ... and to extract from the Commission particular funding to be used, for and by, the voluntary sector in Northern Ireland for community development'* [emphasis added]. She also shows how a more facilitative policy approach and ethos began to emerge from government that led in turn to the establishment of an 'effective policy network' in the form of a new tripartite arrangement involving local civil servants, representatives of the voluntary sector and Commission officials.

The use of the concept of 'community infrastructure' also emerged in the *Strategy for the Support of the Voluntary Sector and of Community Development* (DHSS, 1993), which stated that 'All departments recognise the importance of an infrastructure for the voluntary sector ...'

On 2 December 1992, only a few months before the publication of the Strategy, the Department of Finance and Personnel had held an important consultative conference in Belfast to assist with the preparations for the Structural Funds submission to be made in early 1993. Hodgett reports the view of a senior civil servant that the workshop on Community Infrastructure at this conference had a 'gargantuan impact' (1996: 75). A number of key Commission officials were present at the workshop. Esben Poulsen, a senior Commission official, paid tribute to the 'multiplicity and dynamism' of Northern Ireland's voluntary and community sector. Three priorities were identified of which the first was 'community infrastructure'. 'Participants felt that Northern Ireland's economic, social and political development greatly depends on the development of community infrastructure and the elaboration of methods of co-operation and partnership between people' (Hodgett, 1996).

The workshop was followed by the publication of a NICVA document: *Proposals from the Voluntary Sector on the Structural Funds Plan* (NICVA, 1992). It advocated the defining of 'a major new programme ... Developing Community Infrastructure' which would establish a remit for investment in community development alongside investment in industrial development and investment in agricultural/rural development. It further recommended that Community Infrastructure might be contained within the Physical and Social Environment [PSEP] priority.

On 7 July 1993 the Draft Structural Funds Plan was published and included community infrastructure as a theme. In a comment on the Draft Plan

NICVA noted that 'The inclusion of community infrastructure as a theme is particularly interesting to the community and voluntary sector *who developed this concept during consultations last year*' [emphasis added] (Hodgett, 1996: 80).

The Northern Ireland Programme for Building Sustainable Prosperity 2000-2006 and the EU Programme for Peace and Reconciliation in Northern Ireland and the Border Counties of Ireland 2000-2004 (PEACE II) also provide a source of funding for community groups.

Action for Community Employment (ACE)
On the domestic front, a major spur to community development came through the Action for Community Employment (ACE) scheme introduced in 1981 by the then Department for Economic Development as a counter-unemployment measure. Voluntary and community groups were eligible to apply for funding to offer jobs to previously unemployed people for up to one year to undertake work of community benefit. A similar scheme, later known as Community Employment, was developed in the Republic. The scheme had a huge impact on the sector and McCready (2001) regarded its introduction as 'the single, most significant decision by government that changed the face of community work during the 1980s'. Donaghy notes the fact that:

> ACE in many cases virtually redefined what constituted community work and community organisations. One clear example of this could be seen in the large scale environmental ACE schemes that grew up in many towns and villages throughout Northern Ireland under the umbrella of 'community' organisations when in fact such organisations had been especially established for the purpose of administering the programme (Donaghy, 2000).

A key feature of the ACE scheme was that it was delivered largely through a parallel set of new voluntary organisations set up specifically for that purpose in each of the two main communities in Northern Ireland with substantial involvement by both the Catholic church and most Protestant denominations (Morrow, 1995). While the other voluntary and community organisations were also substantial users of the ACE scheme, the preponderance of jobs was in the large specialist schemes. This had the effect of recreating the sectarian division in the delivery of social welfare by a parallel set of voluntary agencies divided along ethno/religious lines and thus tended to undermine government policy of reinforcing a single identity voluntary sector, organised primarily around social issues. This was a very large scheme (at its peak running at over £50m a year supporting more than 10,000 jobs) that was the responsibility of a government department with no previous history of involvement with the voluntary sector and, at that stage, with no responsibility towards the sector as a whole. Its focus on labour market management meant that it was able to ignore some of the implications of its search for reliable partners.

The ACE scheme was also the setting for the 'political vetting' controversy. For more than 10 years from June 1985, it had been government policy not to provide funding for voluntary and community organisations if by thereby doing so, support might be seen as going to paramilitary organisations. The wording of the policy, announced by a parliamentary written answer, was broad: organisations would not be funded if they were perceived by government to have 'sufficiently close links with paramilitary organisations to give rise to the grave risk that to give support to these groups would have the effect of improving the standing, or furthering the aims, of a paramilitary organisation, whether directly or indirectly' (Hurd, 1985). Very few grants were in fact withdrawn for these reasons (probably in the region of 30 to 40 in total) before the policy fell into abeyance during the 1990s. However, it soured relationships between government and community groups, particularly those operating in strongly republican or loyalist areas, and was to remain an issue of contention between NICVA and government. The former was obliged to stand up for the principle of the independence of the voluntary sector in the face of what appeared to be a very opaque set of funding criteria that seemed to operate quite independently of the work being done.

The demise of the ACE scheme in favour of the government's New Deal initiatives caused a very significant reduction in the amount of funding available to community groups. For many groups, ACE was a financial lifeline, and the sector vigorously opposed the decision to end the scheme, since it was not certain that groups in receipt of ACE funding would be eligible under the provisions of New Deal.

The political context of community development in the late 1980s and early 1990s

The political vetting controversy should be understood as a partial government response to the emerging power of Sinn Féin as a political party in working-class Catholic areas, particularly in Belfast during the latter half of the 1980s. Sinn Féin had become a significant political force in the aftermath of the hunger strike of the IRA prisoners in the Maze prison that had taken place in 1981 during which one of the hunger strikers, Bobby Sands, had won a by-election in a constituency to the Westminster parliament. Sinn Féin was able to capitalise on the traditions of self-help and community organising within the Catholic community where it rapidly established a power base. In this context it is important to note that from the early 1970s to the early 1990s, in the estimate of the leadership of Sinn Féin, more than 10,000 people had passed through the ranks of the IRA. Former volunteers and former prisoners on release from the Maze prison formed a well-educated and highly motivated leadership cadre that was both to energise and politicise community-based voluntary action in these communities. The government's initial response was to attempt to marginalise Sinn Féin by directing public funds through organisations closely associated with the Catholic church. But by the early 1990s, there had been an important reversal of policy. The groundwork of the process that led later to the IRA ceasefires of 1994 was based in a move by the state to legitimise voluntary action closely linked to Sinn Féin and to bring it within the framework of the urban regeneration initiatives that were then getting off the ground (see below).

The Communities in Action Programme
Another example of a funding initiative that was to have a significant impact on community development was the Communities in Action Programme of the International Fund for Ireland (IFI). The initial work of the IFI was primarily associated with economic development. The Fund considered the concept of a specific social programme and in June 1996, the Communities in Action Programme was launched as a three-year pilot programme based on community-development principles and practices. The programme's overall aim was to stop the drift of a new generation of young people into social exclusion, and to support women in their own social and personal development and in their role as parents. It was based on three principles: harnessing local energy for lasting effects, a partnership approach, and the recognition of local diversity; and it focused on children, young people, and women. With an annual budget of £2.5 million for each of the three years, the programme eventually funded 30 projects: 23 in Northern Ireland and seven in the border counties. Despite a very positive evaluation of the programme, it was not continued by the IFI beyond its pilot phase, though finance was provided by the Fund for a transition period pending funding from other sources (LRDP, 1999). However, the good practice emanating from the programme has helped to inform the development of other programmes and some of the projects are still in operation today.

Urban regeneration
In 1987 the Direct Rule government established nine Belfast Action Teams (BAT) consisting of small teams of civil servants who were located in offices in communities and had grant budgets (typically from half to one million pounds per annum) to support local community projects. Part of the purpose of BAT was to pump-prime other government departments and agencies to target their own, much larger, funds on the acute social and economic problems of action team areas. BAT worked closely with local voluntary and

community groups and was an important source of funding to them. During its first three years the BAT teams supported 868 local projects of which 69 per cent were associated with community benefits. Birrell and Wilson consider that BAT proved to be 'a flexible and accessible source of funding for projects [that] help[ed] community groups to develop solutions to local problems' (Birrell and Wilson, 1993).

The following year, BAT was supplemented by the much larger Making Belfast Work (MBW) programme. MBW was a further funding programme that was created to support government's work in the field of urban regeneration, and to identify disadvantaged areas of Belfast where the efforts of community and the private sector would be harnessed to tackle the social, economic, educational and environmental problems. MBW began with four main themes: economic measures geared at training and enhancing job skills; educational initiatives that included support to schools and the establishment of a new further education college; health and environmental initiatives including immunisation; environmental improvement schemes designed to enhance the attractiveness of the urban areas. Both Making Belfast Work and the Belfast Action Teams emphasised the importance of community engagement and the involvement of the local voluntary and community sector (though in some cases that proved to be impossible owing to the policy of security vetting of community groups, discussed elsewhere in this report). Gaffikin and Morrissey (1990) note that the promotion of voluntary groups in the urban renewal process was in accord with the anti-statist ideologies of Thatcherism; furthermore the fact that the bulk of the resources were spent on training was underpinned by supply-side assumptions about unemployment in west Belfast. Birrell and Wilson (1993) point out that economic objectives were paramount in MBW and note that 'three ideas underpinned the strategy – the need for job creation, local community involvement and central government control'. MBW emphasised the multi-dimensionality of social deprivation and the need for co-ordinated social and economic policies. It had some success in facilitating community involvement despite the complex situation in west Belfast.

In Derry, the Londonderry Development Office played a key role in co-ordinating the urban regeneration drive in the city. This included the management of the Londonderry Initiative, an inter-departmental mechanism for skewing mainstream programmes and budgets towards the areas of greatest need, which was launched in 1989. A central role was accorded to the partnership ethos and to the facilitation of partnerships involving business, government, elected representatives and the community sector. City Partnership Boards were set up to develop and then to oversee the realisation of long-term visions for Belfast and Londonderry. Within Belfast, five area-based partnerships made up of representatives from the community, public and private sectors were also established. The sums of money that were channelled to local community organisations were substantial over a significant period of time. Between the Belfast Action Teams and the Making Belfast Work office, for example, about £25m a year was made available to the most socially and economically depressed areas of the city for more than ten years. In addition, the establishment of outposts of the civil service in the midst of these communities was to play an important role in opening up new channels of communication between politically alienated communities and government.

Rural Community Development

The Community Worker Research Project, 1978-1982
The Community Worker Research Project (CWRP) is generally identified with the beginnings of rural community development in Northern Ireland. Under this initiative community economic development projects were set up in Crossmaglen in south Armagh, in the Knockinny area of Co. Fermanagh and in several other rural areas. CWRP was evaluated by the Department of Education (which assumed responsibility for community development following the abolition of the Ministry of Community Relations in the mid-1970s). The evaluation noted the very slow pace of work in the field of rural development and the administrative and other obstacles that had inhibited the development of projects (Caven, 1982). Following the conclusion of CWRP there were few sources of funding for community development in rural areas during the 1980s apart from the Northern Ireland Voluntary Trust (NIVT, now renamed the Community Foundation for Northern Ireland) under its innovative Rural Awards Programme. NIVT also assisted the Northern Ireland Rural Association which was set up in the mid-1980s to bring together representatives of local rural community associations and interested statutory bodies.

The Rural Action Project, 1985-1989
The Rural Action Project (RAP) was Northern Ireland's first rural community-development initiative at a regional level. The project was established through the joint efforts of four voluntary organisations: the Northern Ireland Rural Association, the Northern Ireland Voluntary Trust, the Northern Ireland Council for Voluntary Action, and Strabane Citizens' Advice Bureau. It was well-researched and locally-rooted and proved to be both an important pilot for later initiatives and a significant influence on the development of government policy for rural areas. RAP was funded by the EU's Second Anti-Poverty Programme and by the Department of Health and

Social Services. It ran for a period of four years as a partnership between rural community organisations and district councils. Its report, *Rural Development: a Challenge for the 1990s*, was published in 1989. This document's main recommendations were for: a bottom-up approach to rural development; the formation of a rural development centre, and the creation of a special fund for rural development. RAP was influential in shaping the then Department of Agriculture's policy on rural development and it also influenced the establishment of the Secretary of State's Inter-departmental Committee on Rural Development in 1989, a Rural Development Division and the Rural Development Council (Armstrong and Kilmurray, 1995). The fact that RAP was sponsored by the EU meant that its staff and management were closely involved with debates in the Commission about the principles and practices of rural community development across Europe. These debates included the concepts that shaped the EU's key policy document, *The Future of Rural Society*, published in 1988.

The Rural Community Network
RAP contributed to the founding of the Rural Community Network (RCN), a voluntary organisation established in 1991 'with a mission to identify and voice issues of concern to rural communities in relation to poverty, disadvantage and community development' (Greer and Murray, 1999). More than a decade later RCN has developed into a highly effective representative and lobbying organisation on behalf of disadvantaged rural communities throughout Northern Ireland. Starting with 60 members in 1991, by 2002 it had more than 500 members and twelve Rural Support Networks providing support at sub-regional level for local rural community development groups. Its Rural Support Networks have an important role to play in building up the cohesion of the community sector at local level by overcoming fragmentation, sectarianism and isolation. Funding for this infrastructure was provided through the EU's PEACE programmes. RCN's central Community Development Support Unit, which is funded by two government departments and by that policy, remains philanthropic funding, provides support for the Rural Support Networks, promotes the development of policy at a strategic level, and runs a pilot programme in areas of low community infrastructure.

The development of the rural community and voluntary sector in Northern Ireland is inhibited by the lack of a comprehensive rural policy framework. England, Scotland and the Republic of Ireland have had their rural development needs and policies reviewed in a white paper. In Northern Ireland the absence of an adequate strategic framework means problems of underdevelopment in the countryside and other rural questions are often overwhelmed by pressing agricultural priorities.

Towards a strategic approach by Government to voluntary action and community development

The 'Efficiency Scrutiny', 1990

A further, major policy development in Northern Ireland was to flow from the report of the *Efficiency Scrutiny of Government Funding of the Voluntary Sector: Profiting from Partnership*, published in April 1990 (Home Office, 1990), a development which was to move partnership beyond issues of grant aid and the provision of services to the involvement of the voluntary sector in policy formulation. One of the key recommendations was that clear, general aims for government funding should be formulated and stated. In his announcement of the publication of the *Scrutiny* report, the then Home Secretary, the Rt Hon. David Waddington, made a definitive statement of the principles by which government funding would be governed.

Responsibility for co-ordinating Northern Ireland's involvement in the *Scrutiny* and the preparation of an implementation plan had significantly fallen to the Department of Health and Social Services, the Department which had cultivated constructive links with voluntary organisations and had cemented those relationships, based on partnership, in the various policy documents mentioned above. The *Scrutiny* provided an opportunity to break new ground in the UK by developing a specific, government strategy for the voluntary sector on an inter-departmental basis. A draft Strategy was issued for consultation in 1992. At the same time, government was considering, again on an inter-departmental basis, two reports on community development that had been submitted to the Secretary of State for Northern Ireland by the Community Development Review Group (CDRG, 1991a, 1991b). While the draft Strategy had been well received, a number of respondents had commented on the absence in it of any specific reference to community development. The results of the inter-departmental community development review were eventually reflected in the Strategy in its final form and the *Strategy for the Support of the Voluntary Sector and for Community Development in Northern Ireland* published by DHSS in 1993 contained not only a Northern Ireland strategy and a sectoral strategy for each area of business, but also an important statement of principle on government's support for the community development process in Northern Ireland.

A key initiative in the Strategy was the announcement that a Voluntary Activity Unit would be established within the Department of Health and Social Services to provide a clearly defined focal point within government for voluntary activity in Northern Ireland and that the existing inter-departmental co-ordinating machinery would be strengthened. The Voluntary Activity Unit was established in June 1993 and the Inter-Departmental Voluntary Action Group was replaced by a higher level Inter-

Departmental Group on Voluntary Activity and Community Development.

The Strategy was widely regarded as a model of its kind (Elliott, 1998) and as paving the ground for the compacts with the voluntary sector that were subsequently to be developed throughout the UK under the Labour administration.

Continuity and change

The 1990s and into the new Millennium represented a period of both continuity and change in the development of public policy towards the voluntary and community sector in Northern Ireland. The 1990s were also years of momentous change in the constitutional, institutional and funding environment in which the sector operates.

The *Strategy for the Support of the Voluntary Sector and for Community Development in Northern Ireland* (DHSS, 1993) helped lay the foundations for the *Compact between Government and the Voluntary and Community Sector in Northern Ireland* (DHSS, 1998), with its subtitle, *Building Real Partnerships*, reflecting the spirit and principles underpinning it. This set out the respective roles of both sectors, which were seen as complementary, inter-dependent and mutually supportive. It articulated the shared values and principles and the commitments that would underpin the further development of the relationship. Uniquely in the UK, the *Compact* recognised the importance of translating the principles and commitments into practical action and gave an undertaking both to produce a supporting document to replace the 1993 *Strategy* and to keep it under review.

The supporting document, which would define the current strategic public policy framework, was not to emerge in draft form until 2001. In the intervening period, the Belfast (Good Friday) Agreement heralded the ending of civil unrest. In June 1998, members were elected to the new Northern Ireland Assembly, which agreed the functions of 11 new departments in February 1999. Direct Rule by the UK government at Westminster ended on 2 December 1999 when power was devolved to the Northern Ireland Assembly and its Executive Committee of Ministers, though the institutions were subsequently suspended on several occasions. The Secretary of State for Northern Ireland remained responsible for Northern Ireland Office matters and criminal justice, not devolved to the Assembly. A number of other new institutions were set up, including the Civic Forum to act as a consultative mechanism on social, economic and cultural matters.

While devolution raised the possibility of a tension between representative and participative democracy, this proved not to be a major issue. On the contrary, the Northern Ireland Executive endorsed the *Compact* as the basis of its relationship with the sector. The key role of the sector and the importance of involving it in policies and programmes aimed at strengthening community well-being were clearly stated in the Executive's first Programme for Government (2001) for the three years from April 2001. It also stated the Executive's commitment to working in partnership with the social partners:

> In tackling many of the Programme for Government issues, we have the advantage of a vibrant and extensive community and voluntary sector which makes a significant and crucial contribution to many aspects of the social, economic, environmental and cultural life of Northern Ireland. We are committed to sustaining the work of the sector, building stronger relations with the voluntary and community sector and working together as social partners to maximise benefits to society.

The Programme for Government also committed government to sustain and enhance local communities, to support community infrastructure, to encourage and support greater community participation, particularly from those groups under-represented in volunteering activities and to increase the number of active community groups and volunteers.

The reform of Health and Social Care

A major reform of health and social care was undertaken in the first half of the 1990s which was to have a profound impact on the way voluntary organisations involved in welfare services were to develop. The impact of these changes is dealt with in detail in chapter six. The changes confirmed voluntary organisations as important providers of government-funded welfare services (apart from large-scale residential and nursing home schemes). Relationships were managed through contracts or service agreements that specified the purposes for which the funding was being provided, and set out quality standards and arrangements for monitoring performance. The goal of achieving transparency through service level agreements had been clearly set out in the 1991 *Scrutiny* report. The reform of health and social care provided both the money and the mechanisms for managing the relationships that led to a large-scale increase in the role of the voluntary sector in social care. One unintended consequence of these reforms was to establish this area as the main funding flow from government to the voluntary sector that was managed in ways that were unsuitable for developing the sector's role as representing the interests of welfare users in the policy environment. As a result commentators have suggested that the largest and most powerful part of the sector is the least fit to play this participative role.

Church-related voluntary action in Northern Ireland

Religion is a major motivating factor for organised voluntary action at local level (Greeley, 1997). Religious congregations are usually rooted in communities and tend to have an interest in promoting positive values, the potential to deliver much needed community services and the capacity to provide opportunities for volunteering for their members and others (Sarkis, 2001). During the 1990s church-related voluntary action became a subject of research in the United States and Britain. Writing of the United States, Drucker (1994) described churches there as 'an integral part of a potent and largely unseen "third force" of volunteer productivity and philanthropy'. In Britain, Harris (1998) and Cameron (1998) produced ground-breaking studies that highlighted church-related voluntary action as a significant, but largely hidden, part of the wider welfare system. In 1998 Derek Bacon at the Centre for Voluntary Action Studies undertook a ground-breaking study of churches (*Splendid and Disappointing*) and their contribution to social capital in Northern Ireland. He audited the roles performed by volunteers in 87 churches in the Coleraine local government district. Bacon found that people associated with those churches gave approximately 3,200 voluntary hours each week in a wide range of activities including pastoral care of members, youth work, sporting and recreational activity as well as occupying roles in the formal services of the churches (Bacon, 1998).

Bacon's research continued and his *Communities, Churches and Social Capital in Northern Ireland* was published in late 2003. This reports on the findings from an extensive study of 12 churches and para-church organisations in Belfast and Derry and in four provincial towns across Northern Ireland during 2001and 2002. In the organisations that he studied Bacon found that some 2,000 people were involved in performing volunteer roles. There was a wide range of innovative measures and approaches to promoting positive community change and meeting community need. Analysing his findings in the context of the eight domains of social capital identified by Forrest and Kearns (2001) Bacon reported that local faith-based organisations were empowering local people; promoting participation, associational activity and common purpose; supporting networks and reciprocity; promoting collective norms and values as well as promoting trust, community safety and a sense of belonging for marginalised people. Bacon's book concludes with a series of recommendations to the churches and to policy-makers. He suggests ways in which the voluntary action work of churches and other faith-based organisations could be developed. Deploring the fact that policy-makers are largely unaware of, and seemingly uninterested in, the work of churches and faith-based organisations, he urges that they should 'invest energy, resources and time in uncovering how these bodies encounter and minister to people' and recommends that they should also 'make themselves aware of the work of such bodies towards transformation and regeneration at many levels ...'

In a forthcoming publication *Acting in Good Faith: Churches, Change and*

Regeneration (2004) Bacon et al present a case study of church-based voluntary action in a rural area. A chapter entitled 'Working at peace-building within and across the boundaries', considers Derry and Raphoe Action, a faith-based voluntary organisation that is associated with the Anglican (Church of Ireland) diocese. Since 1997 this initiative has been actively encouraging the engagement of Protestant people with local community, cultural and social issues. This project spans the border dividing Counties Derry and Tyrone and County Donegal. It is partly supported by the Combat Poverty Agency in Dublin, the Community Foundation for Northern Ireland, the Department of Foreign Affairs in Dublin and the Special EU Programmes Body. Bacon points out that for the Protestant community in Donegal the local parish church is a focal point of community life. Derry and Raphoe Action embraces capacity building, training, networking, developing links and helping people to address local concerns. It has developed a role in partnership approaches and has been active in working with local networks, district councils and community-development agencies. It involves 140 groups of which approximately 60 per cent have been formed with its assistance. These groups address a wide range of community issues in the lives of young people, women, farmers and victims of the conflict.

Norman Hamilton (2002) undertook a study of Protestant churches in North Belfast while he was a Visiting Fellow at the Centre for Voluntary Action Studies. His primary focus was on their relations with their local communities and on their work to benefit their local community. North Belfast is an area of acute social need and community division; it experienced some 600 sectarian murders from 1968-1994 (nearly 20 per cent of the sectarian murders that took place in Northern Ireland during that period). Hamilton's study considered the contribution of local churches to the community infrastructure of North Belfast and he identified a wide range of hitherto undocumented community-benefit voluntary activities being provided by the churches. He also considered volunteering among church members and found that in one of the churches that he surveyed approximately 8 per cent of its members were active formal volunteers in wider society (apart from any church volunteering roles they may have had).

The work of Bacon and Hamilton provides clear evidence of the importance of church-related voluntary action within both urban and rural communities. They document many examples of work across a number of different fields including work with young people, children, senior citizens, and the provision of buildings for community activity. Some church-related, or faith-based, organisations run extensive programmes in fields as diverse as promoting economic development, providing affordable housing and promoting local cultural development. Some have formally embraced a community relations and anti-sectarian policy. Some span the two jurisdictions of Ireland and provide valuable opportunities for people from both parts of the island to meet and to work together. Recent financial support has come from the Voluntary and Community Unit of the Department for Social Development for the Churches' Community Work Alliance (CCWA) for an eighteen-month study into the nature and practice of community work from a Christian perspective in areas of disadvantage and where good community work is weak. The outcomes will be presented in the forthcoming publication *Acting in Good Faith: Churches, Change and Regeneration* (Bacon et al, 2004).

Eddie McDowell, Northern Ireland development worker with the Churches' Community Work Alliance, also considers that the work of the churches and other faith groups is often not recognised. He attributes this in part to the fact that most church-related community work is done without significant external funding. McDowell stated:

> To attain the outcomes that church-related community development can deliver, the government and other bodies should seek to understand the values that underpin the method and inform the process. To do this, long-term relationship must be built on trust and mutual understanding (McDowell, 2002).

The importance of the role of the churches is also noted by Langhammer (2003), who argues that 'in grass-roots social and community life there is a less active "civil society" in Protestant than in Catholic districts' and that 'in most predominantly Protestant districts today, most of the "social cement" is provided by, or within the sphere of influence of churches.' He notes, however, that:

> The influence of both the churches, particularly in urban areas and the trade unions in the world of work are declining within Protestant communities. This is undoubtedly a factor in the 'unhinged' nature of Loyalism. However, they both remain important influences and should form the core and basis of an alliance with government in the delivery of social and community services in the Protestant community (Langhammer, 2003).

Human rights, the Good Friday Agreement and Northern Ireland's
voluntary sector
By ensuring the centrality of human rights in the Good Friday Agreement civil society organisations have exercised a shaping influence on the development of the Northern Ireland Peace Process. Mageean and O'Brien (1999) note that less than three months after the paramilitary cease-fires were

announced in the late summer of 1994, on 10 December a coalition of four leading voluntary sector human rights organisations launched *The Declaration on Human Rights, the Northern Ireland Conflict and the Peace Process*. This event marked the formal beginning of a process that has made a fundamental contribution to reshaping civil and constitutional rights in Northern Ireland. The organisations that launched the *Declaration* were the Committee on the Administration of Justice, the Irish Council for Civil Liberties, the Scottish Council on Civil Liberties and the British-Irish Human Rights Watch. These voluntary organisations called for human rights to be made central to all efforts to arrive at a political and constitutional settlement of the Northern Ireland problem. Their careful work and skilful lobbying contributed to ensuring that this took place in the settlement arrived at in 1998.

The December meeting was quickly followed by a further event, held in Belfast under Chatham House rules. Influential policy-makers and senior officials from the British and Irish governments were present and the meeting received representations concerning a proposed Commission on Policing, a Criminal Justice Review, and new measures to promote equality. All of these measures were subsequently incorporated into the Good Friday Agreement. Further briefing meetings ensured the centrality of rights to the peace process. The organisations, and in particular the Belfast-based Committee for the Administration of Justice, maintained a consistent flow of press briefings, meetings and submissions to international fora.

Mageean and O'Brien record their view that: 'There is little doubt that the broad agenda that the non-governmental organisation community was articulating emerged onto the political agenda in Northern Ireland' (1999: 1503).

These writers analyse the contribution of the two governments, the political parties and other key bodies and figures to advancing the human rights agenda, and note the contribution of republicanism and nationalism to the debate. Whereas the Official Unionist Party made little contribution, the loyalist political parties that were associated with the loyalist paramilitary organisations participated effectively and these parties share responsibility for the extent to which the rights agenda made its way so significantly into the final text of the Agreement. Mageean and O'Brien record the view that 'some of the proposals from the loyalist parties went beyond those which were finally included in the Agreement ...' (1999: 1510). They suggest that the process in Northern Ireland was informed by the experience of non-governmental organisations in other jurisdictions. They point to the experience of South Africa where the relatively rapid and successful transition from apartheid to a multi-racial democracy has been facilitated by the centrality of human rights. This has also been the case in Guatemala and Bosnia where, as in South Africa, rights were central to the peace process. By contrast, in the Middle East where human rights remain peripheral to attempts to achieve a settlement there has been little progress of a substantial nature.

It is not yet possible to provide an accurate assessment of the relative influence of the various factors that contributed to the formulation of Northern Ireland's Good Friday Agreement and the subsequent legislation that gave effect to its provisions. It is clear, however, that civil society organisations, and in particular the Committee on the Administration of Justice (CAJ), encouraged by a number of sister organisations elsewhere in Ireland and in other parts of the United Kingdom, played a central role in shaping the agenda for change (Committee on the Administration of Justice, 1994).

An important consequence of the Good Friday Agreement, and the 1998 Northern Ireland Act that followed, was to embed parts of the voluntary sector in the administration of the legal requirements of the Act. This has been particularly noticeable in the operation of the equality provisions of Section 75 of the Act. This requires public bodies to consult on their equality impact statements with representatives of nine categories of people whose rights to equal treatment are enshrined in the legislation. This has imposed a significant consultative burden on those voluntary organisations (some say to little effect) that have a claim to represent these groups but in doing so has provided them with a legal function unique to Northern Ireland. There has also been a marked growth in voluntary action around the equality agenda, some of them self-interest groups, which one of our interviewees described as a particular skewing of the sector that the sector itself needs to address. In addition, the amalgamation of the equality concerns of an otherwise heterogeneous set of categories of people into one Act, supervised by a single equality body, has drawn these organisations into a closer formal alliance, with the CAJ providing the secretariat. While these are contemporary events in which we lack the distance needed to properly evaluate them, this changing policy environment is driving change in what appears to be one of the fastest developing parts of the voluntary sector.

Partnership and new forms of governance
Since the early 1990s, the idea that the complex and multi-faceted nature of social problems requires collaboration between stakeholders among public and private institutions and bodies at regional and at local level has acquired widespread acceptance. Recent reforms in Northern Ireland have been particularly concerned with developing forms of network governance as a way of addressing profound problems of accountability in the structures of public administration that had developed over the years of Direct Rule from London (Hughes et al, 1998). These reforms and their policy context have roots both

in reforms within the UK, which have gathered momentum since Labour came to power in 1997, and in reforms to the way that the supra-national institutions of the European Union have understood their task.

Governance by self-steering networks is conceptualised as an organic consequence of the institutional fragmentation of state institutions driven by the market and 'new public management' reforms of the institutions of government during the 1980s and 1990s, which were more wide-ranging and deeper in Britain than in any other developed state with the exception of New Zealand (Stoker, 2000).

The idea of community governance emerged from a parallel reconceptualising of local government from delivering services to securing the well-being of the area which it covered (Stoker, 2000). The new vision emphasises working in partnership with other agencies and actors. 'The aim is not only to work with others in the formulation of shared objectives but also to work with and through them to achieve implementation' (Stoker, 2000: 15). Governance is thus defined 'as a concern with governing, achieving collective action in the realm of public affairs, in conditions where it is not possible to rest on recourse to the authority of the state ... Governing becomes an interactive process because no single actor has the knowledge and resource capacity to tackle problems unilaterally' (Stoker, 2000: 3).

In Britain, a Labour Party document on relationships between government and the voluntary sector, *Building the Future Together,* published in March 1997, shortly before the general election of that year, made an explicit link between the social exclusion/inclusion approach to social policy and partnerships in stating: 'Partnership with the voluntary sector is central to Labour's policy of achieving social cohesion in a one nation society' (cited in Plowden, 2001: 19).

Labour's approach to the participation of voluntary and community organisations in governance structures was heavily influenced by the Deakin Commission Report for England (Deakin, 1996) and the equivalent Kemp Report for Scotland (SCVO, 1997). These reports envisaged a recognition by government through an agreed set of general principles of the positive role of voluntary action in society – campaigning as well as service delivery. Both reports had laid considerable emphasis on the role of voluntary action in securing social cohesion. These themes chimed with the intellectual underpinning of Labour's approach at that time in which the place of voluntary and community sector interests was interpreted in the light of the need for government to play a lead part in the fostering and renewal of civic culture (Giddens, 1998).

This British policy background was to be very influential in Northern Ireland in the years from 1997. However, there have been important differences between Northern Ireland and the rest of the UK. The main reason for this is that the policies and instruments of the European Union have played a more important role in shaping the development of governance in Northern Ireland than in the rest of the UK. In the context of other Western European states the partnership model emerged from a much more corporatist tradition of government than that which had developed in the UK, whereby the state and both sides of industry collaborated in the management of economic development. However, as outlined in chapter one, from about 1990 onwards partnerships as instruments of policy at a European level through the institutions of the European Union came to include the idea of engagement with voluntary and community sector interests within civil society (McCall and Williamson, 2000).

The third European Anti-Poverty Programme proved to be particularly influential in Northern Ireland. Based on the experience in the Brownlow initiative funded through the programme, the Northern Ireland administration adapted its regeneration policies and established a series of area partnerships with inter-sectoral representation as the main mechanism for channelling regeneration initiatives and money (Spence, 1995). The area-based urban regeneration partnerships that were established had representation from local councillors, but the structures largely bypassed local government (Hughes and Carmichael, 1998; Cebulla, 2000).

The relative weakness of local government in Northern Ireland and the growing ability among voluntary and community organisations to influence the development of policy during the 1990s is illustrated particularly clearly by the experience of the European Union Special Support Programme for Peace and Reconciliation. The first Peace Programme ran from 1996 to 1998 with an extension until 1999. Williamson, Scott and Halfpenny (2000) draw attention to the way that voluntary and community organisations were able to decisively influence the priorities of the programme, and to the programme's emphasis on innovative delivery mechanisms. They conclude that the district partnerships gave: 'Northern Ireland's community and voluntary sector a more central role in regard to issues of local development and regeneration than any of the European Union's partnership initiatives in other countries' (Williamson, Scott and Halfpenny, 2000: 61).

The district partnerships comprised one-third elected representatives from the local Councils, one-third voluntary and community-sector representatives, and one-third other social partners – trade unions, business, farmers' interests. Furthermore, the allocation of the voluntary and community sector places in individual partnerships was the responsibility of NICVA. NICVA organised and oversaw the selection of individuals to fill the available places and was responsible for finding replacements when people dropped out. In doing so, it was concerned to ensure that as far as possible the people selected were well connected to voluntary sector networks and infrastructure. The aim was to ensure that those who sat on the partnerships were able to speak with authority and create a synergy with developments within the voluntary and community sector itself. Built on the principle that each constituency within the partnerships was responsible for its own partnership members, this structure simultaneously both limited the power of elected representatives and maximised the power of the voluntary and community sector.

The second European Union Special Support Programme for Peace and Reconciliation (PEACE II) was established in 2001 and runs until 2006, with the commitment of funds to be completed by the end of 2004. PEACE II emerged in a very different context to that of PEACE I. That programme had been self-consciously experimental and was agreed, negotiated and instituted during the period between the first paramilitary cease-fires in 1994 and the signing of the 'Good Friday' agreement in 1998. It was largely written by officials in the European Commission, and at that time voluntary and community sector interests were among their most effective lobbyists. One result was that voluntary and community organisations were very influential players in the funding mechanisms and were to play a leading role in the delivery of projects funded under the programme. In contrast, the PEACE II programme was negotiated by the devolved Northern Ireland Executive and was written by Northern Ireland civil servants. In his careful analysis of the background to the programme, Harvey (2003: 34) notes that:

> There was a feeling in the political and administrative establishment that the PEACE I programme had been captured by the (voluntary and community) sector. There was strong pressure to push back the territorial gains of the sector, which were resented by some elected representatives. PEACE I was too populist and civic society was 'getting out of hand'.

As a consequence, the local strategic partnerships (LSPs) have been constituted differently. First, the division of places between the different social partners has been changed. The partnerships have been conceived as having two strands:

- local government and the main statutory agencies operating at local level
- the four pillars of the social partners: private sector, trade unions, community and voluntary sectors, agriculture and rural development sector.

The minimum number of people on each partnership is 16, but most have opted for higher numbers to ensure good representation from each of the social partners. For example, the LSPs might have six councillors, six representatives from local statutory bodies, six representatives from the voluntary and community sector and two each from business, trade unions and farming interests. Some are larger to allow for more business representatives.

The negotiations over the make-up of the new partnerships strengthened the influence of the local statutory bodies, which played a quite nominal formal role in the district partnerships at the expense of the voluntary and community sector. The latter has seen its numerical influence reduced from one-third to one-quarter. Indeed the initial proposal was that the partnerships should be constituted from one-third local councillors, one-third local statutory bodies, and one-third the other partners. However, the social partners, themselves organised as an *ad hoc* alliance known as Concordia, succeeded in getting these guidelines rewritten to reduce the government side from two-thirds to one-half.

Concordia was established within the context of the negotiations over the second Peace Programme. Constituted of NICVA, the Irish Congress of Trade Unions, the Ulster Farmers Union, the Northern Ireland Agricultural Producers' Association (NIAPA) and the Confederation of British Industry, its formal role was to agree the make-up of the transition teams from PEACE I to PEACE II, agree the selection process for partnership members on the new LSPs, and finally endorse the selection outcome. The process of lobbying at the level of the European Union was a crucial background factor in this development, where the relationship was mediated by staff at the Northern Ireland Centre in Europe, a government-funded lobby point for Northern Ireland interests in Brussels (NICVA, 2003). It now has its own secretariat and continues to have a formal monitoring role in respect to all current EU Structural Funds.

The relative strength of the voluntary and community sector on the LSPs has also been influenced by changes in the manner in which their representatives have been selected. Unlike the district partnerships where NICVA retained control, for the duration of the programme, responsibility for the selection process was devolved to the transition teams that remained in place in each partnership to oversee the changeover from PEACE I to PEACE II. Most went to public advertisement for applicants to fill the voluntary and community sector places. People were appointed either on the basis of the information on their application forms, or after interview. This appears to have resulted in a further reduction in the influence of the voluntary and community sector as many of those who are filling the places are poorly linked to voluntary and community sector networks and structures. NICVA suggests that there is evidence of individuals putting themselves forward and labelling themselves without reference to any voluntary organisation, and there are partnerships where the formal local voluntary and community sector networks are not involved at all. Using the voluntary and community sector as a recruiting ground for individuals to serve on the partnerships is vitiating the meaning of the term 'partnership'.

While the research evidence is incomplete and anecdotal, there are signs that the relative influence of the voluntary and community sector partners in these structures will come to resemble the position in England where Craig and Taylor (2002) have argued that local partnerships tend to be dominated by local authority priorities. They conclude:

> Research suggests that the rules of the game are set from above; the cultures and structures of public sector partners are not compatible with effective community involvement; and communities themselves do not necessarily have the organisational capacity and resources for effective involvement (Craig and Taylor, 2002: 229).

Conclusions: 1922-2003, eighty years of growth and change

How the story of the development of voluntary action in Northern Ireland since 1922 is read depends to a large extent on how the jurisdiction's history as a whole is read. The major stages of the story do, however, seem quite clear and have provided the broad structure of the account related here.

- First was the period before the end of the Second World War where both state and voluntary institutions that had emerged in the Victorian and Edwardian era had to struggle on, meeting overwhelming social need without major reform. State action was limited by an obsession in the Department of Finance on balancing the books. Innovation was evident among voluntary organisations, both within BCSW and later from the newly formed NICSS.
- The second period (the remaining years of the unionist government at Stormont until 1972) coincided with the heyday of the Welfare State. The most striking aspect of this period is how the policy framework of the British Welfare State (together with its unstated assumptions about the role of the state in guaranteeing the welfare of citizens) was imported into and imposed on top of a deeply conservative, unchanging and deeply divided society. The reforms of the 1940s produced the first statement of public policy towards voluntary organisations, but the latter remained essentially organised along ethno/religious lines with very little intercourse between the two communities.
- The third period, covering the start of the years of 'the Troubles' to the peace process of the 1990s, began with the destruction of the old order in the violence of the early 1970s. What happened subsequently was grounded in two rather contradictory processes. The first, which drove the

development of community-based voluntary action, reflected the very different ways in which the cataclysm of the first years of the 1970s impacted on the two main communities in Northern Ireland. It is possible to argue that the high point of Protestant community action was the Ulster Workers Strike of 1974 since which time the Protestant working class has consistently lost influence (Darby and Williamson, 1978). This was symbolised at the political level by the failure of an attempt at similar mass action to prevent the implementation of the Anglo-Irish Agreement of 1985. Catholic social action on the other hand moved out of the influence of the church and gained steadily in confidence. (For an assessment of the contribution of the voluntary and community sector to the Peace Process, the reader is referred to Couto, 2001 and Guelke, 2003.)

The second process consisted of the way in which the institutions of the Welfare State shaped the development of voluntary action. Part of this influence came from the role given to voluntary organisations in delivering welfare services, and this continuing tradition has provided a coherent place for philanthropy. More significant was the way in which the so-called 'third wave' voluntary organisations emerged around the rediscovery of poverty, and disillusionment with the ability of the Welfare State to live up to its initial promises. These organisations brought with them a set of secular values and organising principles that were not grounded in the ethno/religious divisions in Northern Ireland. These newer organisations were thus focused on what were perceived to be state failures, but in a way that was politically neutral in the Northern Ireland context. The political neutrality underpinned the utility of the concept of a single voluntary 'sector' (imported from North America via Britain), but the anti-statist orientation provided a basis for an alliance with Catholic community-based voluntary action that was similarly, although for different reasons, driven by demands on the state for reform.

The content of the concept of a single voluntary and community 'sector' in Northern Ireland has been largely (although never entirely) shaped by a coalescing of interests between these two aspects of voluntary action, each with roots in a very different type of struggle. Protestant philanthropy has been able to make its own way, its continuing relevance now sustained by the degree of contracting out of state-financed social care and other services. Protestant working-class community action turned in on itself, but produced a political leadership who, it has been argued, were a crucial factor in achieving a successful outcome in the negotiations that led to the Good Friday Agreement. But its relatively weak community base and weak links to generalist voluntary sector networks such as NICVA have remained a problem for the sector, evidenced by continuing debate about 'weak community infrastructure'.

- The fourth historical period takes the narrative up to the present and coincides with the peace process and the reform of social welfare in the early 1990s. Developments in the 1970s and 1980s had been in part a response to the efforts by the state to find a way of using voluntary action as a means of managing the conflict and minimising some its effects. Deficiencies in the accountability of the Direct Rule administrations enhanced the development of more participative forms of governance in which voluntary sector organisations became increasingly sophisticated and influential in policy formulation.

The 1990s were a time in which the long-standing agenda of reforming the state on the basis of equality, respect of difference and human rights (which had been at the heart of the declared value base of the voluntary sector) was finally achieved in the Good Friday Agreement of 1998. The social policies of the European Union with their emphasis on social partnership provided an institutional context for the development of relationships between the voluntary sector and the state. Chapter six will consider the institutionalisation of the voluntary sector in the governance of Northern Ireland and will show how this has also been underpinned by the large-scale transfer of resources from the state to enable it to deliver welfare services.

The story of voluntary action in Northern Ireland can thus be usefully understood in the context of the struggle over the legitimacy of the state and its institutions, most particularly the institutions of the Welfare State. The struggle over the future of the Welfare State and the role for voluntary action within it was imported from Britain. But what has shaped the development of the voluntary sector in the past 30 years has been the way in which struggles over the Welfare State have intersected with the indigenous struggle over the state itself.

The nature of this intersection remains a matter of some controversy, particularly when considering the role of voluntary action in relation to 'the Troubles' and the extent of its contribution to the peace process. This was reflected in the range of responses from our interviewees. There was wide agreement that this role was central to defining the distinctive characteristics of voluntary action in Northern Ireland, but there was less agreement on how crucial this was. Some felt that the claim that it filled the 'democratic deficit' was overstated, but there had nevertheless been an important contribution in which voluntary sector networks had been able to broker relations between politicians. Others pointed to the role of the sector as a form of democratic opposition to the Direct Rule administrations. Several interviewees noted that a number of individuals in leadership roles had pursued careers in voluntary organisations where otherwise they might have developed political careers as a result of the way in which political parties are structured around the single issue of national identity. One interviewee noted that the voluntary sector in Northern Ireland was both quasi-political and state dependent.

The legacy of this history will impact on the further development of the relationship between voluntary and community organisations and the state as the consequences of the Good Friday Agreement. A number of key themes stand out from our interviews. The first is a growing perception that the client relationship of many organisations with government is not healthy and will have to change. Interviewees suggested that one of the consequences of the way these relationships have developed is a lack of capacity for strategic policy interventions by the sector, fragmentation and 'me-too-ism'. While the sector has developed a close and effective relationship with civil servants in the administration of public policy, a number of our interviewees noted an immaturity in dealing with political decisions informing stategic reforms. This is in part, as one interviewee observed, a consequence of the nature of politics in Northern Ireland in which political parties have never operated to convert interest group lobbying on social and economic issues into programmes for government. But a consequence noted by some observers is that organisations appeared ill-equipped to lobby effectively in the face of the enormous changes that are now under way in the administration of Northern Ireland and driven by globalisation. On the government side, interviewees identified a similar lack of strategic vision in most departments, evidenced by an over-riding concern with audit that was strangling many smaller voluntary organisations.

A second important theme was the ability of voluntary and community organisations to respond effectively to the restructuring of government and the development of partnerships. Several interviewees noted that many organisations were not resourced properly to do this work and that this had the danger of overloading the capacity of organisations while achieving little benefit. One interviewee suggested that many voluntary organisations had unrealistic expectations of what they could do.

A third consequence of this history is the development of a leadership in the voluntary and community sector that is effectively 'stuck'. Many appeared to have been in their current posts 'an incredibly long time', in the view of one interviewee. There was a lack of movement into politics that was having consequences for the development of the devolved institutions of government. Several interviewees noted that the lack of engagement of local political parties in social issues, and what they perceived to be a dysfunctional party political system, meant that people with strong ideological commitments ended up in leadership roles in the voluntary sector rather than in politics.

══════════ 3 ══════════

Voluntary Action in the Republic of Ireland

Introduction

Chapter three traces the key points in the evolution of voluntary organisations in the Free State and the Republic until the end of the twentieth century. As will be seen, the theories and practice of Catholic social action played a key role in shaping the sector in the 1940s. The chapter then traces the emergence of self-help, campaigning and federative organisations. In the 1990s, the voluntary sector made its 'long march through the institutions', eventually achieving national social partnership. Other key features of the voluntary sector are then examined, such as the issue of the cohesion of the sector, patterns in the evolution of its funding, Europeanisation and the level of political engagement. At the end of chapter three, concluding comments are made and points of comparison are made between the evolution of the voluntary sector in Northern Ireland and the Republic.

It took the new state 78 years to define its formal relationship with the voluntary sector. The Minister for Health and Social Welfare, Brendan Corish, first proposed a policy framework for the respective roles and relationships of statutory and voluntary organisations in 1976 (Dáil Éireann, *Debates*, 29 April 1976). As we will see later, it took from 1976 to 2000 to actually produce the new policy. The relationship between the state and the voluntary section was a marginal consideration in the few landmark points of the new state's social policy such as the Commission on the Relief of the Sick and Destitute Poor (1927), the white paper on social security (1949) and the Commission on Social Welfare (1985). These tended to focus on the important issues of poverty, incomes and welfare, neglecting institutional relationships (Curry, 1993). Not until the 1980s did the state give much attention to institutional issues in policy-making. That said, the absence of a formal relationship for the first 80 years of the state's existence did not mean that there was *not* an implied set of relationships between the voluntary sector and the state, for there was.

It is reasonable to say that the new Irish Free State had not given much thought or attention to the respective roles of the government and voluntary sector. An examination of the state of the voluntary sector in 1922 would have found the descendants of the eighteenth-century Protestant philanthropic societies; the voluntary hospitals; the extensive social and institutional services provided by the Catholic religious orders; and early forms of youth movements (principally the scouts and girl guides).

The new state had been forged out of the struggle for independence, a movement in which social policy goals had been subordinate. One exception where social movements had been influential was in cultural and language policy. Here, Irish language and cultural organisations had made a prominent contribution to the new national project, but they declined in importance as the new state whole-heartedly adopted the policies they had long advocated.

It might be expected that some pressures for new voluntary activity might come from the many unresolved social questions that remained from the British period. After all, a Soviet had been established in Limerick in 1919, the only one west of Prague during the European post-war upheavals. In the event, the voice of social policy and social movements played a minor role in the new state. Only a minority, principally those in the labour movement, questioned the purposes for which independence should be achieved in the first place. Some of their concerns were echoed in the Democratic programme of the first Dáil (1919), which expressed a number of worthy social policy objectives. Their concerns continued to be voiced from time to time, but were confined to a relatively small, politically marginalised sector on the left of Irish politics. A national association for the unemployed was set up over 1923-6 but the project fizzled out (Kilmurray, 1989). A revival was attempted in 1932, modelled on the National Unemployed Workers Association in Britain – indeed its Cork to Dublin hunger march echoed the Jarrow march in England. The association won broad support, taking in the Labour Party, some clergy and the republican left. The de Valera government responded with a mixture of minor concessions in the operation of unemployment assistance, followed by coercion. The association's street meetings were baton charged and some of its leaders deported or interned. Tenant leagues were also formed during the 1930s as a voice for tenants living in poor conditions and at the mercy of slum landlords. They were sufficiently effective to promote the coming into existence of a counter organisation, the Property Owners Association (Powell, 1992).

The new Irish state was not characterised by new, or original, social thought. Indeed, a more austere social policy had already been heralded by Irish resistance, led by the hierarchy and supported by Arthur Griffith, to the social reforms of the last Liberal government (Barrington, 1987). The Free State governments of 1922-32 did not come with a strong social policy agenda, nor any views as to the proper relationship between the state and the voluntary sector. The small supply of social policy ideas provided by civil servants and the colleges far exceeded demand (Lee, 1989). At a time of post-civil-war reconstruction, social policy questions were not government priorities, especially when some outstanding constitutional questions still had to be resolved with the British government and when the state still faced a crisis of legitimacy with anti-treaty opinion. In the view of Barry (1992), the new government chose instead to assume a role of moral management, to reinforce the relatively small capitalist ruling class and to centralise administration. The new government inherited intact the British colonial administration, which it did little to change. To the regret of many, the new government pruned some of its more useful parts, like the Congested Districts Board, the economic and social development agency for the western districts. The hated workhouses were closed down or adapted as hospitals, asylums, infirmaries, district or county homes (O'Sullivan, 1996). The industrial schools were unaffected by reform.

Early voluntary action in housing
Leaving aside social movements associated with the political left, voluntary action during the Free State period was not a complete desert. The voluntary housing movement developed in the pre-war years was sustained, although it was poorly chronicled. The movement was all the more important due to the low level of Free State investment in public housing. These were called public utility companies and no less than 400 were established in the first forty years of the new state. Public utility companies were registered as friendly societies and built houses for sale or rent 'to the working class and others' and were eligible for and received grants, loans and subsidies from the local authorities towards each home completed. Some local authorities worked extensively with public utility companies (e.g. Dublin Corporation), providing land and even serviced sites for them. From 1933 to 1938, fifteen public utility companies built 1,878 homes in Dublin alone, so the scale of their contribution was significant. Nationally, 125 societies built 9 per cent of all homes from 1922-7. One of the best-known leaders of this movement was Canon David Henry Hall of St Barnabas, Dublin, called 'the building parson' who modelled the St Barnabas Public Utility Society on the British garden-city model, constructing garden suburb projects of 40 semi-detached homes at a time, inspiring similar schemes as far away as Carlow and Monaghan (Fraser, 1993; McManus, 1996, 1998, 1999; Williamson, 2003).

In the event, the thinkers who did most to shape the social policy of the Free State came not from the people's movements or the revolutionary left, but from the right of the political spectrum. They were also, in the institutional form of the Catholic church, in much the strongest position to act on their views. The impact of Catholic social theory on the political evolution of the Free State has been well documented at this stage (Lee, 1989; Browne, 1986; Whyte, 1971), although less attention has been given to its practical effects on voluntary action.

The era of Catholic social action

Before dealing with the manifestations of Catholic social action, it is worth saying a little about the theoretical context. The key documents were the encyclicals *De rerum novarum* and Pope Pius XI's later *Quagragessimo anno* (1931) which formally articulated the principle of subsidiarity, the delivery of services at the lowest possible level in society and the minimising of the role of the state.

It would be wrong to presume that Ireland alone became a model of Catholic social action in the 1930s, for the principles of subsidiarity enjoyed widespread application throughout Europe, from Christian socialists like Mounier, right across the spectrum to theories of vocationalism and corporatism adopted in moderate and sometimes more extreme and aggressive forms in Italy, Spain and Portugal. Ireland's flirtation with vocationalism was institutionally expressed through the quasi-vocational character of the new senate under the 1937 constitution and through the Commission on Vocational Organisation, which sat from 1939-43, even as war ravaged continental Europe. The Commission proposed a National Vocational Council to guide economic and social policy, informed by an actively participating citizenry. The senate had provision for the representatives of voluntary social activities to be nominated to a panel of candidates.

Archbishop John Charles McQuaid and the Catholic Social Service Bureau

The man most prominently associated with the theory of Catholic social action was also its leading practitioner. Within weeks of becoming archbishop of Dublin in 1940, John Charles McQuaid embarked on a flurry of intense organisation building, whose legacy remains to the present day (Cooney, 1999). Although some of the organisations, groups and bodies he set up were initially a short-term response to wartime and post-war hardship, they showed a remarkable flexibility to adapt their mission once the war ended and move out to the suburbs. McQuaid had an unmatched organisational energy and *élan*, combined with a concern for the poor (observers contrasted the terror of the clergy summoned to the archbishop's house with the numbers of destitute people who regularly called to his door, quite unafraid of him). During his time, the number of religious communities in his diocese rose from 180 to 297. He supervised a more than doubling of Catholic secondary schools. The history of voluntary action, with its focus on collective activity, often understates the impact of individuals. Here, Archbishop McQuaid exercised a dominant personal influence for over thirty years and without him, events might have taken a quite different turn.

The Catholic Social Service Bureau (1941), a merging of forty diocesan charities, was his main instrument designed to meet the needs of Dublin's poor. This it did through food distribution, emergency works, cash relief and the provision of fuel and clothing. McQuaid prompted the religious orders in the city, over whom he had moral rather than ecclesiastical authority, into the setting up of schools, services for the deaf and blind, homes for girls at risk, probation services, flats for young married couples, services for adults with learning difficulties, and homes for the elderly. The Catholic Youth Council (1941) began by providing clothes and food for underfed, ill-clad children, then expanded into summer camps and educational youth clubs.

Within the Catholic Social Service Board, a bureau for emigrants was set up in 1942, with a hostel for girls in Dublin, designed to accommodate, advise and direct them from the country trains *en route* to Britain. This later grew into the Irish Episcopal Conference for Emigrants (IECE) which stimulated and co-ordinated the establishment of services for Irish emigrants in Britain and later in the United States and Germany. It would be a misreading of Catholic social action to assume that the church, in the name of subsidiarity, always preferred to provide these services and dissuaded government action. On the contrary, Archbishop McQuaid peppered government with demands, requests and proposals for government action. The case that the ever-impatient McQuaid developed these services out of frustration with government lethargy and even complete inaction is persuasive. Indeed, services for Irish emigrants had to wait thirty-two years between when they first applied for a government loan in 1948 and the arrival of a structured funding scheme in 1980. The Irish government was more concerned about the infiltration of the Irish community abroad by communists (the Connolly Association) than about the need to provide social services, and these fears were more likely to spark it into action than objective social need.

Not all services were set up by the clergy. The Legion of Mary for example became one of the main providers of services for homeless women. It was set up by the lay Catholic activist Frank Duff, also a civil servant in the Department of Justice. Although he was treated with initial suspicion, he won over official support through the devotional and obedient ethic of the Legion.

Catholic social policy was monopolistic and stridently denominational. McQuaid in particular would tolerate no groups outside the fold, especially to the political left. When the unemployed tried to organise in the early 1950s, the *Catholic Standard* pressed the claims of a rival group, *Deo Duce*, open to all – except for communists and their fellow travellers. When the unemployed tried to organise in the late 1950s, the Catholic Unemployed Association quickly sprung up to rival it. When a representative of the unemployed, Jack Murphy, was elected to the Dáil in 1957, McQuaid persuaded him to ask communists to leave his association, setting in train a series of events which led to its collapse (Kilmurray, 1989).

Denominationalism was most evident in the field of youth activities and the denominational boundaries established in the 1930s persist to the present. At the foundation of the state, the new scouting and guiding associations had just begun their work. In the 1920s, the rival Catholic Boy Scouts of Ireland and the Catholic Girl Guides of Ireland (1928) were set up, with visibly distinct uniforms and colours (blue rather than green). The withdrawal of many young boys and girls from the existing troops into the new associations caused dislocation, especially in the rural areas: the existing associations being labelled 'Protestant' and 'unionist' in justification. The latter was no longer true, while the former became a self-fulfilling prophecy. As a result, youth activity, which was one of the most prominent forms of voluntary activity in the new state, streamed into a denominational pattern, which it still partly maintains.

McQuaid, to put it mildly, was highly protective of the Catholic character of the pre-existing hospitals and voluntary organisations: not only that, but expansive as well, for there is evidence that he and his associates sought to infiltrate and take over, one way or the other, the declining number of 'Protestant' organisations, such as the St John's Ambulance, the ISPCC and the voluntary hospitals (Cooney, 1999). The denominational imperative applied to informal youth work as well. In Dublin, the prominent youth clubs association was the Catholic Youth Council (1944); in the rural areas it was called the National Federation of Catholic Boys Clubs. In the 1960s, the federation tried to rename itself the National Federation of Boys Clubs, but the archbishop refused it permission to do so. In 1971, it did so anyway, becoming the National Federation of Youth Clubs (1971) and the National Youth Federation (1987) or 'the fed' for short. In practice it still operated on a parochial basis, not least because the Catholic parishes had the one facility most prized by youth clubs: a hall.

Despite this, some of the largest voluntary movements in the country managed to operate outside strictly denominational reference points (though in practice, many depended on, sought and obtained the blessing and co-operation of rural clergy). Two of the most successful youth movements in the new state's history were Macra na Feirme and Macra na Tuaithe. Macra na Feirme (1944) became a large, club-based organisation promoting rural development, social and cultural education and leadership training throughout the rural areas (despite its title, not all its members are farmers) (Miley, 1994). Macra na Feirme was complemented by Macra na Tuaithe – the National Youth Development Organisation (1952), subsequently renamed Foróige. This had a strong educational, self-developmental orientation and rapidly expanded throughout the rural areas and provincial towns.

Muintir na Tíre is another example (Devereux, 1992). In practice, the organisation, which was championed by a priest (Canon Hayes), fitted in well with the ideals of contemporary Catholic social policy and enlisted the co-operation of parish priests in the rural areas for its development (indeed, its symbol was the cross and the plough). Muintir na Tíre was founded in 1931 to promote community, rural and parish development in general and co-operatives in particular, later focusing on community facilities, recreation and educational courses. It advocated the self-help principle and worked to improve the rural infrastructure through group water schemes, electrification and community schools. The key leaders tended to be parish priests, teachers, doctors and professional people. The movement was criticised, despite its accomplishments, as conservative, over-consensual and avoiding the class divisions that had such an important bearing on rural life (Kelleher and Whelan, 1992).

Features of Catholic social activism

One feature about Catholic social activism was its professionalism. If we take as our example the services provided for Irish emigrants, they had a strong focus on the most excluded emigrants (e.g. the mentally ill and single mothers). These services set standards for social provision far ahead of their time, employing social workers from an early stage and setting standards for documentation and accountability. They provided a joined-up set of services in the area of accommodation, work, integration into the host community, and advice and recreation, long before such approaches were formally articulated as good practice. They campaigned vigorously to address the underlying causes of the poverty among Irish emigrant communities and were not tardy in relaying back the policy issues arising, either to the Irish or host governments (Harvey, 1999b). McQuaid was far-sighted in many ways. He warned against the Ballymun high-rise project and in his latter years in the 1960s began to tackle the problems of drug addiction and the need for adult education. He fought hard for the best equipment for the Catholic hospitals in the city: Crumlin Children's Hospital being one of his most cherished projects (1956). Some of his projects addressed the toughest social problems, like severely disturbed youngsters or people with profound disabilities such as the deaf blind (McMahon, 2000).

Ironically, Catholic social activism came to turn full circle by the end of the century. The institutions set in place by McQuaid came, in the course of time, to assail government policy from the left. The precise reasons for this are uncertain, but these changes may be attributed to progressive papal encyclicals and the influence of missionaries returning to Ireland, some of whom began to re-evaluate their work in the context of global liberation theology (Flynn and O'Connell, 1990). The Irish Commission for Justice and Peace (1970) began to develop critical commentaries of government in the areas of human rights, prison and Irish adherence to international conventions. In the 1980s, the Conference of Major Religious Superiors (CMRS) began to make critical commentaries on the government's work in the area of social policy and poverty. By the late 1990s, reorganised as the Conference of Religious in Ireland (CORI), its commentaries were cited repeatedly in the Dáil, the government even seeking its approval for its policies in the area of social inclusion. This mutation in the role of Catholic social action was mirrored by a change in another part of the voluntary sector closely associated with nation-building: Irish language organisations. Their vigour had diminished as the state put their policies into effect. By the 1960s, the shortcomings and failures of language policies prompted the Irish language organisations to reconsider new approaches and persuaded members to distance themselves from reactionary social policies with which they had previously associated. Instead, they focused on new educational methods, championed new types of projects (e.g. Gaeltacht television) and, adopting a pluralist political model, modified their role to represent the needs and views of the minority Irish-language speaking community (Donoghue, undated).

Traditional features of Catholic social action fell into disrepute at the end of the twentieth century. Investigations by Raftery and O'Sullivan (1999) uncovered disturbing histories of personal, physical and sexual abuse of those placed in institutions, exacerbated by a lack of oversight by the state. Several priests were convicted of abuse in these institutions and a compensation fund was set up by governments and the religious orders.

Although by the century's end the Catholic church was much less prominent as an institutional generator of voluntary sector activity, there was evidence that its role had changed, but not necessarily declined. Many of the more active religious orders, even as they contracted in size, deployed their considerable skills, talents and resources in community-based settings. Several of the religious orders, wishing to discard burdensome institutional bases and similarly wishing to become more relevant, moved into disadvantaged communities. Their activities ranged from informal casework services provided by parish sisters to stimulating the establishment of community groups, women's centres, youth groups and local social and family services (Ó Cinnéide, 1999).

An analysis of 244 women's groups funded by the Allen Lane Foundation in Ireland over 1989-91 found that no less than 72 per cent had been set up by the church, often by a religious sister (Mulvey, 1992). Faughan and Kelleher (1993) in their analysis of 42 significant voluntary organisations, found that 57 per cent had an important religious involvement, that involvement being defined as having a religious founder, director or funder or provided with facilities by the religious. This is what Powell and Guerin (1997) say in a lengthy and telling observation:

What appears to be happening is that religious involvement in the voluntary sector is mutating and evolving from its traditional ownership of the institutional voluntary sector to community participation, frequently in a leadership role. There is very little evidence of a decline in religious influence in a more secular society, rather there is evidence of a remarkable ability to adapt and to continue to exercise a hegemonic role. The underlying aspiration of the voluntary and community sector to promote democratic pluralism is fundamentally challenged by this on-going religious hegemony that remains the most durable influence in the Irish voluntary sector. It defies the long-term trend toward secularisation and secular values within Irish society as a whole. What is evident is that traditionalist influences continue to be highly influential in defining the concept of community in Ireland.

Peillon (2001) probably agrees, seeing the leftward move in the church's political position as a successful means of relegitimisation, one gliding over many contradictions and U-turns.

Industrial schools
This might be an appropriate moment to return to the ugly subject of the industrial schools. When the new state was formed, there were 7,000 children in the schools, a number that had fallen only a little by the 1950s (over 6,000 children). A striking illustration of the isolated, conservative social philosophy of the state was that the system of industrial schools was preserved intact, even as it was being speedily dismantled in Britain and in Northern Ireland. As early as 1924, there were more children in industrial schools in the Free State than in the entire UK; by 1933 the system was gone in Great Britain and by 1950 in Northern Ireland. During the 1960s in the Republic, the courts lost their zeal for putting children into the industrial schools and by 1969, the numbers had fallen to 2,000 children in thirty-one schools. In 1970, the child care system was investigated by Justice Eileen Kennedy. Her report brought about substantial changes and the system of industrial schools collapsed as quickly as it had come into place. Not until 1999 did the government acknowledge some of the horrific damage that had been done (Raftery and O'Sullivan, 1999). In 2003, a related new issue emerged with the discovery of unmarked graves of unidentified girls from the Magdalen laundries (Raftery, 2003).

The emergence of self-help groups, campaigning groups and federations
The high summer of Catholic social action was the 1940s, though it continued to find new expression even at the turn of the new century.

Voluntary sector formation began to broaden out in the post-war period alongside a more active role on the part of the state. A small number always functioned independently of the churches and denominational-based action (e.g. Association of Women's Societies, Adoption Reform Society). The ten years after the European conflict ended saw the reorganisation of health services, the forming of the Department of Social Welfare and the drive to eliminate tuberculosis. The setting up of the Rehabilitation Institute and Central Remedial Clinic was paralleled in the voluntary sector by the formation of the National Association for Cerebral Palsy (1948), the Polio Fellowship (1949), and Cork Polio (1956). Later came the Cheshire homes, the Irish Wheelchair Association (1960), and the National Association for the Deaf (1963).

The political context began to change in the Republic of Ireland from the late 1950s. The 1960s decade saw a temporary slackening in emigration, which meant that social problems, issues and contradictions were more likely to be addressed at home, rather than abroad. The prospect, through the initial efforts of Taoiseach Seán Lemass, of the hitherto insular and isolated state joining the European Economic Community, meant that the country was more alert to international social, economic and political developments and trends.

It is very possible that voluntary organisations contributed to some of the success of the Lemass years. In the mid-1950s, unemployment and emigration hit record levels. The Dublin Unemployed Association (1953) and the Unemployed Protest Committee (1957) organised monster marches and presented a range of policy proposals not only for a better treatment of the unemployed but also for domestic economic reform (Kilmurray, 1989). They contested the 1957 general election, their candidate Jack Murphy being elected to the Dáil. It is more than likely that their proposals stimulated the white paper *Programme for Economic Expansion* (1958) which led to a successful reorientation of the country's economic policies (Allen, 1998).

The emerging women's movement was one of the first signs of change, as it was to be in Northern Ireland. Women's movements had never entirely disappeared during the early days of the Free State, although they operated in a political climate ill-disposed to women's participation in public life (Tweedy, 1992). A women's perspective had been kept alive by the Irish Women's Citizens Association (1923), the Women Graduates Association, the Women's Social and Political League, and the Irish Housewives Association (1942). Women's organisations were outspoken critics of the *Kinder, Küche, Kirche* sentiments of the patriarchal constitution introduced by de Valera in 1937. An umbrella federation of 17 women's groups functioned in the 1950s, called the Joint Committee of Women's Societies and Social Workers, the leading members being the Irish Countrywomen's Association and the

Mothers Union. Irish women were formally disadvantaged within Irish law and administrative practices in ways that mirrored Britain and continental Europe. However, the Free State and the Republic kept such laws and practices in operation for much longer (as late as 1972, women were obliged to resign from the public service on marriage; as late as 1975, pay rates for women were formally set at lower rates than men). A significant breakthrough was the appointment by the government of a Commission on the Status of Women in 1970, which reported two years later and this began the process of lifting some of the formal barriers to women's participation in public life and the labour market. A Council for the Status of Women was duly established with 17 founder members in 1972 to ensure that women's issues could be formally articulated and presented to government.

The prohibition of contraception both by the Catholic church and by the criminal law was a crux point for the women's movement, the highlight being the famous 'contraceptives train' when women publicly attempted to import contraceptives from Belfast, inviting arrest for their wrongdoing. The Irish Women's Liberation Movement was formally founded in 1970, but lasted in that organisational form for only four years (Irish Women United took up many of its concerns). The Women's Liberation Movement, a member of the Council for the Status of Women, articulated a radical feminist perspective, one directly confrontational of the oppression of women and the many forms of discrimination that existed, successfully using direct action to highlight injustice.

Other women were not prepared to see their situations addressed within the traditional boundaries of Catholic social care. Single mothers were a particular source of social stigma. From the early 1960s, the birth rate outside marriage began to rise. Fewer single women were prepared to see their children adopted through Catholic (or other) welfare societies or associations and formed Cherish. This organisation was different insofar as it was an association of those most directly affected, set down the principle of non-judgemental support and believed in campaigning for an end to the discriminations endured by single mothers (for example, in access to housing, welfare benefits, and the legal status of their children). New groups arose to express women's needs and to provide acutely needed social services, such as the Rape Crisis Centres, the Well Women clinics, AIM (Action, Information, Motivation), ADAPT (Association for Deserted and Alone Parents) and Women's Aid. The Women's Political Association worked to secure the election of women as public representatives both in the political parties and as independents. The National Association of Widows in Ireland was an early group established to address the problems of widowed and, in practice, older women.

Other groups in this new tradition of self-help, non-judgementalism and advocacy followed. In 1969, the first of the Simon Communities was established in Ireland, based on the twin principles of non-judgemental support for the homeless and campaigning for an end to homelessness. Their untraditional approach attracted the support of the political left and they were treated with suspicion by some (but not all) among the traditional charities (Coleman, 1990). Among the Traveller community, the well-meaning but assimilationist model, led by the settled community, was challenged by the Itinerant Action Group (1963) led by Travellers themselves which sought political responses to their situation (Fay and Crowley, 1990).

Campaigning groups and providers with a campaigning dimension went on to achieve much over the subsequent years. Some groups were associated with legislative success. For example, Cherish and the Federation of Services for Unmarried Parents and their Children achieved the abolition of the status of illegitimacy of children (1988). Simon and the National Campaign for the Homeless obtained legislation defining the responsibilities of local authorities to the homeless (Housing Act, 1988). The Simon Communities actively and publicly supported the election of a senator committed to this and related causes, Brendan Ryan. The Irish Haemophilia Association engaged in a 15-year long campaign through the political system and the courts to get justice for those whose blood had been contaminated. Coalitions of voluntary organisations twice defeated inadequate government legislation in the area of disability (2002). In *Working for Change: a guide to influencing policy in Ireland* (1998), the Combat Poverty Agency published case studies of voluntary sector campaign successes.

The Republic of Ireland was affected by the growth in environmental activism that characterised the continental European countries. Individual battles over crux issues such as the Hume Street Georgian houses, the Wood Quay Viking site and the proposal for a Carnsore nuclear power station led participants and others concerned with environmental protection into a range of single-issue and broad-based NGOs in the 1970s onwards, such as Friends of the Earth/Earthwatch, Greenpeace and An Taisce. The first Green party deputy was elected in 1989, more following in subsequent years. Environmental campaigning became a distinct subset of the activities of all the social movements (Gormley, 1990). In the 1990s, the Republic saw the emergence of groups concerned with gay rights, lesbians, anti-racism and what are known as identity-based social movements (Powell, 2001).

O'Donovan and Varley (1992) caution us against overstating the campaigning role of the voluntary sector, expressing the view that it is a minority activity. A further warning is that several voluntary organisations, for example in the disability area, came to use the term 'advocacy' – but they tend to refer less to organisational campaigning, more to aggressive casework designed to ensure that individuals received their statutory entitlement to services.

The growth of federations was an important feature of the voluntary sector in the 1970s and 1980s. Until then, voluntary organisations tended to function in isolation from each another. Federating offered a number of advantages: access to government, the opportunity to make the case to government for improved resources, sharing of knowledge and information, a place where well-established organisations could help newer smaller organisations to find their place and grow. The following are some of the federations that developed over the period.

Federations of Voluntary Organisations from the 1960s to 1980s

Disability	Union of Voluntary Organisations for the Handicapped, later Disability Federation of Ireland
Learning Difficulty	National Association for the Mentally Handicapped in Ireland
Housing	Irish Council for Social Housing
Homelessness	National Campaign for the Homeless
Poverty	European Anti-Poverty Network
Unemployment	Irish National Organisation of the Unemployed
Single Parents	Federation of Services for Unmarried Parents and their Children (FSUPC, later Treoir)
Youth	National Youth Council of Ireland
Travellers	National Council for Travelling People
Women	Council for the Status of Women (later National Women's Council of Ireland).
Children	Children's Rights Alliance
Credit Unions	Irish League of Credit Unions

The value of such federations was recognised in the early 1990s when the Combat Poverty Agency introduced a system of annual grant-aid for national networks. From the mid-1990s, the agency funded on a long-term basis seven national networks: the Community Workers Co-operative, European Anti-Poverty Network, Irish National Organisation of the Unemployed, Irish Rural Link, Irish Traveller Movement, Forum of People with Disabilities, One Parent Exchange and Network.

A sub-theme of the development of federations was the creation of national advocacy platforms. This was most evident in the field of disability, where people with disabilities were dissatisfied with organisations which represented people with disabilities but were not disabled themselves. The idea of self-help or advocacy groups of people with a particular concern was nothing new, but the idea of a national organisational platform for this purpose was new. Examples of these groups are:

- Disability: Forum of People with Disabilities
- Older people: Senior Citizens Parliament
- Travellers: Irish Travellers Movement

These platform-type organisations often operated in a manner similar to the national federations. Their patterns of activity were sometimes little different. What distinguished them was their emphasis on putting forward the authentic voice of the individuals and groups most directly concerned by the issue. They were happy to welcome the support and involvement of those not personally affected, but made it clear that they must play a subordinate role.

Community development
Community development was a feature of the voluntary sector in the Free State and the Republic. Indeed, it could be said that its role was an ambiguous one. At one level, the state was strongly supportive of notions of community and group action, for it was seen as a low-cost, effective means of binding and reinforcing the social fabric, especially in the rural areas. At another level the state was suspicious of, and quick to react against, community action that took place outside the conventional channels of public administration, local government and the main political parties.

In the first half of its history, community development was most evident in the rural areas, especially in the form of Muintir na Tíre. In the urban areas, community-development projects were, some argue, the descendants of the historic battles of the urban labour movement, where conflicts of class and place had always been closely linked. The Dublin Housing Action Committee, for example, a protest movement from the 1960s, addressed issues not dissimilar from the appalling housing that came to light during the great lockout of 1913 – indeed, it was in many of the same streets that the new protests now took place. In the 1970s and 1980s, two of the first community action groups, North City Centre Community Action Project and Fatima Development Group, arose from tenant action groups in the two areas concerned. Others followed in different parts of the city, such as Ballymun, Tallaght, Blanchardstown and the south inner city (Kelleher and Whelan, 1992). These community-development groups operated under a range of different names and titles, such as 'action group', 'community coalition', 'development association', but they had in common the local community confronting the consequences of national patterns of unemployment, educational disadvantage, lack of public services, uneven urban development and irresponsible planning. In 1982, a 'community candidate', Tony Gregory, was elected to Dáil Éireann, to find himself immediately holding the balance of power in the new hung Dáil. He used this to advantage to stream up to IR£200m (€635m) in projects into the inner city, dramatically succeeding in redirecting resources where mainstream political representatives had failed.

The 1980s saw the establishment of the first community resource centres. The first family resource centres were set up by the Catholic Social Service Conference in 1976 (Blakestown, Killinarden, Fettercairn, Jobstown, Neilstown, Loughlinstown) and by the Irish Society for the Prevention of Cruelty to Children in 1977 (Darndale, Cork, Wexford, Drogheda) (Nic Giolla Choille, 1982). By 1990, about 55 resource centres had been established (Harvey, 1990). Some served the broadest possible range of groups in a given locality (e.g. community resource centres) while others focused on specific groups such as children (e.g. family resource centres), women or unemployed people (e.g. centres for the unemployed). Resource centres were important for the provision of information, training and facilities for deprived communities or groups; as a means of empowerment; and as a focus for voluntary and community activity. The Irish National Organisation of the Unemployed, established in 1989, worked with local groups to establish local centres for the unemployed in most of the large towns in the country, providing resources, information, assistance and a focus for protest. Studies of communities suggested that local action, based on community-development principles, had become a well-embedded part of the economic and social landscape by the 1990s, especially in deprived communities. A study of Tallaght, for example, found no less than 91 active local groups, raising serious questions as to how the Irish state should respond to the new political space that these groups now occupied (Duggan and Ronayne, 1991).

Community work with women was an important theme of voluntary and community sector development from the 1980s. The reasons for this had to do with the impact of the women's liberation movement, the changing nature of the labour market, the employment of women community workers, the situation of women in deprived urban satellite communities and the struggle against unemployment (Tobin, 1990). By 1989, a total of over a hundred women's groups had come into existence. Their number exploded from this point, rising to 400 in 1992 and 600 by 1993. The UK-based Allen Lane Foundation ran a funding programme in Ireland from 1989 to 1991, providing £82,740 (€105,058) to 132 projects run by 110 different women's organisations: this was a considerable stimulus to the development of a women's sector within the voluntary movement (Mulvey, 1992).

Many of the early groups were established to promote women's education, though they also had important secondary roles in bringing women together around a broad set of needs in the area of training, the labour market, child care and social exclusion. A typical early example was KLEAR (Kilbarrack Learning Education and Renewal). The election of Mary Robinson as President of Ireland in 1990 was a moment of special significance, since she had been closely associated with women's groups and made continued contact with them a priority of her presidency. Estimates of the numbers of women's groups rose from 166 in 1989 to about 1,000 in 1997 and 2,631 currently, though these figures should be treated with some caution because of the definitions and methodologies used (Kelleher Associates, 2001). No one would dispute the overall trend or its significance.

The period of community development probably marked the largest single phase of expansion of the voluntary and community sector in the history of the state. A picture of the expansion of the voluntary sector in recent years is confirmed by independent research. Ruddle and Donoghue (1995) found that the average age of voluntary organisations in Ireland in the mid-1990s was 17 years, indicating that most had been established from the 1970s onwards. Powell and Guerin (1997) similarly found that only 18 per cent had been established before 1960, 14 per cent in the 1960s, 26 per cent in the 1970s and 34 per cent in the 1980s. Data are not yet available on the rate of voluntary sector formation in the 1990s, but there are no indications that it is slowing down.

State agencies and the voluntary sector
So far, this history has told one side, the voluntary and community side of the story. How did the state respond? Two state agencies played an important role in the development of voluntary activity during the last quarter of the twentieth century: the National Social Service Board (since renamed Comhairle) and the Combat Poverty Agency. The Combat Poverty Agency's role can be traced to the first European programme against poverty in 1975 (see below: Europeanisation) and it will be discussed shortly. The role of the National Social Service Board came to reflect, over time, some of the problems experienced by the Irish state in its attempt to establish a relationship with the sector.

The National Social Service Board (NSSB) was established in 1970, originally as the National Social Service Council (NSSC), at a time of health reform and the setting up of the eight regional health boards. Some see the formation of the NSSC as the first serious indication by government of an interest in a social policy that involved voluntary action. The Minister for Health concerned, Erskine Childers, also appointed external advisors for the department at the time. Childers envisaged the NSSC as providing a focal point for voluntary services (Faughnan, 1997). Its functions included support of the work of social service councils and the community information centres that had emerged in the 1950s.

At the time, these were seen as one of the main lines of development of voluntary activity in the Republic. Social service councils were umbrella bodies bringing together voluntary and community organisations in a town, city or region; community information centres were small offices, generally staffed by volunteers, providing a range of services on social welfare entitlements and related matters. Despite high hopes, social service councils did not realise their promise and the NSSC was apparently unable to support them in a strong and visible way. Except in a few towns (e.g. Galway, Kilkenny), social service councils did not reach their full potential and their importance declined rapidly (Duffy, 1993). The Minister for Health announced in 1979 that his department would draw up a policy document for their development, but this did not appear and the work of the NSSC declined (Ruddle and Donoghue, 1995).

The NSSC was reconstituted as a board in 1981 (the NSSB). The brief of the board included, *inter alia*, the encouragement of voluntary community action. From 1984, the board employed development officers to work with local voluntary and community groups. Apparently this created tension with health boards, though the precise nature of the problems was never publicly made clear (Powell and Guerin, 1997). This coincided with the election of a Fianna Fáil government determined to severely prune government spending. A memorandum circulated by the government in 1987 asked departments not merely for the reduction of spending but for the wholesale elimination of agencies whose continuation could not be justified in the national interest or where savings could be achieved through mergers or integration into government departments. The government decided to abolish the National Social Service Board and to integrate its functions into the Department of Social Welfare. There was a howl of protest from voluntary organisations, largely because the government decision was seen to undermine the promotion of voluntary action, which was the aspect of the board they valued the most. In the event, the government backed down. The board survived the crisis, though its terms of reference were amended and trimmed to take account of the reported earlier objections of health boards. The board was ordered to concentrate on information-giving functions and the support of citizen's information centres, its community-development role emasculated. In a further organisational mutation, the board was transferred to a new parent, the Department of Social Welfare, in 1995. Faughnan (1997) concludes that the board did not have the scope or opportunity to fulfil its brief with the voluntary sector originally envisaged at its start. Despite these limitations, the board carved out a niche for the support of the communications and informational role of voluntary organisations as well as the promotion of volunteering and the provision of a social mentoring scheme (Comhairle, 2003). In retrospect, the mid-1980s represented a redrawing of the boundaries of the state and voluntary action, but not the last.

It is an intriguing counterpoint that in Northern Ireland at the same time, the government perceived that the community-development movement had become undisciplined, had overstepped the mark and was out of hand. As McCready (2000) wrote later in an aptly entitled chapter 'The state strikes back', the government attempted to neuter community development by making it the responsibility of largely indifferent district councils.

The Republic's government had an equally uneasy relationship with the other state agency that worked with the voluntary sector. In 1975, the Fine Gael/Labour government had run the first programme against poverty, co-ordinated by a national committee on pilot schemes to combat poverty, or 'Combat Poverty' for short. When Charles Haughey became Taoiseach, the schemes were allowed to lapse (1980-81). In March 1982, the Fianna Fáil minority government resolved to abolish Combat Poverty and replace it with the National Community Development Agency. Legislation for the new agency actually completed its passage through what was one of the shortest Dála in the history of the state, a new board even being appointed. The government appeared to signal its distaste of the work taken by voluntary organisations against poverty with the political agenda that this implied. It was prepared to support community development, an outwardly softer concept with less political baggage, even though community development could be a radically transforming concept.

In the event, the Fine Gael/Labour incoming government in December 1982 abolished the short-lived National Community Development Agency, re-establishing the Combat Poverty Agency, although its founding legislation took an astonishingly long period to pass, not until 1986. When the Fine Gael/Labour government collapsed the following year, Fianna Fáil was prepared to allow the agency to continue to develop, despite its desire to pare down government across the board. Fianna Fáil governments made no further attempt to trim the agency's role in community development for another fifteen years.

The Combat Poverty Agency's importance in supporting voluntary activity was not because of the size of its budget, which was small and, compared to health board funding for voluntary organisations, minuscule. Rather it lay in the agency's support for community-based and voluntary sector action that confronted social policy issues. The agency's research programme in its early years provided a solid basis for subsequent campaigning work by voluntary organisations. The agency helped to form, in the public mind, a strong connection between 'voluntary action' and the new battleground of 'social inclusion'.

Social partnership: the long march through the institutions

Despite this difficult background, social partnership was to emerge as a key theme of voluntary sector development. National social partnership in its present form may be dated to 1993 with the National Economic and Social Forum and to have matured as the fourth pillar of the national agreement in 1997 (see below). However, it would be wrong to portray social partnership as something that happened with a 'big bang' in the 1990s. Incipient social partnership was evident in a number of individual sectors some time earlier, as government drew individual voluntary organisations and sectors into the political process or as voluntary organisations managed to infiltrate the political decision-making process. Some of the key steps in the process are outlined.

As far back as 1963, the national trust, An Taisce (established 1948), was given a statutory role in the planning process. A requirement was laid down in the planning Act of that year that all planning applications be passed to the trust, thereby giving it an opportunity to appeal against environmentally undesirable proposals. Although this might seem a small step, it recognised the primacy of access to information as being the first step in political engagement. In the course of time, this role was to become controversial, with many elected politicians objecting to the role played by An Taisce in the planning process, especially in the west of Ireland. Despite this, the government was otherwise slow to extend the social partnership role of voluntary organisations in the environmental fields. In the early 1990s, Earthwatch asked for and was refused representation on the Industrial Policy Review Group, the Tourism Task Force and the Jobs Forum. An Taisce was invited to nominate a member of the Environmental Protection Agency in 1990, the government giving the impression that it was prepared to do business only with safer voluntary organisations. This view was subsequently relaxed. Partly encouraged by foreign example, the government established in 1999 Comhar, the National Sustainable Development Partnership, as a broad forum for the country's debate on how best to make progress on sustainable development. It had 25 members, drawn from government, the economic sectors, environmental NGOs, the community and voluntary sector, and professionals and academics. Its work was conducted through four working groups – national policy, spatial planning, waste management and prevention and local sustainability, participation and education.

From 1975, the government gave an early version of social partnership status to the National Youth Council of Ireland. This meant the right to nominate a member of the National Economic and Social Council; nomination rights to the state training agency, FÁS; annual meetings with government departments at Secretary General level and monthly meetings with the minister responsible for youth affairs. One youth organisation obtained a privileged form of access to the political system: in 1989, Macra na Feirme was awarded representation on the county enterprise boards and the monitoring committees of the structural funds.

When the government passed the Child Care Act, 1991, provision was made for the appointment of child-care advisory committees in each health board area, with places set aside for representatives of voluntary and community organisations. The operation of these committees has not been well documented and they are known to have got off to a problematic start. In the case of the Eastern Health Board, the board itself chose the voluntary sector representatives, avoiding some of the most prominent (and noisy) child-care providers in the region (Harvey, 1994a). In 1990, co-ordinating and advisory committees for mental handicap committees were established in most (but not all) health board areas. Seven or eight voluntary organisations working with people with a learning difficulty were invited to participate, but the criteria for deciding which ones should be so invited and which ones excluded were unclear (Harvey, 1992). A report on disability, *Toward an Independent Future* (Government of Ireland, 1996), recommended regional co-ordinating committees for disability services, including health board personnel, service users and voluntary agencies. The Health (Amendment) Act, 1996 required health boards to have regard to the need for co-operation with voluntary bodies. Regional co-ordinating committees for persons with a physical or sensory disability now exist in each health board according to national guidelines, paralleled by consultative and developmental committees in the area of learning disabilities. Key voluntary service providers are represented on both.

Under the Housing Act, 1988, the local authorities were required to establish consultative fora with voluntary organisations in their areas in order to consult over the housing of homeless people. In the event, the local authorities were very slow to do so. Cork and Dublin, the two largest local authorities, failed to establish such fora until 1992 and in other areas they took even longer. Some just ignored the legislation outright (Leonard, 1992). Local government appeared to voluntary organisations to be a reluctant and limited participant in this consultative process, preferring to focus discussions on liaison and casework rather than longer-term or strategic issues. Such fora were eventually established in most local authorities by 2002-3.

In 1984, the idea of a national jobs forum was first proposed as one means whereby those most directly concerned with unemployment could gather to try to address the escalating problem of unemployment and agree some common solutions (Kerins, 1991). The Irish National Organisation of the Unemployed pressed the idea forward, arguing that the traditional social partners could not reasonably be expected to devise successful policies to combat unemployment, while shutting out the representative bodies of the unemployed themselves. In 1989, the idea won support from two political extremes, the Workers Party and the Progressive Democrats, the latter becoming less enthusiastic when they entered government that year. When John Bruton became leader of Fine Gael, he adopted that idea as a 'forum on employment' and put forward a Dáil resolution accordingly. In response, the government set up a Joint Oireachtas Committee on Employment, which, for the first time invited in as participants not just the employers and trade unions but voluntary organisations, the Irish National Organisation of the Unemployed, and the Conference of Religious in Ireland (Allen, 1998).

Political recognition for the sector was strengthened following the election of Mary Robinson as President of the Republic in 1990. She appointed to her Council of State, the founder of the Forum of People with Disabilities and the director of the Northern Ireland Council for Voluntary Action.

National social partnership was the next stage. From the 1960s, the government had negotiated wage rounds with employers and trade unions, farmers later joining the process. From 1987, there had been formal triennial framework agreements between government, employers, farmers and trade unions, formalised as the *Programme for National Recovery* and subsequent agreements (*Programme for Economic and Social Progress*, 1991; the *Programme for Competitiveness and Work*, 1994; *Partnership 2000 for Inclusion, Employment and Competitiveness*, 1997; the *Programme for Prosperity and Fairness*, 2000; and *Sustaining Progress*, 2003). These triennial agreements between what were called 'the social partners' were driven by three factors. First, the analysis of the Republic's poor economic performance pointed to what had been achieved in other European economies (e.g. Austria) when governments negotiated comprehensive deals with their social partners. Second, the government offered an attractive trade-off, namely that in exchange for economic 'responsibility', the partners could negotiate a broad range of government economic and social policy far outside the traditional parameters of wages, terms and conditions. Third, several theorists articulated the notion of 'voice' – namely that social and economic development would be forever hindered unless a structure could be found to give 'voice', or a say, to its key players on core socio-economic issues (Mjoset, 1992). Here, this was termed social partnership – but it was only for employers and trade unions. Voluntary organisations were not part of this process. In 1993, the new government of the 27th Dáil appointed a national policy consultative body, the National Economic and Social Forum (NESF), and invited voluntary organisations to become full members. Whilst in retrospect, NESF looked logical and inevitable, its political birth was a confused coming together of difficult political forces and trends. Allen (1998), a close spectator at the time, described it as a 'strange mongrel' which attempted, at one swoop, to address a series of concerns about the social partnership process, such as the exclusion of members of the Oireachtas from the national agreements and the diverse interests of the voluntary and community sector.

In NESF, voluntary organisations were called the third strand, alongside the other strands of members of the Oireachtas (strand 1) and the traditional social partners of trade unions, employers' and farmers' organisations (strand 2). The initial voluntary sector representatives were the Council for the Status of Women, the Irish National Organisation of the Unemployed, the National Youth Council of Ireland, the Disability Federation of Ireland, An Taisce, the Irish Travellers Movement, the European Anti-Poverty Network and the Community Workers Co-operative. These tended to be representative, rather than service-providing organisations. Voluntary organisations quickly played a lead role within the forum and drove the agenda of many policy reports presented during its first term of office. The ability of the voluntary and community sector representatives to reach agreed positions, argue their case and write coherent text made an impression on the existing social partners and civil servants in attendance. In an initial burst of activity, later called 'the glory days', NESF produced a series of short but thoughtful, hard-hitting and provocative reports. NESF got the voluntary sector a seat at a consultative top table, but this was still some stage short of full social partnership in the determining framework policies. At a 1995 plenary meeting of NESF, the Taoiseach was formally asked to offer the voluntary and community sector full partnership process. Although the government side put forward a series of formal reasons why this could not happen, it was soon apparent that the will to hold out against the sector was weakening.

The final breakthrough of the voluntary and community sector into national agreements was, in the end, remarkably sudden. The body which unlocked a door, already loosened by others, was the Irish National Organisation of the Unemployed (INOU) which met the Taoiseach in May 1996 to discuss the idea (it was actually the first time that a representative body of the unemployed had ever met the Taoiseach). In August, voluntary and community organisations received an invitation to join negotiations as a pillar of the next framework agreement, which began two months later and concluded that December as *Partnership 2000*. Voluntary organisations had addressed the committee monitoring the *Programme for Economic and Social Progress* some years earlier on an *an hoc*, once-off, invitation-only basis, but the new arrangement offered participation as of right. For the INOU and its allies, this represented the culmination of what Allen (1998) later called 'the long march through the institutions'. That *Partnership 2000* was more than a token arrangement became clear as consternation followed the initial refusal of the Irish National Organisation of the Unemployed to sign the agreement. This pillar was defined by the government as having eight constituent parts: the National Youth Council, the Irish Congress of Trade Unions Centres for the Unemployed, Protestant Aid, the Conference of Religious in Ireland, the Irish National Organisation of the Unemployed, the National Women's Council, the Society of St Vincent de Paul and community organisations grouped as the Community Platform.

The Community Platform brought together 25 or so of the country's most prominent policy-focused voluntary and community-based organisations operating at national level. They shared a common broad commitment to promoting equality, solidarity and social justice and in combating poverty and social exclusion. Specifically, they worked to organise the involvement of the voluntary and community sector in national decision-making arenas and in the national agreement. Although the primary purpose of the platform was representation in the partnership negotiations and the subsequent monitoring of the national agreement, platform representatives were also appointed to a range of other bodies (e.g. National Economic and Social Council, structural fund monitoring committees). The impact of the voluntary sector on the first national agreement in which it participated was plain, with one of the five parts or frameworks of the 132-page current plan entirely devoted to policies for social inclusion and equality.

National social partnership put the voluntary sector in the Republic of Ireland in a more advantaged situation than the voluntary sector in almost any other European country. National social partnership sparked a considerable amount of comment for what it said about the voluntary statutory relationship and the relationship between decision-making through elected representatives on the one hand and the representatives of peak organisations on the other. National social partnership coincided with a period of extraordinary economic development and some commentators believe that it made at least a modest contribution. National social partnership has been broadly, albeit not universally, welcomed as a form of nascent corporate pluralism: a hybrid governance that brings in a diverse network of interest groups in more inclusive relationships to the political system (O'Donnell and Thomas, 1998). Some even see it as the late working out of the theories of social corporatism that date back to the 1930s. Others have pointed out some of its imperfections, for example its lack of full representativity (O'Sullivan, 1999/2000). They questioned its consultative base, noting that the process was led by a relatively small number of people concentrated in a few key organisations.

Social partnership reconstructed

In spring 2002, the groups belonging to the Community Platform made a token and temporary walk-out from the *Programme for Prosperity and Fairness* because, they said, the government had taken a number of important economic and social decisions that ran counter to the provisions of the agreement, highlighting new laws to restrict Travellers. Negotiations for the next national agreement, later called *Sustaining Progress 2003–5*, proved to be tense. Although six members of the Community Platform voted in favour of the new national agreement, 16 voted against, as did the National Women's Council of Ireland. Even those in favour were critical of the lack of social commitments, targets and funding in *Sustaining Progress*, but preferred to 'play a long game' and stay on the inside.

The withdrawal of significant organisations from social partnership had two immediate consequences. First, those organisations that voted against social partnership lost their place on a broad range of national monitoring, consultative and negotiating bodies. They argued that whilst it was not unreasonable for them to leave bodies specifically linked to *Sustaining Progress*, it was unfair for them to be removed from all national consultative forums. By early 2003, the community pillar had achieved representation on no less than 39 national forums, so a considerable number of expulsions was involved. This was not an unprecedented situation, for the Irish Creamery Milk Suppliers Association had rejected a much earlier national agreement and lost its seats (it eventually returned). The government stated that it was still prepared to deal with the dissident organisations on an individual basis.

Second, the withdrawal of the National Women's Council and the Community Platform created gaps in the structure of social partnership. Of the five key groups that had driven the original social partnership process, two were now gone (National Women's Council, Community workers Co-operative), but three remained inside (Conference of Religious in Ireland, Irish National Organisation of the Unemployed, National Youth Council). The government took advantage of the opportunity to restructure social partnership. The government appointed six individual organisations as members and selected seven member strands. These were as follows:

- Conference of Religious in Ireland
- Congress Centres for the Unemployed
- Irish National Organisation of the Unemployed
- National Youth Council of Ireland
- Protestant Aid
- Society of St Vincent de Paul
- Care: The Carer's Association
- Children: Children's Rights Alliance

- Local and voluntary: The Wheel
- Rural: Irish Rural Link
- Older people: Age Action Ireland and the Irish Senior Citizen's Parliament
- Disability: Disability Federation of Ireland
- Housing: Irish Council for Social Housing/National Association for Building Co-operatives.

This opened the door to a number of new groups, especially in the area of care, children, the elderly and housing. The Wheel, a body bringing together a broad range of voluntary and community organisations, achieved representation, marking its arrival on the national stage. Two additional organisations applied for membership, but were turned down: the Union of Students in Ireland and Women in the Home.

Local social partnership

The move to social partnership at national level was matched by progress towards social partnership at county and local level. This happened in two stages. In the first half of the 1990s, structured partnerships were developed around local economic development. In the second half of the 1990s, initiatives were taken to bring voluntary and community organisations into the broad range of decision-making in the local authority system.

The seeds of local social partnership went as far back as the 1930s with the idea of the parish councils. Parish councils arose from a confluence of circumstances: the desire to reform local government; continental concepts of vocational organisation; and the emergence of new axes of rural and community development. The Local Government Bill, 1939 proposed the establishment of voluntary local committees for the development of local facilities, sports and agriculture. The Local Government Act, 1941 encouraged the local authorities to work with communities in their area through approved advisory committees. After a brief burst of activity, this early effort at democratic local involvement quickly foundered on strong opposition from the beleaguered local government system which saw such committees as a direct threat (Daly, 1997). Despite this, the idea of local partnership between voluntary and community organisations on the one hand and reformed local government was raised again by the white paper on local government in 1971, but it was many years before a fresh start was eventually made. Local social partnership, as it eventually developed, was the meeting point of quite different cultures, approaches, concepts and mindsets. For central government, local social partnership was the means whereby local government made itself more relevant and responsive; but for the community sector it was about much bigger issues of participation, accountability, social inclusion and integrated development (Community Workers Cooperative, 1990).

Present-day partnership for local economic development may be formally traced to the *Programme for Economic and Social Progress (PESP)* (1991-3), which (section VII) piloted 12 Area-Based Responses (ABR) to unemployment. Their origins were opportunistic, being devised to meet a combination of criteria for European global grant funds. The ABRs were called the PESP or partnership companies and they brought together state agencies and the social partners at local level to develop responses to unemployment and social exclusion. Their brief was to combat unemployment and to promote community development. The partnerships built links to community groups and voluntary organisations, inviting them to participate on their boards as community directors. The evaluation of the work of the partnerships was favourable (Craig and McKeown, 1994), later winning approval from the Organisation for Economic Co-operation and Development (Sabel, 1996). The partnerships demonstrated, teething troubles notwithstanding, that local social partnerships not only contributed to social cohesion but had immediate practical value in providing training opportunities, job placement and job creation for thousands of unemployed people. Commentators now explain the new local partnerships throughout Europe as due to the coming together of a number of different factors: a recognition of the cost-effectiveness of voluntary organisations, a commitment to the local, a rediscovery of subsidiarity, and an appreciation of the merits of the social economy in combating joblessness and social exclusion, all with lower costs than traditional regional policies (Williamson, 1999b).

Originally, there were 12 PESP companies or partnerships. Because of their success, the concept was extended to 38 areas, with partnerships formed in each, in the 1994-9 round of the structural funds under the programme for local, urban and rural development and later in the 2000-6 round under the local development social inclusion programme. This was a strong impetus for local development, community-led social action and new structures, leading to concrete results. The local partnerships brought new resources to deprived communities, gave those communities a seat at the table with the other social partners and state agencies and brought an element of planning to bear on local economic development. In concrete terms, between 1992 and 2000, the partnership companies assisted 23,500 people to find work, 13,100 people to set up their own businesses, 17,000 people to enter education, and 1,400 community, environmental and infrastructural projects. By the late 1990s, it was estimated that between PESP and other initiatives about 150 local social partnership bodies were now functioning. A critical analysis by the Combat Poverty Agency recommended ways in which their operation could be further refined to increase their effectiveness. It saw the partnerships as a considerable challenge to the professionalism, management capabilities, strategic thinking and capacity of the community and voluntary sector (Walsh, Craig and McCafferty, 1998).

Even as the community sector engaged in local economic partnership, it sought out a challenging political role. With the reform of the European structural funds in 1988, voluntary and community organisations sought representation on the structural fund monitoring committees. Such representation, they argued, would give them opportunities to obtain information on the structural funds, ensure that voluntary and community organisations could apply for funding, and modify the funds so that they were more effective instruments in combating social exclusion. Some parts of the voluntary and community sector became involved in the issue of the structural funds in order to mount a direct political challenge to what they regarded as the wholly inappropriate use of the funds by the Irish political élite (Community Workers Co-operative, 1989).

Progress was made: the 1989-1994 round saw the Irish Countrywomen's Association and Macra na Feirme invited to sit on the monitoring committee of the operational programme for rural development. The operational programme for the occupational integration of disabled people invited as monitors the National Association for the Mentally Handicapped in Ireland, the Disability Federation of Ireland and the Federation of Providers of Services for the Handicapped. For the 1994-9 round of the structural funds, 16 places were given to voluntary organisations out of a total of 264 places on national monitoring committees; with two seats on each of the regional monitoring committees (16 places out of 368). On the first Programme for Peace and Reconciliation, which covered both jurisdictions, voluntary organisations obtained two places out of 45 on the main monitoring committee and a larger number of places on the 109-strong consultative forum.

A broader involvement of community and voluntary organisations was one of the outcomes of local government reform at the end of the 1990s. The landmark policy document was *Better Local Government – Programme for Change* (Government of Ireland, 1996). This established city and county development boards of state agencies, social partners, voluntary and community organisations in each local authority to plan the economic and social development of the area concerned. Within each local authority, five or so strategic policy committees were established, to which voluntary and community organisations were elected. Within a few years, voluntary and community organisations achieved representation not only on the city and county development boards and on the strategic policy committees but also on county child-care committees, child protection committees, the local drugs task force, monitoring committees for the RAPID programme, the young people facilities and services fund, and local integrated planning committees.

The engagement between the voluntary and community organisations on the one hand, with the local authority elected representatives and officials on the other hand proved to be a difficult one. The organisational cultures of community groups and local authorities were quite different from one another. Although most local authorities welcomed the participation of voluntary and community organisations, some elected representatives felt quite threatened by the process. Some voluntary and community representatives experienced bureaucratic, procedural and personal resistance to their participation, though there was optimism that the process would settle down over time (Harvey, 2002b).

The reform of local government prompted voluntary and community organisations to organise themselves formally at local level. In the early 1990s, some of the partnerships had set up community fora so that they could establish a process of consultation with the community. From 2000 (under the white paper for the development of voluntary activity) the government made available €1.27m each year to resource community participation in local social partnership. This sum was allocated to the 34 main local authorities on a *per capita* basis (with a minimum for each county) and distributed by the city and county development boards. Several community fora were set up in the late 1990s, examples being Blanchardstown and Northside Dublin, Donegal, Roscommon, Kerry and Galway city. These took different organisational and lexical shape.

Some local authorities had broad-based fora, bringing together all the voluntary and community groups in the county or city concerned. In other local authority areas, the structures divided between a large forum open to all voluntary and community organisations and a smaller grouping designed to represent those groups concerned with social exclusion. These often called themselves platforms. These community structures had varying degrees of autonomy. In some cases, they functioned as entirely free, self-sustaining bodies. In others, they were closely tied in to the work of a parent body that might be the local authority or the partnership. By 2002, operational fora had been set up in most local authority areas (Cosgrove and Ryder, 2001). However, when spread across 34 local authorities, the €1.27m, especially when further subdivided between the respective fora and platforms, meant that the process was quite under-resourced.

For the voluntary and community sector, local social partnership posed a difficult set of challenges. National partnership was a formal, visible process in which aims, objectives and results were open to tangible analysis and from which the sector could ultimately withdraw. The complex mechanisms and set of relationships around local social partnerships were more labyrinthine and elaborate. Local social partnership, although portrayed by governmental commentators as the benign outcome of a natural course of development, was at times quite conflictual, especially when local groups were politically aware, ably led and seeking specific changes (Rafferty, 1992). As far back as the early 1980s, political parties, public representatives and local authorities saw community organisation as an unwelcome threat to their accustomed ways of doing business (Linehan, 1984). During the 28th Dáil, several deputies expressed unease about the proliferation of local development groups. One of the most uneasy of them, Éamon Ó Cuiv, subsequently became the Minister for Community, Rural and Gaeltacht Affairs and he quickly announced plans to rationalise the many layers of local development. Many community organisations suspected he had a more sinister agenda: to curb the influence of the sector.

Opinion within the voluntary and community sector (and even within parts of the state sector), while welcoming the principle of social partnership, was wary of ensnarement in a series of relationships that would ultimately poorly serve the disadvantaged communities whose interests they sought to defend. Community representatives warned that the gains from social partnership were likely to be limited as long as the underlying economic and class relationships within society were unchanged.

> Partnership with the state as a basis for access to funding could end up excluding groups with a more radical critique of the state or communities in conflict with the state. It could also end up being part of a process of coopting of the community sector into a state-imposed agenda and thus of silencing a dissenting voice. Then there is always the possibility that it could be structured and pursued in a way that empowers community groups (Community Workers Co-operative, 1992).

This echoes the ambiguous role of community development referred to earlier. Here, the co-operative made clear the need for space for civil society to articulate an independent voice and to have the rights associated with this space recognised. It also articulated the natural concern of any political group that it not be co-opted into the governmental policy community, for fear of losing its identity, thrust, values and sense of purpose.

Now we turn to a number of other features of voluntary sector development in the Republic over the period 1921-2000. European funding has already been mentioned and now is the time to examine its influence in more detail.

Europeanisation

Ireland's accession to the European Communities in 1973 was to have significant implications for the voluntary sector. In the first instance, the main impact was financial, but its overall impact proved to be much more significant and subtle than the immediate financial benefits. (The growing influence of the European Communities, later the European Union, is referred to here as the process of Europeanisation.)

The European Communities established in 1975 a set of pilot action projects against poverty, sometimes called the poverty programme. The programme was very much an Irish initiative, proposed by the Parliamentary Secretary to the Minister for Social Welfare, Frank Cluskey, in the Fine Gael/Labour government of the period. This €20m European programme provided funding for a range of projects, generally run or led by voluntary and community organisations. Although these developments were retrospectively called the first programme against poverty, their proper title was the *Pilot Schemes to Combat Poverty*, overseen by the National Committee on Pilot Schemes to Combat Poverty mentioned above. The programme's work had an important long-term effect on the development of voluntary and community organisations in Ireland, for the following reasons.

The programme recognised voluntary and community organisations as having a centre stage role in the combating of poverty. It funded a range of research studies concerning community and voluntary activity. The programme supported the development of resource centres, then a new form of activity (e.g. Waterford Area Resource Project, Dublin South City Area Resource Project, Cork Education Rights Centre) and began structured welfare rights work. The programme had a strong focus around community development, empowerment and community participation. It was the beginning of a programmatic response to social questions.

The role of NGOs was one of seven areas of study within the European programme as a whole. The programme compiled a report on the role of non-governmental organisations in Europe (Northern Ireland was a case study area). This drew up a typology of non-governmental action on poverty in Europe, making a distinction between larger, older service providers and smaller, newer, more politicised groups. The former, while being professional, it criticised for being ameliorative rather than preventative, lacking in innovation, bureaucratic, conservative and safe. The latter it commended for tackling root causes, though they could be woolly, extreme and narcissistic (Commission of the European Communities, 1981).

The poverty programme raised the awareness of voluntary and community organisations of the possibility opened up by the European Union for funding and external recognition. European Social Fund resources began to find their way into projects for people with disabilities at around the same time. The poverty programme also indicated the preparedness of Europe to fund areas of work which the domestic governments found difficult, as seen when Fianna Fáil closed down the projects in 1981.

In the end, the idea was to have a second chance, for the second poverty programme got under way in 1985, by which time Fine Gael and Labour were back in government. The second programme funded nine projects in Ireland over 1985-9 while the third programme a further three over 1989-94. The second programme funded projects under thematic headings: rural development, urban policy, single parents, the unemployed, youth, homeless and marginal groups and the elderly. Poverty III had three themes with, in Ireland, one project each: integrated rural development (Forum in Connemara), integrated urban development (PAUL in Limerick) and innovative projects (Pavee Point Travellers project). These projects established a level of co-operation with the Brownlow Poverty III project in Craigavon, Co. Armagh.

With the reform of the structural funds in 1989, additional resources became available through Community Initiative Programmes such as HORIZON and NOW. Voluntary and community organisations initially perceived the benefits of European participation as financial, but they were much more extensive than that. First, European funding made possible a significant expansion of a number of existing voluntary organisations. Because of their low level of development and of the scarcity of Irish funding, European project funding was comparatively large and sometimes even greater than the existing size of the project itself. Second, the European Union required projects to make themselves 'visible'. As a result, these projects and the issues they promoted (e.g. rural development, Travellers) came to have a much higher profile on the national stage. Third, projects were expected to confront policy issues and contribute to policy development. The issues arising from their work were presented to national policy-makers (e.g. Barry, 1988; Harvey, 1994b). Fourth, the nature of European funding led to a professionalisation of the sector. The European Union required much tougher standards of accounting, reporting and auditing than had been the case hithertofore. The European Union required the evaluation of projects, a phenomenon virtually unknown in the Irish voluntary sector up to that point. The requirement of evaluation was willingly embraced as a tool for the improvement of the sector and did have the effect of prompting voluntary organisations to think, act and plan more strategically. These disciplines and approaches began to spread to other parts of the sector, whether in receipt of European funding or not.

State and voluntary sector: a conflictual relationship?
The conflict between state and the voluntary sector evident around the National Social Service Council (and Board) and around the pilot schemes to combat poverty suggested that relationships between the two were uneasy. Such a tension appears to have been a dominant theme of the relationship throughout the whole period, as a series of examples illustrates. It took the new state a long time to devise a policy for the voluntary sector. One of the reasons was an ongoing history of difficulties between them, as the following case studies illustrate.

The hospital sector provides an interesting picture of the shifting boundaries of church-state-voluntary provision at the end of the twentieth century. This was documented in detail by O'Ferrall (2000). Unlike the case of social services, the new state felt obliged to extend health services and this process brought these relationships under some strain. The Free State inherited two types of hospitals: those run by Catholic religious orders and institutions; and what were termed 'voluntary' hospitals, run by voluntary committees associated with the Protestant community. The new Irish state established, as the health services grew, an infrastructure of local hospitals later run under the aegis of the appropriate regional health board, so now there were three streams.

By the 1920s, the religious and voluntary hospitals had exhausted their endowments and found it harder to provide a service for anyone other than paying patients. The government, for its part, was anxious to ensure that hospital care be extended as widely as possible, especially to those unable to afford it. Financial squeeze brought voluntary hospitals to the verge of closure and they were only saved by a government betting monopoly, the hospitals sweepstakes, introduced in 1930. The government, through the Hospital Commission established in 1933, required the voluntary hospitals to accept a certain level of state direction and standards in return for public money. The voluntary hospitals, both Protestant and Catholic, resisted such state direction, guarding their autonomy, while still making a claim on public funds so that they could meet public needs. The Protestant voluntary hospitals' resistance was based on the idea of maintaining pluralist provision in a Catholic state; that of the Catholic hospitals was based on the ideal of subsidiarity and the prevention of state interference.

In an effort to preserve their autonomy and to achieve economies of scale, the seven Protestant teaching hospitals that were associated with Dublin University, federated in 1961 as the Federated Dublin Voluntary Hospitals (Coakley, 1992). However, the pressure by government for rationalisation proved relentless. Three of the voluntary hospitals closed, their functions and services transferred to a government-appointed board under the name of St James' Hospital. The 1980s saw severe retrenchment in health services compounded by rationalisation, leading to further closures of voluntary hospitals, the final assets being transferred to government (this happened to some of the Catholic hospitals too). The surviving voluntary hospitals saw state attitudes to their record, role and assets as downright predatory and found it ever harder to attract a voluntary input when their freedom of manoeuvre was evermore restricted. O'Ferrall (2000) attributes the decline of the voluntary hospital sector to the lack of a secular theory to come to its defence, religious protestations finding less and less sympathy among the public as a whole and administrators in particular. The voluntary hospitals certainly failed to make a convincing public case in the face of Department of Health insistence on their greater 'co-operation'.

These closures set the scene for an epic clash between government and the voluntary hospitals in the late 1980s. The occasion was the merger between the Meath Hospital (estd. 1753), the National Children's Hospital (1821) and the Adelaide Hospital (1839) who came together to move to a new campus at Tallaght. These hospitals were all that was left of the tradition of Protestant medical philanthropy of the nineteenth century. The Adelaide, the key player of the three, was voluntary in so far as it had an open membership (the Adelaide Hospital Society), an extensive scheme for the involvement of volunteers in the work of the hospital, its own fund-raising programme and its own views on the development of health services (e.g. making submissions on health strategies). It had a self-elected lay board of about 30 people, some in practice being drawn indirectly from the society. The board was not directly accountable to the membership: originally some voluntary hospital boards were so accountable, but following the attempted take-over of the Meath Hospital by the Knights of Columbanus in 1953, a barrier was established between the society and the board to prevent such a recurrence.

Planning for the new hospital was made the responsibility of a body appointed by the Minister. The Department of Health originally envisaged that the Minister would appoint the board of the new Tallaght Hospital. The Adelaide fought a long, difficult, but ultimately successful battle to protect the concept of a lay board outside ministerial control and its own consultative style of management. This was especially difficult, granted ministerial control of financial flows, one which the department used to the full. The Department of Health appeared to have great problems with the concept of voluntary management and a voluntary sector space, adhering to a command style of management through ministerial appointees. So too did the Department of Social Welfare, which dismissed these hospitals as outside the scope of the 1997 green paper (Donnelly-Cox, 1998). O'Ferrall (2000) suggests that despite the use by the Department of Health, health boards and others of the language of 'partnership' and 'voluntary', they had little grasp of its meaning or implications. He characterised the authorities as seeking to structure their relationships with voluntary organisations as dependent, rather than active partnerships. He saw the battle as a contest in which, through the Adelaide, values of diversity, pluralism, citizenship, social capital and democratic management managed to hold out against managerialism, centralism and command-and-control public administration. Indeed he argued (2003) that it brought into play much broader issues of citizenship and the core values of public services (O'Ferrall, 2003).

O'Ferrall's analysis is intriguingly counterpoised with the fate of the voluntary hospitals in Britain during the same period. Although the post-war period saw the establishment of a universalist national health service, Britain still had room for a voluntary hospital sector supported and part-funded (in London) through an independent umbrella, intermediary body: the King's Fund. Whilst the fund had, at times, a difficult existence, the value of voluntary sector management at arm's length from central government appears to have been more valued there, even in a more collectivist political environment (Prochaska, 1999). In Northern Ireland, the Mater Hospital remained outside the National Health Service until 1971, eventually joining by agreement between the two parties (see chapter two, above).

The uncertain boundaries between the state and the voluntary sector could also be seen in sharp relief but in a different way, through the story of the Free Legal Advice Centres (FLAC). FLAC was set up in 1969 by law students (some later rose to legal and political prominence), conscious of the fact that most people on low incomes could not afford legal advice. The students resolved to provide a *pro bono* law service themselves, whilst simultaneously campaigning for the introduction of a comprehensive state scheme which, they were confident, would eventually make at least some of these services redundant. FLAC's aggressive and effective campaigning led to the appointment of a committee which recommended the scheme they sought (the Pringle committee). The government, in the event, introduced in 1980 an extremely limited, under-funded state scheme with a restricted scope and tight means tests, eschewing both comprehensive and community-based services and discontinuing its limited funded of FLAC. FLAC resolved to continue in existence, meeting the needs of the huge numbers of people unserviced by the government scheme, defining a niche role in case and employment law and continuing its campaigning work. The government found enormous difficulty in funding FLAC or community-based services (e.g. Coolock Community Law Centre, 1975), apparently taking the view that it should only fund a limited, residual state scheme and seeing little or no merit for critical, community or broad-based services provided by voluntary organisations. Here, the Irish state tolerated, but certainly did not welcome, some forms of voluntary activity.

Eventually, after protracted lobbying, the government came to fund both FLAC and Coolock in the mid-1990s. The two systems, state and voluntary, now continue in uneasy, parallel existence (Whyte, 2002). When in 1995 the government legislated for the appointment of a civil legal aid board, the Minister for Equality and Law Reform strenuously and successfully resisted proposals to have voluntary organisations represented on its board, despite (or possibly because of) their knowledge and experience. Not until 2001 was a third voluntary law centre established, in Ballymun, Dublin, the key funder being an English foundation concerned with rights and justice issues (FLAC, 2002). To this day, they remain the only independent legal advice centres, complementing an inadequate state service.

Between these episodes, the story of the National Social Service Council and Combat Poverty, we get a picture of tension, unease and points of clash between the state and the voluntary and community sector. Despite this, the voluntary sector grew, from Catholic social action in the 1930s and 1940s to the emergence of new providers in the 1950s, from self-help groups in the 1960s to campaigning groups in the 1970s, leading to community-development activity in the 1980s. In most, but clearly not in all, respects the new state provided substantial *scope* – though little formalised *support* – for voluntary social activity. There was little recognition in state legislation for the voluntary sector, but too much should not be read into this, since the overall level of social activity by the new state was low. The role of voluntary organisations received some acknowledgement as providing ancillary services to those of the health boards (Health Acts, 1953 and 1970) though in reality voluntary organisations were often the primary providers.

Toward a policy
Not until the 1970s with the commitment given by Brendan Corish did the state show an appreciation that there should be a policy for the voluntary and community sector. The *Programme for Government* of the short-lived Fine Gael/Labour government of 1981 gave a commitment to drawing up a charter for voluntary services that would provide a framework for relationships between government and voluntary agencies (Curry, 1993). The government changed twice more in the next 18 months and no more was heard of the proposal. The 1976 and 1981 commitments were renewed in 1990 when the Minister for Social Welfare, Dr Michael Woods, announced that there would be a white paper and charter for voluntary social services and voluntary activity in Ireland. He launched an extensive process of consultation. Other government departments were questioned about their involvement with the voluntary sector. Advertisements were placed in the national press, inviting organisations and individuals to file questionnaires relating to the key themes

of the charter. Three hundred questionnaires were sent out and 72 returned. The department met 95 voluntary organisations and experts and received policy submissions from seven. Voluntary sector structures in England and Northern Ireland were studied. The Department of Social Welfare set up a task force to get agreement on the white paper from government departments, health boards, local authorities and vocational education committees. In 1992, the government appointed an 18-strong expert committee to assist in the process. The consultative process received a positive response from voluntary organisations: they raised a mixture of individual, sectoral and broad concerns. Several saw this as an important opportunity to clarify and redefine the relationship between the state and the voluntary sector. For example, the Community Workers Co-operative, in *Toward a Charter for Voluntary Action – a Voluntary Sector Perspective* (1992) laid down the principles that should guide the actions of state and the sector in this relationship (e.g. accountability, partnership, resourcing, non-discrimination). A short paper is available summarising the key issues raised by voluntary organisations (Department of Social Welfare, 1991). These were questions of definition and terminology; funding, the overwhelming issue; the provision of supports such as training and premises; staffing, principally community employment; taxation; and involvement in policy-making, including social partnership.

The white paper process was given a deadline of June 1993. This came and went. Within a short period of time, it became evident that the process was in trouble. The exact points of contention were never identified and until such time as the papers from the period are declassified, we are unlikely to know for certain. It appears that both the Department of Justice and the Department of Health blocked the white paper, the latter possibly because of turf disputes as to who should fund the voluntary sector for what activities. Although there were regular questions in the Oireachtas about the slow progress of the white paper, no minister ever referred publicly to the precise nature of the difficulties encountered.

Did the absence of a formal structured relationship between the voluntary sector and the state actually matter? Faughnan and Kelleher (1993) suggested that it did matter. In their study, they described a voluntary and community sector that was under pressure, embattled, lacking recognition and denied a voice in policy-making, making it difficult for it to operate effectively. O'Ferrall (2003) would presumably raise a broader range of concerns about the importance of the state to recognise a public space apart from the state, and the wasteful destruction by the state of its social capital in the health services.

When the government changed in 1995 the new minister, Proinsias de Rossa, attempted to salvage what he could from the process by producing the stalled white paper as a green paper instead. This was eventually published in 1997 as *Supporting Voluntary Activity*, shortly before that government went out of office. A certain level of disillusionment had set in within the voluntary sector, reflecting the seven-year gestation period of this document. The Combat Poverty Agency organised a day conference on the green paper, but it was one of the few exercises organised in what was supposed to be a new period of structured consultation. Overall, the green paper was welcomed for the political framework it provided, its acceptance of the role of the sector, the proposals for the respective roles of the sector and the state, and its promise to redress inequities in consultation and funding. There were, however, a number of criticisms of the green paper. The sections of funding were inadequate, understating the sector's own fund-raising, over-stating the level of government contribution (inflated at IR£487m, €615m) and defining the funding problem as weaning the sector from dependence on the state. The proposal for a community foundation, while welcome, lacked detail. The green paper dodged the issue of legal status for voluntary organisations and the baleful influence of the national lottery. Research and our knowledge of the sector were not even mentioned. The green paper focused on the role of smaller, community-based organisations combating poverty to the detriment of the role of larger social and health service providers and intermediary bodies (Donnelly-Cox, 1998).

In 1997, when the government changed again, the new minister appointed by the long-running Fianna Fáil/Progressive Democrat coalition of 1997-2002, Dermot Ahern, resurrected the concept of a white paper. A fresh round of consultation was organised. The response from the voluntary sector was muted this time, though as many as 66 submissions were received. This was much less than the response to the Commission on the Family and the Commission on the Status of People with Disabilities (over 500 for each), probably reflecting the sector's frustration with the lack of outcome for its earlier efforts. The submissions were recorded discursively this time (Tubridy and Colgan, 1999), but the authors chose not to weigh the concerns raised, making it difficult to assess their relative priorities or urgency.

Once again, there were further delays and the publication date was put back again and again. In the end the white paper did not represent a quantum leap forward from the green paper – on the contrary, some felt that it was a step backward. The lines of development of the white paper were, in retrospect, well flagged in the green paper (both bore the same title, *Supporting Voluntary Activity*). When the twenty-ninth Dáil was elected in May 2002, the new government's principal commitment in the area of voluntary activity was 'comprehensive reform of the law relating to charities to ensure accountability and to protect against the abuse of charitable status and fraud'. This is a subject addressed in chapter five.

Cohesion of the sector

Despite its professionalisation, the Republic of Ireland lacked an umbrella body for the voluntary sector akin to those in Britain or Northern Ireland. This is a source of some puzzlement to outsiders, since the UK has umbrella bodies in England, Wales, Scotland and Northern Ireland, some dating back to the early twentieth century.

The reasons for this are unclear. One explanation is that the UK bodies were prompted by government, which saw the advantages in resourcing and negotiating with a single umbrella body representing the whole sector. The governments of the Free State and the Republic were slower to see the advantages of such a body and even slower to offer it resources.

The lack of a representative umbrella body for the voluntary sector may be a contributory factor to the under-development of the sector in the Republic. The absence of such a body means that there is no point at which unified views may be presented to government on policy issues that directly affect the sector. There is no point of engagement between the voluntary sector on the one hand and the corporate, trust and foundation sector on the other concerning funding issues. It is doubtful if the long period of time (78 years) for the preparation of a government policy for the sector would have been permitted had a strong umbrella body been in existence. Unlike Northern Ireland, the Republic's much larger voluntary sector lacks even a newspaper of its own, also impeding information flow.

In 1993, a study was carried out on the issue. *Prospects for an Umbrella Organization for the Voluntary Sector in Ireland* by the Enterprise Trust found that two-thirds of national voluntary organisations favoured such a body (Harvey, 1993). In the smaller community organisations, support ran even higher at 85 per cent. Those who favoured a national umbrella body argued that it would provide a negotiating link with government, achieve cohesion in the voluntary sector, expand the resources available, make the sector more strategic and provide services hitherto unavailable. Although the level of opposition to an umbrella body was small in size, it was vigorous and included a number of influential players in the sector. They argued that such an umbrella body would be quickly captured by government and divert resources that could better serve organisations directly. The voluntary sector should be left to organise itself in its own diverse way, which, whilst outwardly chaotic to uninformed observers, in fact was cohesive. Interestingly, opinion within government was split, some favouring the concept of negotiating with a united voluntary sector body, others reluctant to provide a platform for potential critics of government policy.

In the late 1980s, the Carmichael Centre became a model of how voluntary organisations could function effectively together. In 1987, when the Richmond hospital was decommissioned, Dublin Corporation made the building available to voluntary organisations (a second nearby building, Coleraine House, was subsequently available). The concept of the centre was that it would provide office space for small voluntary organisations, with common areas for meetings and the provision of common services (e.g. training, copying). An initial 30 groups joined the centre, the number subsequently rising to 50. In the course of time, the centre began to extract the policy issues common to the groups working in the centre, many revolving around the funding relationship between the voluntary sector and the state.

The development of common purpose here may work well with organisations of similar size and concentrated on a particular sector. Some commentators doubt whether the gap between small, community-based organisations and large, politically traditional voluntary service providers can be bridged and a common viewpoint emerge. On the other hand, other countries have overcome this challenge.

New attempts to reduce fragmentation and promote cohesion

Fresh efforts have now been made to bring together voluntary organisations with a view to promoting the cohesiveness, identity, visibility and authority of the sector in a body called The Wheel. The first meeting was held in 1999, being convened by Dr Mary Redmond, the founder of the Irish Hospice Foundation, with 200 people attending. Since then, The Wheel has operated as a network to form a collective voice enabling the sector to identify common cross-cutting issues as well as sectional ones, called 'spokes'. 'Spoke' activities are areas of work where groups organise around common interests. The health spoke is the most active, reflecting the number of voluntary organisations working in this field. Thematic meetings have been held on such topics as civil society, volunteering, the Internet and regulation. By 2003 The Wheel had a budget of €600,000 and a staff of seven, a database of 2,900 organisations and 4,200 individuals, with plans for substantial expansion over the following three years.

The Wheel has now become organisationally well established. The logic of the project is that it becomes, over time, the representative body for the voluntary sector in the Republic. This is something it formally eschews, emphasising that its role is limited to co-operation, networking, facilitation and the exchange of views. It will be even more difficult to resist, now that The Wheel has been given responsibility to represent the 'local and voluntary' strand in the system of restructured social partnership.

A specialised umbrella body for the voluntary sector is the Irish Tax Reform Group (ITRG). This was set up in the late 1980s to campaign for a more favourable tax environment for the voluntary sector, achieving success when the government made provision in the Finance Acts for individuals and companies to set donations to charitable voluntary organisations against tax.

Since then, the group has campaigned for comparable reliefs in indirect tax. Over 95 national voluntary organisations belong to the ITRG (e.g. Cancer Society, Rehab, Trócaire, Barnardos, St Vincent de Paul, Cheshire Homes).

Whatever the cohesion of the sector, its infrastructure has continued to develop. Many organisations have expanded their publishing programmes and embraced the new technologies. At least a quarter of national voluntary organisations were known to be publishing regular newsletters by the mid-1990s. Eighty-three per cent had fax services and 41 per cent were on e-mail (Harvey, 1997b). Inevitably perhaps, some parts of the voluntary sector moved ahead to purchase and use the new technologies more quickly than others – larger, national organisations, especially those in the environmental area first, followed by the smaller, community-based groups, especially those most involving women, later (O'Donnell, Trench and Ennals, 1998; O'Donnell and Trench, 1999). What we lack, but need, is information on the way in which voluntary organisations now play a role in fostering a more inclusive information society (O'Donnell, 2002).

Funding the voluntary sector
Developments of the funding of the sector are now examined in some detail, for they tell us much about the sector's evolution and pattern of development and shed light on its relationship with government, the private sector and the rest of society. Government funding for the voluntary sector in the Free State and Republic developed on an *ad hoc* basis. Government bodies tended to respond to individual requests for funding, rather than by setting up a set of strategic funding lines (this did not happen until the arrival of programmatic European funding). The 1953 Health Act (Section 65) made provision for the health boards to provide resources for voluntary organisations providing health or related services. Section 65 was defined in a curiously residual manner and stated:

A health board may, with the approval of the minister, give assistance to any body which provides or proposes to provide a service similar or ancillary to a service which the health authority may provide.

In other words, such funding might complement state funding, but it was not designed as a specific scheme to support the sector in its own right. Until the 1970s, such Section 65 funding was limited. Most voluntary organisations depended on extensive voluntary fund-raising. Insufficiency of funding was a predictable criticism of state funding for voluntary and community organisations. This was a criticism made by voluntary and community organisations the world over, but it took on a special significance in the

Republic of Ireland, where social spending was lower than average and where concepts of standards of public services were poorly developed. Voluntary and community organisations found the health boards difficult to deal with, for the boards' funding was discretionary, year-on-year and lacked any open systems for application and accountability. It was very difficult to develop services in a planned, strategic way. The Irish Society for the Prevention of Cruelty to Children, for example, attempted to pioneer the development of family resource centres in the late 1970s, Wexford being one of the flagship projects. After three years, the South Eastern Health Board withdrew its funding without explanation and the centre had to close. This was not a system that rewarded strategic development.

The system was also slow to change. In 1989 the Combat Poverty Agency drew attention to the manner in which voluntary and community organisations must always 'make do with bits and pieces from different agencies' and that much time was spent pursuing different sources. Their work was perceived as a residual activity, the agency said (Combat Poverty Agency, 1989). The Independent Poverty Action Movement (IPAM), in its aptly named *To Scheme or not to Scheme?* drew attention to the manner in which groups must find considerable energy for protracted negotiations, the mismatch between funding schemes and the needs of groups, and the high level of skills required, often for meagre results, describing the process as one of 'negotiation without dialogue'. Faughnan and Kelleher (1993) found that funding remained a serious problem, many networks lacking any statutory funding while other voluntary organisations could not obtain core grants.

The introduction of social employment schemes
The introduction of social employment schemes provided an unexpected influx of resources into voluntary organisations. As originally introduced in 1985, it was called the Social Employment Scheme (SES), then the Community Employment Development Programme (CEDP) (1991-4) and finally the Community Employment Scheme (CES), or Community Employment (CE) for short. The scheme was controversial and problematical for voluntary organisations. Under social employment, voluntary organisations and some parts of the semi-state and state sector were encouraged to take on unemployed people for a limited period. Within a few years, it became their main source of funding staff in voluntary organisations, in some cases the only source (Harvey, 1990; Faughnan and Kelleher, 1993). The widespread use of community employment, on which 44,000 workers were engaged at one stage (of whom 80 per cent (35,200) were estimated to work with voluntary organisations), raised the question that the state had created thereby an important but secondary labour market (Powell and Guerin, 1997).

The principal attraction for voluntary and community organisations was that social employment salaries, which were set above the unemployment level, were paid for by the state training agency, FÁS, and its predecessors, though there were some costs incurred for the organisations concerned. Social employment proved to be remarkably successful, with high take-up rates both by unemployed people themselves and by voluntary organisations as sponsors. For the latter, though, there were disadvantages. First, social employment workers required, by definition, a certain level of supervision, something which not all organisations were then well equipped to provide. Second, social employment workers stayed for a limited period of time, a year being the norm set by government, meaning that voluntary organisations lost their services at a time when they became effective employees. Third, voluntary organisations contrasted the relative ease with which they could obtain social employment staff with the near impossibility of obtaining core staff.

Following a controversial review by Deloitte and Touche consultants in 1999, the government cut the scheme to 37,500 places and then to 28,000 places. By 2003, it had flattened out just above 20,000 places. Funding of social employment places in schools was terminated, despite opposition from groups like the Society of St Vincent de Paul. Voluntary organisations strongly resisted these cuts, because they destabilised their staffing. They also argued that so long as there were unemployed people in a position to take advantage of such schemes, they should be maintained.

The late 1990s saw the government formally establish a social economy programme, one that would benefit the community and voluntary sector. In a sense, community employment was a form of social economy programme, but this was formalised, arising from commitments given by government in the *Programme for Prosperity and Fairness*. The initial programme was designed to provide 2,500 places by 2003 at a cost of €52m a year in the areas of community businesses, what are called 'deficient demand social enterprises' and enterprises based on public service contracts. Although some effort went into the design of the programme, it was much less ambitious than that originally proposed. By March 2003, 331 social economy enterprises had been approved for start-up support, with 1,738 full-time equivalent jobs, the budget set for the year being €30.7m. The programme appeared to plateau at this stage.

The first area of state funding specifically directed to the voluntary and community sector was youth services. This coincided broadly with a period of investment in higher education, recognition of the political role of youth, the renewal of the country's political leadership, and the reduction of the voting age to 18 (approved in 1972). In 1969, the government decided to allocate IR£100,000 (€126,973) for the funding of national youth organisations. The Department of Education, which was responsible for the funding line, drew up a system of applications, criteria and procedures for its allocation. Funding went to about 30 national organisations, based mainly on the size of groups serviced, but this marked the opening of systematic, regular, negotiated funding between the Irish state and the voluntary sector.

The beginnings of funding from the European Union for voluntary action
Programmatic funding may be said to have begun in Ireland with the introduction of the European Union programmes against poverty (see *Europeanisation*, above). It is no coincidence that programme-based funding was to emerge from the department that oversaw the programme against poverty, the Department of Social Welfare. The department became the third funder of voluntary and community organisations, after the health boards and FÁS. Although the amounts provided were small compared to the health boards and social employment, the department's schemes followed model procedures, had high visibility, the outcomes were published and many of the schemes were subject to evaluation. The Community Development Programme, one of the first, was originally set up to find a home for projects that would otherwise have been left financially stranded by the end of the European Poverty II programme. The programme was warmly welcomed by the voluntary and community sector and followed what would then have been considered good practice in programme funding, organisation, management and scrutiny. The Community Development Programme represented a formal recognition and legitimation of the value of community-development approaches by the Irish state. The projects were considered effective means of addressing the local dimension to poverty and social exclusion and an important elaboration of the principles of community development in Ireland (Cullen, 1994).

The Department of Social Welfare schemes went through many evolutions over the period, the details of which are not necessary to recount here, but they included the Community Development Programme, a programme for women, a programme for men, miscellaneous grants, and a respite care fund. This funding had some interesting territorial aspects. The respite care fund provided grants for organisations providing relief for carers. In normal circumstances, this was the type of support that could have been introduced by the health boards and the Department of Health, but was not. The Minister for Social Welfare found it possible to introduce it as an open, trans-parent, cost-effective scheme of funding for appropriate voluntary organisa-tions. After two years, in a departmental trade off, the scheme was repatriated by the Department of Health and the health boards, disappearing into the general pot of health board spending. Enquiries to some health boards in the mid-1990s as to how they allocated such resources to voluntary organisations were then met with the response that they were now 'confidential'.

In 1993, the level of government support for the voluntary sector was calculated at €271.8m. Funding for the sector trebled over the next eight years, up 289 per cent (Harvey, 1993, 2000). The main areas of growth were: community employment (although this has peaked and is now falling); substantial growth in the funding of health organisations (up from €143m to €495m); significant expansion of programmes by the Department of Social, Community and Family Affairs; and much increased investment in social housing by voluntary bodies (up from €20m to €60m).

Contracts and service agreements
The contracting of voluntary organisations to carry out particular services, a feature of voluntary sector development in the UK from the 1980s, did not impact on the Republic of Ireland until the late 1990s. The term used was 'service agreement'. The idea of service agreements emerged in the Department of Health in the national health strategy *Shaping a Healthier Future* (1994) which announced that 'larger voluntary agencies will have service agreements with the health authorities which will link funding by the authorities to agreed levels of service to be provided by the agencies'. The strategy pledged that the identity and autonomy of the voluntary agencies would be fully respected and that they would continue to have a direct input into the overall development of national policy. The health strategy stated that these agreements would be for a number of years, would give voluntary organisations a greater degree of continuity than had been the case in the past, and would be able to specify precise levels of funding. It went on:

> It is recognised that formal agreements of this type would not be appropriate for the smaller voluntary groups who receive some financial assistance toward their activities. While it is important that they too are accountable for the public funds which they receive, the reporting procedure will be simplified and tailored to their circumstances.

The introduction of service agreements took place in the specific context of the anomaly whereby, since 1970, all funding of health-related voluntary organisations had been routed through health boards. Fourteen voluntary organisations, mainly religious orders delivering what were then called mental handicap services (e.g. St John of God), were exempt, arguing that they provided a national service and should continue to be funded nationally and centrally by the department. Over the years, Ministers of Health sought ways to divest the department of these fourteen agencies and the final push was announced by *Shaping a Healthier Future*. Service agreements promised the advantage of providing the voluntary agencies concerned with some protection from what they regarded as the capricious funding systems of the health boards. So well entrenched were these agencies that an inter-departmental committee was convened to oversee the process, issuing a report *Enhancing the Partnership* (Department of Health, undated).

Enhancing the Partnership confirmed the transfer of the fourteen agencies to health boards and the arrangement for service agreements, outlining a model service agreement (schedule 2). The model was a four-page text specifying the joint principles agreed between the two parties, the obligations of the voluntary agency (eleven points), the obligations of the health boards (six points), a system for resolving differences, and provision for more detailed arrangements to be made specifying the quantum of services to be provided. At a planning level, *Enhancing the Partnership* recommended that each health board establish a Mental Handicap Services Consultative Committee and a Mental Handicap Services Development Committee. *Enhancing the Partnership* led to a sequel, *Widening the Partnership* (Department of Health, undated), set up to apply these principles to a broader range of health board funded voluntary organisations in the mental handicap area. This recommended that service agreements should be extended to all such agencies funded by health boards able to meet standards of good practice, accountability and organisation.

The first service agreements are understood to have been made between the Eastern Health Board and voluntary organisations from 1997. Other boards followed (e.g. East Coast Area Board) but it is not clear if their use is now universal. *Enhancing the Partnership* appears to have acted as the basis on which service agreements were extended to a broad range of voluntary organisations in the late 1990s and early 2000s. The model agreement drafted in the schedule appears to be widely used and was specifically cited by several health boards. Service agreements are also used by the Homeless Agency as the basis on which it funds organisations working with the homeless in Dublin.

Health boards set about the introduction of service agreements in different ways. In July 1998, the Southern Health Board reviewed its relationship with the voluntary and community sector within its area (*Funding Mechanisms for Voluntary Agencies – Review Group Report*). This found that the board did not operate service agreements, that there were no standard criteria for assessing grant applications, and that the board did not have a formal structure for reviewing the performance of the voluntary organisations it funded. The review group recommended that new procedures should be set down whereby voluntary organisations provided accounts, that standard assessment criteria be put in place, and that a formal service agreement should be framed with funded organisations setting down accountability systems and requirements for quality of service. A draft service agreement was subsequently proposed. This took the form of a 7-page text setting down: the values underlying the provision of services; the responsibilities of the voluntary organisation to be funded; obligations of the health board (e.g. to respect the autonomy of the voluntary organisation); a system for resolving differences; the specific services to be provided; arrangements for review; the nature of the financial commitment to be entered into by the board; and referral, admission and discharge criteria as well as catchment areas, designated officials and contact persons. The development and implementation of service level agreements became a specific objective of the board's subsequent *Corporate Development Plan, 2002-5.*

By 2003, in the Western Health Board area, service agreements covered 78 per cent of the board's voluntary sector allocations and it was expected that the rest would be covered in 2004. This is a longer, 14-page document outlining agreed principles, the obligations of the voluntary organisation concerned (25 points), the responsibilities of the health board (six points), the specific details of the services to be provided, catchment areas, employment control systems, monitoring arrangements, the funding to be provided by the health board, staffing details, and arrangements for review. A similar document is in operation in the Midland Health Board. Here, the obligations on the voluntary organisation are smaller in number (14), while detailed provisions are to be agreed following further consultation and the voluntary organisation is expected to file monthly financial and employment control reports, with quarterly service activity reports.

No research yet appears to be available on the impact of the service agreements on health boards, voluntary organisations, or those for whom they provide services. The process is still at an early stage (Boyle and Butler, 2003). Some observations can, however, be made about the process at this stage.

Service level agreements were introduced in what might be described as an oblique way. The vehicle for introducing them was as a mechanism to formalise new relationships between 14 mental handicap service providers and the health boards (*Enhancing the Partnership*). They were then extended to all mental handicap providers (*Widening the Partnership*). Health boards then began to extend them to the rest of the voluntary agencies they funded. The model outlined in *Enhancing the Partnership* was adapted by health boards to provide a greater level of control by health boards over voluntary organisations. The original model listed six points of obligation on the part of the health boards and eleven on the part of the voluntary agencies. The model adapted for the Western Health Board lists six points of obligation on the health board, but the obligations on the part of voluntary organisations have risen to twenty-five. Some of these adapted models required a high level of monitoring and reporting and are very specific about staffing levels and responsibilities. The original health strategy document *Shaping a Healthier Future* expressed the view that service agreements were designed for large organisations and made it clear that these were too formal for smaller organisations. Here, simplified procedures should be adopted. This does not appear to be the case and health boards do not seem to have felt inhibited in extending the full rigour of service agreements to smaller voluntary organisations as well. Although *Shaping a Healthier Future* promised that voluntary organisations would continue to have a direct input into the overall development of national policy, arrangements do not seem to have been specifically put in place to do this. Overall, it may be said that the outcome of the exercise has favoured a higher degree of board control, promoted greater accountability by voluntary organisations, but given little to the voluntary organisations in return.

The lottery
The introduction of the national lottery in the Republic in 1987 had largely negative effects on the voluntary sector. When the lottery was established, explicit commitments were given by the government that the new revenue, calculated at between €10m and €50m a year, would be used to fund new voluntary sector activity. In the event, only 37 per cent went to the voluntary sector and this was for voluntary activities already funded by government. Only between 7 per cent and 11 per cent of lottery allocations represented genuinely new activities or additionality, in contrast to the situation in the United Kingdom. The vast bulk went to support mainstream government funding programmes, in many cases being directly subsumed into existing budget lines. Unlike the British lottery, which was distributed by independent boards, the national lottery in the Republic of Ireland was distributed by government departments and their subsidiary agencies.

The amount of money raised by the lottery was magnitudes greater than expected, levelling out at €495m in 2000. This money would have made a big difference to the voluntary sector had it been made available in the manner promised. The lottery was reviewed by the government in 1997. Commitments were given to make the system more transparent, and to give the entire revenue to the voluntary sector (like the previous commitments, these have not been kept either). In the 1999 government estimates, budgetary headings were reorganised so as to maximise lottery allocations under headings apparently attributable to voluntary sector support, though the essential basis of lottery decisions remained as opaque as ever. A reading of the estimates in 2000 showed that substantial parts of the lottery continued to go on spending on state services. Two compendia of lottery spending were published. These were far from transparent: for example, substantial allocations to health boards were listed as 'block grants', giving no clue as to how the amounts concerned were finally spent. Most politicians in Fianna Fáil, Fine Gael and the Labour party strongly resisted reform to the system of lottery allocations, some vigorously attacking the concept of independent boards. The chairman of the lottery review group later regretted that he had not recommended an independent distribution board for lottery funding.

The lottery came under fire for corruption. Research by Fine Gael in 2001 found that allocations per constituency were far above average in those counties represented by the Minister for Finance and the Minister of State at the Department of Finance (the two Ministers responsible for the lottery). Whereas in Dublin the average lottery allocation was €11.42 per head, the allocations were €32.43 per head in Waterford (the Minister of State's constituency) and €28.56 in Kildare (the Minister's constituency).

The lottery had additional effects on the voluntary sector. Until the advent of the National Lottery, several voluntary organisations (e.g. Rehab) had run their own lotteries, though they were tightly restricted in their scope, size and operation (see chapter five). These lotteries came under serious pressure with the arrival of the national lottery in 1987. Thirteen years later, the Department of Justice (2000) was to comment on the extraordinary situation whereby the state severely restricted certain forms of gambling (for voluntary organisations) while on the other hand actively encouraging the public to buy a wide range of state lottery products. A study of the impact of the lottery on the voluntary sector found that 62.5 per cent of voluntary organisations believed the lottery had impacted on their fund-raising abilities: 87 per cent believed that this impact had been negative. A third of voluntary organisations noted a fall in donations to them since the start of the lottery, two-thirds observing that they had had to increase their fund-raising efforts (Harvey and Kiernan, 1993). In 1991, 16 charities came together to try to put the playing field on a more level basis. Eventually, the government set up what was effectively a compensation fund, valued at €6.35m. In a final irony, this compensation fund was drawn from the national lottery itself! In 2001, 12 voluntary organisations received compensation of €7,618,429 for the loss of revenue to their lotteries for having to compete with the National Lottery. The main recipient was Rehab, which had run the most prominent lottery in the pre-national lottery days.

Funding for north-south activities
In the context of this study, funding for north–south activities takes on a special significance. The outbreak of 'the Troubles' in 1969 led to the establishment of a small part of the voluntary sector in the Republic concerned with issues of peace, reconciliation and north–south contact (see chapter seven). The importance of this work eventually received some financial recognition in 1982 when the Department of Foreign Affairs established what was termed the Reconciliation Fund, to support the work of organisations engaged in reconciliation work and efforts to create a better

understanding between people in both parts of Ireland and between Ireland
and Great Britain. This fund was poorly publicised and details of its
beneficiaries did not become available until the Freedom of Information Act
required disclosure. The fund started at €88,881 in its first year, rose to
€336,481 by 1997, and increased substantially in 1999, with the allocation of
€2.53m in an expanded programme. In the early years, the principal
beneficiaries were Co-operation Ireland, Glencree Centre for Reconciliation,
the Irish School of Ecumenics and Anglo-Irish Encounter, but as many as 60
groups benefited each year in the expanded programme. The funding was
hardly programmatic, being geared to one-off projects, rather than to the
strategic development of a sector dedicated to north–south co-operation.

Additional funding emerged from two important bodies concerned with
north–south work: Co-operation Ireland and the International Fund for
Ireland. Co-operation Ireland was originally called Co-operation North
and it aimed to promote improved north–south understanding through
events and funded activities, with a brief covering the whole island. Although
many people saw it as funding body, it was actually much more than that,
promoting networking and co-operation in its own right. Its activities
were directed principally to supporting co-operation in the areas of youth,
schools, business, culture, be that through voluntary organisations or
otherwise.

The International Fund for Ireland (IFI) was set up in 1986 following the
Anglo-Irish agreement. Although structured as a private funding body, it was
funded by the governments of the United States, New Zealand, Australia,
Canada and the European Union. Its board and advisory body were appointed
by the British and Irish governments. Although it used a post box address, its
operating base was in reality Iveagh House, base of the Department of Foreign
Affairs. Its brief described it as an independent international organisation
with the twin objectives of promoting economic and social advance; and
encouraging contact, dialogue and reconciliation between nationalists and
unionists. For the Republic, the principal beneficiaries were in the border
counties. The fund came under some fire in the 1980s for excessively funding
private projects and supporting some inappropriately. From the 1990s, the
fund could be seen to take a much greater interest in the regeneration of
deprived areas and community development. Between 1986 and 2000, the IFI
provided funding for 4,600 projects to the value of €604m in both parts of the
island (most in the north).

The Peace Programme (the European Union Special Support Programme
for Peace and Reconciliation in Northern Ireland and the border counties of
Ireland) was an important stimulus to parts of the voluntary sector in Ireland.
The Peace Programme was a substantial investment in Northern Ireland and
the border counties of the Republic. Although the programme was originally

supposed only to fund work directly concerned with the conflict and issues of reconciliation arising therefrom, it was colonised in the course of the consultation process to the extent that it became a programme of regional reinvestment in the border counties. The determination that social inclusion should be a prominent theme of the programme virtually guaranteed that voluntary and community organisations would see a large slice of the programme. In the border counties of the Republic, the programme was delivered by the Combat Poverty Agency and Area Development Management. The thrust of the programme was on the delivery of a large number of small grants (Harvey, 1997a). In the Republic, the outcome was a substantial growth in the size of the voluntary and community sector in the border counties around Northern Ireland, an area where it had been weak. Because the focus of the programme was on the border counties, it probably had little impact on the level of networking between national voluntary organisations (e.g. on the Dublin–Belfast axis) which were not eligible for programme funding.

Foundations, trusts and philanthropy
Philanthropy played an important role in the very early development of the voluntary sector in Ireland as has already been noted. Philanthropic giving was not a feature of funding developments in the Free State and the Republic until near the end of the century. The level of organised and formal giving from foundation, trust and philanthropic sources for the voluntary sector was estimated at only €8.5m in 1993 (Harvey, 1993). Voluntary and community organisations depended largely on informal giving – by calling door to door, flag days, wills, unsolicited individual donations, fund-raising events, table quizzes and so on (see chapter five). Donoghue (2003) makes the point that the voluntary and community sector in the Republic was able to develop and survive without significant foundation support, that the size of foundations is small by international comparisons, and that there is still considerable potential for its growth.

The first sign of organised philanthropic giving was the Ireland Funds, established in 1976 (not to be confused with the International Fund for Ireland, 1986, above). The Ireland Funds sought to raise money abroad and at home for projects in both parts of the island in such areas as arts and culture, community development, peace and reconciliation and education. The amounts raised were, until the late 1990s, quite small, but they set a pattern whereby giving on the one hand and funding for voluntary organisations on the other might become more planned and systematic.

The year 1979 saw the establishment of a foundation to support voluntary and community organisations, the Katharine Howard Foundation, which provided small grants for educational, community development and research purposes. The Irish Youth Foundation was established in 1985, specifically as a development trust for the National Youth Federation and more generally to support the development of youth services in Ireland. It had a particular interest in improving the situation of disadvantaged young people. Reflecting the exodus of Irish people to Britain in the 1980s, it developed a funding programme in Britain to support the work of voluntary organisations assisting Irish young people there.

Probably the largest philanthropic funder of the Irish voluntary sector was Atlantic Philanthropies. The founder was Charles F. 'Chuck' Feeney, an Irish American businessman who made his money in the duty free and airport shopping business. When he sold his interest in the duty free shops, he made the money available for charitable causes, principally for universities, education and the non-governmental sector. Between 1986 and 1997, €76m was spent in the Republic in the areas of education and community development, going to such bodies as the universities, Disability Federation of Ireland and the Limerick Community-based Education Initiative. Further grants worth €358m were given in the Republic of Ireland over 1998-2000. The funds were previously distributed in Ireland anonymously through Tara Consultants, with a small staff identifying suitable organisations for funding, making payments and subsequent monitoring.

Another organisation that operated in a similar way was the St Stephen's Green Trust, a Catholic-affiliated trust which provided financial support for groups working with the socially excluded. Like Tara/Atlantic, it eventually operated more openly. The Jesuit Solidarity Fund was set up following the sale of Rathfarnham Castle and, until its closure in 2001, provided grants for groups working with the unemployed and the most excluded.

A novel development in organised giving was the telethon, set up in 1988 and subsequently organised under the title of *People in Need*, the main promoter being the national radio and television service, RTÉ. The telethon was an American idea whereby people were encouraged to respond to a day-long television entertainment programme by giving money to good causes. The trust aimed to distribute the revenue to organisations working with deprived and disadvantaged people such as the homeless, elderly, children and mentally and physically handicapped. There were two important features of the telethon: first, it operated on the principle that money raised in one county should be allocated back proportionately to that county; second, it consulted with health boards in making its allocations. In 2000, the seventh telethon raised €7.75m, distributed to 879 groups in small to medium-size grants.

Several British trusts operated in the Republic at the end of the century. The Allen Lane Foundation ran a small funding programme. In its first phase, it supported groups working with women and organisations combating violence against women; in its second phase it assisted offenders and ex-offenders. The Gulbenkian Foundation operated a small part of its funding programme in Ireland, supporting groups working in the areas of the community arts, rural development, peace, reconciliation and literacy. Perhaps the most striking British foundation to come to Ireland in the 1990s was the Joseph Rowntree Charitable Trust. The trust had originally been set up in 1908 at a time when all of Ireland was part of the United Kingdom. The trust's funding of activities in the Free State and then the Republic had gradually withered away, though it had never been formally abandoned. The trust's funding of activities in Northern Ireland made it aware of how political developments in one part of the island were linked to the other and in 1992 the trust began to investigate whether it should formally reinstitute a programme in the Republic. Following the publication of a baseline document in 1993, voluntary organisations in the Republic made it clear that they would welcome a funder operating in the rights and justice area. Accordingly, over 1994-9, the trust ran its first full funding programme in the Republic, approving 49 grants valued at over €1m for 36 different organisations. A particular feature of the programme was that it provided core funding for a small number of rights and justice organisations working in areas of activity unlikely ever to receive government funding (e.g. civil liberties). The programme was adjudged to have been a success in building up the rights and justice sector from a low base, making an impact on the political and administrative system and placing rights and justice issues more firmly on the national agenda.

The end of the century saw the establishment of the first community trust. The success of the Northern Ireland voluntary trust made the absence of a comparable funder south of the border ever more conspicuous, especially in a time of growing economic prosperity in the Republic (Everett, 1998). The entity that emerged was a government initiative, announced in a green paper in 1997. The setting up of the trust proved to be a painfully slow process, for it experienced difficulties in determining its composition, membership and priorities (Donoghue, 2001d). In the end, it was established as a three-part organisation – the Community Foundation for Ireland; Business in the Community to encourage corporate social responsibility; and a National Children's Trust, to provide funding for voluntary organisations working with children. By 2003, the Community Foundation for Ireland had built an endowment of €3.5m and was in a position to provide grant assistance of €200,000 a year. Its target is to establish an endowment of €10m by 2005. By the end of 2001, the Community Foundation had distributed 41 grants valued at €369,379 to community groups, offering grants in the €600 to €1,200 range but not more than €5,000. Funding priorities over 2001-3 were in the areas of new communities, isolation, diversity, lone parents and homosexuality. With a core staff of six, the foundation is much smaller in size than the Community Foundation for Northern Ireland.

Business in the Community, a separate organisation with its own board drawn from industry and the top Irish companies, works with companies to help them develop policies for corporate social responsibility and community involvement. Business in the Community enlisted the support of several companies which encouraged their staff to volunteer for voluntary and community work (e.g. National Irish Bank, KPMG, AIB, Cantrell and Cochrane, Bank of Ireland, Iona Technologies). Business in the Community developed a School Business Programme (providing mentoring and other supports for a local school) and a Linkage Programme (jobs, training and education for ex-offenders). Trusts and foundations in the Republic come together as the Irish Funders Forum, established during the 1990s. This provides a meeting place for these organisations, about 25 in number, to share and reflect together on their work. An organiser was appointed in 2002 to develop the forum's work and bring the concept of philanthropy to a wider audience. The total number of personnel working in foundations and trusts giving money in the Republic was estimated at 133 (Donoghue, 2001d).

Funding by the business community
Very little is known about the evolution of funding for the voluntary and community sector by the business community in the Free State and the Republic in the twentieth century. In the face of such a paucity of information, it is difficult to describe trends, patterns or events of significance. The first attempts to measure the level of corporate or business support for the sector were not made until the 1990s (e.g. Curry, 1990; Manley, 1991). They established three key facts: companies were reluctant to give any information on their donations (all but a small number refused outright); donations were small and localised; and companies did not have giving plans. Some companies operated payroll giving schemes.

Not until 1997 were any satisfactory data available and these are reviewed in chapter seven. Most businesses were still extremely reluctant to provide any information about their giving to charity. Very few actually promoted their giving to charity in a formal programme. One that did was Allied Irish Banks which developed the programme of Better Ireland awards, designed to improve the quality of life in local communities. Groups could enter projects, that, if they were successful, received an award which they could put to further good use. These awards were worth about €380,921 annually, with 660 projects supported during the 1990s under such headings as arts/communications, community development, heritage, the environment and youth. The awards varied from €1,270 (100 awards) to €63,486 (the winning award).

Attempts to bring coherence to business giving to the voluntary sector have been limited. The level of engagement evident in Business in the Community in the UK has not yet been matched in the Republic, although this may change as the work of the Community Foundation for Ireland and Business in the Community matures. The enormous growth in the economy in the late 1990s did not appear to lead to an apparent increase in giving (Donoghue, Ruddle and Mulvihill, 2000). In 2002, the Ireland Funds analysed patterns of business, foundation, trust and individual giving, and noted the very considerable effort expended by voluntary organisations in fund-raising, but took the view that this could be done much more efficiently and effectively, with far greater return. They proposed the establishment of a new entity to assist the voluntary sector in its fund-raising efforts (Colgan, 2002).

A final note on the issue of funding concerns the professional fund-raiser. From the 1980s, a number of voluntary organisations began to employ professional fund-raisers (Sheriff, 1999). Their overall number was probably small and limited to the largest voluntary organisations (e.g. development agencies). The Fundraising Institute of Ireland was established as a national body committed to promoting standards of ethics and practice in the fund-raising field and to act as a self regulatory body for the profession. However, it does not appear to have or to be prepared to part with any information on the number of fund-raisers or the scale or nature of their activities. The only information available here comes from Colgan (2002). In her survey, she found that 31.5 per cent of national organisations surveyed had salaried fund-raisers, 50 per cent had trustees engaged in fund-raising and 52 per cent had other staff engaged in fund-raising. These figures indicate a significant professionalisation of fund-raising.

Political engagement with the voluntary and community sector

As already observed, many voluntary organisations in the Republic of Ireland have had a sense of political engagement. Voluntary organisations have served an important and probably underestimated function of providing the country's political élite. A personal interest or ambition in mainstream political action is by no means considered anathema within voluntary organisations. Many of those prominent in Macra na Feirme have subsequently become members of the Oireachtas (in the mid-1990s, for example, 64 out of 164 deputies had a background in Macra). Others have emerged from community action in disadvantaged communities (for example, the long-serving deputy for Dublin Central, Tony Gregory). Other individuals, either party or non-party, have had close associations with individual voluntary organisations.

Whereas most voluntary organisations are providers of services, a small number has emerged to take up a politically challenging role. The Irish state has generally been politically uncomfortable about such organisations and has been slow to resource voluntary organisations that contribute to the policy-making process. On the other hand, the state has taken few efforts to actively restrict such a role. Typical of organisations that have developed an adversarial role are the Council for the Status of Women (1972), the Irish Council for Civil Liberties (1976), the Community Workers Co-operative (1981) and the Irish Penal Reform Trust (1994).

There is some evidence that the ability to engage in a policy-making role is closely related to the size of the organisation concerned. When the first baseline report of rights and justice organisations was carried out in the Republic in 1993, it was found that most were so small they were unable to achieve the critical mass necessary to make a meaningful engagement with the policy-making process. A study of 40 voluntary organisations in the Carmichael Centre, many of them engaged in the provision of health-related social services, found that their ability to engage in policy-making was similarly crippled by chronic under-resourcing, a competitive, Darwinian territorial funding environment and over-extension of existing resources (Harvey, 2000). Many other factors apart from size will also play a part in achieving a critical mass, such as the human resources available, the level of networking and the advocacy profile.

Although the constitution makes provision for representatives of professional associations and voluntary social services to be nominated as candidates to the Senate, remarkably few such organisations take advantage of this provision. The exact clause must be qualified by the term 'candidate', since the electorate consists of public representatives of local authorities who vote along party lines. Nevertheless, the clause offers voluntary organisations some leverage with party candidates, or the threat of nominating a non-party candidate who might pick up votes from independent councillors. Voluntary organisations known to have registered as nominees of Senate candidates are the Irish Georgian Society, the Library Association, the Irish Countrywomen's Association, the National Youth Council, the Irish Wheelchair Association, the National Association for Cerebral Palsy, the National Association for the Mentally Handicapped of Ireland, the National Association for the Deaf, the Multiple Sclerosis Society of Ireland, the Irish Kidney Association and Comhaltas Ceoltóirí Éireann. Candidates associated with the voluntary sector have contested the Senate panels on this basis. Kathryn Sinnott, prominently associated with campaigns for people with disabilities, almost broke the monopoly of the main political parties in the 2002 Seanad election.

The study by Faughnan and Kelleher (1993) is one of the few to have analysed the forms of political engagement of the voluntary organisations under study. This found that the preferred form of engagement was delegations to ministers, officials and other politicians (used by 85 per cent of the group), followed by policy submissions (75 per cent), the use of the media (55 per cent), conferences (40 per cent) and research (35 per cent). Up to 20 per cent engaged in direct action (e.g. demonstrations). The experience of these voluntary organisations was that although there was a good level of informal access to politicians, the lack of a more formal consultation mechanism, coupled with lack of resources for policy work, meant that the impact of this engagement was limited.

Emerging parts of the Irish voluntary sector
Finally, in this examination of the history of the voluntary sector in the Free State and the Republic, it may be worth looking at new trends that may be evident. Two stand out: the new immigrant communities; and social housing.

As many as 10,000 people sought asylum in Ireland in 2001. The arrival of relatively large numbers of immigrants, refugees and asylum seekers in the mid to late 1990s led to the establishment of the first embryonic groups representing these new communities. Most of the organisations are at the earliest stages of development and some have progressed little further than establishing a contact point. Several bodies working with the immigrant community are beginning to emerge, dedicated either to specific groups (e.g. Congolese Irish Partnership) or to the sector as a whole, e.g. Association of Refugees and Asylum Seekers in Ireland (ARASI). Over time, some may disappear while others will emerge as strong, representative associations. A study conducted in 2001 found that as many as 42 voluntary and community organisations now worked directly with new minority communities, refugees or asylum seekers either as part of their work or as its exclusive focus (Faughnan and O'Donovan, 2002).

Housing was a major growth area in the Irish voluntary sector toward the end of the twentieth century. Public utility societies, active in the 1920s, declined, receiving little encouragement from the state in the post-war period. They did not die out entirely, for between 2,500 and 3,000 such homes were built by 25 co-operatives or public utility societies in the period 1950-80, concentrated on a number of localities, such as south Dublin. The government focused its interest, attention and support on municipal housing and by 1983, voluntary housing associations comprised only 1,850 dwelling units, 0.4 per cent of the national housing stock (O'Sullivan, 1996). Not until 1984 did the government introduce a scheme for the funding of voluntary housing associations. An 80 per cent subsidy was provided and the first 700 projects had been sanctioned by 1989 (Harvey, 1990). The change of policy

in 1984 was less the result of a deliberate government re-evaluation of the role
the voluntary sector could play in social housing but rather a response to the
campaign by building co-operatives and voluntary housing bodies for a more
level playing field in relation to housing subsidies.

From 1987, following the decimation of local authority housing, a switch
of emphasis toward provision by voluntary organisations became attractive to
government. This was formally adopted as policy in 1991 (the *Plan for Social
Housing*). For government, voluntary housing, even with improved subsidy
rates of 95 per cent, saved planning, acquisition and management costs,
catered for hard-to-manage groups and could make a worthwhile dent in the
ever-lengthening housing waiting lists. The impression that the voluntary
sector was to be the servant, rather than the partner, of the state in this
process was hard to avoid, for the same plan failed to give the voluntary sector
a direct role in either policy-making or the planning of the process.
Indeed, where consultation systems were set down by the state, they were
often ignored by lower-ranking state and local bureaucrats (Leonard, 1992).
A second large expansion was heralded in 1999, when the government
proposed that the output of voluntary housing associations should rise to
4,000 units a year. The associations responded positively, but set down the
conditions which they felt were necessary for such targets to be reached.
The outcome was positive, for the government duly established a voluntary
and co-operative housing unit in the department concerned, dedicated
to the support of the sector, and fully revised the legal and financial
environment in which the associations operated (Mullins, Rhodes and
Williamson, 2003).

Even still, the proportion of social housing need met by voluntary
organisations probably disappointed the government, reaching only 950 units
a year in 2000. By 2003, the overall total had risen to between 12,000 and
13,000, about 1 per cent of the national stock and 10 per cent of the social
housing stock (Kenna, 2000; Mullins, Rhodes and Williamson, 2003).
Government investment in voluntary housing enabled a substantial
expansion of organisations already caring for groups such as older people,
the homeless and people with disabilities (e.g. Respond, Focus Ireland).
It also attracted several UK housing associations to move to Ireland.
Some even received a chauvinistic welcome, the St Pancras Housing
Association renaming itself Clúid in response. By 2003, there were
470 voluntary housing bodies in the Republic, of which 330 were estimated
to be active. Most managed fewer than ten units, with the bulk provided
by six organisations and one organisation providing more than 2,000
homes (Mullins, Rhodes and Williamson, 2003). In his analysis of voluntary
housing in the Republic, Kenna (2000) pointed to its quality, diversity,
independence, innovation, smallness of scale and affirmation of social

solidarity – qualities that fell far short of what he described as the macho role of large-scale social provider envisaged for it by government. Williamson (2000) discussed the anticipated bright future for voluntary housing bodies in the Republic following a statement in October 1999 by Mr. Robert Molloy, the Minister for the Environment, about government plans to enable the sector to produce 4,000 dwellings per annum, and outlined some of the obstacles to be removed if this were to take place. Later work by Mullins, Rhodes and Williamson (2003), funded by statutory and voluntary housing bodies in Northern Ireland and the Republic of Ireland, was the first major comparative study of the voluntary housing movements in Ireland's two jurisdictions.

An Irish voluntary sector abroad
Often overlooked in the development of the voluntary sector is the fact that there emerged an important Irish voluntary sector abroad. These services provided advice, support, services, a meeting place and cultural and recreational assistance to people emigrating from both parts of Ireland. These services were used by significant numbers of emigrants from the Republic (all denominations and none) and by Catholics from Northern Ireland. There was anecdotal evidence of a lower disposition to use these services by economically more successful emigrants, by those seeking a speedy and permanent integration with their host country, and by northern Protestants.

By the end of the twentieth century, there were 216 Irish societies in Britain. Most Irish organisations were cultural and associational, but about 52 could be described as welfare, social service or advocacy groups. In the latter category, a further sixteen could be found in the United States, eight in continental Europe and four in Australia. Whilst they concentrated on providing advice, assistance and support to newly arrived Irish emigrants, many of whom are relatively unskilled and isolated, they also had an important advocacy function in protecting the legal status of emigrants, preventing their exploitation, asserting their identity and ensuring their fair treatment. Most of these services were self standing, but a core group was co-ordinated by the Irish Episcopal Commission for Emigrants. Their services alone within this larger group were estimated to have 150 full-time staff, 20 part-time and 659 volunteers, with an annual turnover of €5m, a hint of the size of the sector as a whole. Contrary to popular views within Ireland that these services might be archaic, they actually expanded in the United States in the 1990s, to meet the needs of freshly arriving Irish emigrants, not all of them legal; while services in Britain reorientated themselves around the needs of the older Irish community, many of whom were in difficult circumstances (Harvey, 1999b).

Comment and conclusions

The development of the voluntary sector in the Republic by the turn of the century presents a picture of contrast and uneven development. Several key phases are evident: Catholic social action, the development of unaffiliated providers of services, self-help and campaigning groups deriving from the social movements of the 1960s, the women's movement, community development, national networks and federation. Distinct features are evident: its lack of cohesion, the importance of the Catholic church, the preparedness of a minority to engage in political action, the lack of a formal policy environment, the limited range of funding sources, and the importance of rural social action in the national picture. The range and richness of its activities are evident.

The bringing of the voluntary and community sector in to national and local social partnership gives the sector a level of leverage and engagement with the political system that must be unique in Europe. It is possible that this reflects the exceptionalism, within Europe, of the Irish state (Lee, 1989), a state that still seeks new ways to re-legitimise itself (Barry, 1992). There have been some questioning voices in the Oireachtas, some members of whom feel they have been by-passed by this new process. Such questions have been raised on the voluntary side too, several complaining that the voluntary organisations involved are small in number and unrepresentative by nature, and that the process has been steered by an inner élite of only four or five people who carved out a national role by the sheer force of their personalities.

The involvement of the voluntary and the community sector in social partnership – 'the long march through the institutions' – has now attracted some examination. McCashin, O'Sullivan and Brennan (2002) analysed the participation of the voluntary and community sector in the National Economic and Social Forum (NESF). This study found that the sector's approach was strongly represented in NESF policy positions and publications. These new sites of governance represented a significant shift in the manner in which aspects of welfare policy were formulated, but they had their limitations. Whether government listened to NESF's opinions, views and policies was of course another matter and there was some doubt that it did. Participation in NESF had strained several of the participant organisations who, although they welcomed the opportunity to bring their views to a new level, were ill-resourced to do so, more so from a human than financial point of view.

Social partnership, with its problems and tensions, may represent an unexpectedly fruitful outcome to a process of voluntary sector/state interaction that was far from promising over the years. The voluntary and community sector that emerged in the new state developed with uneven assistance by government. Its journey was a difficult one. The government was prepared to give it scope, but not support, and even that scope had limitations as the case studies of FLAC, the national pilot schemes, the experience of the National Social Service Council and the voluntary hospitals indicated. The new state suffered a serious problem of social under-capacity and, as Lee (1989) illustrated in such detail, intellectual challenge. The project for the new state did not envisage a role for the voluntary sector, it was not able to accommodate one that was perceived to challenge its authority or its dominant assumptions, and it was not willing to be informed by external example. Not until the 1990s was it allowed some 'voice'. In these circumstances, it is no wonder that the task of drawing up a policy over 1976 to 2000 proved to be almost insuperable. Exposure to new ideas for voluntary and community sector development, be they from Northern Ireland, Britain, continental Europe or further afield, may in future enrich the sector – as the early new ideas of social capital have already done – and give more space for its voice to be heard. But with social partnership and the eventual publication of a policy framework in 2000, maybe the voluntary sector had, at last, emerged from the dark valleys to reach the brighter uplands.

4

Policy, Regulation and Legislation in Northern Ireland

Introduction

The current government strategy for supporting the voluntary and community sector in Northern Ireland is set out in a pioneering document, unique in the United Kingdom, *Partners for Change: Government's Strategy for Support of the Voluntary and Community Sector 2001-2004* (Department for Social Development, 2003). The Strategy fulfils the commitment in the 1998 *Compact between Government and the Voluntary and Community Sector in Northern Ireland* to produce a supporting document setting out how its principles and commitments would be put into practice and kept under review (Department for Social Development, 1998). It is intended also to contribute to the Programme for Government by promoting and supporting the development of innovative, consistent and value-creating relationships between both sectors.

The development of the Strategy began before, and ended after, suspension of the Northern Ireland Assembly in October 2002. A draft of the document, endorsed by the Northern Ireland Executive, was published for consultation by the Department for Social Development in June 2001. In his introduction to the document, the then Minister for Social Development, Maurice Morrow MLA, described *Partners for Change* as 'a strategy for action, not rhetoric – a strategy to achieve coherence and to strengthen sustainability. Over one hundred and fifty action steps have been identified across Government … .' The action steps are set within 'a new strategic context taking account of a range of key policy objectives – the promotion of equality and human rights, and tackling poverty and social disadvantage; areas where the voluntary and community sector is already working very closely with Government to alleviate inequality and help build an inclusive society.'

The consultation document was well received by the sector. Responding to it on behalf of the sector, NICVA commented:

NICVA commends the work of the Voluntary Activity Unit with the help of the Joint Forum in producing what is a major development in the relationship between government and the voluntary and community sector. Collaboration and partnership are key community development principles and it is encouraging to see, in particular within the good practice guides, those philosophies being championed as the way forward for government. It is a developing process and NICVA is confident that *Partners for Change* will have long lasting and tangible effect on the relationship between the voluntary and community sector and government. But like any development there are certain areas and issues that must be addressed.

The *Strategy* in its final form was published by the Department for Social Development in April 2003. It took account of many of the comments received during consultation. For example, it sets out cross-cutting actions in response to comments that there was a need for greater consistency across departments. It places more emphasis on engaging statutory agencies and non-departmental public bodies. District councils, for example, are required to prepare their Community Support Plans under the three cross-cutting themes contained in the *Strategy* and to produce evidence of consultation with the sector before their Plans are approved by the Department. The Strategy pays greater attention to the sustainability of the sector. Of particular significance is the emphasis given to developing relations with smaller community groups. In his foreword, Des Browne MP, Secretary of State responsible for the Department for Social Development, comments:

> Government in Northern Ireland already has good relationships with many voluntary and community organisations. *Partners for Change* provides a cross-departmental mechanism to strengthen these relationships whilst building new ones, particularly with smaller community groups. These grass roots groups help government to better support communities, especially those in greatest need and those whose infrastructure is underdeveloped.

The document itself states:

> *Partners for Change* is driven by a vision of government working with the voluntary and community sector, to build a just and inclusive society which meets the needs of people in Northern Ireland, particularly in those areas of greatest need. This can only be achieved by developing links with a wide range of organisations in the voluntary and community sector. Government particularly seeks to engage with smaller groups who may not previously have been involved in policy making.

Partners for Change commits the eleven departments of the Northern Ireland Executive and the Northern Ireland Office to practical actions that will encourage greater partnership working, enable the sector to contribute more fully to policy making and build the capacity of the sector to strengthen its sustainability. The *Strategy* is intended to be result-driven and for the first time a three-year programme of practical actions is set out, to be pursued across all departments. Each department has offered a case study drawn from key areas of work which require working with the sector to achieve the department's objectives. These will be closely tracked and will form an important part of independent evaluations of the Strategy. Any learning or best practice identified will be included in monitoring and evaluation reports.

To ensure coherence, each of the 12 individual strategies is underpinned by:

- four common aims that derive from the *Compact* and the *Programme for Government: Shaping Policy Development, Building Communities, Promoting Active Citizenship and Tackling Disadvantage*
- three common themes agreed by the Joint Government/Voluntary and Community Sector Forum for Northern Ireland as the essence of a shared working relationship that would result in added value: Capacity Building, Working Together and Resourcing the Sector. To reflect joined-up Government, a set of cross-departmental strategic priorities have been identified under each of these themes
- three Good Practice Guides on Community Development, Funding and Volunteering. A commitment is given that the Office of the First and Deputy First Minister will issue a *Guide to Consultation Methods for Northern Ireland Public Authorities* and that the Voluntary and Community Unit will issue a *Good Practice Guide on Partnership*.

Partners for Change puts in place robust mechanisms for monitoring, evaluation and compliance of the Strategy. These involve Ministers in each Department endorsing an annual monitoring report from their own department prior to submission to the Joint Forum, with the Voluntary and Community Unit bringing added value by generating an annual monitoring report of the *Strategy* as a whole for endorsement by the DSD Minister and presentation to his Ministerial colleagues. The first monitoring report is due by September 2003. The Strategy will also be independently evaluated and the first evaluation report is due to be completed by March 2004. A procedure is in place to deal with complaints about the *Strategy*. Despite ministerial involvement in the monitoring process before submission to the Joint Forum, there is no such involvement in the Forum itself.

The document makes clear that the sector will be closely involved in implementing the *Strategy*, in agreeing issues and new priorities for the future and in monitoring and evaluation arrangements. It notes that the success of the *Strategy* will depend on the sector continuing to embrace its aims and support its implementation and highlights the sector's key role in removing barriers that might inhibit closer working with departments, including their non-departmental public bodies and their statutory agencies.

For the first time, the voluntary and community sector has comprehensive information on government support and plans for the sector. The publication of individual departmental strategies provides the opportunity for the sector to discuss, debate and challenge government objectives and priorities at a time when the funding environment in which the sector works has become more demanding.

The Joint Government/Voluntary and Community Sector Forum for Northern Ireland was set up by the Northern Ireland government in 1998 to provide a formal mechanism for dialogue between both sectors. Representatives of the sector made an important contribution to the preparation of the *Strategy* set out in *Partners for Change* and the Forum itself will have an important role in the monitoring and evaluation of the *Strategy*. The Forum is also the mechanism through which the government and the sector have agreed jointly to monitor the operation of the *Compact* on an annual basis.

The *Strategy* is now being implemented. Action has been taken on, or is in train to develop, some of the key components of policy, for example, a stronger focus within government for voluntary and community activity, sustainability, community development and community infrastructure, volunteering and closer partnership working. Each of these components is now examined.

The Voluntary Activity Unit/Voluntary and Community Unit

The Voluntary Activity Unit, foreshadowed in the 1993 *Strategy* and established on 14 June 1993, provided the first focal point within government on voluntary activity and community development. In December 1993 it added to its remit responsibility for the administration of charity law in Northern Ireland on transfer of those functions from the Department of Finance and Personnel. Its responsibilities were further extended in April 1995 when it assumed the community services functions previously discharged by the Department for Education.

The Voluntary Activity Unit was retained in the new structure for the devolved administration and formed part of a newly created Department for Social Development. The Unit had the task of providing a focus on voluntary and community activity among the 11 new Departments, some of them with longstanding, well-developed relationships with the sector, others with little or no track record of such involvement.

The need to promote a more cohesive, coherent and consistent approach across government in its relationship with the sector added to the pivotal cross-cutting role of the Voluntary Activity Unit. The Programme for Government emphasised strongly the need to develop a more joined up and strategic approach to policy-making than had existed in the past. It also gave notice of action to develop a new role, structure and remit for the Unit to better reflect the Executive's desire to work in partnership with the sector. Following an independent review, the then Minister for Social Development, Nigel Dodds MP MLA, announced a new focus for his Department's work in support of the sector with the launch on 20 May 2002 of the Voluntary and Community Unit, with a new name and remit. He commented:

> This is not just a cosmetic exercise but reflects a significant and planned shift in the department's work to reflect the changing demands of government and to benefit from and support the work of the voluntary sector. These changes reinforce our commitment to working with communities and with community based organisations in particular, whilst continuing to reflect our ongoing support for the voluntary sector.

The Unit now:

- provides guidance and assistance to other departments in their work with the sector
- supports community development
- promotes volunteering and active citizenship
- works in partnership with the sector through the Joint Government/ Voluntary and Community Sector Forum
- researches issues affecting the sector.

The Unit also administers a range of funding programmes. These include support for the regional infrastructure of the sector, the District Councils' Community Support Programme; two EU funding Measures – Advice and Information Services, and Community Stability – under the Programme for Building Sustainable Prosperity; the Outreach Programme; the Local Community Fund and the Executive Programme for Essential Services. Three grant programmes that support volunteering and active citizenship are administered on its behalf by the Volunteer Development Agency.

The Unit was highly regarded by our interviewees, being referred to as the driver and facilitator. One interviewee, however, expressed concern that despite the recommendation in the review of the VCU that it should move away from grant administration and take a more strategic role, it is still involved in grant-making having taken on responsibility for two EU funding measures, with the policy formulation aspect of the work losing out. Another queried whether the Unit had sufficient 'muscle' to effect cross-departmental working.

Sustainability

Sustainability is a critical issue for the voluntary and community sector in Northern Ireland. During the 1990s, the sector experienced significant growth through access to a number of finite funding programmes. The ending of the EU Structural Funds Programme in 1999, with the anticipated contraction in available resources in 2000 and beyond and the likelihood that Northern Ireland would lose Objective One status in the next round of Structural Funds, caused major concern. The then Secretary of State for Northern Ireland, Dr Mo Mowlam, commissioned an inter-departmental review to make recommendations for action by government and the sector, jointly and separately. The result was the issue in April 2000 by the Department for Social Development of a *Consultation Document on Funding for the Voluntary and Community Sector*. Commonly known as the Harbison Report (after the chairman of the Inter-Departmental Group, Dr Jeremy Harbison, then Deputy Secretary in the Department of Health and Social Services), the document identified the key questions that must be addressed with regard to medium and long-term sustainability and made a number of recommendations intended to give a clear focus and way ahead as to how government should respond to the difficulties, particularly driven by short-term funding programmes. The recommendations covered issues such as the need for action to ensure a more co-ordinated strategic approach to funding of the sector, taking account of the development processes involved and the particular needs in areas of weak community infrastructure; to establish a public, voluntary and private sector Task Force to consider the further diversification of funding sources, and to set up a forum of the major funders in the public, charitable and private sectors. Progress has been made on this range of key policy issues.

Performance measurement

Work to develop a set of indicators that could be used to measure the added value of voluntary and community-based activity was taken forward by Community Evaluation Northern Ireland and resulted in the launch in April 2003 of a research report: *Investing in Social Capital: An Evaluation Model for Voluntary and Community Activity*.

Funding to the voluntary and community sector

Informed funding decisions require access to accurate and relevant information, although it is apparent that the appropriate management information systems are not yet in place to provide this. To remedy the situation, a common database of government and other funding of the sector has been developed and is being piloted within the Department of Social Development and the Department of Health, Social Services and Public Safety. Following testing and evaluation, it will be rolled out to other government departments by March 2004. This is a key management information tool and when operational, the database will provide for the first time information on the extent and spread of government funding to the sector and allow a more strategic approach to funding decisions. It will plug a hole identified by many of our interviewees that accurate information on the flow of government funding to the sector was not available.

The Funders' Forum
Following extensive consultation, the Funders' Forum for Northern Ireland was set up in March 2003. It operates at two levels: a Reference Group consisting of a core group of key funders which will meet regularly and a larger group convened through seminars and conferences.

Under its Terms of Reference, the Forum will:

- promote information sharing and co-operation between funders in Northern Ireland at a strategic level
- promote good practice in funding the voluntary and community sector
- facilitate consideration of the complementarity of programmes
- build and maintain an overview of funding to the voluntary and community sector in Northern Ireland
- identify and seek to address any gaps in the delivery of funding programmes.

At the first meeting of the Forum, the majority of funders present was from the statutory sector. This raises an important issue and the Forum has to address the potential between the aspirations to achieve a degree of complementarity among funders as mentioned in the Harbison Report and the independence of funders such as charitable trusts and foundations. For the first two years, the work of the Forum will be evaluated and at the end of that period, its operation as a whole will be reviewed.

Task Force on Resourcing the Voluntary and Community Sector
The setting up of the crucially important Task Force on Resourcing the Voluntary and Community Sector was long awaited, but was eventually announced in February 2003 by the Minister with responsibility for Social Development, Des Browne MP, during the period of Direct Rule that followed the suspension of the Northern Ireland Assembly and the Northern Ireland Executive by the Secretary of State for Northern Ireland on 14 October 2002. Over a period of one year, the Task Force, which held its first meeting on 27

February 2003, is considering how the sector can continue to make a contribution to the achievement of government objectives and to the well-being of society. The Task Force has been welcomed both by Government and by the sector. Mr Browne highlighted the importance of the Task Force in shaping the future of the voluntary and community sector:

In the context of major impending changes to funding programmes, the Task Force will identify action to be taken to ensure that the voluntary and community sector can continue to make a substantial contribution to the achievement of Government objectives and to the well-being of the Northern Ireland Community (DSD press release, 28 February 2003).

Seamus McAleavey, NICVA's Director, welcomed the announcement, commenting:

We have been waiting for this Task Force to be set up since it was recommended in the Harbison review of funding for the sector in April 2000. We now have a year of hard work ahead of us, taking a serious look at the sector and ensuring that we have an infrastructure and funding to take us forward in the long term.

The Task Force has set up working groups to look in detail at government policy and support for the sector, accountability and organisational systems of governance, infrastructure, and sustainability. It has also commissioned research into building sustainable networks, mission drift caused by contract service agreements, and the capacity of the existing fund-raising and income generation skills of the sector. An issues paper was published in November 2003 and the final report will be submitted to the Minister for Social Development by 31 March 2004. The Task Force has a mammoth challenge, against what some may regard as an almost impossible timescale, to make recommendations that will deliver a sea change in funding and support mechanisms, not least before the ending of European Programmes in 2006 and at a time also when the budget of the Community Fund, a major funder of the sector in Northern Ireland, is decreasing.

While the longer term issues concerning funding for the sector are being considered by the Task Force, government has acknowledged the immediate pressures on services provided by the voluntary and community sector by announcing the proposed allocation of nearly £7 million to 154 groups across Northern Ireland from the Social Inclusion and Community Regeneration Fund (DSD press office, 28 February 2003). The allocation followed the Northern Ireland Executive's decision in October 2002, just before suspension, to make £6 million available from the Executive Programme Funds to be used to alleviate the continuing funding difficulties facing the sector. These special funds end in March 2004 and a process has been put in place for considering how such funding might be rolled forward.

To assist the sustainability of the sector, the government donated £3 million to the Community Foundation for Northern Ireland's Endowment Fund on 24 July 2003, with a challenge to raise at least a further £2 million from other sources. In accepting the donation and the challenge, the Community Foundation confirmed that it had already received indications that £2 million will be made available by a major charitable donor to augment the investment in the Foundation endowment and pledged to raise a further £1 million to complement the amounts already assured. Avila Kilmurray, the Foundation's Director, said:

> The increased endowment investment will lay the basis for long term grant-making to community groups and voluntary projects across Northern Ireland. The commitment to funding could not have come at a better time, as it will be delivering real benefits to real people at a time when European PEACE funding is expected to end in 2006 (Northern Ireland Office press release, 24 July 2003).

Closer partnership working
The role of the sector and of civil society was also recognised through its involvement in a range of partnerships and in the Civic Forum, of which more than one third of the seats are allocated to the sector (McCall and Williamson, 2001). The sector has been involved in a range of partnerships delivering urban, rural and social and economic regeneration partnerships. As of right, the sector was accorded a place in the District Partnership arrangements set up under the EU Special Support Programme for Peace and Reconciliation in Northern Ireland 1995-1999 (Williamson, Scott and Halfpenny, 2000). The sector is also involved in the Local Strategy Partnerships established under the successor EU PEACE II Programme 2000-2004.

As noted in chapter two, the Belfast Agreement and Section 75 of the Northern Ireland Act 1998 have significant implications for the relationship between government and the sector. The Agreement itself is based on a commitment to partnership, equality and mutual respect, and a model of participatory, inclusive policy-making was fleshed out in the Equality Commission's *Guide to the Statutory Duties* (Equality Commission, 2002). The process involves the sector both in consultation and as a source of the information that public authorities need to enable them to make a judgement on the extent of equality impacts. Public authorities cannot properly fulfil their statutory duties under Section 75 without input from voluntary and community groups and this is a legislative base for government support of them.

Developments in community development and community infrastructure

As noted above, the Programme for Government commits government to sustain and enhance local communities and to support community infrastructure. There have been a number of recent developments in this area, some of them led by the Voluntary and Community Unit. Its predecessor, the Voluntary Activity Unit, had taken forward the implementation of the community-development agenda set out in the 1993 *Strategy*, which included pioneering work with the Scottish Centre for Community Development to develop a model for the monitoring and evaluation of community development in Northern Ireland.

Following a review of the district council's Community Services Programme by the Department for Social Development (*Beyond the Centre*, 2000), a revised and re-named Community Support Programme has been introduced under which district councils are required to draw up community support plans and provide increased support for local advice centres and community groups. The Community Support Programme is a collaborative initiative involving the Department for Social Development and all 26 district councils in Northern Ireland together with voluntary and community groups and local advice organisations. It supports the provision of resource centres, grants to community groups and the employment of staff in district councils. As noted above, councils are now required to prepare their plans using the three common themes in *Partners for Change* and to provide evidence of consultation with the sector when seeking approval from the Department for Social Development.

To help to address the problem of weak community infrastructure referred to both in the Harbison Report and the Programme for Government, the Department for Social Development launched the Outreach Programme on 28 November 2002. This three-year initiative supported by Executive Funds totalling £2.6 million is designed to assist communities that have not been able to readily access and influence the public services that impact on them. It aims to help public sector organisations across Northern Ireland put into practice the principle of working in partnership with communities and with the voluntary and community sector. The funding is for innovative, demonstration projects that actively involve local communities and test new approaches to meeting community need. The Programme is open to all public sector organisations. While voluntary and community groups are not eligible to apply directly, it is a requirement that communities are involved substantially in the design, development and delivery of projects. Funding for individual projects will range from around £50,000 to £250,000. Ninety-three applications were received, the majority from health and social services trusts, education and library boards, local strategic partnerships and government agencies/departments. Fourteen projects have been selected for support.

Following the renewal of intercommunal violence in 2002, particularly in parts of Belfast, a number of government initiatives were taken to build trust in divided communities and to develop community capacity. On 16 November 2002, Northern Ireland Office Minister Des Browne announced that he would set up and chair a Community Action Group to co-ordinate and drive forward community development and community relations across Northern Ireland. The Minister said:

We want to support and build on the efforts being made to grip those issues that have a practical impact on the daily lives of everyone living at interfaces in Belfast and elsewhere. To play our part requires a co-ordinated approach across government together with other key players from within the statutory sector and beyond and that is what this Action Group will provide (Northern Ireland Office Press Release, 16 November 2002).

Also in November 2002, following intercommunal violence in the area, Des Browne announced a £3million funding package for the development of a programme of community capacity building in North Belfast to enable local people to develop the necessary skills to best represent their areas.

A further major funding package – the Local Community Fund – was announced by the Secretary of State for Northern Ireland, Paul Murphy, on 28 February 2003, with a budget initially set at £3 million for 2003/04. The fund is aimed at creating community capacity and leadership in communities feeling left behind and alienated by the progress made elsewhere. Deployment of the Fund is based on a bottom-up approach, with local communities determining local priorities for action. The first areas to benefit from the Fund, with an allocation of £2.7 million, were announced by John Spellar MP on 10 July 2003 (Northern Ireland Office press release, 10 July 2003).

A programme of measures, developed by the Community Action Group and totalling £7.4 million, to tackle disadvantage in working-class communities across Northern Ireland was announced by Mr Browne on 24 April 2003. Targeted at improving health, education, physical and com-munity regeneration, the measures are intended to build trust and confidence in disadvantaged communities and tackle poor public services in these areas. Not all of this was new money, since it included the £3 million already announced for the Local Community Fund and £2.9 million for the Outreach Programme. On 12 June 2003, the Government announced that it would provide support for local pilot community conventions, based on the success-ful experience of the Shankill Community Convention in May 2002. A series of similar conventions was planned for other areas of the Province over the next two years, facilitated by community leaders with the aim of identifying and resolving practical problems (Northern Ireland Office press release, 12 June 2003).

A further major initiative to improve life for disadvantaged communities was launched on 24 June 2003 with the publication of the Department for Social Development's *People and Places, A Strategy for Neighbourhood Renewal* (Department for Social Development, 2003). One of the vital elements of the *Strategy* is to promote partnerships with key stakeholders, including community and voluntary sector organisations in each area. In launching the document, John Spellar MP signalled a move away from the previous short-term, project-based approach to a longer-term strategy based on well-planned programmes that will work in concert to achieve sustainable renewal.

> I believe the Strategy can act as a catalyst for the transformation of our most deprived urban areas and provide genuine opportunities for developing the potential of local people, many of whom have suffered the worst effects of more than 30 years of conflict and social exclusion.

The move away from short-term funding is crucially important given the difficulties which many groups had experienced as a result of short-term funding provided by the department's Belfast Regeneration Office.

Developments in public policy to promote volunteering

The importance of volunteering was endorsed in the *Compact* and in *Partners for Change*, in which it is the subject of a Good Practice Guide. The *Programme for Government* recognised the need to increase community activity and to broaden the volunteering base. The main plank of public policy to support volunteering is the Active Community Initiative, a United Kingdom-wide initiative launched by the prime minister, Mr Tony Blair, in January 1999, but being implemented in Northern Ireland with the endorsement of the Northern Ireland Executive. The overall aim of the Initiative is 'to help rebuild a sense of community throughout the UK, by encouraging and supporting all forms of community involvement'. Following widespread consultation, a locally tailored action programme – The Northern Ireland Action Plan for the Active Community Initiative (2001) – was published by the Department for Social Development in April 2001 (Department for Social Development, 2001). The objectives are:

- to bring about a change in attitudes in volunteering and community action
- to increase the number of volunteers
- to broaden the base of volunteers to make volunteering an inclusive process
- to act with other initiatives to promote a community empowerment approach.

The Plan sets out a range of action in the areas of research, promotion, policy and practice, volunteering infrastructure, demonstration projects, and monitoring and evaluation. The Department for Social Development provided £1.8m to deliver the Plan over the three years from April 2001 till April 2004. This included funding for the Main Grants and Small Grants Programmes and funding for a number of Demonstration Projects. The Volunteer Development Agency was appointed as managing agent for the administration of the grants process on behalf of the Department.

The Agency also administers three other grant programmes on behalf of government, all of them to promote aspects of volunteering. These are:

- the Community Volunteering Scheme to encourage and support volunteering, targeted primarily at people not in paid work and other groups who are under-represented in the volunteering population, on behalf of the Department for Social Development
- the Volunteer Bureaux Initiative to improve the local organisation and infrastructure of volunteering in Northern Ireland, again on behalf of the Department for Social Development
- millennium Volunteers to promote and develop volunteering by young people between the ages of 16 and 25, on behalf of the Department for Education.

The monitoring of the Active Community Initiative to date reflects progress on the action points contained within the Action Plan. Good progress has been made on the research front in particular, with the publication by the Volunteer Development Agency of the results of research on mentoring (Courtney, 2001), the participation of black and ethnic minority people in volunteering and community activity (Leong, Fee Ching, 2001) and the nature and extent of volunteering in Northern Ireland; by Business in the Community on employer-supported volunteering (Volunteer Development Agency, 2001) and by the Praxis Care Group on the extent, nature and value of volunteer befriending in Northern Ireland (Holloway and Mawhinney, 2002).

The baseline research study by the Volunteer Development Agency revealed that there are in excess of 440,000 formal and 750,000 informal volunteers in Northern Ireland, an increase of 17 per cent and 9 per cent respectively since the previous survey in 1995 (Volunteer Development Agency, 2001).

While acknowledging the role and the achievements of the Volunteer Development Agency in promoting volunteering, some of our interviewees considered that there remains an issue of image and of class, with volunteering still being regarded as a philanthropic concept and volunteers as 'do gooders'. Volunteering is not widely seen as an expression of active citizenship, and what people do in their own communities is not really seen as volunteering. Volunteering was not seen to reflect the nature and diversity of the sector or of a society coming out of conflict.

The social economy

The social economy, with its double bottom-line of social and economic goals, has a long history in Northern Ireland. It is diverse, comprising for example, credit unions, co-operatives, housing associations, commercial/trading arms of charities, community businesses etc. It includes organisations such as Ulster Community Investment Trust, which adopts a commercial approach to profit generation but recycles profits to lend to community economic development associations, and the John Hewitt Bar where profits from the bar go to support the Belfast Unemployed Resource Centre. The social economy accounts for an estimated 5 per cent of employment or 30,000 jobs and is a significant and growing sector in its own right. Much of what can be identified as the social economy has until recently evolved independently from government and other public sources. However, it is clear that newer social economy projects are involved in the delivery of publicly funded services.

Stutt, Murtagh and Campbell (2001) found that despite employing more people than in textiles, agriculture and fisheries, there remains no mainstream public policies or programmes in Northern Ireland which explicitly target the social economy as a matter of intention. In 2003, the figures are on a par with the tourism or construction sectors. The social economy is now a fast-growing policy area. Its importance in strengthening the local economy was recognised by the Economic Development Forum in its medium-term strategic projects (Economic Development Forum, 2002). It has been espoused by government, the Corporate Plan of the Department of Enterprise, Trade and Investment (DETI) (2002-2005), which identifies the social economy as a new priority issue, noting that social economy organisations 'are distinct in their flexibility, closeness to communities and ability to focus on disadvantaged areas'. The Plan commits DETI to spearheading an integrated approach to the social economy and its work to create a new policy approach to, and a structure for, maximising its potential in Northern Ireland. Another key driver has been the EU, with over £55 million being allocated under the PEACE II Programme to Local Strategic Partnerships for the development of local social economy initiatives within each district council area.

On 22 January 2003, the DETI Minister, Ian Pearson, announced that a £600,000 four-year funding package from a consortium of DETI, DSD and IFI was being put in place to enable the Social Economy Agency to take forward a comprehensive programme of work focusing on the social economy. This will deliver, among other things, an inclusive Social Economy Network; promotion of the Network, and the benefits of social enterprise (throughout Northern Ireland, but particularly in areas of under investment and economic deprivation); the identification and better understanding of social enterprise policy issues, and the establishment of a research capability to assess and identify new opportunities for increased social enterprise activity in both private and public services (Pearson, 2003). The Minister also announced that a first draft of a framework for a cross-departmental strategy for the social economy sector should be available for consultation with interested parties this year. *Building on Progress – Priorities and Plans for 2003-2006* (Office of the First and Deputy First Minister, 2003) gives a commitment to develop and implement agreed priorities to maximise the contribution of the social economy by March 2004. Two new structures have since been put in place: the Social Economy Network to represent and act on behalf of the social economy sector in Northern Ireland; and the Social Economy Forum, which has been formed to deliver a more integrated and co-ordinated response to the needs of the sector. The Forum, which held its first meeting on 25 June 2003, is to be chaired by the Minister for Enterprise, Trade and Investment and comprises members of the Network and officials from relevant Government Departments.

While it is a positive development that structures and a financial package to promote the social economy have been put in place, it should be noted that most social economy projects in Northern Ireland have been funded from EU sources. As a result, many projects are heavily reliant upon the continuation of that funding. Morrissey (2003) notes that the social economy

> is an area that will always require public subsidy and given the retreat of welfare states, will probably be a permanent feature of modern economies. It may nurture small business development in the longer term. However, the level of subsidy required to sustain it should be legitimated not on business principles but on the social and fiscal costs of long-term unemployment.

If the potential which government has identified in the social economy as a means of sustaining the local economy (and indeed of contributing to the sustainability of the voluntary and community sector, and to building social capital) it is to be realised, it will be essential that support for such projects is mainstreamed when current European Union funding sources end in 2006.

A shared future
A key policy development that is likely to have a significant impact on the voluntary and community sector in its social capital building role and on the

relationship between community development and community relations is the government's consultation exercise on improving relations in Northern Ireland. Chapter two noted the impact of 'the Troubles' on the voluntary and community sector and the role that the sector played – and continues to play – in embedding the peace process. It noted also the role played by community development. While some progress has been made, Northern Ireland remains a deeply divided society, with little change in the extent of inter-community friendship patterns and evidence that, in some urban areas, further divisions are emerging within local communities. The government has sought to deal with this in a consultation document *A Shared Future: Improving Relations in Northern Ireland* (Office of the First and Deputy First Minister, 2003), which sets out a vision for 'a peaceful society in which everyone can freely and fully participate, achieve their full potential, and live free from poverty'.

This exercise is likely to have a significant impact on the sector. The aim is for a shared society (in which people are encouraged to make choices in their lives that are not bound by historical divisions and are free to do so) and a pluralist society (with respect and tolerance for cultural diversity where people are free to assert their identity). The paper makes clear that 'our policy must be long-term and strategic, based on a clear vision, values, principles and objectives. Above all, it must tackle the fundamental divisions in our society directly.' It sets out policy aims, fundamental principles that should underpin any policies, strategies or actions undertaken, and the actions that might be taken at central and local government level. The aim following consultation is to develop a new cross-departmental strategy and framework to promote better relations between and within communities in Northern Ireland.

The Paper does not explicitly mention social capital, yet evidence from research shows that bridging social capital can stabilise areas facing, or in danger of, conflict. Varshney (1998), for example, in his study of communal violence in India, examined the role of voluntary associations and informal community networks. He concluded that areas with low levels of communal strife are characterised not only by high levels of associational activity but also by high levels of cross-cutting engagement between Muslim and Hindu. He also stated that: 'There is no evidence in our material that the state alone can bring about lasting peace in violence-torn areas. The state should begin to see civic society as a precious potential ally and think of the kinds of civic linkages that can promote the cause of peace.'

The Paper does, however, acknowledge that the voluntary and community sector is a critical stakeholder in future actions to promote greater sharing, contact and communication between and within the different communities. It also acknowledges the important role of churches and other faith-based organisations, a contribution which one of our interviewees described as dramatically understated.

In its response, NICVA (2003) endorses the vision in *A Shared Future* as the right one, but notes:

> The vision needs to be central to the work of all government departments and the issue of good relations should be core within departmental objectives. This is not so much an issue of formulating a strategy and a budget for community relations; this should be about using government's entire budget, all the resources at its disposal, in such as way as to facilitate sharing rather than separation. It should be ensured that no government department has policies or objectives which reinforce separation (NICVA, 2003).

Consultation has now closed and the government's response is awaited. Of particular relevance to the voluntary and community sector will be whether the absence of specific reference to social capital in the consultation paper will be remedied in the response. And if it is recognised, will government promote the development of social capital through, for example, assessing policy developments for their impact on social capital? Will the performance measurement of voluntary and community organisations funded by departments take account of their capacity to build bridges and link social capital? Will there be a closer alignment or integration of community relations with community development, since, as one of our interviewees told us, progressive community development is dependent on improved community relations, not an alternative to it?

The supervision of charities in Northern Ireland

From common beginnings
Charity law on the island of Ireland, for most of its history, has been provided within a unified legislative framework. Its statutory roots lie in the twin pieces of early seventeenth-century legislation: the Statute of Charitable Uses 1601 and the Statute of Pious Uses 1634, which were judicially construed as legislative equivalents. Neither statute provided a definition of 'charity'. In the final phase before partition, this framework consisted of the Charities Procedure Act, 1812 and the Charitable Donations and Bequests (Ireland) Acts, 1844, 1867 and 1871. Despite partition into the two jurisdictions in 1920, this nineteenth-century legislation continued to provide a common governing framework until the 1960s. The Charitable Donations and Bequests (Ireland) Act, 1844 was the principal act governing the law relating to charities on the island of Ireland. The legislative intent was to centralise responsibility for responding to charity law issues. Establishing the

Commission of Charitable Donations and Bequests (the Commissioners) proved to be the most important and lasting contribution of this legislation.

Post-partition in Northern Ireland and a convergence with England
From partition in 1920 until 1964 the Minister of Finance continued to bear much the same responsibilities as the Commissioners in the Republic of Ireland as defined by the Charitable Donations and Bequests (Ireland) Acts. The introduction of the Charities Act (NI), 1964 broke the link with the Republic and tied development of charity law in the jurisdiction with that of England. Prior to the proroguing of the Stormont Assembly in 1972 there were two legislatures with territorial jurisdiction in Northern Ireland. Firstly the Stormont government itself, which passed a considerable amount of the laws affecting charities, most importantly the 1964 Act. This was primarily an attempt to assist the operations of charities by providing various facilities. Other important legislation was the House to House Collections Act (NI), 1965, the Recreational Charities Act (NI), 1958, which extended slightly the definition of 'charitable', and the Charitable Trusts (Validation) Act (NI), 1954. Most of these pieces of Stormont legislation very closely followed English legislation passed around the same time.

After Stormont was prorogued in 1972 all legislative power reverted back to Westminster. Once more, jurisdiction was exercised in two ways. Firstly through Northern Ireland Orders in Council, for example the Charities (NI) Order 1987. Secondly there is United Kingdom-wide legislation which applies also to Northern Ireland (for example part of the Charities Act, 1993 applies in Northern Ireland).

Since devolution of power to the Northern Ireland Assembly in 1999 and its suspension in 2002, only one piece of legislation affecting charities was enacted. This was the Trustee Act (NI), 2001, which reformed the powers and duties of trustees and was based closely on the Trustee Act, 2000.

Charity and legal forms
A large proportion of charity law is concerned with the definition of charity. For an object to be deemed charitable at law it must be within the 'spirit and intendment' of the 1601 statute which gives a list of charitable purposes, which must be for the public benefit and be exclusively charitable. Attempts have been made by the courts to classify the objects listed under statutes, and poverty, education, religion and other purposes not included in the first three are now recognised as constituting the four heads of charity. Statute law in Northern Ireland has, in effect, added recreation as a fifth head. To satisfy the public benefit test, the charitable purpose must benefit the public and the benefit must be available to the public or a sufficiently important section of it.

What constitutes a charitable purpose has never been strictly defined in law and courts have sought to interpret it in accordance with contemporary social conditions. However, Northern Ireland has been disadvantaged by the fact that the twin agencies for determining what constitutes a contemporary charitable purpose are based in England. In deciding such matters, the Inland Revenue takes its lead from the rulings of the Charity Commission which are then transferred by proxy to determine similar issues in Northern Ireland. The Commission's remit does not extend to Northern Ireland, so it has had no opportunity to consider the distinctive characteristics of contemporary social conditions in this jurisdiction. Therefore, the merits of viewing purposes such as promoting peace and reconciliation or facilitating cross-community initiatives as charitable have never arisen for consideration and remain non-charitable. Given the fact and nature of social divisions in Northern Ireland, a strong argument exists for ensuring that a mechanism exists to test the worthiness of such purposes for charitable status.

The three most common structures are the trust, the company and the unincorporated association. Other legal forms exist such as Industrial and Provident Societies, a Friendly Society, a charity created by act of parliament, a charity created by royal charter, charities whose trustees are given a limited incorporated status under Section 10 of the Charities Act (NI), 1964 and an eleemosynary corporation. With the exception of the latter, charities exist in all the other forms.

The charity authority
The charity authority is now the Department for Social Development (DSD). In December 1993, responsibility for the administration of charity law was transferred from the Department of Finance and Personnel to the Department of Health and Social Services (DHSS). The transfer followed and was justified by the establishment of the Voluntary Activity Unit (VAU) within DHSS with a remit to facilitate and encourage the development of voluntary action. Administratively, the charities' functions were assigned to the new Unit as a separate Charities Branch, with the intention of enabling a more co-ordinated approach by government to voluntary action. Following devolution, the VAU was transferred to the Department for Social Development, and Charities Branch remains part of the renamed Voluntary and Community Unit.

Registration of charities
The powers of the Charity Commission do not extend to Northern Ireland and no explicit system of registration of charities exists, though several bodies fulfil elements of a registration system. For example, a charity may apply to the Inland Revenue for tax exemption and the Inland Revenue determine

whether or not the body is a charity for tax purposes. If successful, the applicant receives an exemption number and, in the absence of a registration
system, the number is used almost as a proxy for registration. The Department
for Social Development carries out certain functions of a registration system
such as facilitation, assistance and monitoring, but it has no explicit role in
regulating and monitoring charities. It has no register and does not create
definitions of charity and does not decide whether a particular body is a
charity.

A framework fit for purpose?
Much has changed in Northern Ireland since the 1960s, yet the jurisdiction,
according to Cormacain, O'Halloran and Williamson (2001) 'has the most
dated, least relevant and non-interventionist legislation relating to charities
in the United Kingdom'.

The basis for this assessment was a major study undertaken by the Centre
for Voluntary Action Studies in the University of Ulster. Its purpose was to
place on the record a history of the development of the law governing
charitable activity in Northern Ireland; to identify and assess the distinctive
characteristics of the law in the jurisdiction as it relates to emerging trends in
charitable activity, and to consider the appropriateness of Northern Ireland
charity law in relation to sustaining and regulating voluntary activity and
promoting the development of civil society. The findings were based on and
informed by a literature review, a postal questionnaire survey of 250 voluntary
organisations, a series of interviews with chief executives of charitable bodies
and, in relation to practice issues, with solicitors, accountants, a high court
judge and relevant officials.

The research report made a telling case for the urgent review of charity law.
It found, for example, that the statutory basis for charity law in Northern
Ireland is now very dated and out of touch with some practice. It found the
law particularly deficient as regards systems for registering and regulating
charities and for supervising fund-raising activities. It noted that definitional
issues exist, specifically the fact that peace and reconciliation is not a
charitable purpose. The Report called for a formal review of charity law as a
matter of some urgency, 'if this jurisdiction is to avoid being relatively
disadvantaged by legislative developments occurring in all other jurisdictions
of these islands'. It recommended also that the review 'should seek
opportunities to maximise parity of legislative provision with all other
jurisdictions of these islands'.

Review or not to review?
It should be noted that following new charity legislation in England in the
early 1990s, Northern Ireland charity law had in fact been reviewed with a

Consultation Paper issued in November 1995 (Department of Health and Social Services, 1995). The key proposal was to introduce a system of registration of charities. There was little support for such action. In 1997, the Government announced that a decision on the content of proposed new legislation would be postponed. This was to allow time to consider the implications for Northern Ireland of the recommendations on charity law in the *Deakin Report* (NCVO, 1996) and the indication in the government response *Raising the Voltage* (Department of National Heritage, 1996) that some of them would be seriously examined. Since then, Northern Ireland legislation has fallen further behind and there have been significant developments in charity legislation in England and Wales, in Scotland and in Ireland.

In England and Wales, Government has recently published its response (*Charities and Not-for-Profits: A Modern Legal Framework*, Home Office, 2003) to the recommendations in the Strategy Unit's review *Private Action, Public Benefit* (2002). The recommendations for reform aim among other things to modernise charity law and status so as to provide greater clarity and a stronger emphasis on the delivery of public benefit and to improve the range of available legal forms enabling organisations to be more effective and entrepreneurial. A Charities Bill is to be published in draft as soon as possible.

Scottish law was reviewed by the Scottish Charity Law Commission in the McFadden Report (Scottish Charity Law Commission, 2001). The Scottish Executive in its response (Scottish Executive, 2002) accepted the thrust of the McFadden Report that there should be better regulation of and support for charities in Scotland. This will be provided through a new Office of the Scottish Charity Regulator – as an agency of the executive, with functions of registration, monitoring and supervision, investigation and support and information. Charitable status will continue to be granted by the Inland Revenue. The Executive is now pressing ahead with modernising charity law, with tighter regulation and proposals for legislative reform promised later this year.

Charity laws in the Republic of Ireland have a similar heritage and characteristics to those in Northern Ireland and are also in need of modernisation. A commitment was given in the Dáil on 26 March 2003 that a consultation paper on new charities legislation will be published this year and the draft bill in 2004.

Preventive action?
A recent development affecting a charity in Northern Ireland pointed up the absence of a system for registration. In December 2002, Mr Des Browne, the then Minister for Health and Social Services, appointed a review team chaired by Sir Graham Hart, to examine the past and current management of the Northern Ireland Hospice (NIH) and to make recommendations on the

way forward. The review was to examine the circumstances surrounding the suspension and dismissal of the Administrative Director and his subsequent reappointment as Chief Executive. In its Report (Department of Health, Social Services and Public Safety, 2003) the Review Team noted that:

> It is clear that the NIH has suffered from the lack of a body in Northern Ireland with powers like those of the Charity Commission in England and Wales ... It seems to us reasonable to suppose that the Charity Commission would have been able to exercise a constructive influence at an early stage in the history of the difficulties at NIH and, if not, would have adjudged the threshold for intervention crossed if it had not had a satisfactory response from the NIH at some point as the events which led to the present review unfolded. We therefore consider that the Government should take urgent steps to remedy this gap in the arrangements for the supervision of charities in Northern Ireland.

Interestingly, the review was appointed by the Health Minister, not the Minister with responsibility for charity law in the Department for Social Development. The Health Minister in accepting all the recommendations that were relevant to her Department, announced that the question of a Charity Commission for Northern Ireland was a matter for the Department for Social Development Minister and that she had written to him for his views (Northern Ireland Office news release, 24 July 2003). The outcome is awaited.

Towards a modern framework (at last)?
In spring, 2004, the Voluntary and Community Unit launched a review with a commitment to move ahead as soon as the government's response to the *Private Action, Public Benefit* is known. That response has now been published. The Department for Social Development's proposals, which will presumably take account of any recommendations on charity law by the Task Force, are awaited. Perhaps a modern enabling legal and regulatory framework for Northern Ireland that is fit for its purpose and that takes account of developments in Great Britain and Ireland is at last in prospect?

The need for reform was widely supported by our interviewees who generally regarded the framework as archaic and in danger of impeding developments such as the entrepreneurial activities of the sector. Concern was also expressed about the impact on the sector of wider policies and of a range of statutory or legal requirements. There was widespread unease about what was seen as a growing preoccupation within government with audit and accountability, reflected in disproportionate and bureaucratic demands on the sector for formal accountability that can crowd out all other considerations.

This is an issue being addressed by the Task Force and it is clear from our interviews that a transparent, proportionate and consistently applied framework of accountability is urgently needed.

Other recent developments
Two other developments are relevant to charities in Northern Ireland. The first relates to sustainability, the second to the position of United Kingdom organisations with branches in Northern Ireland. *Private Action, Public Benefit* made recommendations for changes in legal forms to develop the sector's potential and to enable it to be more effective and entrepreneurial. One of these is a new legal form of 'community interest company' which pursues social enterprise in the public interest and dedicates profit to the public good. Government has accepted this recommendation which relates to company law and it is being taken forward by the Department for Trade and Industry, separately from the proposed Charities Bill. Corresponding action in Northern Ireland is the responsibility of the Department of Enterprise, Trade and Investment who are understood to be considering a similar legal form in Northern Ireland company law. This would be a particularly welcome development in view of the funding crisis facing charities in Northern Ireland with the ending of European funding in 2006.

Government also accepted a recommendation that a new umbrella committee, on which all United Kingdom charity regulators are represented, should be created to ensure a consistent regulatory approach UK-wide and commented: 'Now that charity law and regulation are devolved matters in Scotland and Northern Ireland – and are, or have been under review – there is an even greater need for strategic co-ordination of regulatory approaches' (Home Office, 2003, para 6.23). If the DSD review considers the scope for convergence of the regulatory frameworks in Northern Ireland and in Ireland, this should assist those charities that operate on an all-Ireland basis.

Overview

With the publication of *Partners for Change*, Northern Ireland has an up-to-date policy and strategy for the support of the voluntary and community sector, developed on an inter-departmental basis and in consultation with the sector. In this regard, it is unique in the UK. Northern Ireland also has a specific government initiative – the *Active Communities Initiative* – to promote community involvement.

Many challenges lie ahead and, drawing on our own review and comments made by our interviewees, a number of reservations and comments can be made. While the values and principles in the 1998 *Compact* underpin much of *Partners for Change* and the associated Good Practice Guides, it remains an important, living document. It contains important safeguards that must continue to be upheld, e.g. respecting the sector's independence and right to campaign. This is crucial. Knox (2003) in his paper *Resourcing the Voluntary and Community Sector*, comments that the principle of voluntary and community sector independence is fundamental.

> The *Compact*, *Partners for Change* and the prominence given to public sector collaboration with the voluntary and community sector in delivering the Programme for Government in Northern Ireland could, in the round, be seen as an agenda of incorporation and ultimately a dilution of the independence of the sector.

Achieving the aims and targets as set out in *Partners for Change* will require an unprecedented degree of cross-departmental co-operation ('joined-up government') and also an understanding of voluntary and community sector issues. The difficulty of achieving this should not be underestimated. Effective partnership working by departments will also require a culture change. Lyner (2003) comments that endless examples of the lack of joined-up thinking abound. 'While *Partners for Change* does lay before us the plans of all departments under agreed heads to pursue the partnership, we already know that departmental styles and inputs are greatly affected by the personality of our departmental champion.' Alcorn (2003) argues that despite the sea of government rhetoric about partnership and *Partners for Change*, there is reluctance across most of the statutory sector to enter into genuine partnerships with voluntary organisations and to develop meaningful working relationships with respect of information, training, liaison and service delivery.

While the Voluntary and Community Unit is well regarded, there is concern that other departments need to own the *Strategy*. There is concern also that there is often a marked distance between the policy framework and its outworking. The interviewees for this project remarked that those making the policy know the sector but those implementing it often do not. Right across government, there needs to be a much greater understanding of the sector, its nature and diversity, and of the issues it faces. There was concern that policy changes are slow to effect and percolate slowly to groups on the ground. The three-year delay in setting up the Task Force was cited as an example.

With regard to volunteering, the three-year Active Communities Initiative came to an end in March 2004. This raises questions as to whether there will be a further dedicated initiative to promote community involvement. It provides the opportunity for a more strategic approach to supporting volunteering at local level and for a radical look at the image issue in volunteering to ensure that volunteering reflects the diversity of the sector and the needs of a society coming out of conflict.

As the outworking of a range of policy and strategic documents and initiatives which have highlighted the partnership role of the sector and its status as a social partner, the involvement of the voluntary and community sector in the structures of governance in Northern Ireland is increasing steadily. In their review of developments in the sector in Northern Ireland in the five years since the Report of The Commission on the Future of the Voluntary Sector in England (The Deakin Report), Kearney and Williamson (2001) drew attention to the fact that while the opportunities for involvement in the structures of governance were welcome, the number and diversity of partnerships place significant demands on the sector both in terms of workload and skills. They also raised some policy issues.

It is important to recognise and acknowledge the sector's need for further capacity building, including the skills necessary for participation. Partnership also involves risks. Will, for example, partnerships become collusive? Will the sector's closer involvement in the formulation of policies, programmes and projects, as well as, in some instances, their delivery, put at risk its traditional and distinctive features such as challenging, opposing, campaigning and advocacy? Can the very real potential of conflict of interest be accommodated? This remains a major issue and the promised publication of a Good Practice Guide on Partnership by the Voluntary and Community Unit by 2004 is welcome.

The policy framework is not, of course, static. The Task Force on Resourcing the Voluntary and Community Sector, which is examining current government policy and support for the sector, could well recommend changes. The sector could be affected by the outcome of the current review of public administration in Northern Ireland. This was announced by the Northern Ireland Executive in the spring of 2002 and its continuation is being facilitated by the government during the period of the suspension of the Northern Ireland Executive. It is examining the structures for the delivery of public services, including health and social services boards and trusts, education and library boards, district councils etc. It is looking also at the scope of public services, asking questions about which functions should or should not be delivered by the public sector. Specific mention is also made of the need to consider the role of the sector in contributing to better public services. The Review could, therefore, have a major impact on the voluntary and community sector both in terms of its future role in delivering services and of the mechanisms through which the sector is funded, since many voluntary and community groups have their main relationships, including funding relationships, not with central government departments but with their agencies, non-departmental public bodies and local councils.

The developments outlined in this chapter reflect both a progression and a cementing of the relationship between government and the sector. But what of the relationship itself? *Partners for Change* notes that the engagement of statutory agencies and non-departmental public bodies is crucial to the implementation of the Strategy and commits the VCU to undertake an audit and compile a report on the relationship between statutory agencies and the sector during 2004. What did we find? Our interviewees spoke of a maturity and mutual respect in the relationship developed over many years of hard work though noting that there were differences among departments. Questions were raised (but not definitively answered) as to whether the relationship was too cosy; if so perhaps this was a consequence of the relationships that had been built up at official level in the absence of a devolved administration. It was noted that there were concerns about a possible tension between participative and representative democracy when the Northern Ireland Assembly was set up but this had not been an issue. The importance of maintaining a critical voice while working in partnership with government was repeatedly noted as expressed by one interviewee who said that the sector needed to make sure that its critical edge stays well honed.

A more detailed analysis of main developments in the relationship between government and voluntary and community sector in Northern Ireland since 1995/1996 can be found in Kearney and Williamson (2001), *Next Steps in Voluntary Action.*

5

Policy, Regulation and Legislation:
Republic of Ireland

Introduction
This chapter examines the policy, legislative and regulative environment of the voluntary sector in the Republic. As in the last chapter on Northern Ireland, this describes and analyses such issues as the legal form of charities in the Republic, how 'charity' is defined, the current tax/financial framework and the nature and quality of oversight of the sector. Policies on citizenship and volunteering are recorded and analysed. At the end, a comparison is made of the two different environments, north and south. But first, the policy framework – in theory and in practice.

The policy
In the Republic, the cornerstone document is the white paper *Supporting Voluntary Activity*, 2000 (for its origins and evolution, see chapter three). The white paper was a logical sequel to the green paper of 1997, making few changes, though some critics felt that it lacked the same depth. The following are its outline features:

- It affirmed the value of the community and voluntary sector as an essential contributor to democratic, pluralist society which provides opportunities for the development of decentralised and participative structures. Voluntary activity was one important expression of active citizenship.
- Voluntary organisations were valued for the contribution that they made toward social inclusion, solidarity, diversity, trust, dialogue and the rights of the individual.
- Specifically, it underlined the contribution that voluntary organisations could make to reconciliation between north and south.
- The government expressed its desire to work with voluntary organisations on a consultative, participative, facilitative basis. This could focus on policy questions as much as services.
- There was an acceptance of the independence of the sector.
- It recognised the role of voluntary organisations in campaigning, lobbying and trying to influence public opinion.

166

The main decisions set out in the white paper were as follows:

- Government committed to consulting with the voluntary and community sector both through the range of channels which existed at present and through *ad hoc* channels which could be developed from time to time
- Voluntary activity support units to be established in all government departments with significant dealings with the voluntary sector
- Each department to make a clear statement of its funding packages for the voluntary sector, with clear procedures regarding funding, criteria, time scales, payments and lists of supported organisations
- Allocation of €507,895 to research to quantify voluntary sector activity and understand its contribution to social development, the economy and employment
- Additional funding of voluntary sector networks, training and support (€8.38m), with measures to support volunteering in connection with the *International Year of the Volunteer* (2001)
- Transfer of responsibility for legislation and regulation governing charitable voluntary organisations and fund-raising from the Department of Justice, Equality and Law Reform to the Department of Social, Community and Family Affairs
- Statutory funding of voluntary organisations to move from a pattern of annual or *ad hoc* funding to multi-annual grants (three or five years at a time)
- Confirmation of the reforms to the National Lottery announced in 1997.

The white paper was not prepared to commit the government to supporting the establishment of an umbrella body for the voluntary sector itself (e.g. along the lines of the Northern Ireland Council for Voluntary Action), preferring to work with the existing, looser, less formal structures. Its failure to address the long-running problem of the lottery (see below) disappointed many people.

Implementing the white paper
Implementation theory is a new feature in the discourse of Irish public administration. Implementation theory confronts an observed phenomenon of government, namely the mismatch between government announcements and what actually happens subsequently. Attention began to be paid to horizontal and vertical mechanisms to ensure that decisions taken actually came to pass. The white paper gave some attention to this problem and proposed an implementation system.

Following the white paper, the government moved in July 2001 to establish an implementation and advisory committee. The voluntary sector was invited to nominate six representatives. Twenty voluntary organisations came together to organise such a process, inviting nominations and setting out a list of desiderata among those candidates to be put forward. This was the first time that the sector had organised such a national collective process in this way. After a lengthy and complex process of consultation, six representatives and six alternates were eventually selected for a term to run until July 2004. The role of the implementation group was as follows:

- Advise on a programme of research, including quantifying the full extent of voluntary and community activity in Ireland
- Agree standard protocols for financial accountability for state funding of the sector
- Monitor administrative mechanisms to underpin the effective functioning of the working relationship and discuss and agree proposals to promote integrated approaches at national level
- Monitor developments in accreditation of training for the sector
- Formulate practical proposals to enhance support and training capacity within the sector
- Advise on its regulatory framework
- Examine areas of overlap or gaps in statutory responsibility in support of the sector and make recommendations to overcome the situation
- Advise on the distribution of the €2.54m proposed funding for federations and networks
- Advise on the allocation of the national lottery surplus
- Oversee the publication of a comprehensive manual of funding and regular updated versions
- Review its own operation after three years

Financial allocations were then formally announced to underpin the putting into effect of the white paper:

- Allocation of €760,000 to support national networks
- €1.27m for community platforms and fora at county level (see discussion under 'Local social partnership' in chapter three)
- Allocation of €508,000 for voluntary sector research
- €1.27m for national committee on volunteering
- €2m for technical and training support for the Community Development Programme
- €2m for national representative bodies.

Implementing the white paper – the immediate issues

Three years after it was published, the process of implementation had slowed to the point that many questioned whether the white paper was, in reality, still an integral part of government policy. Voluntary and community organisations sought, and did receive, assurances from the Minister and senior civil servants responsible as to whether the white paper was still government policy. Appointments in the new government elected in June 2002 were of especial concern for the white paper process. During the 28th Dáil, two government deputies had been particularly critical of the voluntary sector: Éamon Ó Cuiv and Noel Ahern, the former criticising the role of intermediary organisations, and the latter the participation of voluntary organisations in national social partnership. The new government appointed Ó Cuiv Minister for Community, Rural and Gaeltacht Affairs, a reconstituted department; and Noel Ahern as his junior minister. The department was divided into 13 units headed by a principal officer, of which one was responsible, *inter alia*, for the community and voluntary sector and another, *inter alia*, for charities' regulation.

These appointments appeared to set the stage for a relationship of some turbulence. Progress in the implementation of the other decisions of the white paper, especially those relating to funding, was slow (Nic Giolla Choille, 2002). The various funding schemes were advertised but decisions were held up. Eventually, in late 2002, the new Minister for Community, Rural and Gaeltacht Affairs, Éamon Ó Cuiv, announced that the two main funding schemes would be re-advertised, reduced in size and further scrutinised by outside consultants, and that the research funding scheme would be deferred until 2004. He cited legal advice as the need for the programme to be revised, but this was never made public and, apparently, was not even seen by his Minister for State. The first funding was not released until September 2003, well over three years after the white paper had been published. It would be difficult to find anyone who believes that the promised research money will ever be released. The funding for networks and federations was €1.9 million a year for three years (34 organisations) and, for training, €600,000 a year for three years (24 organisations).

Ministers spoke repeatedly about the need to rationalise local development work, an activity in which voluntary and community organisations played a prominent role. They promised streamlining to ensure better value for money and the more efficient delivery of local services. Some have suggested that the Minister had an ulterior agenda on the basis of the public service estimates for 2003. Éamon Ó Cuiv announced to the Dáil that there would be overall reductions of 17 per cent in funding for voluntary and community activities in 2003, even though the overall state budget was to grow that year. Additionally, when existing contracts for community-development projects expired at the end of 2002, these groups would be offered interim funding and a one-year contract thereafter, subject to satisfactory progress over the previous period and receipt of a one-year work plan. The Minister announced that, concerned with the multiplicity of structures, all agencies involved in local development (e.g. community development projects) must now submit their plans to city and county development boards for approval. In August 2003, the three government bodies involved (Community, Rural and Gaeltacht Affairs; Justice, Equality and Law Reform; Environment and Local Government) came together to issue details of the precise channels and procedures to be followed in this process of endorsement, adding a layer of some complexity to a process supposedly undergoing simplification.

The Minister announced that given the tighter economic situation, it was necessary to refocus resources and identify priorities for the continued funding of programmes that benefit local communities. The intervening period would be used to review 'optimal coherence' across the range of the department's schemes. This review, formally called the optimal coherence review, got under way in the course of 2003. The Community Workers Co-operative, in its comment on the review, emphasised the importance of the state supporting community-development work that could 'constructively challenge, critique and inform' and that it was not there to manage local dissent or organise local consent for national decisions made elsewhere.

Implementing the white paper – the broader issues
These developments, many of them dealing with the immediate and practical concerns of the sector, primarily affected voluntary and community organisations engaged in local development. What about the broader issues? Despite the enlightened sentiments expressed in the white paper, it seems that the problems experienced with the immediate issues were reflected more widely. In theory, the white paper applies across all government departments and its principles were indeed echoed in strategy documents and practice elsewhere. Whether this has fully been taken on board elsewhere is uncertain. Although the pre-white paper, the health strategy, *Shaping a Healthier Future* (1994) recognised 'the integral role of voluntary organisations in the provision of health and personal social services in Ireland', its successor strategy, *Quality and Fairness for All* (2001) made no specific reference to the development of relationships with the voluntary sector at all.

A key area of the white paper – and, arguably a test of government commitment – was the decision to establish voluntary activity units in government departments that had a significant relationship with the voluntary sector. By late 2002, apart from the parent department, only one government department had established a new voluntary activity unit (the Department of Health and Children) although several other departments had designated officials responsible in other sections. One department (Environment and Local Government) already had such a unit in support of voluntary housing, predating the white paper. Table 5.1 sets out the response of departmental spokespersons regarding the establishment of voluntary activity units.

Table 5.1. Establishment of voluntary activity units by October 2002

Gov't Dept	Progress on establishing a voluntary activity unit, October 2002
Health & Children	Voluntary activity unit with staff drawn from health services, services for older people, mental health services, environmental health unit, finance unit, child-care policy unit, acute hospitals, health promotion, community health and blood policy. So far, the unit has commented on applications for funding, is participating in the white paper implementation group and meets regularly with voluntary organisations. Overall responsibility for co-ordination of communications with the Disability Services Unit.
Enterprise, Trade & Employment	Responsibility for co-operation with voluntary and community organisations resides primarily in the Employment Services Section of the Labour Force Development Division.
Environment & Local Government	The voluntary and co-operative housing unit has been designated as responsible for co-ordinating liaison between the department and the community and voluntary sector. The unit comprises 50 per cent of the time of a principal officer, an assistant principal officer, a higher executive officer, executive officer and clerical officer.
Justice, Equality & Law Reform	The department has a broad remit and interacts with many voluntary organisations. Given the complexities of the issues involved and the number of divisions of the department which would be involved, the department considers that it would be quite difficult to implement the recommendation of the white paper which proposed the establishment of voluntary activity units and at this point in time. No plans to establish such a unit.
Foreign Affairs	The department does not have a dedicated voluntary activity unit but co-operates with a wide range of voluntary and community organisations. The department has an excellent relationship with Dóchas, the umbrella bodies for Irish development NGOs.
Education & Science	Responsibility for voluntary activity spans a number of units within the department but primarily youth affairs and further education sections.
Finance	The department does not intend establishing a full-time voluntary activity unit. It considers that a more effective approach is to appoint senior personnel from this department to work with inter-departmental and voluntary groups to set up and implement agreed national policies.

Table 5.1. Establishment of voluntary activity units by October 2002

Gov't Dept	Progress on establishing a voluntary activity unit, October 2002 (contd)
Arts, Sport & Tourism	A unit responsible for co-operation with voluntary and community organisations has not been formed to date, but the matter is under review.
Agriculture and Food	The department's main contacts with the voluntary and community sector were transferred to the Department of Community, Rural and Gaeltacht Affairs, leaving the department with minimal contact with the community and voluntary sector and therefore no voluntary activity unit has been established in this department. Co-ordination on matters arising out of the white paper is handled by the staff of the department's management services division.
Transport	The department has very limited involvement in funding voluntary and community sector activity. It was not deemed necessary, considering the department's limited involvement in the area, to establish a dedicated voluntary activity unit.
Defence	No unit. The department provides financial support for the Red Cross and the *Asgard*.

Source: Dáil Éireann, Debates, 9 October 2002.
Note: In October 2002 the original host unit for voluntary and community issues was in the process of transfer from the Department of Social and Family Affairs to the Department of Community, Rural and Gaeltacht Affairs which is now the lead department.

Several government ministers appeared to have problems answering the question raised. Several had appointed unidentified officials to deal with the sector. Others referred to the quality of their informal relationships with the sector – despite the fact that the aim of the white paper was to put that relationship on a more formal, structured basis. Only one department actually seemed to have established a dedicated unit as a result of the white paper decision (Health and Children). By summer 2003, the unit had 14 members drawn from a range of services and divisions within the department meeting monthly and with formal terms of reference for its work. Two others said that responsibility lay primarily with a particular unit (Enterprise, Trade and Employment; Education and Science), implying that this was something less than a formal dedication. Several Ministers took the view that they had insufficient dealings with the voluntary sector to merit such a unit being established, although all did have dealings with voluntary organisations. The Minister for Finance stated outright that he was following a different approach, which is interesting considering that the white paper decision was one binding on all departments and Ministers. Perhaps the most intriguing is that of the Minister for Justice, Equality and Law Reform. Whilst some of his colleagues justified the absence of a voluntary activity unit because of the simplicity of their relationships with the voluntary sector, he justified the lack of such a unit because of their complexity. While some departments might have some legitimacy in arguing that their contacts with the voluntary and community sector were not significant, this was hardly true in the case of the Department of Enterprise, Trade and Employment, or the Department of Foreign Affairs, both of which were significant funders of the sector in the areas of community employment and development aid respectively.

The white paper held out the promise of an improvement in consultative arrangements. It had given clear commitments that voluntary organisations would have structured opportunities to contribute to the policy-making process. So far, it may be said that there have been two such tests as to the improved quality of that relationship. In summer 2001, the government decided to establish the Family Support Agency. Little advance notice had been given. Furthermore, all the family resource centres in the community development programme would be transferred to the new agency. This aroused great concern among the family resource centres, who feared that their focus on social exclusion might be dissipated under the new régime. At least as important, they felt that key decisions had been taken about their role and future without any consultation and contrary to the letter and spirit of the white paper. The Minister, in response, made it clear that he was happy to engage in a consultation process *after* the decisions had been taken, making it clear that the key elements in his decisions were not open to change. During the discussion on the subsequent Family Support Agency Bill, opposition deputies and senators presented amendments to make the transfer of the family resource centres to the new agency optional and to provide for representation of the family resource centres on the board of the new Family Support Agency. Several times the opposition pressed these views to a vote, but the Minister strenuously and successfully resisted these amendments in the Dáil and Seanad. A second such test came with the National Action Plans for Social Inclusion, 2003-5. Here, the government consulted widely, but, the European Anti-Poverty Network commented acidly, the views of those consulted was hardly reflected at all in the draft or final document. The draft document was circulated to a narrow group of government departments and agencies and pro-social partnership voluntary organisations, who were given an equally narrow time frame in which to respond (Hanan, 2003). Hanan explicitly says that the government's behaviour was contrary to both the spirit of the white paper and the European white paper on governance.

So far, the pattern of white paper implementation appears to have been extremely problematical where voluntary organisations work in the areas of community and local development and against poverty and social exclusion. Another view is given by Donoghue (2002), who made a detailed analysis of the relationship between the state – in the form of the health boards – and the voluntary sector coinciding with the period of the introduction of the white paper. She did so at a time of transition within the health boards, with the Eastern Health Board giving way to three regional area boards (northern, east coast and south western) under a unified authority (Eastern Regional Health Authority). Her paper, *Reflecting the Relationship*, confirmed that relationships between voluntary organisations and the health boards focused on questions of funding rather than strategy or planning. She highlighted the informality of those relationships and how voluntary organisations worked through key individuals rather than formal procedures. She also outlined how the broadening of channels of communication could do much to improve relationships between voluntary organisations in the region and the new area boards. Again, the process of change that the white paper was expected to catalyse appears to be slow.

Thus if we summarise the key developments that have taken place in the implementation of the white paper process, they are as follows:

- Funding promised in 2000 was not released for over three years
- Research funding was deferred and is unlikely to be made
- Voluntary and community sector budgets were cut by 17 per cent in 2003
- Local development projects must obtain the approval of city and county development boards for their work plans
- Annual funding was restored in the place of three-year funding
- The role of the sector in local development is now under further examination, with a view to its rationalisation (the optimal coherence review)
- Voluntary and community organisations engaged in anti-poverty, community or local development work find that governmental approaches to consultation have not changed
- *Reflecting the Relationship* suggests that the voluntary–statutory relationship still retains many of the characteristics of the period before 2000.

In summary, it is difficult to reach the view that the white paper has made any significant difference or that the government has followed its conclusions with any conviction. Some voluntary and community sector activists paint an even blacker scenario, one in which the government may even row back on the new relationship heralded in the first place. They mark a sharp contrast to the current state of play between the voluntary sector and government in Northern Ireland. How can one make sense of this strange turn of events? Here, Peillon (2001) may help us. In his analysis of social policy at the turn of the new century, he makes a number of interesting broad observations about the Republic: its semi-peripheral location, intellectual isolation, a government based more on informal clientelism than formal rules, a civil society with some weaknesses and especially a centralising but weak state. The state, he says, 'possesses only low capabilities and finds it difficult to mobilise the kind of resources that would be required for proactive policies'. If he is right, then the white paper may be a casualty of these many deficits of governance.

Legal form

Among the issues raised by the white paper were legal form and oversight: these are now examined. The following is the standard, classic body of legislation governing the legal form of voluntary organisations. It is quite extensive. Much of it relates to the period before partition.

Classic legislation governing charitable voluntary organisations in the Republic
- Charitable Donations and Bequests (Ireland) Act, 1844
- Trustees Act, 1893
- Industrial and Provident Societies Act, 1893, 1894 (Amendment Act, 1913)
- Friendly Societies Acts, 1896, 1908. Minor amendments were made by the Registry of Friendly Societies Act, 1936 and
- Friendly Societies (Amendment) Act, 1953
- Friendly Societies (Amendment) Act, 1977, 1978
- Companies Acts, 1963, etc.

Voluntary organisations as such are not required to register or seek formal approval for their existence or operation. It is perfectly possible for voluntary organisations to operate without state sanction, permission or registration. Legally, those so doing are regarded as executing internal contracts between groups of individuals and are not subject to external supervision. Once voluntary organisations collect or spend money, provide services or employ staff, they do of course fall within the normal requirements of taxation and employment legislation and must be organised accordingly.

First, we deal with the question of legal form. Unlike many other countries, there is no specific purpose-designed, tailor-made legal form for voluntary organisations, or for foundations for that matter. The following are the forms most familiar to voluntary organisations in the Republic:

- A company limited by guarantee under the Companies Act, 1963 and subsequent legislation
- A friendly society
- A charitable trust
- An incorporated body
- An unincorporated association, with or without a constitution.

Each is examined in turn.

A company limited by guarantee

In practice, most voluntary organisations that adopt a legal expression to their identity use the first form, the company limited by guarantee. This distinguishes them from companies limited by share capital. 'Limited by guarantee' means that its members guarantee to pay a certain limited portion of its debts should it collapse, and that it does not distribute profits. In 1993, there were 130,000 companies limited by share capital and 3,500 limited by guarantee (not having share capital). The Companies Act, 1963 requires companies to state whether they have or do not have share capital and to state this on their letterhead. Those who do not are formally called a 'company limited by guarantee and not having share capital'. A company limited by guarantee may drop the term 'limited' from its title only with the permission of the Minister for Enterprise, Trade and Employment. These companies may obtain an exemption to state this and to omit 'limited' on their letterhead because of its commercial overtones. In 1999, 4,739 companies had the exemption not to use 'limited' in their title. Under Section 24 of the 1963 Act, such companies must have as their objectives the promotion of commerce, art, science, religion, charity or other useful object and be non-profit-distributing.

To be a company limited by guarantee, a solicitor draws up a standard *Memorandum* and *Articles of Association* that specify the aims and objectives of the organisation, its means of operation and the founding members, called the subscribers. These articles normally provide for the appointment of a board of directors, who retire on a phased basis, being eligible for re-election. The Companies Act lays down their duties. They must notify changes in name, office, board membership or its objects. The financial responsibility of the directors is limited to €1.27, but they are fully liable for failure to comply with the law in the areas of employment and accountability. Board members have a common-law duty to act honestly and with due diligence. They are liable, under the 1963 Act, for fraudulent trading and, under the Companies Act, 1990, for reckless trading.

In essence then, the governing of a voluntary organisation is the responsibility of the directors elected on a phased basis. Typically, these comprise seven or more people, one of whom is the company secretary and is responsible for the return of accounts to the companies office. The board of directors may be called different things by different voluntary organisations, such as directors, governors, trustees, management committee, council or executive. It is not unknown for a voluntary organisation to comprise a core of directors, those with the formal legal responsibility, with an outer group of non-directors, functioning together as a management committee. This has the disadvantage that in the event of a conflict, the non-directors will find themselves without legal standing. In the case of a legal challenge, the courts would rule the *Memorandum* and *Articles of Association* as decisive.

The Companies Acts require all companies to make annual returns to the Companies Office. In theory, the office should contain the records of all such companies going back to the establishment of the Act. Historically, there seems to be little evidence that these requirements were actually enforced. This changed in the early 2000s when, following a series of investigations into fraudulent trading by commercial companies, new requirements were laid down on all companies, commercial or not. Voluntary organisations are now required to file annual returns within months of the end of each respective financial year, with heavy penalties and daily fines imposed for late returns.

The format of a company limited by guarantee has a number of drawbacks for voluntary organisations. It is a format originally designed for trading companies and is a cumbersome one for non-profit associations. The directors have no direct line of responsibility to the members and it is possible for an oligarchy of founders and directors to retain power indefinitely. Some voluntary organisations attempt to surmount these problems by the adoption of a constitution that establishes lines of accountability and control, with their operation governed by two documents operating in parallel.

A Friendly society
There are three types of friendly society: industrial or provident societies, credit unions and mutual insurance friendly societies. All come under the aegis of the Registrar of Friendly Societies. The format of Industrial or Provident Society (IPS) was designed to suit trading and co-operative organisations. There are currently over a thousand such bodies, including, for example, group water schemes. Organisations wishing to become an IPS must apply to the Registrar of Friendly Societies, who will then determine the application and have oversight of the IPS thereafter. To be approved, an IPS must have a constitution, though it is normally called 'the rules'. Generally, such rules follow a simplified form of the memorandum used for companies limited by guarantee For example, the Irish Co-operative Organisation Society (ICOS) has set out model rules in order to assist approval by its member organisations. There are 1,078 industrial or provident societies, which may be subdivided into various agricultural and distributive categories. In 1999, the government approved in principle the drafting of fresh legislation to govern the operation of industrial and provident societies.

The second form is the credit union. These register under the Credit Union Act, 1997, which is in effect legislation operating in a subsidiary way to the Industrial and Provident Societies Act, 1893-1971. Credit unions are exempt from paying income tax under the Finance Act, 1972. There are currently 530 credit unions in operation, with assets totalling over €8bn (Irish League of Credit Unions, 2003).

The third form is that of small mutual insurance societies set up to provide insurance, assurance, and hardship, sickness and death benefits for their members (e.g. parish priests, Gardaí, sugar factory workers, prison officers). This is the core group of 'friendly societies'. During the 1930s, the Fianna Fáil administration consolidated 65 friendly societies into a unified health insurance society (Barrington, 1987). This might have brought this legal form to an end, but many still survive, some with archaic titles, such as 'working men's clubs'. They are not generally suitable for voluntary organisations, although a small number has taken this form (e.g. Tallaght Welfare Society, Limerick Rape Crisis Centre). The legal form of friendly society includes trade unions, which are also defined under the Trade Union Act, 1913 and subsequent legislation. The Republic has 71 registered trade unions, of which over 60 are affiliated to the Irish Congress of Trade Unions. Under law, they are exempt from income tax on interest earned and dividends.

Table 5.2 is a summary of the number of societies, organisations and bodies governed by the Registrar of Friendly Societies as of 1999.

Table 5.2. Types of voluntary organisations operating as Industrial Provident Societies or Friendly Societies under the Registrar for Friendly Societies

Credit Unions	439
Friendly Societies	982
Trade Unions	71
Industrial and Provident Societies	1,078
Total	**2,570**

Source: Registrar of Friendly Societies, Annual Report, 1999

A charitable trust
The law also makes provision for the establishment of trusts. The principal legislation dates to the period of the British administration and the Trustee Act, 1893. This makes possible the payment out of money for defined purposes and would suit funders or those dispersing scholarships. It is not a form suitable for voluntary organisations themselves, despite some terminology which might indicate that it is. One must be careful of language here. The Irish Penal Reform Trust, for example, despite its name is not a trust, but a company limited by guarantee. A trust is more a procedure than a form: being set up as, or called, a 'trust' does not of itself give a voluntary organisation a legal personality.

An incorporated body

For the sake of completeness, one should mention that voluntary organisations can apply to the Commissioners of Charitable Donations and Bequests to be incorporated. To comply with this, a voluntary organisation must have a deed of trust, a charity number and the opinion of a barrister that it is of a charitable nature. It is then called an incorporated scheme. This is an obscure form of legal personality, used by 25 voluntary organisations.

An unincorporated association, with or without a constitution

Many voluntary organisations function without any of these forms. These are likely to be new, small or rather informal groups. They may or may not have a series of rules or a constitution. Most voluntary organisations now operate under a constitution although there is no legal obligation on them to do so. A constitution is simply a contract between members agreeing to conduct their business in a certain way. Funding agencies will sometimes ask for a constitution from organisations applying for money, as it gives them a better idea of the nature of the organisation concerned and an assurance as to its stability. For a small organisation operating without staff or extensive budgets or exposure, then a constitution may be the only form of organisation required.

Commissioners of Charitable Donations and Bequests

Finally, in discussing legal status, the Commissioners of Charitable Donations and Bequests were established in 1844 to distribute resources made available to them following the winding up of charities or the redistribution of their resources to related causes (the application of the *cy pres* principle). Their powers were subsequently amended by the Charities Act, 1961 and 1973. The Commissioners comprise eleven commissioners appointed by the government (almost all are eminent judges and legal experts) and a small staff. The Law Society (2002) explains that it has powers rather than duties; it is reactive, not pro-active; it may give advice, if requested; it is facilitative, rather than regulatory (the cost of running the office was €401,000 in 2002, giving an indication of the scale of its operation). In 1998, the last year for which information is available, it received 494 applications and made 333 orders, though for some reason these are not formally identified (Commissioners of Charitable Donations and Bequests, 1998).

Status of 'charity', or 'charitable'

The question of legal form presupposes a definition of 'charitable' voluntary action. Charity law in the Republic of Ireland has, historically, much in common with English (but less with Scottish) law, and much in common with systems operating in Northern Ireland (Cormacain, O'Halloran and Williamson, 2001). English law applied in the island of Ireland from 1495 to 1920, with a further subordinate layer of legislation enacted by the Irish Parliament until 1800. Legislation from the 1495 to 1920 period is still in effect in the Republic, except insofar as it has been specifically overturned since 1920. In some specific areas of detail, the legal situation is quite complex, exacerbated by the fact that there is no standard legal code or single statute book in place, so that legal experts must search through dispersed statutory and case law over four centuries within three distinct jurisdictions (College Green Parliament, Union parliament and the Oireachtas) to ascertain the precise legal situation in a given case.

There is, legally and strictly speaking, no such thing as 'charitable status' in the Republic of Ireland's law. However, the concept does exist in various non-legal forms. The Revenue Commissioners will, under certain specified circumstances, provide an exception from certain taxes when they are satisfied that an organisation is engaged in charitable activities. These are defined under English and Irish case law (respectively 43 Elizabeth I c IV (1601) and 10 Charles I c. I (1634)) and under *Income Tax Special Purposes Commissioners vs Pemsel* (1893) as:

- the relief of poverty
- the advancement of religion
- the advancement of education
- other purposes beneficial to the community not included above.

In practice, the last phrase has been understood to apply to organisations concerned with illness, disability, public utility, the environment, sport and recreation. These terms will be familiar to students of charity law in the other UK jurisdictions. In *Incorporated Society vs Richard, 1841*, it was ruled that the 1634 listing was to be treated as analogous to the 1601 Act. The 1634 listing was quite extensive, referring for example to:

the relief of the aged, impotent and poor persons; the maintenance of sick and married soldiers, sailors and mariners; the maintenance of schools of learning, free schools and scholars in universities; the education of orphans; relief and maintenance of houses of correction and the relief and redemption of prisoners and captives; the marriage of poor maidens; support, aid and help to young tradesmen; persons decayed; the maintenance of any preacher or minister of the word of God; and the relief of bridges, ports, havens, causeways, churches, sea banks and highways.

The principle that charities should be exempt from income tax dates to the first Income Tax Act (of the Union parliament), 1799. It was restated when the income tax was reintroduced in the island of Ireland in 1853. The Republic's statement of the exemption is to be found in Sections 333–4 of the Income Tax Act, 1967 and subsequently in 1972 (for industrial and provident societies), with more amendments in 1975, 1976, 1979, 1986 and 1987. These exemptions were subsequently extended to capital gains tax (Section 22, Capital Gains Tax Act, 1975), corporation tax (Sections 11, 13 of the Corporation Tax Act, 1976), capital acquisitions tax (Section 54, Capital Acquisition Tax Act, 1976), deposit interest retention tax (Section 38, Finance Act, 1986) and stamp duty (Section 50, Finance Act, 1979) (Rafter, 1992). Nowadays, voluntary organisations believing that they fulfil the criteria of charitable status may apply to the Revenue Commissioners for exemption from income, capital gains, capital acquisitions, corporation, gift, inheritance taxes on income, stamp duty, probate tax, savings (e.g. Deposit Interest Retention Tax, DIRT) and property, but not for exemptions from Value Added Tax or payroll taxes.

Such applications are normally successful and the organisation is allocated a 'charity number' or a 'CHY number'. Many voluntary organisations call this 'charitable status'. This operates under a guide issued by the Revenue Commissioners in 1996 (*Applying for relief from tax on the income and property of charities*). Organisations applying for a charitable number are required to indicate under which of the four headings they apply. From 1992 to 1996, the following was the proportion of the four headings:

- Religious purposes   7 per cent
- Poverty   12 per cent
- Education   24 per cent
- Beneficial to the community   57 per cent

The Revenue Commissioners do not accept all works beneficial to the community as necessarily charitable, for example social and recreational purposes. The Revenue Commissioners do not consider sport *per se* to be charitable, even if linked to an educational body. Athletic, sports and games bodies apply for a separate exemption. Despite this, the Commissioners will, under the Tax Consolidation Act, 1997, provide exemption from income and corporation tax if its sole purpose is the promotion of amateur sport, it is non-profit, controlled and owned within the state.

Applicant organisations are required to submit copies of their governing instruments, statement of activities to date, future plans, financial statements and lists of officers or trustees. According to parliamentary records, in 1998, 535 organisations applied for tax-exempt status. A total of 359 applications were granted and 16 refused. The average time for processing an application was six weeks. There were 5,106 organisations with this status in 2002.

Under the Valuation Acts, 1852-4, now reformed by the Valuation Act, 2001, charities are exempt from commercial rates in respect of buildings and land used for charitable purposes. Here there has been some case law, principally revolving around those portions used for charitable purposes (vide Law Society, 2002, for details). Under the Scientific Societies Act, 1843, organisations existing exclusively for the promotion of science, literature or the finer arts may be exempt from rates. Charity shops are commercially rated, a situation which the Irish Tax Reform Group would like to change.

Case law on charitable standing in the Free State and Republic of Ireland has been limited – indeed, the Law Society (2002) described the situation as stagnant – and has tended to focus on the definition of 'religious' and 'educational' 'purposes' or situations where part of an organisation was charitable, but not all. By way of example, in 1957 the supreme court restated the 1634 definition in the case of *Barrington Hospital vs the Commissioner of Valuation*. Here, the court ruled that the hospital was charitable, even though some patients were paying fees.

It is probably the case that there are many voluntary and community organisations, especially the latter, who have not tried to obtain such a status. Legally, they are liable for company taxes on their excess of income over expenditure in a given year (this would be deemed as 'profit'); however, there are no cases known of small voluntary or community organisations being so pursued. If they had not organised themselves to apply for a charity number, it is reasonable to assume that they may not have formed themselves into a limited company either, so their existence would be unknown to the Companies Office, the Revenue Commissioners or other enforcement authorities. This is not illegal in itself, providing they are not trading or taking in income. Generally, voluntary organisations applying for statutory or trust funding are now expected to have some form of legal recognition, so such organisations are likely to be small.

There are no known cases in which the right of a voluntary organisation to campaign has been formally challenged or for which a charity number has been denied or revoked (for not devoting its work to charitable purposes). The controversies in England in the early 1990s concerning the role of groups such as Oxfam have not been echoed in the Republic. Having said that, there is a supposition that an organisation engaged *solely* in campaigning might not be able to obtain a charity number (Randon and 6, 1992). One organisation, the Irish Council for Civil Liberties, takes two legal forms in order to address this potential problem: the Irish Council for Civil Liberties Ltd and the Irish Civil Liberties Trust, the latter having a charitable number. In a dispute between the Revenue Commissioners and a voluntary organisation concerning charitable status, those parts of the Constitution relating to freedom of expression (40.6.1) and the provision for the representation of the interest of voluntary social service organisations in the Senate (18.7) would be key texts.

The financial environment
Until recently, there were few provisions in Irish tax law to encourage giving to charities. Most legislation comprised controls restricting how people might lawfully give money to charitable organisations (e.g. lotteries and street collections) rather than trying to create a more positive financial environment. Donoghue, Ruddle and Mulvihill (2000) point out that the government has generally approached financial questions reactively, responding to pressure, not generating pro-active strategies on its own.

In the 1960s, provisions were introduced for tax relief for covenants of up to 5 per cent of a person's income for three years or more for research conducted in universities, teaching in universities colleges and schools in the area of natural sciences; and bodies devoted to the promotion or observance of the universal declaration of human rights or the implementation of the *European Convention of Human Rights*. It is not known to what degree any voluntary organisations may have benefited as a result. Relief at the marginal rate was available for donations to the arts between IR£100 (€127) and IR£10,000 (€12,697) if given to bodies approved by the Revenue Commissioners. Approval to be a receiving body could be obtained from the Department of Finance. Similar tax relief was also available for gifts by individuals to companies for third-level educational projects approved by the Minister for Education and involving projects in the areas of research, equipment and infrastructure, provided the donation was more than £1,000 (€1,270) (CAFE, 2000).

In the 1990s, important changes were made to the tax regime for charitable voluntary organisations, as follows:

- From 1995, persons and companies were permitted to offset donations to development charities against their income tax liabilities (Finance Act, 1995). Under the Taxes Consolidation Act, 1997, this applied to donations valued between €253 and €952.
- From the Finance Act, 1998, tax relief was provided for corporate donations to voluntary organisations with a charitable tax number. Companies donating between €127 and €12,700 or up to 10 per cent of their income were allowed tax relief as an ordinary business expense on each charity to a maximum of €63,486.
- From 1998, tax relief at the standard rate was available for personal or company donations to designated disadvantaged primary and post-primary schools for gifts between IR£250 (€317) and £IR50,000 (€63,487) (according to category).

- Under the Finance Act, 2001, donations over €318 may be offset against income tax liabilities by companies, sole traders and individuals. In order to benefit, voluntary organisations must register with the Revenue Commissioners and be in operation at least three years. These procedures also apply to educational bodies.
- Under the Local Government Act, 2001, local authorities are enabled and encouraged to establish local community initiative funds for community facilities and community development. It is not known if any have actually done so.

These successive changes represent an achievement for the Irish Charities Tax Reform Group, which battled strong resistance by the Department of Finance which feared large tax 'leakages' (in reality, the 'leakage' was predicted to be €29m in 2002). Despite their potential importance, few data are available on the impact of these changes. By 1998, 26 organisations had been recognised as eligible for receiving corporate donations. Donoghue, Ruddle and Mulvihill (2000) suggest that there was a sharp increase in donations to overseas charities when the first set of tax reliefs was introduced – in other words, that the stimulus worked.

The next objective of the Irish Charities Tax Reform Group is to permit charities to reclaim Value Added Tax (VAT), which is currently estimated to be worth €63m to the exchequer from the voluntary sector each year. Value Added Tax in the Republic of Ireland is lower than some other European countries (e.g. Denmark, where there is a universal 25 per cent rate) but higher than the UK. Voluntary organisations find that many of the key products they buy not only attract VAT but the standard, highest rate of VAT (21 per cent) (e.g. newsletters, most office requisites). Rafter (1992) calculated that for several leading voluntary organisations, 8 per cent of their annual spending went on VAT, in some cases worth more than the value of their government grant. The government has resisted the removal of VAT from charities, both on financial grounds (loss of revenue to the exchequer) and legal ones (the sixth European VAT directive prohibits any further zero rating).

As chapter three outlined, voluntary organisations in the Republic have relied extensively on fund-raising from the public. Here, a legislative régime does exist. The regulations for charitable fund-raising are the Gaming and Lotteries Act, 1956 and the Street and House to House Collections Act, 1962, quite apart from the injunctions in the companies legislation to act honestly (Dolan, 2000). For public money collecting, either for charitable or non-charitable purposes, a permit is required from the Gardaí under the Street and House to House Collections Act, 1962. Such permits are normally limited to a defined police area and the Gardaí are entitled to set down restrictions on the number of collectors, the times of collection and the nature of the boxes used (e.g. that they are sealed). Refusal of a permit may be appealed to the district court. Collectors must carry a copy of the permit when collecting (CAFE, 2000). In 1988, the last full year for which information is available, 27,289 permits were issued under the 1962 Act (Costello, 1990). Requests for permits to the Gardaí are rarely refused. Permits are not required for people selling tokens on the street (e.g. €1 for a daffodil). Permits are not required to raise money by standing orders.

Voluntary organisations were and are permitted to run some limited lotteries under the Gaming and Lotteries Act, 1956. The legal approach was to ban all lotteries, but then to permit them under certain limited circumstances. Section 27 permitted the issuing of occasional licences for non-profit purposes and section 28 the issuing of periodical licences for charitable purposes. The 1956 Act took a fairly austere view, which was that gaming was something that should be tolerated rather than encouraged. However, government several times permitted its own lotteries with privileged positions operating outside the scope of the 1956 Act, such as the hospitals sweepstakes (see chapter three). Several voluntary organisations did run lotteries under the 1956 Act and as late as 1998 these raised €10m a year (Department of Justice, 2000). In 1998, 5,786 occasional permits and 1,636 periodical lottery licences were issued under the 1956 Act. Much the largest and best known of these was the Rehab group lottery.

Voluntary organisations may run competitions without permission. A competition is different from a lottery insofar as winning requires skill (for example, completing a slogan) while a lottery is based on chance. Voluntary organisations may hold, without the need for a permit, a lottery confined to their own members only. These are called private lotteries. A lottery held in connection with an event is called an event lottery or a raffle. Such lottery tickets may be sold to non-members, provided that they are limited to a single event (e.g. during a pub quiz) and provided the prize does not exceed IR£25 (€31.74). Any other, wider lotteries require the permission of the Gardaí and, in certain cases, the issuing of a licence by the district court.

Although several voluntary organisations trade through charity shops, there is no dedicated legislation to cover this area. Charities are only entitled to the standard set of charitable exemptions insofar as the trading activity is carried out for the primary purpose of the charity or its beneficiaries. The Revenue Commissioners do not regard most trading of second-hand shops as being trading, since the items sold were donated: they are legally considered to be realising the value of a gift (CAFE, 2000). But, as noted earlier, they are nonetheless rated for commercial rates.

The nature and quality of oversight

'Oversight' is a broad term, covering a spectrum from financial and legal responsibility to the manner in which society expects voluntary organisations to give account of the stewardship of their role, especially of how they look after those entrusted to their care. Oversight is a term preferable to 'surveillance' or 'supervision', the former having sinister overtones and the latter suggesting a degree of control over the autonomy of the organisation concerned. 'Oversight' recognises the autonomy of the organisation, but suggests more than a minimal degree to which the political and administrative system has the right to enquire about the activities of voluntary and community organisations and the welfare of its clients.

It is difficult to give a qualitative answer to the question: how well are charities regulated in the Republic? One's initial reaction is to assume that, granted there are no external or self-regulating bodies, not well. The legislative régime comprises a mixture of archaic, classic and modern legislation, whose impact is uneven. Many voluntary organisations operate under legislation designed for different kinds of bodies (e.g. commercial companies), while considerable numbers may, quite legally, operate without a regulatory framework at all. It is not that legislation is not there: it is, but it is uneven, in many cases inappropriate and lacking in comprehensiveness.

Raftery and O'Sullivan (1999) extended our concept of accountability beyond that of financial probity to consideration of the welfare of those cared for by voluntary and community organisations. Traditionally, there was a popular and parliamentary perception that the problem of charitable regulation was a problem of regulating fund-raising only, whereas it is in reality a much broader question. At the first level, there is the issue of *probity*, that voluntary organisations are doing their business honestly, take reasonable precautions against fraud and criminality (it is possible that the industrial schools were models of probity). Second, there is a broader issue of *accountability*: whether voluntary organisations operate openly, provide government and citizens with adequate information about their work and are prepared to function within a regime that sets reasonable standards (the industrial schools would have failed this test). A good system of supervision will make criminality less likely, but the two are not necessarily the same thing. It is possible that up to now Irish voluntary organisations have conducted their business honestly, but are reluctant to provide public information about their activities. Even a strong, well-founded modern legislative framework will be of little value if the systems and culture of oversight are weak.

The theory and practice of accountability and oversight have not been a prominent feature of politics and public administration in the southern part of the island. Indeed, the Irish Free State marked a long retreat from the oversight characteristic of the British government. During the Victorian period, there was a heavy régime for the inspection of health, social and education services, be that provided by state or local authorities, voluntary organisations or religious orders. Raftery and O'Sullivan point out that nineteenth century standards of oversight were relatively strict, documentation was extensive and inspectors took their job seriously. From 1922, the level of documentation fell abruptly and dramatically in a broad range of social policy areas, not just in industrial schools where documentation almost ceased to exist. Here, by 1929, these lengthy tomes of inspectors' reports had been condensed to a four-page annex in the Department of Health's annual report. The supplement later disappeared and the Department of Health itself ceased producing annual reports in 1957. There was a 30-year gap in the production of reports by the Inspector of Mental Hospitals. When Section 8 of the Child Care Act, 1991 required the compilation of reports on child-care services, these reports were first produced unevenly and then apparently discontinued. Governments showed a notable reluctance to oversee activities in the social sphere. In so far as statutory bodies took the view that the voluntary organisations which they funded should be accountable, accountability took the limited form of providing auditors' proof that grant aid was spent properly and for the purpose for which it was intended (Donoghue, 2002).

Raftery and O'Sullivan (1999) made oversight a core issue in their study of the industrial schools, arguing that had sufficient systems of oversight existed, then most of the horrors they describe would not have taken place. Raftery and O'Sullivan point out that the schools were relatively well funded by state (some even made profits), yet they persistently failed to provide financial details about how they spent the money. There was a showdown in 1951 when the Department of Education announced an inquiry into the operation of the schools. The schools objected vigorously, the government backed down, increased the grants and made no further efforts to obtain accounts. Except for short periods on the initiative of individual officials, there was little effective policing or inspection of the schools and complaints were not investigated or pursued. Even to this day, the two religious orders that ran most of the schools, the Sisters of Mercy and the Christian Brothers, refuse to make their records available. They at least kept their records: on the government side, the records of the only two investigations into industrial schools, the Cussen committee (1936) and the Kennedy committee (1970) subsequently 'disappeared' (Raftery and O'Sullivan, 1999). Reflecting their disappearance, institutional amnesia returned to government in 1999: when a new body was appointed to inspect children's homes that year (the Social Services Inspectorate), homes managed by voluntary and religious agencies were excluded. That this was more than an academic or historical issue became evident in 2003, when a report was issued concerning conditions for mentally and physically disabled people cared for by the Order of St John of God in Drumcar, Co Louth. Residents were locked in at night without means of escape and straightjackets were routinely used (Hennessy, 2003). The report was, to its credit, commissioned by the order itself, but if the health authorities had been aware of these conditions – and there was little evidence that they were – they had kept their concerns to themselves.

Likewise, in her contemporary study of voluntary statutory relationships in the Eastern Health Board region, Donoghue (2002) found that there was very little monitoring of the voluntary organisations funded by the board. In 59 cases examined, 20 voluntary organisations reported that there was no monitoring, eight did not know what form it took and for 17 it was limited to the return of annual accounts. The image painted by Peillon (2001) of the new state as centralised but weak in asserting its authority is hard to argue against.

The white paper on the voluntary sector put forward the notion that voluntary organisations should be more accountable to society, largely as a *quid pro quo* for receiving funding. O'Sullivan (1999/2000) states plainly that many voluntary organisations are 'unaccountable to a high degree' and in the case of the industrial schools, tens of thousands of children paid a high price for the lack of accountability. In publishing his 2001 report, the ombudsman argued that public voluntary hospitals should be brought within his remit. However, few commentators have dealt with these broader issues.

Most of the discussion of the oversight of voluntary organisations has focused on the more immediate and practical issues of probity, rather than broader issues of accountability. Undoubtedly, probity is the more urgent public concern: a 1999 survey found that 50 per cent of people considered charities to be honest, but one-third expressed concern (Cullen, 2002). How justified are these concerns? As the earlier discussion indicated, there is no single, dedicated regulatory body for the sector, the role being performed by a number of organisations covering distinct, although sometimes overlapping areas:

- The Registrar of Friendly Societies, which has authority over friendly societies who must file returns to the registry. Documents returned there are considered public and may be accessed. As we noted already, the number of bodies falling within its remit is small (2,570).
- The Commissioners of Charitable Donations and Bequests. It is not the regulatory body its title suggests, being limited to the application of charitable funds which come into its possession.
- The Companies Registration Office. Here, companies limited by guarantee constitute only a small proportion of its overall brief (about 3 per cent).

- Revenue Commissioners, who approve voluntary organisations for charity numbers for tax exemption purposes (and may deny it if they feel it is no longer lawful) (5,106 approved at present).

As may be seen, only two of these four bodies exist to supervise voluntary organisations, but those that they do supervise are only a small proportion of the voluntary sector as a whole. In the case of the Companies Registration Office and the Revenue Commissioners, the reverse picture is true: voluntary organisations comprise only a small part of their business. None is established with the dedicated purpose of oversight of the voluntary sector as a whole. The Law Society (2002) has pointed out, citing the Minister for Finance, that the closest thing to a regulatory body is the Revenue Commissioners. However, the function of the Revenue Commissioners is to collect taxes and determine exemptions, not to regulate or supervise charities. Even the nature of its regulatory operation was, until recently, carried out behind closed doors. Until 1999, the Revenue Commissioners considered the very identity of voluntary organisations with a charity number to be a state secret, until a change was forced by the Freedom of Information Act. The practice of the Revenue Commissioners is to investigate charities only if someone else draws an irregularity to their attention or as a result of random audits. According to the Minister for Finance, the Commissioners do carry out random checking of bodies to confirm their continuing exemption. In 2001, of the 5,603 tax-exempt charities, 251 were checked to ensure their compliance with the terms of the exemption (in the event, these reviews revealed a high standard of compliance (Dáil Éireannn, Debates, 9 October 2002, question 430). From what we know (Law Society, 2002), 98 per cent of voluntary organisations prepare annual accounts, 19 per cent do so in accordance with UK Standards of Recommended Practice.

These figures tend to indicate a high level of formal compliance, albeit within narrow criteria. They may tell us little about broader concepts of accountability. We do not know the proportion of charitable organisations who actually *publish* meaningful accounts. For those who do, accountants tend to aggregate both incomes and spending under headings that make such accounts uninformative.

There have been several visible individual cases of fraud within voluntary organisations, but these have been pursued by the Gardaí as part of their normal work, not arising specifically from the regulatory regime concerning charities. Recent irregularities in voluntary organisations have been uncovered not by statutory inspectors but by the media and the Gardaí. The arrest of the director of the ISPCC in January 1999 followed investigations by the *Sunday Business Post* and the whistle blowing of volunteers in *The Irish Times*. Goal's funding was suspended in 1997 because of suspected irregularities that were not later confirmed (funding was restored); Concern apologised for passing on details of its donors to a marketing agency, a breach of the Data Protection Act (Cullen, 2002). In 1998, 136 cases were taken to court for breaches of the Gaming and Lotteries Acts, 1956-86, leading to 96 convictions. These figures tell us little, for they do not tell us the proportion of charitable organisations implicated, if any.

Government concern about the probity of voluntary and community organisations has been evident for over a decade, although, as we shall see, it has been remarkably slow to act on these concerns. In 1989, the government appointed a committee on fund-raising activities for charitable and other purposes chaired by Mr Justice Declan Costello (1990), which resulted in what is popularly called the Costello report. This is a summary of the main points presented by Costello:

- Voluntary organisations with an income over IR£10,000 (€12,697) should be required to register. Only registered voluntary organisations could lawfully fund-raise. Registration should be with chief super-intendents locally and, for organisations taking in over £50,000 (€63,486), with the Commissioners of Charitable Donations and Bequests centrally. They should be required to make annual returns. The Commissioners should have responsibility for proper oversight of the whole sector.
- There should be a ban on street and door-to-door selling of lottery tickets and lines, prohibition of payments for collectors, a ban on open-bucket collections and tighter regulation and accounting for existing systems of fund-raising and lotteries.
- Changes should be made to more strictly control the system of running private, occasional and event lotteries and telethons.
- There should be a system for the regulation and registration of professional fund-raisers and professional fund-raising consultants.
- In effect, the Commissioners of Charitable Donations and Bequests would become the watchdog of probity for the voluntary and community sector. They would have powers of investigation, the authority to deregister charities (and thereby deny them the right to raise funds), the power to set standards, the power to require charities to take remedial steps and the power to refer charities that failed to carry them out to the High Court. The report envisaged that charities would be overseen by spot checks, a requirement to make accounts publicly available and powers given to the Gardaí to investigate complaints.
- There should be a new legal form for charities, called Charitable Incorporated Organisation (CIO), along the lines proposed by the UK Charity Commission.

The programme for government for the Fianna Fáil/Labour government of 1992 contained a commitment to introduce tighter controls on charities and street collections in line with the Costello report. Although the Minister for Justice repeatedly assured the Dáil that the matter was in hand, it appears that little if any work was done for the following ten years. Tighter requirements were imposed on voluntary and community organisations during the 1990s, but these were part of broader efforts to curb tax evasion and were not part of the Costello process. Voluntary organisations were required to provide, in order to receive grants, such details as their tax reference and district number; confirmation that their tax affairs were in order; their charity number; and tax clearance certificate. Voluntary organisations employing contractors must be able to provide tax clearance certificates for them and other details of their tax affairs (e.g. reference numbers and districts) (CAFE, 2000).

To resume progress on the Costello report, the Minister of State in the Department of Justice, Joan Burton, convened a seminar in 1995 (*Ad hoc working group*, 1998). She explained that its aim was to work toward legislation that would promote accountability by voluntary organisations (but do so without imposing undue burdens) and inspire public confidence in fund-raising. Twenty voluntary organisations subsequently made proposals to the department as to how this might best be done. An advisory group was appointed and some of its members came from voluntary and community organisations. Its report, called *Report of the Advisory Group on Charities and Fund-raising Legislation* (sometimes also called the Burton report) proposed a national fund-raising authority and register (prohibiting fund-raising by voluntary organisations not properly registered), assisted by an advisory body drawn from the Minister's office and the worlds of finance and voluntary organisations. The advisory group's recommendations were in most respects a reiteration of Costello, with the additional recommendations to include categories excepted by Costello (e.g. religious bodies) that controls apply to bodies which received government grants even if they did not participate in traditional fund-raising methods. The group dealt with a number of specific issues, such as nuisance callers, saturation collections and collectors without *bona fides*. A point of difference was that the advisory committee saw as the watchdog not the Commissioners of Charitable Donations and Bequests but a new body similar to the Companies Registration Office, assisted by an advisory body which would act both as an appeal board and as a consultative body for information and advice. The advisory group also recommended the use by Irish charities of the UK Statement of Recommended Practice (SORP).

In effect, the purpose of the exercise was to accelerate progress on one core area within the Costello report. In this it failed completely, for despite the work invested, the hoped-for acceleration did not take place. Its formal fate

was that it was referred to the Dáil select committee on legislation and
security, where it seems to have subsequently disappeared. The report of the
advisory committee was followed by another review, that of the
interdepartmental group to review the Gaming and Lotteries Acts, 1956-80
(Department of Justice, 2000). This review was carried out by an inter-
departmental group comprising departmental officials, passing up an
opportunity to involve voluntary organisations in the process. About 70
groups and individuals made submissions to the committee, of which four
were identifiable as national voluntary organisations or associated with them.
This reported in June 2000 and proposed a rationalisation of the system of
charitable lotteries, with four new categories (category 1, 2, 3 and 4), graded
according to size and brought within a standard regulatory framework.

In 2000, the white paper on the voluntary sector *Supporting Voluntary
Activity* was published. The white paper reached no verdict on regulation,
announcing that responsibility for the new regulatory environment would
now pass to the Department of Social, Community and Family Affairs. Even
the simple matter of transferring the responsibility proved to be almost an
insuperable challenge and the process of issuing the transfer order took a year
and a half. Meantime, in 2001, the Law Reform Commission began its own
review of charity law. On commencing its review, the Commission had to
start from the very beginning, since little or no preparatory work had been
done in the Department of Justice when it was supposedly progressing the
Costello report. The review sought examples of good practice from other
jurisdictions to determine how they might most usefully be applied here.

The programme for government for the Fianna Fáil/Progressive Democrat
coalition, re-elected in June 2002, gave a commitment to a comprehensive
reform of the law of charities to ensure accountability and to protect against
charitable abuse and fraud. However, no sooner was the process under way
than there was a further change in course. Within months of responsibility for
regulation being transferred to what was now the Department of Social and
Family Affairs, responsibility for the legislation was moved to another
government department, the new Department of Community, Rural and
Gaeltacht Affairs. Here, the new department announced a fresh timetable for
regulatory reform, confirming the government's intention to complete the
process during its lifetime. A consultants' report on regulation was completed
jointly by Arthur Cox (Solicitors) and the Centre for Voluntary Action
Studies at the University of Ulster and a consultation document was in
preparation by the end of 2003.

Besides Costello, several other bodies have expressed views as to how the
probity of charities may best be ensured. These include the Revenue
Commissioners Internal Audit Team (1988) and the Comptroller and
Auditor General (1992). The most substantial recent contribution to this

debate came from the Law Society (2002), which issued a report on the status of charitable organisations called *Charity Law – The Case for Reform*.

This recommended the following:

- The government should establish a Charities Office, Charities Board and Charities Registrar. The board would include the reconstituted Commissioners of Charitable Donations and Bequests.
- All charitable voluntary organisations with a turnover of more than €2,000 would be required to register. The Charities Office would have powers of deciding status, maintaining a register, public accountability, regulation, support services, monitoring and investigating abuse. Larger charities should operate to SORP standards.
- The new Charities Office would be empowered to investigate fraud and misconduct. It would have powers similar to the Companies Office and could carry out audits and inspections, refusing charitable status if appropriate. Reviews of charities would be triggered if they failed to complete timely and full returns. There would be a public complaints procedure.
- Charitable voluntary organisations would be required to file annual accounts and publish them on the Internet.
- There would be a national database of charity collection permits. The Charities Office would issue these permits, no longer the Gardaí.
- Fresh regulations would cover the operation of charity shops and fund-raisers (e.g. requirements to state proportions going directly to charities themselves).
- There should be a new legal definition of charity to take account of the work of charities in the area of social inclusion.
- Charities should be permitted to act politically, though not so far as to support political parties or individual candidates.
- In a recommendation of particular interest in the context of this study, the Law society recommended that there should be reciprocal recognition and registration arrangements with Northern Ireland. Granted the current consideration of the issue, there now was 'an exceptional opportunity' to co-ordinate and harmonise the two systems.

The Law Society made a strong case for reform and that the issue should be tackled promptly. There was a hint that some voluntary organisations might be coming to Ireland from abroad because of its lax regulatory regime. Several foreign charities had begun to arrive in Ireland or are planning to do so (Tear Fund from Britain, *Médecins Sans Frontières* from France). Some had already successfully raised money in Ireland even without a base in the country, doing so by television and Internet advertising (Cullen, 2002). The Law Society took the view that there were many good reasons for maintaining a comprehensive register of charities. Most of those it cited were informational – ensuring that information about charitable work was available to the public, the government, planners and researchers.

The general effect of the Law Society proposals would be to move the Republic closer to or back to UK legal norms. Indeed, its whole report was very tightly referenced within the context of the law of the three UK jurisdictions (England and Wales, Scotland, and Northern Ireland) with broader reference to the other English-speaking common law countries. There was little reference to the European context.

The Law Society not only analysed the legal situation of charitable voluntary action in the Republic, putting forward proposals for reform, but provided up-to-date information on the views of voluntary organisations themselves. The society was forward looking in working into the exercise some distinct questions on accountability as well as probity. The survey went to 2,300 charities (the study does not specify precisely how they were selected) and had a response rate of 11.5 per cent. Table 5.3 illustrates some key responses:

Table 5.3. Attitudes among charities on the issue of accountability: the Law Society's survey, 2003

Question	Yes %	No %
Do you think the structure for registration and regulation works effectively?	10	47
Do you think the current legislation for public collections is adequate?	14	44
Should charities be required to give information on fundraising, including the costs of professional fundraisers?	82	5
Do you think an Irish charities register should be established?	94	1
Do you think all charities should be on a central register?	94	1
Should this publish details of directors, management, places of operation?	87	11
Should charities annually send in details of income/spending?	77	21
Should the registrar annually publish such accounts and balances?	53	41
Should there be a register of those involved in running charities?	82	4
Should there be a register of those disqualified from running charities?	86	4
Should all charities prepare full accounts irrespective of their legal form?	71	17
Should all charities prepare full accounts irrespective of their size?	61	24
Do you think it would be good to have quantitative standards set by the registrar?	44	18

Note: Balance of responses are undecided. Questions slightly abbreviated for reasons of space.
Source: Adapted from Law Society (2002).

This shows clearly that the current limited regulatory environment lacks the confidence of voluntary organisations and charities. There is a very high disposition to the setting up of a formal and effective system of oversight in almost all the areas questioned. The one question where the answer presented an intriguing divergence was whether the registrar should publish the details submitted (italicised, 41 per cent opposed). Almost half the voluntary organisations seemed content to send these details to the registrar, provided the information went no further. There seemed to be a preparedness to act with full probity, but shyness as to the same level of accountability. An initial formal view of the sector was presented in 2003 by the 'CV12' – the twelve voluntary and community sector representatives on the white paper implementation group. The group argued in favour of a new regulatory structure encompassing the whole sector, characterised by a light touch, working in an enabling, supportive way.

Policies to promote citizenship and volunteering

Volunteering policy is an essential complement to policies for the sector and its regulation. It is increasingly recognised that 'volunteering' to work for voluntary organisations does not happen in isolation but is intrinsically linked to civil, social and political values and prevailing conditions. It does not just happen. There is a danger that as society becomes more atomised, fragmented and individualised, volunteering will decline. Indeed, there is some evidence that this happened in the Republic in the 1990s, coinciding with the economic boom (Powell and Guerin, 1999).

There is a long-standing belief that the level of volunteering in Ireland is exceptionally high. There has been little critical debate on the quality, nature and level of volunteering in the Republic. With few exceptions (Hewitt, 1985), the issue of volunteering had been little studied critically until very recently. As recently as 2002, *The Irish Times* proclaimed, in a supplement dedicated to volunteering, that 'volunteering is alive and well in Ireland today and opportunities abound'.

Heady rhetoric to the contrary, the Republic of Ireland has a poor record on encouraging, enlisting, supporting and training volunteers. Faughan (1997) drew attention to these problems when she criticised the level of support for volunteers by Irish voluntary organisations. There was a low level of support structures, volunteer management procedures were informal and little training was provided for them. Her findings were supported by other evidence which showed that well into the 1990s, few voluntary organisations had systematic policies in place for the recruitment of volunteers, exceptions being St Michael's House, Focus Ireland, the Simon Community and CASA (Caring And Sharing Association) (Harvey, 1992). One of the few initiatives was undertaken by the National Social Service Board in 1994 setting up the Social Mentor Programme which had a panel of volunteer mentors to provide specialised advice for voluntary organisations.

The Volunteering Centre estimates that the total amount of time given by volunteers was the equivalent of 96,454 full-time workers a year (Ruddle and Mulvihill, 1999). The centre says that 65 per cent of those who do not volunteer at present would be willing to give at least some time to voluntary organisations (Powell and Guerin, 1997). Despite these positive indicators, some voluntary organisations found it harder to recruit volunteers, possibly associated with economic expansion and growing pressure of time and money. The Simon Community, for example, was recruiting 80 per cent of its volunteers for working with the homeless from abroad by 2001. Others also noted a falling roll of volunteers (e.g. AFRI).

Government responses to promote volunteering were slow to develop. Indeed, a first step was for government to remove disincentives to volunteering. Voluntary work was effectively prohibited to people in receipt of social welfare benefits, especially the unemployed, as such work would undermine the principle that unemployed people must be ready, at any time, to take up work offered to them by an employer and must spend their time genuinely seeking work. Not until the 1990s was this requirement eased when the 'voluntary work option' permitted them to do work of benefit to the community, provided that they had suitable endorsement by voluntary organisations. The Department of Social Welfare introduced a procedure (VW1) whereby voluntary work by unemployed people was authorised on application from the voluntary organisation concerned, without it negatively affecting entitlements. People on disability and injury benefit were also permitted to do light work for voluntary organisations without it affecting their payment. The Volunteer Centre (2002) nevertheless has warned such prospective volunteers of the care they must take in complying with the procedures involved.

A positive initiative was the introduction in 1993 of the Students Summer Jobs Scheme, which enabled students to work with voluntary organisations during the summer. These organisations were given a subsidy to take students on for such temporary work. Although the scheme was a success, it coincided with the removal of unemployment assistance from students during the summer holidays and was politically controversial, criticised as motivated more by a government desire to make financial savings. The scheme ended in 2002.

A landmark in the promotion of volunteering in the Republic was the opening in 1998 by the Carmichael Centre of the first volunteer resource centre in the state. The centre was able to offer support, advice, information, training, consultancy, placement and the matching of volunteers with suitable organisations (it is now called Volunteering Ireland). Since then, local volunteer bureaux were established in Tallaght, Swords, Blanchards-town, Clondalkin, Lucan, Ballyfermot and Drogheda (Kelly, 2002). In November 2000, Volunteering Ireland launched, with National Irish Bank, the *Social climbing* programme, aimed at encouraging people to consider volunteering and publishing a list of 150 voluntary organisations keen to attract volunteers.

To mark the United Nations *International Year of the Volunteer, 2001*, the Minister for Social, Community and Family Affairs appointed a 38-strong National Committee on Volunteering and allocated a budget of €1.27m in support. Membership was drawn from government departments, voluntary organisations, academic bodies, foundations and training bodies. The Minister charged the committee with responsibility for devising policies in the areas of recognition, training, accreditation, widening the pool of volunteers and supports. The committee invited proposals for projects to demonstrate the potential of volunteering that could be replicated by others. Grants totalling €444,408 were allocated to 95 community and voluntary groups and a joint north–south conference was held in Cavan in November 2001. Awards were given to recognise organisations and individuals that had done most to promote volunteering.

The committee invited submissions and proposals on ways in which volunteering policy and practice might be improved. An encouraging figure (given the low level of development) of 67 organisations and individuals responded. The committee's work led to the principal outcome of the year, publication of *Tipping the Balance – Report and Recommendations to Government on Supporting and Developing Volunteering in Ireland* (National Committee on Volunteering, 2002). This was a thoroughly researched, substantial, sophisticated, balanced and thoughtful approach to the issue. The main report was reinforced by a series of informative background papers on accreditation (Unique Perspectives, 2002), international approaches (Larragy, 2001), young people and volunteering (National Youth Council, 2001), organisational aspects (Conroy and McDermott, 2001) and a look to the future (Donoghue, 2001e). Larragy's report (2001) was especially useful in setting volunteering policy in the Republic in an international context. He emphasised the importance of state policies to enable volunteering quality control, and a national centre to promote volunteering accompanied by local centres – features that he identified as common to successful approaches abroad. The principal recommendations were, in summary, that:

- there should be a national policy to support volunteering
- one government department should be explicitly responsible for promoting volunteering (the Department of Community, Rural and Gaeltacht Affairs)

- specific funding should be allocated in the support of volunteering.
- there should be systems for the protection of volunteers and those with whom they work
- volunteering policies should be socially inclusive and representative of all sections of the community
- voluntary organisations should develop systematic policies for the support, training, management, accreditation and recognition of volunteers, underpinned by national systems
- there should be continued research into the nature of volunteering and the promotion of good practice
- there should be a national centre to promote volunteering. This should, preferably, be an independent statutory body with a substantial representation for volunteer-involving organisations
- local volunteer centres should be established, promoted, supported and funded.

Although there was strong support for the idea of a national body to promote volunteering, its location proved to be a point of contention on the national committee. Several voluntary organisations argued for the reinforcement of the existing national voluntary organisation, Volunteering Ireland. Statists successfully argued for the task to be undertaken by a statutory body, a proposal which, in the view of voluntary sector activists, demonstrated state fears that it would lose control over the voluntary sector.

The government seemed to find some difficulty in responding to the *Tipping the Balance* report, which was referred for discussion within the new Department for Community, Rural and Gaeltacht Affairs and to the cabinet sub-committee for social inclusion. The department's strategy, published in 2003, promised that departmental recommendations would be made that autumn. Nothing is known as to its fate in the cabinet sub-committee, nor presumably will it be until the state papers are eventually released in 2033.

Comment and conclusions

The white paper is the key policy document setting forth the role of the voluntary sector in the Republic of Ireland. Despite criticisms of points of detail, the white paper received a positive – if exhausted – welcome across the sector. Until the political change in 2002, commentators on the development of the voluntary sector had been relatively upbeat. They pointed to the development of local and national social partnership, the resolution of voluntary statutory relationships offered by the white paper, the much improved financial environment and the seamless endorsement of the role of the sector by the country's political and administrative elites (Hayes, 1999).

A year later the principles and practices set down by the white paper seem to have come adrift. The failure to establish voluntary activity units across departments was clear evidence that these proposed initiatives had failed to enlist strong support outside an immediate circle. One of the few departments that did establish such a unit was, ironically, the Department of Health, the department that had, it is said, been most resistant to the white paper in the first place. One such unit already existed in the Department of the Environment and Local Government, where the voluntary sector had a key role in the delivery of social housing programmes.

Even within its parent department, the white paper's principles were adopted only to a superficial degree. The fiasco over the Family Support Agency, where the minister made plain that consultation was something that happened *after* he had taken key decisions, was ample evidence. Even when the state organised extensive consultation around the National Action Plan for Social Inclusion, there was little evidence of the consultative input in the outcome. The white paper seemed to have been adopted with little conviction and was soon vulnerable to ministerial and departmental reconfiguration. Of the three strands of the funding package accompanying the white paper, one was deferred to the distant future while the two others were reduced in size and delayed. Voluntary and community sector budgets were cut up to 17 per cent, the move to triennial funding arrangements was reversed and community groups had to submit their development plans to city and county development boards for approval. How these developments squared with the commitments of the white paper to support the sector, move to triennial funding and respect the independence of community organisations was never explained satisfactorily. The sector faced the prospect of further changes under the optimal coherence review launched in 2003.

Some take the view that the voluntary sector in the Republic is largely to blame for the situation in which it finds itself. In his refreshingly heretical essay, O'Sullivan (1999/2000) made many pertinent points about the self-righteousness, conservatism, chaos and irresponsibility of voluntary organisations in the Republic. At this point in time, it is difficult to judge where the battle between the sector and the state will end over the spectrum of control and regulation, independence and accountability, consultation and dialogue, supervision and maturity. It is possible that the principles of the white paper will, against the odds, prevail. Powell (2001) envisaged a situation in which the sector rediscovered a critical, adversarial role and where creative tension between the state and the sector worked for the best of both. Either way, a fresh redrawing of the boundaries between the two appeared to be taking place.

Regulatory issues were parked by the white paper and they remain unresolved. Some of the focus of government moved on to the new regulatory

environment, in line with the commitment in the *Programme for Government.*
So far, there has been little indication of the current line of government
thinking for the oversight of the sector. Cousins (1994) appealed for a simpler
legal form for voluntary organisations that might replace the existing
inappropriate and archaic classical legislation. Leadbetter (1997) also
appealed for simple forms of governance that would facilitate voluntary
organisation and social economy organisations. Whether government will
accept this proposition remains to be seen. There remain many similarities
between north and south despite 80 years of political separation. The
jurisdictions share some of the classic legislation and case law. Although, in
some details, the law governing charitable voluntary action may be more
comprehensive and up to date in Northern Ireland, the two parts of the
country share common features in regard to charitable status, registration,
legal form and oversight. The Law Society (2002) saw this as an opportunity
for a simultaneous, common and co-ordinated reform, one in which the
Republic would move closer to the UK (and specifically English) model of
regulation. Granted the number of charitable voluntary organisations that
operate in overlapping jurisdictions (UK-based ones in both parts of Ireland;
Republic-based ones operating in the north), this would seem to have some
merit. Above the important legal, technical and regulatory issues, the two
sectors would both appear to have much in common in the need for more
effective oversight and public accountability.

   In Britain, the role of the voluntary sector was determined in reference to
the project of the welfare state. In the Free State and the Republic, there was
no welfare state project and the role of social policy was a residual one at best.
Only in 1949 did the newly declared Republic briefly flirt with the welfare
state after the Labour minister for social welfare, William Norton, issued the
white paper *Social Security.* Its fate, Ó Cinnéide (2000) reminds us, was a
timely warning to politicians not to engage with issues bigger than themselves
– and the country returned to its slower, pragmatic, extremely incremental
path of policy and state building – one which did not give much space to
encouraging voluntary sector development. Indeed, the *Report of the
Commission on Social Welfare* (1986), having considered and rejected other
approaches, formally endorsed such an incremental model. Little wonder was
it then that the Republic did not engage with broader issues of the nature of
the modern state in the Republic, the boundaries between citizen and
government, the welfare state and the role of the civil society and a non-
governmental sector. Faced with a lack of government articulation of the
roles of the state, welfare, citizenship and voluntary action, academics sought
to redefine the voluntary sector within what they consider to be an Irish
model of the 'mixed economy of welfare' (Duffy, 1993) or welfare pluralism –
but without generating much of a political reaction or response.

How can we compare the overall situation between Northern Ireland and the Republic? Looking at the formal policy picture, the Republic's white paper is, at first impression, broader, more aspirational; the northern strategy is more concrete and precise. But if one looks at the terms of these two foundation documents, there are many points of convergence. The northern strategy came sooner, doing so within a United Kingdom framework of considerable reflection on the role of the voluntary sector within the welfare state project. The Republic's white paper emerged tortuously, from a difficult political background and from a more constricted social model and failed to quickly embed itself in the political system. Whether these two documents represent a brief coming together at slightly different points in time before the two parts of the island moved apart remains to be seen. European and global pressures for a more mature relationship between the state and the sector may still force a reconvergence and the scenarios currently predicted for the voluntary sector in the Republic may prove to be only a temporary difficult phase.

6

Towards a Profile of the Voluntary and Community Sector in Northern Ireland

Introduction

Rigorous research on the Northern Ireland voluntary sector is relatively recent, with a few notable exceptions. In common with the worldwide increase in academic interest in voluntary and community organisations, new empirical data and an associated analysis only started to emerge in the 1990s. During the 1980s there were a number of important 'reports from the field', and the earliest serious attempts to either construct a database of voluntary and community organisations in Northern Ireland and then to assess their size, fields of activity and resource base date from the late 1980s. However, these earlier attempts were hampered by the lack of an adequate sampling base, difficulties in gathering financial information, and the absence of good analytical tools to make sense of the data.

Voluntary Action and Social Policy in Northern Ireland (1995) was the first book-length study of the voluntary sector in Northern Ireland. Its twelve chapters were contributed by academics and by leading figures in the voluntary action field in Northern Ireland. Its publication coincided with the establishment of the Centre for Voluntary Action Studies (CVAS) at the University of Ulster. Since that time CVAS has generated a stream of new research on many different aspects of the voluntary sector. In addition to generating new empirical material the research undertaken at CVAS has developed analytical approaches geared to local circumstances, while reflecting developments in international scholarship. The CVAS website presents the research undertaken at the Centre for Voluntary Action Studies (www.ulster.ac.uk/cvas).

Research capacity was also greatly strengthened by the establishment of an effective research function at the Northern Ireland Council for Voluntary Action where, since the late 1990s, the research department has pioneered and refined the *State of the Sector* studies, replicating in Northern Ireland work done by its sister Councils in England, Scotland and Wales and has completed a number of other key studies. In addition, the Northern Ireland Volunteer Development Agency has commissioned important research on volunteering in Northern Ireland (see below).

A considerable volume of research has been generated by the emergence and consolidation of evaluation as a concern within the sector and within government. Heavily promoted as a tool by government, pioneering methodological work on evaluation was commissioned by the Voluntary Activity Unit, particularly in measuring the outcomes of community development. The establishment of Community Evaluation Northern Ireland has significantly enhanced the quality of data available on the practice of voluntary and community organisations in Northern Ireland. Another source of data is available from a number of research reports either commissioned directly by government in relation to the development of policy or on occasion conducted in-house.

There has, in short, been a great deal of research on the Northern Ireland voluntary and community sector since 1995. This is of varying quality and was initiated for a variety of purposes. Taken as a whole, it has increased knowledge of the sector to a significant degree although there remain significant gaps.

The main sources of data on Northern Ireland Voluntary and Community Organisations are set out in Table 6.1. The focus is on new empirical data generated since 1995. Earlier material is of historical interest and, where relevant, is referenced in the historical chapters of this study.

The overall dimensions of the voluntary and community sector in Northern Ireland

Definitions
The series of three reports published by NICVA from 1996 to 2002 under the title *The State of the Sector* provide a good overview of the size and structure of the voluntary and community sector. The data for each were derived from responses to a postal questionnaire sent out on each occasion to the population of qualifying organisations and associations to be found on a database of voluntary sector organisations in Northern Ireland maintained by NICVA. The population size sampled and the number of returns for each of the three surveys are set out in Table 6.2.

The analysis reported by NICVA on each occasion refers to the respondents only and no attempt has been made to establish confidence intervals for population estimates. In the light of the relatively low response rate on each occasion this means that trends are difficult to establish, as there is no way of knowing the extent to which the same respondents appear in each survey. However, in the absence in Northern Ireland of any other central charities register, the *State of the Sector* series provides the best available overview of the sector as a whole.

Table 6.1. Some key sources of data on the Northern Ireland Voluntary and Community Sector

Date	Research agency	Study	Nature and source of data
1995	Centre for Voluntary Action Studies (CVAS), University of Ulster	*Voluntary Action and Social Policy in Northern Ireland*	Twelve chapters presenting overviews of fields of voluntary action including a study of government funding for the voluntary sector
1995	Volunteer Development Agency/ Williamson and Associates	*Volunteering in Northern Ireland*	The first of two population surveys of formal and informal volunteering in N. Ireland
1998	Social Services Inspectorate, Department of Health and Social Services	*Adding Value: the Contribution of Voluntary Organisations to Health and Social Welfare*	Survey of 106 voluntary organisations receiving core grant aid from the Department of Health and Social Services
1998	NICVA	*State of the Sector II*	Survey of 768 respondent voluntary organisations in NI
1998	CVAS	*Training and Development Needs of Board Members of Housing Associations*	Survey of training needs of 187 board members
1998	CVAS	*Splendid and Disappointing*	A study of the voluntary action work of 87 churches in the Coleraine Borough Council area
1999	School of Law, Queen's University, Belfast	*Advice Services in Northern Ireland*	A study for the Lord Chancellor's Legal Aid Committee
1999	Community Evaluation Northern Ireland (CENI)	*The Story of Community Infrastructure in Northern Ireland*	Evaluation of the EU Community Infrastructure measure, 1994-1999. Includes 18 case study 'stories'
2000	Department for Social Development	*Consultation document on Funding the Voluntary and Community Sector* (the Harbison Report)	Three studies of funding support this document. (unpublished)
2000	CVAS	*The Voluntary and Community Sector and District Partnerships*	A study of 3 district partnerships created and funded under the EU Peace Programme
2001	Volunteer Development Agency (VDA)	*Volunteering in Northern Ireland*	Interviews with a representative sample of 1,312 Northern Ireland residents

Table 6.1. Some key sources of data on the Northern Ireland Voluntary and Community Sector (contd.)

Date	Research agency	Study	Nature and source of data
2001	CVAS	*Charity Law Matters*	A study reporting on the responses of 82 voluntary organisations concerning the adequacy of charity law in N. Ireland
2001	School of Education, University of Ulster	*Co-operative Enterprises and Social Disadvantage in Northern Ireland*	A research-based study of the co-operative and credit union movement in N. Ireland
2001	CENI	*Evaluating Community-based and Voluntary Activity in Northern Ireland*	Interim report on developing an evaluation framework commissioned by the Department for Social Development
2001	CVAS	*From Welfare to Citizenship: A Study of Voluntary Organisations, Disability and the State in Northern Ireland.*	Survey of 56 regional voluntary organisations. Interviews with a sub-sample of 15
2001	CVAS	Jenny Sproule, unpublished PhD thesis: 'Voluntary Action, Health and Social Well-Being in the Derry City Council Area.'	Survey of 294 voluntary organisations and associations in Derry
2001	VDA	*Volunteering in Organisations – A Northern Ireland Survey*	Survey of a sample of 895 organisations
2002	NICVA	*State of the Sector III*	Survey of 851 respondent organisations plus public attitudes to giving survey
2002	NICVA	*Are You Being Served?*	Analysis of training and support mechanisms for management committees
2002	CVAS	*Community Involvement in Rural Regeneration Partnerships*	A study of 3 rural partnerships in N. Ireland
2002	NICVA	*Scoping the Voluntary Social Care Sector*	Analysis of social care sector based on SoS III dataset
2003	NICVA	*Squaring the Circle*	Analysis of networking organisations based on SoS III dataset

Table 6.1. Some key sources of data on the Northern Ireland Voluntary and Community Sector (contd.)

Date	Research agency	Study	Nature and source of data
2003	Universities of Birmingham, Ulster (CVAS) and Dublin (Trinity College)	*Non-Profit Housing Organisations in Ireland, North and South*	Study of the housing association movement in N. Ireland and the Republic of Ireland
2003	CVAS	*Local Area Partnerships, Social Exclusion and the reform of Local Governance*	Qualitative data from case studies of two District Partnerships/LSPs
2003	VDA	*Committee Matters*	A survey of voluntary management committees and 12 focus groups.
2003	CVAS	*Communities, Churches and Social Capital in N. Ireland*	A study of 12 faith-based organisations in N. Ireland and an assessment of their contribution to building social capital.

Note: This list is provided for reference only and cannot be exhaustive. Other research is published in books and scholarly articles in journals. An attempt has been made to list additional resources in an appended select bibliography.

Table 6.2. NICVA *State of the Sector* surveys showing populations surveyed and numbers of respondents

Date of Survey	Population surveyed	Achieved responses	Percentage response
1995	450	N/A	
1997	3,000	968	32
2001	3,400	851	25

It has since been supplemented by a 'census' of the Sector conducted by NICVA on behalf of the Department for Social Development, which has further refined some of the instruments used. In particular, the census ranked purposes, beneficiaries and activities, whereas the *State of the Sector* survey had not asked respondents to prioritise among the options. More importantly, the census returns were far higher than the earlier *State of the Sector* surveys. This was partly as a result of a simplified questionnaire, but it was also boosted by making a survey response the only way to access a unique reference number that organisations would subsequently have to use in making applications for funding from government. By August 2003, 2,066 responses had been received. The census data thus provide a more accurate assessment of the voluntary sector's own ranking of these dimensions. Indeed by adding data on organisations that had responded to earlier surveys, NICVA has generated an achieved sample of over 3,000 for many of the key variables.

The census and the most recent report in the *State of the Sector* series are based on the General Charities Classification devised by the United Kingdom Office of National Statistics. Organisations and associations on the NICVA database of organisations that were identified as falling within this classification were surveyed. The Classification is set out and compared to the structural/operational definition that underpins the ICNPO (Kendall and Knapp, 1996).

As noted in Table 6.2, NICVA identified 3,400 organisations and associations in Northern Ireland that fell within the definition used. Population estimates of this kind are subject to bias through both double-counting where projects may appear as separate organisations, and under-counting, where there may be unknown others that simply do not appear on the radar of those responsible for identifying the population.

As far as can be estimated this population has not increased since 1998 to any identifiable extent. The 1998 data showed that half of all organisations surveyed in 1997 had been founded since 1986. This very steep rise in the numbers of organisations and associations at the end of the 1980s and the start of the 1990s thus appears to have levelled off. The reasons for the steep rise and the subsequent levelling off have yet to be analysed. Government policy and a favourable funding environment do, however, appear to have been important drivers of this growth. However, the growth has not been exceptional in the light of international comparison from developed economies as diverse as those of the United States of America and the Netherlands (Burke, 2001; Burger and Veldheer, 2001). Indeed Salamon and Anheier (1994) referred to a 'virtual global associational revolution'. It is thus likely that the growth in Northern Ireland was also triggered by factors that are shared elsewhere.

Purposes, beneficiaries and activities
As already noted, NICVA has adopted the classification system devised by the Charity Commission for England and Wales in order to determine the range of purposes, beneficiaries and activities of the survey respondents. The 2002 Census findings are reproduced below. The tables report the numbers and percentages of respondents ranking each category as being the most relevant.

Table 6.3. Primary purpose of organisations in the voluntary and community sector in Northern Ireland

Purpose	Count	%
General charitable purposes	352	10.0
Education/training	632	18.0
Medical/health/sickness	236	6.7
Disability	225	6.4
Relief of poverty	41	1.2
Overseas aid/famine relief	14	0.4
Accommodation/housing	131	3.7
Religious activities	61	1.7
Arts/culture	235	6.7
Sport/recreation	123	3.5
Animals	20	0.6
Environment/conservation/heritage	174	5.0
Economic/community-development/employment	501	14.3
Cross-border/cross-community	110	3.1
Rural development	51	1.5
Urban development	10	0.3
Advice/advocacy/information	259	7.4
Community transport	34	1.0
Other	129	3.7
Youth work/development	87	2.5
Volunteering development	9	0.3
Counselling/support	48	1.4
Playgroup/after schools	18	0.5
Search and rescue	4	0.1
Total	**3,504**	**100**

Source: NICVA (2003) Census: Personal communication

Table 6.4. Main beneficiaries of voluntary and community organisations in Northern Ireland

Beneficiaries	Count	%
Children/Young people	773	34.8
Older people	209	9.4
People with disabilities/special needs	226	10.2
People with a particular ethnic or racial background	14	0.6
Other charities/voluntary bodies	51	2.3
Mental health	43	1.9
Parents	35	1.6
Drugs/substance/alcohol abuse (general)	18	0.8
Unemployed	61	2.7
Victim support	42	1.9
Women	119	5.4
Adult training	44	2.0
Gays/lesbians	10	0.4
Carers	17	0.8
General public	367	16.5
Volunteers	40	1.8
Other	155	7.0
Total	**2,224**	**100**

Source: NICVA (2003) Census: Personal communication

Table 6.5. Activities of voluntary and community organisations in Northern Ireland

Activity	Count	%
Makes grants to individuals (includes loans)	78	2.3
Makes grants to organisations (includes schools, charities, etc)	65	1.9
Provides other finance (e.g. pensions/investment fund)	11	0.3
Provides human resources (e.g. staff/volunteers)	588	17.3
Provides buildings/facilities/open space	341	10.0
Provides services (e.g. care/counselling)	1091	32.1
Provides advocacy/advice/information	526	15.5
Sponsors or undertakes research	38	1.1
Acts as an network/umbrella or resource body	166	4.9
Other or None of these	495	14.6
Total	**3,399**	**100**

Source: NICVA (2003) Census: Personal communication.

In summary:
• The *purpose* cited most often is education/training, followed some way down by economic/community-development/employment, which is closely followed by advice/information and advocacy.

- The main *beneficiaries* are children/young people, followed some six percentage points behind by older people and people with disabilities.
- The single most frequent reported *activity* is the provision of services to people (not other organisations), followed by the provision of buildings and facilities, followed by advice/advocacy and information.

Networks, resource bodies, membership/umbrella organisations
Further analysis of the SoS III dataset was carried out in 2002 to assess the extent of networking organisations in Northern Ireland. Preliminary analysis had suggested that over half of the survey respondents fell into this category, but in a discussion paper, NICVA argues that this result was a consequence of confusion between networking as an activity or process, and a network as a formal structure. Respondents, it argues, may have used the network term as a 'flag of convenience' in the absence of a definition. NICVA suggests the following working definition: 'A network is any formal organisation whose main focus is the promotion and development of the sector itself, a sub-sectoral grouping, a defined membership or a specific issue'.

NICVA estimates that 18.8 per cent of all voluntary and community organisations and associations in Northern Ireland are networks by this definition. In comparison with other organisations in the voluntary and community sector, these organisations are:

- more concerned with the provision of advice, advocacy and information services
- more involved in economic, community development and employment activities
- more involved in education and training activities
- more involved in urban and rural development than other types of activities
- more involved in providing services to other organisations in the sector
- more focused on women, adult education and the unemployed.

Further qualitative research with a number of network organisations was unsuccessful in exploring problems of definition any further, due to a reluctance among the case study organisations to discuss the issues the research wished to raise, which in some cases, amounted to 'incomprehension' (McCarron, 2003: 29).

However, these preliminary findings do suggest that there is a substantial infrastructure of network organisations in Northern Ireland. Many of these appear to be very small and local. Their reported profile suggests they are largely a legacy of community development. NICVA suggests that they are both more fearful of the consequences for the sector of extending the role of voluntary organisations as providers of government-funded services, while at the same time being more concerned that this will happen than are those organisations that are already providing such services. There may be a hint here of the split in perceptions between community-based organisations and service-providers that is much more evident in the Republic of Ireland where the sectoral perspective embodied by NICVA itself has never developed to the same extent.

Location of voluntary organisations

The Northern Ireland voluntary sector appears to be largely constituted of organisations and associations based only in Northern Ireland. Even where these local structures mirror those found in Britain, they tend to maintain formal independence. Thus, the most recent *State of the Sector* survey reported that just under 85 per cent of the survey's respondents were based solely in Northern Ireland – only 15.4 per cent were found to have direct links with organisations in Britain, Ireland or internationally.

Within Northern Ireland, one-third of all the respondents were based in Belfast City Council area (although this figure will include the head offices of organisations that operate elsewhere as well) and a further 9 per cent in Derry. The other 58 per cent of organisations are fairly well spread out, but a slight bias towards the more western district council areas is apparent.

Employees

Based on the returns to the 2001 *State of the Sector* survey, NICVA estimates that 29,168 people are employed by the voluntary and community sector in Northern Ireland (4.5 per cent of the workforce). The breakdown of full-time and part-time employees, by gender, is set out in Table 6.6.

Table 6.6. Employment in voluntary and community organisations in Northern Ireland: full-time and part-time, by gender

Paid	Full-time	%	Part-time	%	Total
Males	5,180	17.7	2,908	9.9	8,088 (38%)
Females	10,912	37.6	10,168	34.8	21,080 (62%)
Total	**16,092**	**55.3**	**13,076**	**44.7**	**29,168**

In presenting these figures, NICVA notes that while at the time of the 1997 survey, 25 per cent of all jobs in voluntary and community organisations were supported by the Action for Community Employment (ACE) scheme, the proportion of the current workforce supported by its replacement, New Deal, remains unknown. But it is likely to be smaller since the New Deal schemes are spread across all employer categories.

The figures show an increase of 13.4 per cent on the numbers reported in the 1996/97 survey. The number of part-time posts reported showed an increase of 25.5 per cent, whereas the number of full-time posts reported showed a much smaller increase of 3.9 per cent.

Volunteers
Northern Ireland is fortunate in having fairly up-to-date comparative data on participation in volunteering. The first survey, *Volunteering in Northern Ireland*, was published by the Volunteer Development Agency in 1995. The second, *Volunteering in Northern Ireland 2001*, also published by the Agency, reported on the nature and extent of volunteering in that year.

Both surveys used common definitions, thus allowing trends to be identified:

- volunteering and volunteers – individuals and the work or action they undertake for the benefit of others or the community (outside one's immediate family), undertaken freely and by choice and not directly in return for wages
- formal volunteers – unpaid voluntary work carried out with or under the auspices of an organisation
- informal volunteering – unpaid voluntary work carried out outside organisations, often at neighbourhood level, but outside the immediate family.

The 2001 survey found that there were 448,116 formal volunteers, aged 16 or over and 759,000 informal volunteers aged 16 and over; 125,472 of the formal volunteers were also participating informally. Formal volunteering had increased by 17 per cent since 1995 and informal volunteering by 9 per cent. In terms of profile, volunteers were more likely to be female (58 per cent), white, married (59 per cent), aged between 35 and 49 (28 per cent) or 50 and 64 (23 per cent), in full-time employment (39 per cent), in the middle classes (55 per cent), to have no disability and with no young children (63 per cent). From 1995-2001, no significant change was detected in the profile of those who volunteer. The survey estimated that the economic contribution of this level of formal volunteering was in excess of £452 million over a twelve-month period, while informal volunteering contributed more than £370 million over a similar period.

The average number of volunteer hours per year amounted to 50,330. This is around 181 for each formal volunteer per year. Almost two-thirds of volunteers working with an organisation did so at least once a month, a finding relatively unchanged since 1995. However, more volunteers were concentrating their efforts with one organisation as opposed to 1995, when people were more likely to volunteer with a range of organisations. The most popular type of volunteer activity, as in 1995, was raising money. Other popular activities included organising or running an event, helping in church or religious organisation, committee work and visiting and befriending people, again largely unchanged since 1995. The 2001 survey showed that over 30 per cent of volunteers were involved in sport and recreation, an increase of 7 per cent since 1995. Religious organisations were the next most popular type of organisation with 27 per cent of volunteers, though reflecting a 10 per cent decrease from 1995. When asked why they volunteer, 41 per cent of formal volunteers cited a need in their community. Thirty-eight per cent said that they had personal reasons connected to their own lives or to someone they knew. A further 38 per cent said they volunteered because they had time to spare. A religious or moral duty was given as a reason by 29 per cent and 25 per cent said they volunteer because they are good at what they do. These reasons were similar to this given in 1995. A range of benefits of volunteering was cited, including personal enjoyment, meeting people, satisfaction with results and using skills and knowledge. A similar range was reported in 1995, though the chance to learn new skills was more frequently cited in 2001 than in 1995.

For the first time, the 2001 survey contained a new set of questions in relation to civic participation. Almost 1 in 10 (9 per cent) had attended a public consultation event and the same number had been involved in raising an issue in person or in writing with an MP, MLA, MEP or local councillor. Formal volunteers were found to be more likely than non-volunteers to engage in all the defined forms of civic participation.

The 2001 survey briefly compared the Northern Ireland findings against the 1991 and 1997 National Surveys of Volunteering (United Kingdom) carried out by the Institute for Volunteering Research. (No comparison was possible of levels of participation in volunteering in the Republic of Ireland.) The 1997 National Survey reported a formal volunteering rate in the previous year of 48 per cent (which is higher than the Northern Ireland figure of 35 per cent but lower than the 1991 National Survey figure of 51 per cent). In 1997, the informal volunteering participation rate for the United Kingdom was 74 per cent compared to 65 per cent in Northern Ireland. The national figure for 1997 was a decrease of 2 per cent from the 1991 National Survey. Twenty-nine per cent of formal volunteers in the United Kingdom in 1997 volunteered at least once a month. This was lower than the Northern Ireland figure of 31 per cent and slightly lower than the 1991 figure of 31 per cent. The profile of formal volunteers is broadly similar in the United Kingdom and Northern Ireland samples, though in Northern Ireland, females are more likely than males to be formal volunteers, whereas in the United Kingdom study there was no difference in volunteering across gender. The age structure of formal volunteers is also somewhat different, with people in the 45-54 age range being more likely to volunteer in the United Kingdom study, whereas in Northern Ireland the most common age range is 35-49.

The findings demonstrate that a range of issues still need to be addressed in areas such as promotion and publicity, policy and practice, the volunteering infrastructure, and testing new approaches to volunteering and research. On the premise that community participation is an indicator of social inclusion, the survey noted the importance of broadening the volunteer base and the need to ensure that volunteers reflect the widest diversity of profile.

Some further sources of data on volunteers in Northern Ireland should be mentioned. *State of the Sector III* (NICVA, 2002) revealed that there are approximately 72,908 volunteers engaged in some form of formal volunteering for voluntary and community groups across Northern Ireland. This figure is lower than that in the Volunteer Development Agency Survey. However, it excludes volunteering that is carried out on an *ad hoc* and more informal basis. It should also be noted that the estimates in *State of the Sector III* concentrate only on general charities and as such, bodies such as state organisations, sports organisations, religious organisations and mainstream schools are excluded. The majority of volunteers are female (70 per cent), which is similar to other studies that have attempted to define the gender mix of volunteering.

As a follow-up to the population-based *Volunteering in Northern Ireland 2001*, the Volunteer Development Agency commissioned research focusing on organisational aspects of volunteering in Northern Ireland, which resulted in the report *Volunteering in Organisations: A Northern Ireland Survey 2001*. The survey, the first of this nature undertaken in Northern Ireland, sought to provide an understanding of organisational practice and needs in relation to volunteers, highlight significant issues around volunteering, and provide a baseline against which to monitor future trends.

There were 895 responses from organisations throughout Northern Ireland. Of these, 82 per cent were voluntary/community/non-profit organisations, 33 per cent were local independent groups and 24 per cent were neighbourhood or community groups. A total of 83 per cent of the organisations involved volunteers. In addition to a range of data on organisational aspects, the survey also provided data on the profile of the volunteer pool. While there is a range of ages among the volunteers, the age range 25-54 represents the core volunteer base for most groups. The gender balance among organisations involving up to 20 volunteers is even between males and females, but there is a significant difference in favour of females among those organisations involving more than 20 volunteers. Minority ethnic groups and those with a disability are well represented in the body of volunteers and there is a balance between those in employment and those not working. However, half of the respondents consider that there is under-representation within their organisations from some groups in society, mainly in minority ethnic groups, young people, people with disabilities and males. Just over half of the groups target specific types of volunteers mainly because they are under-represented in their organisation or in order to match the needs and requirements of particular clients.

A study of the extent, nature and value of volunteer befriending in Northern Ireland was carried out by the Praxis Care Group and published in 2002. Demographic data were gathered on all the 115 befrienders who completed a Volunteer Functions Inventory. While the befrienders who participated were not drawn from a representative sample, the data gathered indicated that:

- the befrienders were predominantly female (72 per cent)
- their ages range from 16 to 75 years, with an average age of 45 years; 50 per cent were between 35 and 64 years of age
- almost half of the befrienders were married or cohabiting (49 per cent)
- twenty-seven per cent of the respondents were retired, 20 per cent were in full-time education and 16 per cent were in full-time employment
- most had been living in Northern Ireland for 10 or more years (94 per cent)
- all respondents were white.

As part of its research initiative on Building Active Communities through Governance, the Volunteer Development Agency commissioned NICVA to undertake a research project to provide baseline information on the characteristics, role and support needs of management committees across Northern Ireland. A sample of 1,600 voluntary and community organisations was constructed from NICVA's database, *SectorNet*. A questionnaire was issued to each organisation requesting information on composition, structure and procedures of its management committee. Each organisation was asked to forward a number of questionnaires dealing with attitudes and experiences to individual committee members. Seventeen focus groups were held across Northern Ireland. From a sample of 16,000, 558 organisation questionnaires were returned (a return rate of 35 per cent), and 1,094 management committee questionnaires were returned (a return rate of 7 per cent).

The Summary Report (2003) *Committee Matters* was published in June 2003 and provides for the first time a wealth of detailed information on management committees in Northern Ireland. In terms of committee involvement and composition, the research revealed that there are an estimated 42,315 places on voluntary management committees in Northern Ireland. This translates into an estimated total of 33,519 individuals. Fifty-four per cent of all committee members are female (an estimated total of

18,200 females). In organisations with an income of more than £500,000, three out of every four chairpersons are male (75 per cent). Sixty-six per cent of individuals serving on management committees are aged 45 and over. Only 3 per cent are aged under 25 years. Only 28 per cent of organisations monitor the perceived religious background of their management committee members.

The most basic message from the research is that size matters and greatly affects the characteristics and role of management committees. While management committees of larger organisations tend to be more structured, they also appear to hold on to their members for much longer than smaller groups. Larger organisations are more likely to provide a formal induction process and have a budget for committee member training and development. The management committees of smaller organisations tend to have more formalised processes in terms of the election of new members but are more inclined to have difficulties recruiting new members. The formal support available to committee members tends to increase with the size of the organisation.

The report makes a number of recommendations aimed at the Volunteer Development Agency, policy-makers, funders, training providers and the wider voluntary and community sector. These are being taken forward by the Agency in consultation with other stakeholders. The report and the action recommended are timely, since many of our informants highlighted the need for improvements in the governance of voluntary and community organisations.

The finances of voluntary and community organisations

Income
An accurate assessment of the income of voluntary and community organisations in Northern Ireland is impossible to achieve. An internal research paper for the Department for Social Development comments that the way funding circulates within the Sector, lack of consistency in accounting standards, and the sheer complexity of the funding environment in which many voluntary organisations operate conspire against accurate computation (DSD, 2003). NICVA also draws attention to the fact that, unlike in the rest of the United Kingdom, organisations in Northern Ireland are under no legal obligation to provide information on their accounts.

Both NICVA and the Northern Ireland Audit Office estimate that the annual gross income for the voluntary and community sector in Northern Ireland was in the order of £657.1m in the financial year 2000/2001. This represented an increase of 9.6 per cent on the figure for 1996/97. A minority of organisations accounted for most of the income. Of the *State of the*

Sector III respondents, 7 per cent had incomes over £1 million per annum and these organisations accounted for 55 per cent of the total gross income for the year.

The NICVA analysis breaks down income by source as follows:

- *Earned Income (sale of goods and services)*. Income derived from the sale of goods and services where the recipient (or their agent) pays a fee. The recipient is receiving a direct benefit in return.
- *Voluntary Income (grants and donations)*. Income which allows the organisation to provide services at no charge or at a subsidised price. There is no direct benefit to the investor, although the activities supported by the grant will generally be specified by the objects of the grant.
- *Investment income*. Income from investments, including dividends, bank-interest and rent (realised assets).

The reported income broken down into these categories is set out in Table 6.7.

Table 6.7. Annual income for 2000/01 among voluntary and community organisations in Northern Ireland by transaction type

Transaction Type	%	£m
Total earned income	23.5	154.6
Total voluntary income	72.1	473.84
Total investment income	4.4	28.66
Total	**100**	**657.10**

The key findings were reported as follows:

- Individual unspecified donations account for 28.3 per cent of income (United Kingdom equivalent, 34.7 per cent).
- Income from central government departments comes to 19.8 per cent of total, but when all government income is added up, its contribution is 37.4 per cent (United Kingdom equivalent, 29 per cent).
- This proportion has dropped from 48 per cent in 1996/97.
- Almost half of all voluntary income comes from government sources (47.9 per cent).
- The relatively high level of government support underpins the importance of voluntary income as a whole (72.1 per cent of total income).
- Investment income accounts for 4.4 per cent (United Kingdom equivalent 22.6 per cent).

Comparisons with the 1998 data set may be unreliable for the reasons already set out, but it looks as if there was a significant jump in the proportion of total income from earned sources since 1996/7. NICVA calculates this as a jump of 25.6 per cent.

The evidence suggests that the volume of voluntary income has remained fairly constant since 1996/7, but it represents a decreasing proportion of total income (down from about 80 per cent to 72 per cent). Most of the 9.6 per cent increase in total income appears to have been accounted for by the rise in earned income. Earned income is likely to continue to increase in importance as sources of voluntary income remain static, or even in some cases decrease. This trend will not necessarily reduce the importance of the state in the funding mix of the voluntary sector as the most important purchasers of voluntary organisations' services are likely to remain government departments and agencies. Even if this is allowed, it is apparent that the Northern Ireland voluntary sector is relatively more dependent on voluntary income than in Great Britain, and self-generated income through sales and investments is considerably lower. To a greater extent than in Great Britain, the sector remains dependent upon government for its programmes and activities. Although the figures are not readily available, it is likely that the relative rise in earned income over grant income may be in part explained by the reclassification of income from government sources. Much of the earned income reported is likely to be in the form of fees for services provided on behalf of government agencies.

The lack of investment income is likely to be related to the largely indigenous nature of the voluntary and community sector in Northern Ireland. Few organisations are old enough and large enough to have the kind of financial assets that would provide a significant investment income. It is likely that much of the 22.6 per cent of United Kingdom voluntary and community sector income from this source is accounted for by a tiny minority of very large organisations that are not typical of the sector as a whole.

The minority of large organisations holds most resources. *The State of the Sector III* survey found that 55 per cent of total income in the Northern Ireland voluntary sector was accounted for by the 7 per cent of organisations that had a turnover of more than £1m. Based on comparisons with the *State of the Sector II* data, NICVA estimates that the median income for all voluntary organisations has increased substantially between 1997 and 2001. Thus, whereas 82 per cent of respondents in 1997 had annual incomes below £100,000, by 2001 this proportion among respondents had dropped to 60 per cent. The median income group is between £10,000 and £100,000 per annum, with a large dip in the numbers of organisations with incomes above that.

Government support for voluntary and community organisations

Government support for voluntary organisations has, by any measure, grown substantially since the early 1990s. By the end of the 1980s, the state was already playing a very substantial role in supporting voluntary organisations. The evidence available is incomplete, but one survey dated 1986 found that 57.6 per cent of voluntary sector income derived from statutory sources (Sheils, 1986, cited in Acheson, 1989). This figure however excludes state support to housing associations and through the Action for Community Employment (ACE) schemes and Youth Training Programme (YTP) schemes, all of which dwarfed other government support. Discounting housing associations, the latter two together accounted for 78 per cent of all Government support (Acheson, 1989).

Table 6.8 shows the growth in absolute terms of expenditure on voluntary organisations by central government departments in Northern Ireland from 1988/1989 to 2001/2002. While this shows an increase of over 400 per cent, some care is needed in interpreting the figures. The 1988/1989 total excludes expenditure on the ACE scheme of £39.5m, all of which was spent in the voluntary and community sector, and a further £17m on the Youth Training Scheme, much of which was spent in the voluntary and community sector. Their successors, the New Deal schemes, however, have been included in the figures for 2001/2002. The 1992/1993 total, while excluding ACE, includes YTP as the disaggregated figures are unavailable. However, if it is assumed that (based on the data for 1988/1989) this was in the order of £18m, the equivalent total for the year would be around £28m.

Secondly, government was substantially restructured following the 1998 Good Friday Agreement. The DRD, DSD, OFMDFM and DCAL were all entirely new departments, and the responsibilities of the others changed to varying degrees. This means that comparisons in the level of funding activity of individual departments are not easy to interpret. Thirdly, the figures are incomplete and are indicative only. They reflect expenditure that has been traced to government departments. Expenditure by non-governmental public bodies is not included in the figures for 2001/2002. As an example, in addition to the grants from the Department of Culture, Arts and Leisure (DCAL), the Arts Council of Northern Ireland spent £5,556,900 on arts organisations in the voluntary sector. In the case of Health and Social Services, which is discussed in more detail below, expenditure now runs at more than £40m a year. But in many cases, expenditure by bodies such as the Driver and Vehicle Licensing Agency is not easily traced. As a result, the total of over £71m should be considered an under-estimate.

In addition, expenditure on housing associations has also been excluded because its size has a substantial distorting effect on the other totals and is not typical of the pattern of other government expenditure.

Table 6.8. Central Government support for the Voluntary and Community Sector in Northern Ireland 1988/1989 to 2001/2002

Government Department	1988/1989 £ stg	1992/1993 £ stg (to the nearest 100,000)	2001/2002 £ stg
DHSS	4,368,072	5,700,000	9,453,372
DENI/DE	3,998,253	4,200,000	6,987,381
DOE	3,113,753 (excludes £47m to Housing Associations)	9,800,000 (excludes £57.5m to Housing Associations)	2,291,525 277,515
DED	2,896,026 (excludes £17m to YTP and £39.5m to ACE)	19,500,000 (excludes £49.9m to ACE, but YTP figures of at least £17m included)	
DEL			15,555,758 614,010 2,500 118,537
NIO	1,495,017	5,000,000	2,427,540 5,538,259
OFMDFM	–	–	11,700,000
DFP	991,000	1,300,000	
DANI/DARD	47,123	1,100,000	2,776,610
DSD	–	–	1,663,800 6,128,309
DRD	–	–	548,530 791,161 (excludes £126m to Housing Associations)
DCAL	–	–	3,550,393
NITB			686,534
Total	16,909,244	46,600,000	71,111,734

Source: 1988/89, Rolston et al (1991) Community Development Review Group; 1992/1993, Simpson, J. (1995); 2001/02, personal communication, Voluntary and Community Unit, DSD.

A more accurate assessment of changes in government expenditure on voluntary organisations in Northern Ireland can be made by including both expenditure on ACE and YTP, on all health and social services expenditure, and on housing associations. Detailed figures on expenditure by Health and Social Services Boards and Trusts for 2001/2002 were not available, but based on expenditure for 1996/1997, this is estimated at approximately £43m. The estimated totals for the three years 1988/1989, 1992/1993, and 2001/2002 are set out in Table 6.9.

Table 6.9. Estimated total Government expenditure on voluntary organisations in Northern Ireland, 1988/1989 – 2001/2002

1988/1989 stg£m	1992/1993 stg£m	2001/2002 stg£m
126.85	171.17	240.11

This table shows that total expenditure in the period under review increased from £126.85m in 1988/1989 to £240.11m in 2001/2002. A substantial proportion of this increase is accounted for by an increase in housing association grants from about £40m to £126m over this period. However, even if this is allowed for, the pattern of expenditure has changed dramatically. If housing association expenditure is excluded, it is noteworthy that in 1988/1989 and in 1992/1993 ACE and YTP together accounted for almost 80 per cent of total expenditure. The distorting effect of this expenditure is particularly evident in the total for 1992/1993. In 2001/2002, expenditure by health and social services at regional and local levels together accounted for approximately 44 per cent of the total, while ACE and YTP have disappeared. Both tables are useful in interpreting the relationship between government and the voluntary sector in Northern Ireland. There can be little doubt that ACE and YTP were major distorting influences in that their presence hides the levels of other forms of government support at the end of the 1980s, which were at a considerably lower level across all government departments than they were in 2001/2002.

Two trends over the period should be noted. Firstly, there have been significant increases in expenditure from central government to cover the core costs of organisations. Not only has the DHSS figure increased substantially, but it has done so while at the same time losing some of its historic core funding commitments to the Voluntary and Community Unit which moved to the Department for Social Development in 1998. The figures in Table 6.8 show that in 1988/1989 DHSS expenditure was £4,368,072, while by 2001/2002 this had increased to £9,453,372. However, there was additional expenditure on core grants of £6,128,309 by the Voluntary and Community Unit in the latter year. If the new investment of £2,776,610 by the Department of Agriculture and Rural Development is added on, the total core grant expenditure from these three sources came to £18,358,291. This represents a substantially increased investment in the voluntary sector infrastructure over the period.

Secondly, the period has seen the consolidation of voluntary organisations as major providers of publicly funded services in Northern Ireland. Patterns of government expenditure appear to closely match patterns of activities and beneficiary groups within the sector. Thus the main beneficiaries are children and young people, and older people and people with disabilities, reflecting government expenditure on social care, training and youth provision. The dominance of service provision to individuals among the activities of voluntary organisations' activities reflects this pattern also.

Funding from the European Union

Structural funds

The influence of European social policy and its associated funding instruments on the way voluntary and community organisations operate in Northern Ireland has been profound. The history of these developments has been recounted in chapter two. Here we ask whether and to what extent these funding programmes have structured the voluntary sector and the range of activities it has undertaken. Analysis of the projects funded through the 'Northern Ireland Single Programme Document' of 1994 to 1999, which identified the priorities and measures for European structural funds expenditure for that period, shows that just under £50m in EU grants was accessed by voluntary and community organisations supporting projects costing almost £97m. To that should be added the sums accessed through the 'LEADER' and 'INTERREG' Programmes and the first European Union Support Programme for Peace and Reconciliation. The Peace Programme is dealt with separately below.

Relative to total income available to voluntary and community organisations during the six years from 1994 to 1999, Structural Funds remained a small part. But analysis of the Structural Funds expenditure shows three main areas in which voluntary and community organisations were particularly evident. The first and (in terms of resources) by far the most important area was the Physical and Social Environment sub-Programme (PSEP) whose measures were largely delivered through voluntary and community organisations and, in the case of the 'Community Infrastructure' measures, were designed specifically with the voluntary sector in mind.

Table 6.10. EU Structural Funds in Northern Ireland 1994-1999: Voluntary Sector take-up of the Physical and Social Environment sub-Programme

Measure	Total value of approved voluntary sector projects stg£	*Numbers of voluntary sector projects*	*Value of EU derived income for voluntary sector projects stg£*
Community relations	17,451,300	74	9,160,700
Urban regeneration	1,713,000	5	1,272,500
Targeting social need (ERDF)	10,095,500	17	4,726,300
Targeting social need (ESF)	4,339,400	9	2,795,600
Community infrastructure (ERDF)	20,780,435	62	11,553,059
Community infrastructure (ESF)	2,874,435	11	1,923,823
Totals	57,254,070	178	31,431,982

Source: summary table from http://www.Europe-dfpni.gov.uk/Upload/Spd/Approved_projects.pdf Only those recipients listed clearly identifiable as voluntary or community organisations are included. The figures are thus a conservative estimate.

In introducing the Physical and Social Environment sub-Programme (PSEP), the Structural Funds Single Programme Document noted: 'The PSEP is conceived as a unique initiative under the Structural Funds specifically focused on tackling the problems of a deeply divided society where significant socio-economic differentials exist both between and within the principal communities.' The perceived importance of the voluntary sector to making progress on this agenda is illustrated in Table 6.10. This shows that the six PSEP measures drew down over £31m for voluntary and community organisations from Europe, supporting projects valued at over £52m. Voluntary and community organisations were the main beneficiaries of all these measures apart from Measure 2.1.2, Urban Regeneration. In particular the Community Relations and Community Infrastructure Measures were specifically targeted at voluntary and community organisations. While relatively small when compared to the funds that later became available under the Peace Programme, PSEP dominated Structural Funds support for the voluntary sector in Northern Ireland during this period, accounting for over 60 per cent of all the Structural Funds money finding its way to the sector.

The second area of Structural Funds activity, where voluntary and community organisations were shown to have carved out a particular niche with little overlap with statutory services, was in providing training schemes for what the Single Programme Document referred to as 'special target groups'. These training schemes remain an important sub-sectoral industry, which is dependent on the European Social Fund, meeting the needs of disabled adults in particular, although other groups such as single parents, ex-prisoners and school leavers without qualifications also feature to a lesser extent. The importance of voluntary sector provision for these groups is underlined by noting that its projects accounted for almost 75 per cent of the total value of those approved for funding under the relevant measure. In all, 26 projects drew down £17,904,748 from the Structural Funds for this purpose. A further £3m went to eight projects under a different measure, Pathways to Employment.

The third area where the availability of EU Structural Funds has had a significant impact is in rural development. As was noted in chapter two, rural community development was a relatively late arrival in Northern Ireland. The evidence of expenditure shows the importance of the Structural Funds in consolidating the development process at local level and in underpinning a specialist support infrastructure during the latter half of the 1990s. Thus the Rural Community Network accessed both capital and revenue funding through a capacity-building measure under Priority Four, 'The Development of Agriculture, Fisheries and the Rural Economy'. Over £2m went to rural community regeneration projects.

The current Structural Funds Plan, covering the years from 2000 to 2006, is a transitional plan and will mark the end of large-scale EU funding for Northern Ireland. The measures that are particularly relevant to voluntary organisations include a very well-funded Measure 2.3 'Promoting a Labour Market Open to All' with an indicative allocation of over €71m. Based on past experience, this Measure will protect the specialist voluntary sector training industry aimed at special needs groups into the medium term.

The PSEP has been discontinued, but advice and information services (a substantial beneficiary of the PSEP measures) get a small measure of their own with an indicative allocation of €2m. Perhaps of greater significance is the €9m put aside for 'community sustainability'. It is both considerably smaller than the two community infrastructure measures of the PSEP and is more targeted. Its aim is 'to create and strengthen structures and broad approaches leading to greater long-term sustainability where the desired outcome is active, involved and influential communities'.

The European Union Special Support Programme for Peace and Reconciliation
The European Union Special Support Programme for Peace and Reconciliation was first agreed at the Berlin Council of the European Union in 1994. Originally designed to run for three years from 1995 to 1998, the first

Peace Programme was extended for a further two years with additional funds to run to 2000. The perceived success of the Programme led to its redesign and further extension from 2001 to 2004. There are substantial differences in both the aims and mechanisms between the two Peace Programmes that have had a significant impact on the ways in which the voluntary and community sectors have been able to make use of the funds. But in both cases, the Programmes have been predicated to a significant degree on the assumption that voluntary organisations have a core role in their delivery.

The Programmes have been innovative in the Northern Ireland context, not so much because over 50 per cent of the available funds have been spent on projects run by voluntary and community organisations, but because they have institutionalised the voluntary and community sector as deliverers of the Programme objectives. This has been through the establishment of Intermediary Funding Bodies (IFBs) within the sector that are accountable to the European Commission, and through the involvement of voluntary sector representatives on 26 local partnerships where they have sat alongside local district councillors and other local interests. All the money divested through the IFBs and the local partnerships has been spent on projects within the voluntary sector.

The levels of available funding are apparent from Table 6.11. Total expenditure on PEACE I came to approximately 350m ECU (including the two-year extension to 2000). Of this, 58.2 per cent was spent by IFBs and by local partnerships. With a budget allocation of €443.56m, the PEACE II Programme is considerably more generous. In particular, both the new Local Strategy Partnerships and the IFBs have had more money than in PEACE I. However, the proportion of the total allocation given to each of the three types of implementing bodies has remained similar.

Table 6.11. Overall allocations between Implementing Bodies in PEACE I and II

Implementing body	PEACE I	PEACE II
Government Departments	41.8%	39.2%
Local Partnerships	14.7%	19.8%
Intermediary Funding Bodies (IFBs)	43.5%	34.0%
SEUPB	–	7.0%

Source: Hughes et al, 1998; PEACE II Operations Programme, 2000.

In PEACE I there were seven sub-programmes, of which one, sub-programme six, was devoted to the local partnerships. All the other sub-programmes concerned areas of activity, while sub-programme six ring-fenced money for a particular type of implementing body, the District Partnerships.

These were then able to draw up funding strategies based on priorities that dovetailed with the other sub-programmes in PEACE I as a whole, each with its own indicative allocation of money. Table 6.12 shows the distribution of the funds available to District Partnerships. It is immediately evident that social inclusion was both the biggest sub-programme altogether in Northern Ireland and the priority with the largest allocation within sub-programme six.

The consolidation of the significant role for the voluntary and community sector in PEACE I was underpinned by the priority given in that Programme to social inclusion. The voluntary and community sector was seen as central to the delivery of the social inclusion measures under the Programme, but was also seen (and saw itself) as a vehicle through which social inclusion of marginal and excluded communities might be achieved. Thus the Northern Ireland Voluntary Trust defined social inclusion as a process that addresses the needs of excluded people and identifies pathways to ensure reintegration into social, economic and cultural life (NIVT, 1999). The NIVT argued that 'Social inclusion is a pre-requisite for social cohesion and in the Northern Ireland context is therefore fundamental to the ongoing process of embedding peace and reconciliation.' In its summary of the impact of the PEACE I social inclusion measure, the NIVT emphasised outcomes that focused on local voluntary action, community-based participation and dialogue, and active citizenship. In this interpretation, social inclusion measures are by definition only deliverable through these kinds of actions. The allocations to the Programme priorities of PEACE II are set out in Table 6.12.

Williamson, Scott and Halfpenny (2000) point out that the voluntary and community sector achieved an unprecedented level of influence over the make up of the District Partnerships established under PEACE I. The broad definition of the social inclusion measures meant that there was an unprecedented take-up of projects within the voluntary and community sector funded both by the District Partnerships and by the IFBs.

Acheson's research into the transition from PEACE I to PEACE II sets out clearly how changes to the policy-frame and to the role and remit of the successor Local Strategy Partnerships have resulted in a significant decline in the influence of voluntary and community organisations over the management of the Programme (Acheson, 2003b). The current Peace Programme forms half of the Northern Ireland Structural Funds Plan for EU funding for the period to 2006 and, unlike the first Peace Programme, is consequently subject to qualitatively more rigorous audit control. More importantly, its focus on economic development reflects the priorities of the devolved Northern Ireland government, which negotiated and approved the total package. PEACE I was an experimental programme negotiated and agreed in 1994, which in effect was additional to the then current Structural Funds Plan. It largely operated outside of existing policy frames. The

Table 6.12. PEACE II Programme in Northern Ireland.
Distribution of Assistance by type of Implementing Body (€m)

Priority	Departments	Locally Based Delivery	Intermediary Funding Bodies	SEUPB	Total
Economic renewal	24.4%	–	7.7%	–	153.67m
Social integration, inclusion and reconciliation	7.7%	–	17.0%	–	107.04m
Locally based regeneration and development strategies	–	19.4%	–	–	86.05m
Outward and forward looking region	4.7%	0.4%	–	0.1%	25.03m
Cross-border co-operation	2.4%	–	9.2%	3.4%	39.72m
Technical assistance	–	–	–	3.5%	13.49m
Total	173.87m 39.2%	87.82m 19.8%	150.81m 34.0%	31.04m 7.0%	425m 100.0%

Amounts and percentage figures have been rounded to 2 decimal points.
Source: EU Programme for Peace and Reconciliation in Northern Ireland and the Border Counties of Ireland 2000-2004: Operational Programme, p. 41.)

circumstances gave an unprecedented and not to be repeated role for voluntary and community organisations.

Bringing the programme within the context of the Northern Ireland Executive's Programme for Government has had the consequence of shifting some of the balance of power in the administration of the programme towards government agencies and away from the social partners. However, it is also important to emphasise that most of the funds available to the IFBs and the Local Strategy Partnerships will be spent on projects managed by voluntary and community organisations. While at the time of writing, less than 20 per cent of the budget had been committed there was evidence of innovative work within the voluntary and community sector being funded.

Other Funding

Lottery Funding
The United Kingdom National Lottery was established in November 1994 and since then has had a major impact on the funding available to voluntary and community organisations. Its means of operation have been quite different from the system in the Republic. It is currently organised through six distribution bodies, all of which have invested significant sums in Northern Ireland. The six distribution bodies are organised on differing principles. Thus in the cases of the Arts and Sports Councils of Northern Ireland, they are wholly devolved, while in the cases of the Heritage, Millennium and the New Opportunities Fund, they are centrally organised in London. The sixth, the Community Fund (formerly the National Lottery Charities Board) is a single organisation for the whole of the United Kingdom, but with devolved decision-making powers to regional committees (one for Northern Ireland) working to nationally set policies. Only one, the Community Fund, is designed to fund only voluntary and community organisations, although all the other five may. In their cases there are no disaggregated figures so it is impossible to establish an accurate assessment of total funding that has found its way directly to the voluntary sector from the lottery. The Community Fund, however, is the largest distributor – by some way if the Millennium Commission is discounted (the latter has mostly funded large-scale capital projects). Up to March 2003 it had spent more than £111m on voluntary and community sector projects in Northern Ireland. The amount peaked in 1998/1999 when £18,818,639 was spent but has declined since then as total lottery income has declined.

The current mission of the Community Fund is to 'help meet the needs of those most disadvantaged in society and also to improve the quality of life in the community'. When the Fund started work in 1995, one of its early decisions was to announce a series of time-limited grant programmes with a theme, which would give applicant organisations a reasonable idea of when their opportunity to apply would come up. The first six main grant programmes covered: poverty, youth issues and low income, health disability and care, new opportunities and choices, improving people's living environment, and community involvement. These were eventually replaced with continuous grant programmes covering community involvement and voluntary sector development, poverty and disadvantage and a small grants scheme. The Fund also introduced programmes covering international, research and strategic grants. A cross-distributor Awards for All Scheme now provides grants of up to £5,000 to small community groups. The Fund has defined its strategic funding priorities in consultation with the sector. Including Northern Ireland, the current strategic priority groups are black and ethnic minority communities, children and young people, older people and their carers, disabled people and their carers, people living in defined disadvantaged urban and rural areas, and people in areas which have not received their fair share of Lottery income. The Fund continues to fund good quality, generalist projects that meet its overall mission. Since 1995, the £111 million allocated in Northern Ireland has gone to groups, large and small, covering almost every aspect of voluntary activity and in almost every part of Northern Ireland. Since 1995, for example, 95 per cent of Northern Ireland's 552 local electoral wards received funding though one or more of the Fund's programmes.

In July 2003, following a review of the National Lottery, the Secretary of State for Culture, Media and Sport published the National Lottery Funding Decision Document, setting out a number of significant changes to Lottery funding and distribution. One of these is that the Community Fund and the New Opportunities Fund will merge to create a New Distributor, which will be responsible for around 50 per cent of the good causes funding. The Document confirms that among the programmes to be operated by the New Distributor will be an open programme of grants along the lines of those currently offered by the Community Fund. An important guarantee is given that 'the proportion of funding under this programme will be no lower than is presently guaranteed, nor will it be subject to any higher control from the Government.' The sector has expressed concerns about some aspects of the decisions, stressing in particular that the monies distributed should be totally additional to government funding, that decision making should take place in Northern Ireland, and that charities will be hard hit if good causes funding is cut as a result of the decision to introduce an Olympic Fund for a dedicated stream of funding for staging the Olympic Games.

Charitable Giving
A survey of charitable giving of a probability-based stratified random sample of 1,000 of the adult population of Northern Ireland was carried out in September 2001. This showed that 78.6 per cent of those surveyed gave regularly to charity and that, on average, they gave £12.17 a month each, slightly higher than the United Kingdom average of £11.82. This represents a total income from individual giving of £146.9m. Interestingly, women were found to be much more likely to give than men were, but the amount they donated was found to be lower.

Table 6.13 shows the six most popular objects of charitable giving in Northern Ireland. This shows that just over 50 per cent of all charitable donations went to medical research and Third World development and famine relief. Of the remainder, a further 5.6 per cent was devoted to churches. In absolute terms, the survey data suggest that free charitable

Table 6.13. The six most popular 'causes' supported by charitable giving in Northern Ireland

Type of Cause	% of those who give to charity
Medical research	38.5
Other medical/health care	5.6
Children and young people	16.0
Disabled people	8.1
Third World/famine relief	11.8
Religious organisations	5.6

donation income to voluntary and community sector activity within Northern Ireland may only be in the region of £64.78m, or 9.8 per cent of total income.

This chapter will finish by exploring the nature of the relationship between the state and the voluntary sector through more detailed studies of three very important industries: first, social care; second, advice service; and third, housing associations. These cases are illustrative of the ways in which relationships between the state and voluntary sector industries have become closer and more formalised as the organisations within these industries have become more professional in their approach.

Case Study 1: The voluntary sector and social care in Northern Ireland

The important continuing role of voluntary organisations in the provision of social care in Northern Ireland during the 40 years that followed the legislation that established the Welfare State has been highlighted. Government policy formally recognised this contribution from 1949 with the issue of circular letter W28 from the Ministry of Health and Local Government. This circular was updated in 1974 following the restructuring of the administration of health and social care services. Both these circulars encouraged statutory authorities with responsibility for social welfare to support the development of voluntary organisations in the field. However, as discussed in chapter two, there is evidence to suggest that the reality was somewhat different with periodic complaints from voluntary organisations about the lack of dialogue and contact with statutory bodies in practice.

The 1980s saw a process in which relations between government and voluntary agencies were being increasingly formalised as the latter steadily became more visible both in the policy process and in practice. The relative and developing importance and scope of social welfare services provided by voluntary organisations by the end of the 1980s is illustrated by the 954 places in voluntary residential homes for the elderly (16.5 per cent of the total places) and the 158 places in voluntary homes and hostels for people with learning difficulties (19.5 per cent of the total places). The growing importance of the voluntary sector in care services for pre-school children relative to a decline in statutory provision is illustrated in Table 6.14.

Table 6.14. Statutory, and voluntary and private sector pre-school childcare, 1985-1992

| | 1985 | | 1992 | |
	Premises	Places	Premises	Places
Statutory:				
Pre-school playgroups	20	643	11	330
Day nurseries	2	75		
Voluntary and private sectors:				
Pre-school playgroups	395	9617	631	15,827
Day nurseries	8	265	64	1,616

Market reforms and the mixed economy of care

The restructuring of health and social care services by the Conservative administration in the early 1990s had a similarly profound impact in Northern Ireland as it had in Britain. As in earlier major reforms to the Welfare State, once again the underlying principles of welfare reform were imported into Northern Ireland from Britain, but given a local institutional form. Thus the principles of the introduction of quasi-markets and the tenets of the 'new public management' were followed without much deviation from the reforms in Britain.

In 1991, the government published a policy paper for Northern Ireland, *People First: Community Care in the 1990s*. This paralleled the thinking in the British White Paper on Community Care, applied to local administrative circumstances. *People First* promoted the use of voluntary organisations as an efficient and innovative way of delivering social care service. Voluntary organisations, it was believed, would bring flexible ways of working and offer greater choices for service users than had been hitherto possible.

The four area boards were reconstituted as assessors of needs and purchasers of services. The former districts (already and in unlovely fashion renamed Units of Management) were floated off into quasi-independent trusts on a similar model to that introduced to hospital and community health service management in Britain. However, unlike Britain, where personal social services have remained a local authority responsibility, the trusts (or some of them) have also been responsible for social care services. Of the 22 trusts that were established, some are responsible for acute hospitals only, some for hospitals and community-based social care services, and some just for social care.

Underpinning and driving the reforms was the reallocation of substantial sums of money from the social security budget to health and social services for expenditure on new services. In Britain, local authorities were obliged to spend 75 per cent of this 'new' money on independent providers. While this was not the case in Northern Ireland, nevertheless the figures in Table 6.15 shows that expenditure on voluntary organisations by health and social services agencies increased by more than 400 per cent between 1991/1992 and 1996/1997. In addition, funding from the central Department of Health, Social Services and Public Safety (DHSSPS) increased from £3.895m in 1988/1989 to £7.775m in 1996/1997, an increase of just under 100 per cent. By 2001/2002, that figure had climbed again to £9.453m. The increase was from a relatively low base, however. By 1996/1997 expenditure on voluntary organisations by state health and social services agencies accounted for 12 per cent of total expenditure on social care services, a proportion that has remained more or less constant since then. However, taken together, expenditure by the department and by the trusts is, by some distance, the single most important source of government funding for voluntary and community organisations in Northern Ireland.

Analysis of expenditure on voluntary organisations by client group shows that old people were the largest category, followed by families and children, then mental health and finally adult disabled people. This order reflects the order of expenditure on the categories by the state as a whole (NI Social Services Inspectorate, 1998).

The general impact of the reforms on the voluntary sector has been well rehearsed in the literature (Taylor, Hoggett and Langon, 1994; Taylor and Hoggett, 1994; Lewis, 1996, 1999). New players entered the field and many organisations were forced to restructure to meet the demands of the new environment. Of equal significance was the way in which the reforms changed the relationship between the state and the voluntary sector. As funder, the state has retained control over both problem definition and costs. Voluntary agencies are invited to tender to provide services against specifications that indicate both the amount and kind of service to be provided. Such contracts or service agreements have become the main source of funding for voluntary organisations providing social care services and as a result funding mechanisms have become less flexible, if more generous.

Research carried out by the Northern Ireland Social Services Inspectorate in 1995 suggested that the introduction of the new funding mechanisms had given rise to a number of significant problems. These were found to range

Table 6.15. Expenditure on voluntary organisations by Health and Social Services Boards and Trusts in Northern Ireland: 1991–1997

	1991/2 Stg £m	1992/3 Stg £m	1994/5 Stg £m	1995/6 Stg £m	1996/7 Stg £m
EHSSB:					
HQ	5.52	3.77	2.44	2.39	2.09
Trusts	n/a	6.33	11.24	16.57	17.50
Total	5.52	10.1	13.68	18.96	19.59
NHSSB:					
HQ	1.42	0.067	0.046	0.226	n/a
Trusts	n/a	1.89	2.66	6.21	n/a
Total	1.42	1.957	2.706	6.43	n/a
SHSSB:					
HQ	1.76	0.149	0.125	0.192	n/a
Trusts	n/a	2.62	6.23	6.21	n/a
Total	1.76	2.769	6.355	6.402	n/a
WHSSB:					
HQ	1.19	0.352	0.918	0.632	n/a
Trusts	n/a	1.99	3.312	5.78	n/a
Total	1.19	2.342	4.23	6.412	n/a
Totals	9.89	17.168	26.971	38.21	40.253

Note: Figures for 1993/1994 are unavailable. Figures for NHSSB, SHSSB and WHSSB 1996/97 are unavailable in this form.
Source: Northern Ireland Social Services Inspectorate: Annual reports,1991/92, 1992/93, 1994/95,1995/96 and 1996/97

from complaints about a lack of understanding of the nature of voluntary organisations and the need to preserve their character, complex and bureaucratic procedures, and an inability to influence the priorities against which organisations were expected to bid for services. In addition, there were persistent complaints about under-funding and late payment. The SSI research found that many organisations only had sufficient income to fund staff salaries and promotion costs, but were unable to adequately fund activities such as staff training and development work.

More recent research shows that many of these problems have persisted. Acheson found that voluntary organisations still faced significant problems in underfunding, a perceived attitude among statutory organisations that voluntary agencies could get by in ways not open to the state and a feeling of extreme vulnerability among organisations that did not have access to their own free reserves (Acheson, 2003a). However, in a case study of relations between the state and voluntary agencies in one health and social services trust, he also found evidence that relationships were often strong and mutually supportive notwithstanding continuing and persistent problems in under-funding. This was particularly found where there was agreement on both the nature of the social need to be addressed and the appropriateness of the voluntary agency's response.

Level of dependency on the state
Underpinning these perceptions appears to be a very high level of reliance on state funding among voluntary organisations providing social care. This reflects the generally high levels of dependency on the state that have already been noted. It may, however, be a particular problem in this field because of the substantial amount of government funding available and the correspondingly high degree of participation by voluntary organisations in the delivery of state-funded social care services. The SSI research found that among the organisations surveyed, income from central government and the health and social services boards and trusts, together on average amounted to 55 per cent of total income. In contrast voluntary income from donations, membership fees and general fund-raising contributed 18 per cent of total income; only 8 per cent of income derived from the sale of goods and services. Based on a larger sample, the Northern Ireland Council for Voluntary Action found that in 1996/97, 76 per cent of voluntary sector income for social care services in Northern Ireland was in the form of grants and donations. By far the largest proportion of this (59 per cent) was in direct government grants or contracts (NICVA, 1998).

In his later study of a smaller sample of voluntary organisations specialising in adult disability services, Acheson found that almost half his sample received income from health and social services. Of these more than half reported this as the most or second most important income source. Acheson's study is useful for its analysis of the way government expenditure on social care shapes the voluntary sector's range of responses in the social care field as a whole. He found an inverse relationship between levels of government support and degrees of user participation and the extent to which organisations espoused change goals. Government expenditure was largely focused on a minority of large service-providing organisations that generally addressed traditionally conceived categories of need in traditional ways. He concludes that the funding environment is dominated by a paradigm of need and the voluntary sector's role in the relation to that need that largely precludes innovation and change. The further a voluntary organisation positioned itself from that dominant view, the more difficult it finds it to raise income.

The central place of social care activities in the Northern Ireland voluntary sector is emphasised by NICVA's findings that of the 972 respondents to the

State of the Sector III survey, 716 (73.6 per cent) reported that one or more of their beneficiary groups were drawn from the following:

- children/young people
- older people
- disabled people
- mental health
- parents
- drug/substance abuse
- carers.

The reach of this activity into the broader Northern Ireland community is emphasised in the SSI study. This estimated that the 64 organisations in the study that reported providing services reached almost 600,000 people (or well over a third of the whole population).

NICVA defines the social care sector as comprising organisations serving the above beneficiary groups. This very broad definitional approach has the advantage of including those organisations that self-define their beneficiaries and their activities as relating to social care, rather than being defined through recognition by the state. However, in departing entirely from administrative and legislative definitions of what comprises social care, the NICVA approach may include organisations and activities that belong in different policy frames. This may be the explanation behind the finding that the most cited beneficiary group in the NICVA study was children/young people, while government statistics show that older people are the main beneficiary group among those organisations funded through the Health and Social Care system. The children/young people beneficiary group will also receive funding through both the Departments of Education and of Employment and Learning. These departments may be more significant funders than Health and Social Services in this area.

Nevertheless, the NICVA evidence provides useful corroboration of other findings on the range of activities undertaken by voluntary organisations in the social care field. Across all the beneficiary categories, NICVA found that the direct provision of services to individuals was the most important activity. This ranged from 100 per cent of respondents citing people with disabilities as a beneficiary group to 77 per cent of those citing carers as a beneficiary group. Providing advice, advocacy and/or information was almost as popular an activity, cited by at least 75 per cent of organisations in the survey across all but one of the beneficiary categories. The findings reflect that, in practice, services very often include an advice and information component.

The NICVA study also identified the importance of the intermediary function in this field. Activities relating to this role were cited by between just under one-fifth and just over one-third of all respondents across all beneficiary categories.

The SSI study asked organisations to indicate what were their primary, secondary and tertiary roles. While the categories are not equivalent, the findings reflect the NICVA findings closely. They show that just over half of the organisations in the study provided direct services as their primary role, with a further 17 per cent reporting this as a significant function. A further 30 per cent reported their main role as training/information/research/advice/advocacy. In addition, a further 40 per cent reported this as either a secondary or tertiary role. Taken together at 70 per cent of respondents, this is close to the NICVA finding of 75 per cent of respondents citing advocacy/advice and/or information as an activity. It once again emphasises the pattern of service provision being closely allied to advice and advocacy.

The SSI data also emphasise the importance of the intermediary or 'umbrella' function. Over one-fifth (22 per cent) cited this as either their main or a significant role. Together, those that described themselves as intermediary bodies reported a total membership of 5,187 organisations. A larger number (42 per cent) described themselves as regional bodies with local committee-based structures. Together they reported 621 local branches.

Further corroboration of this pattern of activity in the social care field is provided by the study conducted by Acheson who found that 75 per cent of his sample of 56 organisations concerned with adult disabled people provided services, but that 45 per cent of these were also involved in campaigning activities. Just over half of the respondents in this study were self-help organisations, but most of these (72.4 per cent) also provided services. Acheson also found that 28 per cent of his respondents reported an intermediary function.

The three studies cited here thus provide a composite picture of very extensive involvement in social care among voluntary organisations in Northern Ireland. Most of this activity is in the provision of direct services to individuals in identifiable beneficiary categories, but this is heavily overlaid by a commitment to advocacy/advice and information. While most of these organisations operate at local level, there is clear evidence that the field as a whole appears well networked. Between one quarter and one third of regional organisations report fulfilling an intermediary role, providing services that support large numbers of local organisations. Very little is known about the intensity of this support. A substantial part of the social care sector also appears to be structured in regional support organisations with a local branch structure.

However, Acheson draws attention to an important facet of voluntary organisation activity in this field. He found two contradictory sides to the overall picture. On the one hand were sizeable numbers of service-providing voluntary organisations, well resourced by the state that appeared to have limited room for manoeuvre outside their recognised service role. Some of these organisations have grown greatly in relative size since the early 1990s. Among the most notable are Extra Care for the Elderly and the Praxis Care Group, both of which have multi-million pound turnovers and employ hundreds of staff. Others such as Age Concern and MENCAP have added substantial service arms, sometimes including commercial activities such as selling insurance, to their existing portfolios. A few British-based organisations have started operations in Northern Ireland for the first time including the Royal National Institute for the Deaf (RNID). Older indigenous organisations have also benefited, notably Bryson House and the Institute for the Disabled (formerly the Cripples Institute which was founded in 1874).

On the other hand, Acheson found that there has also been an upsurge in voluntary action, based on self-help particularly from the middle of the 1980s onwards. While a minority of these new organisations had developed new types of services, more had retained a core orientation towards achieving social change, focusing on campaigning and information and advice giving. These organisations showed a greater commitment to user participation and were generally smaller than those more focused on service provision. In addition, however, there were a number of smaller self-help associations, run on an entirely voluntary basis with very little money and a very tenuous relationship to formal health and social care systems.

The importance of this latter phenomenon is emphasised in research by Sproule (2001) in the Derry City Council area. Of the 294 organisations and associations she identified, she classified almost 40 per cent as either health and social care related or self-help. In addition there were a number of parent and toddler groups that in her taxonomy were classified as recreation and education.

The growing recognition of the importance of small-scale and local voluntary action around health issues is represented by the rapid development of the Community Development and Health Network. A membership organisation, it was founded in 1995 and by 2001 reported a membership of 368, 60 per cent of which was made up from voluntary and community organisations. It is perhaps unusual in this kind of networking organisation that more than a third of its members were state bodies. This is reflected in its management committee where three of those currently serving are community development managers in health and social services trusts. It also has a small number of individual members. The Network has three strategic aims:

- to develop a significant regional intersectional membership organisation
  that is complementary, democratic, member led, active and influential
- to promote awareness of the links between poverty, inequality and health
  and how community development is an appropriate and valid method to
  support action on health inequalities
- to facilitate the development, application and understanding of tools for
  action in support of community development and health practice

Case Study 2: Voluntary organisations and advice services in Northern Ireland

In Northern Ireland organisations within the voluntary and community
sector provide most community-based information and advice services. It
shares this feature with the rest of the United Kingdom, but this sets it apart
from the Republic of Ireland where this function is largely discharged through
a network of local information centres throughout the state managed by a
state body, Comhairle (formerly the National Social Services Board). The
advice services industry in Northern Ireland has been singled out for
treatment in more detail as it illustrates some of the ways in which voluntary
and community organisations have developed within a different
interpretation of the proper division between the activities of the state and
the voluntary sector in the two jurisdictions in Ireland. It is also of interest
because it is a good illustration of how voluntary organisations have separated
out from their equivalents in Britain, leaving a structure that in many respects
mirrors that to be found in the rest of the United Kingdom, but which is
nevertheless institutionally distinct.

Structure
The advice industry in Northern Ireland is now highly structured, consisting
of two parallel federal structures and a specialist legal and training service, the
three of which share a joint strategic body, the Advice Services Alliance, able
to negotiate with government on key strategic issues.

The two federal structures of advice agencies are at the sharp end of service
delivery. They consist of the Northern Ireland Association of Citizens'
Advice Bureaux (NIACAB) and the Association of Independent Advice
Centres (AIAC). NIACAB provides a number of central services to a
network of 28 local advice bureaux throughout Northern Ireland, offering
services from 87 different outlets. The local bureaux are all formally
independent organisations with their own management committees having a
franchise relationship with the regional body. This means they may style
themselves as Citizens' Advice Bureaux in return for agreeing to use the
central information system, now based on a wide area network IT system, and

buying into a centrally managed quality assurance system. Membership of the Federation is renewable every three years. To remain members, local associations have to show they can meet national standards in respect to the quality of advice, staff training and premises. NIACAB has in turn a similar relationship with the National Association of Citizens' Advice Bureaux in London, enabling it to use the United Kingdom wide CAB logo and image and to access the national information system to support advice giving which it then tailors for Northern Ireland.

AIAC was established in 1995 to provide support for, and to promote and develop the work of, independent advice agencies in Northern Ireland. It currently reports having 73 members, made up of regional and local organisations, generalists and specialists. Many of its members provide other services in addition to advice, typically to a section of the population. These members include, for example, the Chinese Welfare Association, Age Concern, MENCAP and Disability Action. Other members are local community-based organisations and are an aspect of the growing importance of community development. Members sign up to a set of principles, but are otherwise independent. These principles include among others a commitment to give free and independent advice, which is free from statutory or private control and is both non-party political and non-sectarian in nature, and advice services that are aimed specifically towards overcoming social exclusion. It provides a range of professional services including quality assurance, accredited training in advice and guidance, IT support, and some research and social policy work.

The third leg of the advice services industry in Northern Ireland is the Law Centre (NI). The Law Centre provides specialist legal services free to the advice sector in Northern Ireland and to other members through an advice line and referral service. It also provides specialist legal support to other advice agencies in relevant areas of law as well as training and information services. Almost all the local Citizens' Advice Bureaux (CABx) and all the members of AIAC are members. Its core work is a second-tier specialist case-work service staffed by full-time, salaried, legally qualified workers.

These three networks are constituent members of the Advice Services Alliance. Established in 1991, its role is to promote the development of advice services, to act as a forum for discussion among voluntary sector advice agencies and to encourage co-operation.

Workload

According to AIAC's own research, in 2001, a survey of members revealed that during the previous year the 54 respondents indicated that they saw 99,953 people and dealt with 186,050 enquiries. In 2000/2001 the network of CABx saw 145,325 people and dealt with 186,050 enquiries. Social security related enquiries were the biggest single category of enquiries, comprising 55 per cent of CABx and 67 per cent of enquiries among generalist advice agencies that were members of AIAC in 2001. Among the specialist members of AIAC a broader range of issues were dealt with; here social security accounted for 35 per cent of their workload. Other main categories included general consumer advice, particularly at CABx, and employment and housing. The Law Centre's legal casework service covers social security, community care, housing, employment and immigration. In 2001/2002 the Centre had 439 current cases and made 276 appearances in courts and tribunals. Social security issues accounted for 43 per cent of the Law Centre's enquiries. It is notable that immigration equalled the relative importance of employment matters in the year's work, both accounting for 15 per cent of enquiries.

Lundy and Glenn (1999) computed average figures of workload across the industry in 2001. Based on the results of their survey of both CABx and other local advice agencies, they estimated that the industry as a whole deals with 480,375 enquiries a year, or at least one enquiry per 3.3 people in Northern Ireland (including children). The authors note that this represents a 100 per cent increase in the level of service provided in 1990. They suggest that this was driven in part by an increase in demand, but also by a significant change in the capacity of advice organisations to meet that demand.

Funding
In 1991 the General Consumer Council in Northern Ireland published a report on the adequacy of advice services. The report found deficiencies in advice provision and attributed this to a lack of a 'co-ordinated and coherent' funding policy (NIACAB 2001/2). As a result the Department of Education, which was then responsible for funding of local advice as part of its responsibility for supporting the community services budgets of district councils, undertook a wide-ranging review. Following the transfer of responsibility for community services to the new Voluntary Activity Unit in 1995, substantial changes were made to the mechanisms for supporting district councils alongside the centralising of funding of the regional support organisations with the VAU (then part of the DHSS). As a result, more money was made available to developing local advice services through the support of district councils, strengthening relationships at local level and giving advice agencies a much more certain platform on which to plan and manage their work. The funding streams that were available to local advice agencies towards the end of the 1990s are shown in Table 6.16. This confirms the importance of district councils as core funders, accounting for 42 per cent of the funding available in 1997/1998. It also shows that a substantial proportion of the centres surveyed acquired project funding from health and

social services trusts and it shows the relatively large impact of the availability of project funding from the National Lottery Charities Board. The impact of funds from the two urban regeneration initiatives in Northern Ireland, Making Belfast Work (MBW) and the Londonderry Initiative (LI), should also be noted. By definition, this money is only available in Belfast and Derry; its availability has reinforced the dominance of the two cities in the allocation of resources. Lundy and Glenn note, for example that of the £395,600 available to district councils from central government to support advice services, £115,285 (almost 30 per cent) was allocated to Belfast City Council alone.

However, it also shows the exceptional place of the social inclusion measure of the first EU Programme for Peace and Reconciliation administered by the Northern Ireland Voluntary Trust. Together with the smaller amount available from the District Partnerships established under the same programme, this accounted for 18 per cent of total income for the year. With the final end of this programme in 1999, none of this money is now available on equivalent terms.

Table 6.16. Levels and sources of funding in 31 local general advice centres in Northern Ireland in 1997/1998

Funder	Nos of Centres	Total amount stg £	Average	Percentage of overall funding
District Council	26	833,010	32,039	42
HSST	13	185,613	14,278	9
Charitable trusts	16	139,726	8,733	7
Fund-raising	14	16,717	1,194	1
Business sponsorship	9	28,000	3,111	1.4
Lottery	14	249,748	17,839	13
MBW/LI	5	134,144	26,829	7
Peace and Reconciliation (NIVT)	15	300,758	20,050	15
District Partnerships	5	64,738	12,948	3
Other	7	19,021	2,712	1

Source: Lundy and Glenn (1999) p. 30
Total number of centres: 31 (18 CABx and 13 independent centres)
Total funding: £1,970,475; average per centre: £63,563

Regional Advice Networks
A summary of the income of the three main regional advice networks is outlined in Table 6.17. It shows that the total income of the three regional networks amounted to £1,391,636 in 1997/1998, £708,146 of which was in the form of core grants from the Department of Health and Social Services.

Table 6.17. Funding and sources of funds of regional advice networks in Northern Ireland, 1997/1998

	NIACAB	Law Centre	AIAC	Total
DHSS	338,600	360,000	9,546	708,146
National Lottery	28,243		11,404	39,647
Health and Social Services		51,795		51,795
MBW/LI	200,000		13,710	213,710
Charitable trusts	13,950			13,950
ERDF	26,647	71,000		97,647
Business sponsorship	7,584			7,584
NIVT			27,495	27,495
Derry City Council		10,500		10,500
Legal aid		10,000		10,000
Membership, training and management income		45,000	1,146	46,146
Total	615,024	548,295	63,301	£1,226,620

Note: all amounts are pounds sterling; NIACAB = N. Ireland Association of Citizens' Advice Bureaux; AIAC = Association of Independent Advice Centres; ERDF = European Regional Development Fund; NIVT = Northern Ireland Voluntary Trust (now The Community Fund for Northern Ireland); MBW = Making Belfast Work.

The figures are skewed somewhat by the relatively low level of core funding received by AIAC (90 per cent project funding) in the year of the research compared to the other two networks, which received a much larger proportion of their incomes in core funding from the DHSS. In the case of NIACAB this amounted to 51 per cent of total income and in the case of the Law Centre, 57 per cent. AIAC was founded in 1995 and at the time of the research, its core funding relationship with the Voluntary Activity Unit was yet to be established. Its most recently available annual report shows that core funding of AIAC had increased to £101,750 in 2000/2001 (AIAC, 2002). Other features of the funding mix that might be noted are firstly the relatively large sum received by NIACAB from the urban regeneration budget and the significance of the European Regional Development Fund (ERDF). These funds came from the Community Infrastructure Measure referred to above in the discussion of EU funding. A substantial part of the £11.5m available from ERDF under this measure was spent on advice services projects, particularly to specialist regional services, for example Disability Action and as Table 6.17 shows, to both NIACAB and the Law Centre. However, like much other project funding this was short-term and not to be repeated. The current EU Structural Funds Plan for Northern Ireland has no equivalent measure and, as with the impact of the Peace and Reconciliation Programme on local advice centres, it is unclear how in the longer term the advice services industry has benefited from EU funding.

Why is this industry in the voluntary sector and why is it institutionally separate from advice services in Britain?
Northern Ireland's particular relationship to the rest of the state in the United Kingdom has structured the emergence and development of its voluntary sector in precise ways that are clearly delineated by the development of this well-organised voluntary sector industry in Northern Ireland.

It has long been a tenet of public administration in the United Kingdom that information and advice to citizens to help them access the resources deployed by the state should be independent of the state. The CABx were started in Britain in the 1920s and were one outcome of a process of renegotiation of the boundaries of state and charitable activity, which accompanied growing activity by the state in social welfare concerns that had hitherto been the preserve of charity. The settlement that cemented advice and information as pre-eminently the preserve of voluntary organisations in the United Kingdom was secured by the experience of the Second World War in which CABx developed a crucial role in keeping citizens informed and advised. These assumptions were adopted as an axiomatic part of Northern Ireland's adoption of the Welfare State settlement in the 1940s. It was thus never likely that a solution similar to that adopted in the Republic of Ireland could have taken root given that the welfare regime that underpinned the provisions of the United Kingdom Welfare State were an expression of Northern Ireland's continuing status as part of the United Kingdom.

However, as social welfare has always been a devolved matter to the Government of Northern Ireland, the institutional delivery of this principle was always likely to take a separate route. The histories of the development of the Citizens' Advice Bureaux and the independent advice agencies show that both were indigenous applications of models of voluntary action developed elsewhere in the United Kingdom. Indeed, the development of the CABx shows a strong resemblance to the much earlier establishment of the Belfast Charity Organisation Society, outlined in chapter one. In both cases the analysis of the nature of the problem and the appropriateness of a voluntary organisation response, not to mention the name, were imported directly into Northern Ireland, but as the result of local initiative. In the case of the CABx, it was the late 1960s before they emerged in Northern Ireland. A Belfast CAB committee was established and supported as part of the work of the Belfast Council of Social Welfare (BCSW), while at roughly the same time a regional CAB committee was established by the NICSS. These central committees then promoted the development of local CAB outlets. The NICSS CAB committee was to be floated off to become NIACAB as part of the consequences of the Good Review of NICSS in 1985. But it was not until the reorganisation of the funding of local advice in 1995, discussed above, that relations with the separate Belfast group of CABx were resolved. The Belfast group of CABx was finally integrated into the regional network as a result of district councils being given direct responsibility for funding and a rate support grant attached to that funding. District councils then became the natural organisational unit for advice giving, with each district council area ideally supporting a single CAB committee. At the same time NIACAB was being strongly resourced by central government to develop and professionalise its support services for the whole CABx network.

The independent advice agencies largely emerged from two rather different sources. The first was the advice work carried out by the specialist organisations that emerged in the 1970s and 1980s as part of the so-called 'third wave' of voluntary action discussed in chapter two. Organisations such as Gingerbread (single parents) Disability Action, the Belfast Centre for the Unemployed, the Chinese Welfare Association and the Northern Ireland Council for Ethnic Minorities saw the provision of advice and information as a core part of their operations. The second were local community-development initiatives, many as part of the work of local area-based community organisations. The use of the ACE scheme in the 1980s and the first part of the 1990s enabled all these services to be substantially expanded and developed. But a number of problems became apparent due in part to the short-term nature of the available funding and the *ad hoc* way in which much of this work developed. These included a lack of training for advisors and associated quality assurance problems and an uncertain relationship between social need and provision. However, negotiations to extend the work of the English-based support body, the Federation of Independent Advice Centres (FIAC), to Northern Ireland were unsuccessful. Once again, the applicability of British-based support systems to an indigenous voluntary sector in Northern Ireland was called into question due to differences in the nature of the political/administrative environment that a single organisation, based in London, would be unable to bridge. As a result, Northern Ireland acquired in AIAC its own support structure modelled on British precedent, but entirely independent in form.

The structuring of advice services in Northern Ireland closely reflects the way the Welfare State is structured. The Welfare State settlement in Northern Ireland and Britain is essentially the same, in that citizenship entitlements and the fundamental division between private and public action are broadly in line. The respective competencies of the state and the voluntary sector are broadly delineated in this shared settlement. Thus the kinds of support required by citizens to assist them exercise their entitlements and secure their social welfare rights are similar throughout the United Kingdom. So access to free and impartial advice from independent agencies located in the voluntary sector, but substantially supported by the state through arms-length funding arrangements, is a feature common to the welfare system as it has developed throughout the United Kingdom. But the wholly unique state structures in Northern Ireland in the administration of welfare have given rise to the need for separate and indigenous structures in the voluntary sector.

Case Study 3: Housing associations in the 1990s

By 1993, housing associations in Northern Ireland owned 13,226 units of accommodation, of which 11,153 were self-contained and 2,073 were in hostels or other shared accommodation schemes. An important development in funding arrangements was the introduction that year of the Special Needs Management Allowance, which encouraged the development of special schemes for ten categories of disadvantaged people, including frail elderly people, people with a physical or intellectual disability, vulnerable women with children, people discharged from detention, young people at risk or leaving care. Capital and revenue funding were made available to meet the housing element of special needs housing. The funding of the care element was met by a charge to the tenant or by a health and social services board.

By this stage, the government had become very reluctant to register any *new* associations, with a small number of exceptions such as the Rural Housing Association, established in 1992 to tackle the problem of persistent unfitness in rural areas. Increasingly rigorous regulation and decline in the level of housing association grants in the mid-1990s resulted in a number of associations entering into mergers or being taken over by other associations. Here are some examples. In early 1992, NIH and James Butcher Housing Associations merged to form Oaklee. In 1994, Belfast Community, Botanic and Willowfield Associations, which had for some time been sharing some of their staff and functions, merged into Belfast Community. In 1997, Belfast Improved Houses, which had increasingly developed schemes outside Belfast, took over the functions of Ben Madigan, which then ceased to exist. FOLD took over Lisnagarvey. In 1998, Ballymacarrett transferred its assets to FOLD.

To comply with the requirements of the government's Policy Appraisal and Fair Treatment (PAFT), housing associations that were identified with one or other of Northern Ireland's two religious communities were required to take steps to adopt a neutral orientation. This led to a number of changes in the names of associations: the Church of Ireland Housing Association became Choice; the Baptist Housing Association became Abode; the Royal British Legion Association became Clanmill and the Down and Connor Association became Ark. Another name change at the end of the 1990s reflected the further geographical expansion of Craigavon and District Association, which became South Ulster Housing Association. Tennant Street and District changed its name to Filor Housing Association.

The next significant policy milestone was *Building on Success* (1996), a far-reaching review of housing policy in Northern Ireland, published by the Conservative direct rule administration (Department of the Environment, 1996: 89). The review recommended that the Northern Ireland Housing Executive should cease to build new houses for rent, and that registered housing associations should take responsibility for the new-build social housing programme. Largely as a result, the housing association sector grew by about a further 6,000 homes between 1996 and 2002. The Department for Social Development estimates that over 1992-2001, some £155m of private finance was contributed by registered housing associations either by way of loans raised on the money market or from their own reserves.

In many ways the housing association movement in Northern Ireland can be seen as a state/professional project, rather than an example of grass-roots voluntary action. Most of the associations were set up after the Housing Order, 1976 as part of a deliberate strategy to develop an 'independent housing sector' to offset the dominance of the NIHE. Most registered associations have similar origins, common legal structures and strong connections with the NIFHA. There are strong links between the associations and the NIFHA, which was directly involved in the formation of many associations.

The voluntary housing movement is a prominent feature of the social policy scene in Northern Ireland. Recent developments suggest that, as with its counterparts in the Republic of Ireland, its importance may increase in the medium-term future. Questions relating to the voluntary identity of the housing association sector are extensively discussed in *Non-Profit Housing Organisations in Ireland, North and South* (Mullins, Rhodes and Williamson, 2003). As the main provider of social housing, with substantial financial support from government, the housing association sector in Northern Ireland has an unusually close relationship with government. This has led to on-going and extensive monitoring and regulation not only from the Department for Social Development but also from the Northern Ireland Ombudsman and from the Equality Commission. As housing associations have grown and have employed increasing numbers of professional staff, so the role of their voluntary board members has tended to decline and few now appear to involve volunteers at the service delivery stage to any significant extent. Most of the larger associations appear to be planning expansion strategies and many are considering, or implementing, expansion strategies in the Republic of Ireland. A major uncertainty at the time of writing is the impact that Right to Buy legislation will have on the stock of the sector and there are also concerns that the introduction of the government's *Supporting People* legislation may alter established relationships between housing associations and their voluntary sector counterparts who deliver support and welfare services.

Conclusions

The overview of the voluntary and community sector in Northern Ireland in the first years of the twenty-first century presented here suggests that there may be between 3,500 and 4,000 organisations and associations falling within our definitions. An increasing amount is known about the sector, the result of an increase in investment in research at both the University of Ulster and NICVA in particular. A number of themes may be identified at this stage. Analysis based on the General Charities Classification, used by NICVA and reproduced here, is not easy to interpret since it is not very clear where the divisions of all the categories lie. However, it is clear that there is a strong emphasis on service provision to individuals, an emphasis on training and education, and a bias firstly towards children and young people and then towards elderly and disabled people.

The sector is relatively large. It is estimated to employ more than 29,000 people and it has a gross annual turnover of more than £674m. However, most organisations are small, with annual turnovers of less than £100,000, enough to employ (at the very most) four people on very modest salaries. Almost 85 per cent of them have no institutional links outside Northern Ireland, although many are regional replicas of equivalent organisations in Britain. There is very little evidence of consolidation; the sector remains substantially made up of small, local and fragmented organisations.

Our analysis of government support for voluntary and community organisations suggests that there is a strongly symbiotic relationship with the local state in Northern Ireland which still provides much of the funding for most of the organisations within the sector. The evidence of a recent shift from voluntary to earned income suggests a clarification and a maturing of the relationship rather than a more fundamental realignment. Government is likely to remain the main purchasers of voluntary sector services.

A number of themes may be identified from the foregoing account of voluntary and community organisations in Northern Ireland at the start of the twenty-first century. The first that is worth stressing is the size, diversity and pervasiveness of the sector. While there is a minority of large organisations with annual turnovers of millions of pounds, thousands of mostly rather small organisations and associations touch the lives of a significant part of the Northern Ireland population every year. Analysis by NICVA of where they are based suggests that to a large extent their effort is focused on areas of social and economic disadvantage. NICVA's research also reveals that most of this effort is expended on providing services to individual people in expected categories of need such as older people, children and young people and disabled people. To a notable extent voluntary organisations are concerned with managing facilities and buildings. Much of this work is carried on at the level of local communities by community-based associations and it is thus noteworthy that one clear outcome of the investment in community development has been an extension of service delivery. The evidence presented here supports the view that voluntary organisations as a whole function in Northern Ireland as an extension of state welfare either by providing similar services to hard-to-reach sections of the population or, perhaps more typically, providing different but complementary services.

A second noteworthy theme is the indigenous nature of the Northern Ireland voluntary and community sector. The evidence shows that only around 15 per cent of organisations are institutionally linked to other organisations outside the region. However, as is evidenced by the information and advice services industry, many of them replicate and mirror equivalent organisations in Britain, sometimes sharing a name, sometimes a function. Two counter trends would appear to have had little overall effect on this situation. First, reforms in the organisation and funding of social care in the early 1990s did, as noted, encourage some large national voluntary service providers to extend their portfolio to Northern Ireland and has strengthened the position of some, such as MENCAP, that were already established. Second, the national United Kingdom awards provided by the lottery Community Fund on condition that the grants are spent in all countries of the United Kingdom has encouraged some English-based charities to extend services in Northern Ireland. But where this has led to competition with local organisations, the outsiders have generally withdrawn.

A third theme is the well-developed infrastructure with a number of industry-specific support organisations within the voluntary and community sector. In addition to NICVA, and the advice services industry discussed in detail above, we find for example Child Care NI (organisations working with children), the Rural Community Network (rural community associations), Disability Action (disability) and Youth Action (youth). There are also numerous more specific regional networking organisations, some of which, e.g. like the Northern Ireland Pre-School Playgroups Association (NIPPA), have become very large. These support other numerous local associations, sometimes as branches and sometimes as independent affiliates. Examples of these would include MENCAP (local Gateway clubs), Arthritis Care, Age Concern, Gingerbread, the MS Society and many more. In addition the 1990s saw the growth and consolidation of a number of area-based sub-regional networks, notably the North-West Community Forum in Derry, and a series of local-area rural networks that together now cover the whole of Northern Ireland.

Perhaps the most noticeable feature of voluntary action in Northern Ireland is the close relationship with the state in which many voluntary and community organisations appear as extensions to state bureaucracies. The formal recognition of the contribution of the voluntary and community sector to governance in Northern Ireland dates back to the early 1990s with the publication of *Strategy for the Support of the Voluntary Sector and for Community Development in Northern* in 1993, but it appears that the relationship has intensified further since then. The position of housing associations is perhaps an extreme example of one possible end result of this process. But both our other industry studies of social care and of advice services show similar processes at work in which voluntary agencies receive substantial support from government agencies in return for working within a clearly defined and highly regulated policy environment.

The intensification of this trend in recent years has been offset by the rapid emergence of many hundreds of community-based and self-help organisations, a particular feature of the decade between about 1985 and 1995. The evidence, however, suggests that many of these associations are heavily involved in service delivery and the management of local community facilities. Many of the self-help initiatives, particularly in the health care arena, appear to be inward looking and apolitical. The overview of the evidence offered here thus suggests that there has in practice been a four-way split in the structure of the voluntary and community sector, as set out in Table 6.18.

Table 6.18. Typology of voluntary associations in Northern Ireland

Organisation type	Orientation	Relationship with the state
Service delivery	Meeting needs of individuals in clearly defined categories of people	Client/sub-contractor. State defines both needs and methods of intervention
Community associations	Servicing needs of individuals at local level and provision of facilities	Supplicant of state. Outsiders wanting to become insiders
Self-help associations	Inward-looking and supportive of group membership	Outsiders, but making few demands on the state
Networks	Member-orientated and often policy focused	Ambiguous. Critical, but reliant on state sponsorship

As with all systems of classification of this type, these categories are a considerable simplification. They are not mutually exclusive, nor does categorisation cover all the potential functions of voluntary associations. For example, while much of the energies of the committee of a local community association may be absorbed by facilities management, its activities may have a positive impact on both bonding and bridging social capital. But what the table does show is that with the exception of those self-help associations that are self-contained, much of current voluntary action in Northern Ireland now takes place within an agreed policy framework in which the relationship with the state is conducted within mutually acceptable parameters. In this sense the voluntary and community sector is now largely incorporated as part of the system of public administration, operating in a sphere whose parameters are determined by state patronage.

Our interviewees noted some of the consequences. A strongly expressed theme among interviewees based in the voluntary sector was the gap between very aspirational language in policy documents about relations between government and the voluntary sector and the practice of government departments and agencies. This, it was felt, tended to be narrowly focused on departmental or agency function and driven by audit. The problem was made worse by the recent retirement of a number of influential senior civil servants who were considered to have a particularly developed understanding of the sector. Other interviewees felt that relations between government and voluntary agencies were too close and that this had had negative consequences for the ability of the sector to think and act independently. Both government and voluntary agencies, it is suggested, operate in a culture that is strongly risk averse.

7

Towards a Profile of the Voluntary and Community Sector in the Republic of Ireland

Introduction
This chapter first examines the level of knowledge of the voluntary and community sector. Then it considers the various ways in which it has been statistically defined: the size of the sector is assessed. There is a short examination of employment in the sector and sectoral studies thus far completed. Levels of participation in voluntary activity are reported and analysed. There is an examination of funding of the sector by government, trusts and the corporate sector. We look at what is known of the governance of the sector. Some parts of the sector are examined in more detail. This is followed by an examination of the level of north–south co-operation between the sectors.

The state of knowledge of the sector
The level and state and knowledge of the voluntary sector in the Republic of Ireland has improved only in very recent years. As recently as 1993, virtually all the key features concerning its size, scope, activities, funding and composition were unknown, a problem compounded by low levels of self-documentation (Harvey, 1993). The voluntary sector was only one of many aspects of its social self-knowledge about which the new state preferred to remain in the dark, eschewing the development of even the most modest intellectual infrastructure or capacity for self-analysis (Lee, 1989). Thankfully, a series of pioneering studies have since uncovered these key features (O'Connor, 1993; Faughnan and Kelleher, 1993). The key achievements of these researches were as follows:

- Measurement of charitable giving (Ruddle and O'Connor, 1992)
- Mapping of key sectors and regions (Faughnan and Kelleher, 1993)
- Setting the Irish social welfare voluntary organisations in a comparative international perspective (Ruddle and Donoghue, 1995)
- Assessment of the level and nature of volunteering (Ruddle and O'Connor, 1992; Ruddle and Donoghue, 1995)
- Knowledge of the regulatory environment of the sector (Cousins, 1994)

- Situating the Irish voluntary sector in the contemporary European debate on civil society (Powell and Guerin, 1997)
- Preliminary information on the state of governance of the sector (Jaffro, 1998)
- Our first knowledge about private and corporate giving (Donoghue, Ruddle and Mulvihill, 2000).

In addition, in 1997 Burns at the library at University College Dublin compiled a national database of voluntary sector research. The original database had 184 entries, including books, articles and academic theses and was subsequently put on line (www.volsec.ie). Several courses in voluntary sector management were developed in the 1990s, notably in the National College of Ireland, Dublin City University and the Business School of Dublin University (Trinity College) (e.g. course in Managing non-profit organisations). Students on these courses were required to write dissertations, many of which focused on voluntary sector management and development. As a result of these developments, our knowledge has now much improved.

The reasons for this radical improvement in the mid-1990s have not been analysed. It is possible that, with maturity, people in the voluntary sector began to think in cross-sectoral terms. The growth of voluntary sector research in the Atlantic world would have been known to Irish universities and this may have encouraged them to uncover what had hitherto been investigated here. Fresh funding may have been available to them, matching the sudden growth in the Irish economy. Despite these advances, there remain many gaps in our information and knowledge.

- We still lack an agreed, universally accessible, national database of the voluntary sector.
- Histories of voluntary organisations are few.
- Due to non-disclosure, we still know little about corporate giving to the sector.
- The *State of the Sector*-type research developed in the regions of the United Kingdom cannot be directly matched in the Republic.

Defining the sector
Chapter one explored and defined our working model of what constituted 'the voluntary sector' in Ireland. In the Republic, the key studies of the voluntary sector have all used different reference points from which to draw their knowledge of the sector, all with their own merits, and these are summarised below. The lack of a unified, agreed sampling frame is an endemic and challenging problem for voluntary sector researchers (O'Donnell and Trench, 1999). As we have already noted, there is no system for the registration of

charities or voluntary organisations, something which has important implications in the areas of research as well as of oversight. This has obliged researchers to select their own definitions and, for research, their own sampling frames, in chronological order, is set out in Table 7.1.

Table 7.1. Studies of, and information services on, the voluntary sector, Republic of Ireland

Author and publisher	Title	Sample/reference points
Pauline Faughnan and Patricia Kelleher (1993) Community Action Network and Conference of Major Religious Superiors	*The Voluntary Sector and the State*	Sample/reference points 1 in 5 random sample of 366 organisations that applied for funding in the Eastern Health Board area from People in Need (excluding hospitals, schools and small organisations) and 11 national umbrella bodies
Hilary Frazer (ed) (1994) National Social Service Board	*Directory of National Voluntary Organisations*	400 national voluntary organisations in social services, campaigning, caring, charity, support, culture known to the NSSB and from whom information was requested. Note: the directory included a further 135 state and other organisations
Helen Ruddle and Freda Donoghue (1995) National College of Industrial Relations	*The Organisation of Volunteering – a Study of Irish Voluntary Organisations in the Social Welfare area*	50 per cent proportionately stratified random sample of 991 voluntary organisations drawn from NSSB directory, directories for mentally handicapped and older people, categorised as elderly, disabled, chronic illness, humanitarian, homeless, drugs and victims, mental illness, generic, family.
Susan O'Donnell (1996) Dublin City University	*The Voluntary Sector in the Information Age*	300 selected randomly from 20 sources including funders, published sources and databases, in community development environment, development, women, health, youth, religious

Table 7.1. Studies of, and information services on, the voluntary sector, Republic of Ireland (contd.)

Author and publisher	Title	Sample/reference points
Fred Powell and Donal Guerin (1997) University College	*Civil Society and Social Policy*	(1) National opinion poll sample (1020) (2) 579 voluntary organisations drawn from National Social Service Board directory (3) Interviews with 16 voluntary organisation representatives.
Gwen Jaffro (1998)	*Insights into the Boards of Voluntary Agencies*	727 selected from NSSB directory, local area listings from community resource centres, membership listings of umbrella organisations; limited to greater Dublin area
Freda Donoghue, Helmut Anheier and Lester Salamon (1999) Johns Hopkins University, Maryland, USA	*Uncovering the Non-Profit Sector in Ireland – its Economic Value and Significance*	International Classification of Non-Profit Organisations (ICNPO), dividing voluntary sector into 10 categories: culture/recreation; education/research; health; social services; environment; development and housing; civil/advocacy; philanthropy; international; business and professional

As may be seen, with the absence of an agreed, defined, voluntary sector and lacking a national registration system, researchers had to develop their own tools to suit the research. From 1999, the Revenue Commissioners made available an on-line listing of charitable voluntary organisations for whom a charity number had been allocated. However, this listing presents its own problems too, for many voluntary organisations do not have charity numbers and many of those bodies with such numbers are not mainstream voluntary organisations. Probably one of the most influential instruments to define the sector was the International Classification of Non-Profit Organisations (ICNPO) introduced by Donoghue, Anheier and Salamon (1999). This was a systematic attempt to devise a tool for measuring and analysing the voluntary sector worldwide. Its merits and problems will be discussed shortly. In summary, what we know about the voluntary sector in the Republic is based on an imperfect knowledge base using different means of assembling, collating and presenting information within different definitional frameworks. This should be remembered as we examine what we do know about the sector.

Dimensions: The size of the sector
What do we know of the size of the voluntary sector in the Republic? First, some information is available on the number of organisations. This comes from the number granted a charity number for taxable purposes. In 1990, there were 3,793 such organisations (Costello, 1990). This figure rose to 6,305 by 1998. This probably reflected a growth in new approvals only, as no system was in place to check if old approvals were still functional. Efforts were then made to make this listing more accurate and up to date. The Revenue Commissioners weeded out organisations suspected of being defunct. An initial 1,493 were taken off the list in 1998 and a further 539 early the following year. The current number (2002) is 5,106 and may be presumed to be very precise.

Another approach is to look at the number of companies 'limited by guarantee', the standard legal expression used by voluntary organisations. In 1990, the companies office recorded 3,500 such companies (Costello, 1990). By 1999, we had a closely related figure of the number of companies limited by guarantee and having permission not to use the form 'company limited' on their letterhead: 4,739. Allowing for the two-year gap between the two figures of 5,106 and 4,738, these are now quite closely aligned. Table 7.2 indicates our knowledge of the numerical size of the sector, based on these systems. Note that these include overlapping categories.

Table 7.2. Number of voluntary organisations, Republic of Ireland

Number of organisations	Source and date	Notes
5,106	Revenue Commissions (2002)	Number of organisations with a charitable number
4,723	Dept of Enterprise, Trade and Employment (1999)	Numbers of companies limited by guarantee, not having share capital, with permission not to use 'Limited company' in their title
2,750	Registrar of Friendly Societies	Friendly societies, including trade unions and industrial and provident societies
25		Unincorporated societies

Donoghue, Anheier and Salamon's work (1999) is the first direct attempt to size the sector using purpose-designed, objective tools, rather than using various other forms of proxies. The National College of Ireland (NCI) participated in the transnational non-profit comparative project of the Johns Hopkins University, thus measuring the voluntary sector in Ireland within international norms. Their tool, the International Classification of Non-Profit Organisations (ICNPO) had the supreme advantage of making Ireland directly comparable with any and every other country in the study. Its broad methodology has been discussed above (chapters one and six).

The ICNPO, in its sectoral methodology, divided the voluntary sector into twelve categories:

- Culture, arts and recreation
- Education and research
- Health
- Social services
- Environment and animals
- Economic, social, community development, housing, employment and training
- Civil, advocacy, law and legal association
- Philanthropy
- International
- Religious
- Business, professional, trade unions
- Others.

This presents a number of problems. O'Donnell and Trench (1999) found that the system mixed interest and activity areas to the point that some voluntary organisations could belong in up to three categories. To include philanthropy, which involves giving *to* the sector as part *of* the sector, is questionable. Some of the categories, especially the 'business and professional' category, may feel little affiliation with the 'voluntary sector' and might be surprised to be considered part of it.

In the Republic of Ireland, this classification presents a particular set of problems. A broad range of activity was included in the Irish study that would not necessarily be included in other countries. In Ireland, primary and secondary schools are included, as are the universities. In the case of schools, Ireland diverges from international norms in that the government has left schooling almost entirely in private hands, even though the funding pattern may be identical to those countries where the state has formal ownership. It is certainly true that the ownership of schools is private, but they operate according to rules and are largely paid for by funds determined by government: indeed, Donoghue (1998) accepts that whether or not they are self-governing is debatable, since they do not have control over their outcomes, rules or activities and attendance is compulsory. Whilst there is a high level of voluntarism in the Irish educational system, it is doubtful if the member of a board of a primary school management committee would see himself or herself as an integral part of the Irish voluntary sector. O'Sullivan (1999/2000) also questions their inclusion, since they have 'more in common with statist mechanisms for welfare delivery'. Universities, for example, fit the definition by having boards independent of government, but their funding dependence on government means that their freedom of manoeuvre is quite constrained. The level of voluntary activity in a university is, one suspects, quite low compared to the overall level of human activity there. Thirty-two 'public voluntary hospitals' are included, because they pass the 'voluntary board' criterion, even though, as Donoghue points out, 'apart from volunteer input and some fund-raising activity, [they] manifest little other voluntary activity.' (The Adelaide Hospital in Dublin may be an exception here.) O'Ferrall (2000) points out, though in a different context, that several of the listed public voluntary hospitals are now under ministerial control, making their status as non-governmental establishments problematical.

A criticism of the system's application to Ireland is that it lacks a sense of scale or proportion. The ICNPO definition excludes the co-operative movement because it is profit-distributing, even though most historians would consider that it had an integral role in the building of voluntarism in Ireland. Sporting and cultural organisations are included, but not golf clubs, because they are deemed to be profit-making.

> The non-profit sector in Ireland can be said to include the following: hospitals, schools, universities, community groups, trade unions, friendly and benevolent societies, the area based partnership companies and other voluntary organisations such as those operating in the fields of mental health, disabilities and social services. Included, too, are welfare and relief organisations and those involved in the environment. Most important, for purposes of this paper, are those organisations that are excluded. Industrial and provident societies, many of whom are now large agricultural cooperatives that return profits to their members and shareholders are excluded. Excluded too are credit unions because individual members can benefit from an annual dividend. Sporting and cultural organisations are included where it is known that they are non-profit-making. Excluded of course would be the large profit-making sporting organisations like golf clubs (Donoghue, 1998).

This definition adds an additional layer of confusion. It does not distinguish between privately owned schools and publicly owned schools (e.g. Vocational Educational Committee schools, comprehensive schools) or between private voluntary hospitals and the others; nor does it distinguish between mutualised and demutualised co-operatives. The reason for the description of some types of sports as profit-making is unclear for there must be very few sporting groups in Ireland which are shareholder owned (like premier league English football clubs). Most Irish sports groups, large and small, reinvest their surplus in sporting activities and do not distribute financial profit to their members. It is instructive to note that the use of the ICNPO created similar problems when applied to Britain (Whelan, 1999). The exclusion of all industrial and provident societies is peculiar, since they have clearly been an integral part of voluntary sector development and some conventional, mainstream voluntary organisations deliberately choose this institutional form.

These reservations aside, the work of Donoghue, Anheier and Salamon (1999) remains the defining attempt at classification and merits detailed attention. Their task was an inherently difficult one and virtually any instrument decided on is easily open to criticism. Their principal findings were as follows:

- The Irish voluntary sector represented, by turnover, 8.2 per cent of GDP, 9.3 per cent of GNP and 11.5 per cent of employment. Internationally, the sector accounts for 4.7 per cent of GDP and 4.9 per cent of employment, so the Irish voluntary sector is about twice the size of the international norm.
- If we add in the imputed value of volunteers, the Republic's voluntary sector accounts for 9.5 per cent of GDP and 11 per cent of GDP.
- The imputed value to the voluntary sector in the Republic is €4.8bn.
- Within this broader picture, the community and voluntary sector is estimated at 2.14 per cent of GDP and 2.4 per cent of GNP.

These findings show the Irish voluntary sector to be one of the largest components in the economy, larger than public administration, defence, agriculture or fishing. The combined operating expenditure of the voluntary sector with the imputed value of its volunteers is given in Table 7.3.

If we were to strip away 'education and research' and 'health', the size of the voluntary sector would be reduced by 69.1 per cent. If we also remove religion, professional associations and foundations, we would reduce the voluntary sector by a further 7.8 per cent (76.9 per cent). This would give a 'core' Irish voluntary sector of 23.1 per cent of the size indicated, the largest element being 'social services', more in keeping with international norms.

Donoghue, Anheier and Salamon (1999) recognise that there is, within the broad voluntary sector categorisation, a 'voluntary and community' sub-sector. Here, the researchers define the voluntary and community sector to exclude hospitals, hospices, and primary, secondary and third-level

Table 7.3. Turnover of the *non-profit sector* in the Republic of Ireland, 1999

Field	Amount in €	Percentage
Education and research	2,250,812,600	46.8
Health	1,069,886,300	22.3
Social services	485,568,150	10.1
Religion	293,508,840	6.1
Development/housing	272,160,730	5.7
Culture/recreation	244,477,900	5.1
Professional associations	58,269,550	1.2
Environment	52,017,359	1.1
International	28,065,020	0.6
Foundations	25,789,650	0.5
Civic and advocacy	17,019,569	0.4
Other/not classified	9,488,752	0.2

Source: Adapted from Donoghue, Anheier and Salamon (1999)

educational institutions. Included are: culture and arts, sports and recreation, education and research, nursing homes, mental and other health, social services, emergency and relief, income support and maintenance, community development, housing, employment and training, civic and advocacy, legal, foundations, international activities and religion. This is a definition that is much more in tune with the scope of this study. Table 7.4 sets out the turnover of the community and voluntary sub-sector.

Here, the total value is much lower. The value is €1.6bn, compared to

Table 7.4. Turnover of the community and voluntary sub-sector in the Republic of Ireland, 1999

Field	Amount in €	Percentage
Social services	485,568,150	30.1
Religion	293,508,840	18.2
Development/housing	272,160,730	16.9
Culture and recreation	244,479,900	15.2
Health	125,603,760	7.8
Education and research	57,143,292	3.5
Environment	52,017,359	3.2
International	28,065,020	1.7
Foundations	25,789,650	1.6
Civic and advocacy	17,019,569	1.1
Other/not classified	9,488,752	0.6
Total	1,610,971,000	100

Source: Adapted from Donoghue, Anheier and Salamon (1999)

€4.8bn, or about a third of the size of the larger group. It still constitutes, as the authors point out, 2.14 per cent of GDP and 2.4 per cent of GNP.

Dimensions: Employment in the sector
The researchers provided estimates of the quantitative level of employment in the voluntary sector in the Republic. They calculated the level of employment in the sector at 125,584 full-time equivalents (FTE) in 1995.

Table 7.5. Employment in the *voluntary, non-profit sector*, Republic of Ireland, 1999

ICNPO *group*	*Full time equiv.*	*In-kind/ volunteer*	*Combined fte**	%
Education and Research	63,731	896	64,627	40.6
Health	32,739	2,329	35,068	22
Culture/recreation	7,150	8,619	15,770	9.9
Religion	6,921	2,040	8,961	5.6
Social services	5,343	14,265	19,607	12.3
Development/housing	5,079	3,453	8,531	5.4
Professional associations	2,590	–	2,590	1.6
Environment	1,070	234	1,304	0.8
Civic advocacy	459	234	693	0.6
International	370	234	604	0.4
Foundations	133	890	1,023	0.6
Others	–	496	496	0.3
Total	**125,585**	**33,690**	**159,274**	**100**

Source: Adapted from Donoghue, Anheier and Salamon, 1999. * f.t.e. = full-time equivalent.

Table 7.5 shows a total full-time equivalent value of the voluntary sector in the Republic as 159,274. In terms of the country's labour force, this makes it the fourth largest sector, following manufacturing, agriculture, and professional services, and more than all those employed in retail distribution, personal services, building and construction, finance and insurance, transport, wholesale distribution, public administration, defence, utilities and mining. This figure shows Irish voluntary sector employment to be 12.2 per cent of the non-agricultural workforce, the second highest in the European Union after the Netherlands (19.27 per cent) and far above the European Union average of 7 per cent.

The subdivision of the voluntary and community sector within the Irish voluntary non-profit sector, as calculated by Donoghue, Anheier and Salamon (1999), is set out in Table 7.6.

Table 7.6. Employment in the voluntary and community sector, Republic of Ireland, 1999

ICNPO group	Full-time equivalent	In-kind/ volunteer	Combined fte
Social services	5,342	14,265	19,607
Culture and recreation	7,151	8,619	15,770
Religion	6,920	2,040	8,961
Development/housing	5,079	3,453	8,531
Health	3,205	1,371	4,576
Education and research	2,407	83	2,490
Environment	1,070	234	1,304
Foundations	133	890	1,023
Civic advocacy	459	234	693
International	370	234	604
Others	–	496	496
Totals	**32,136**	**31,919**	**64,055**

Source: Adapted from Donoghue, Anheier and Salamon, 1999. * f.t.e = full-time equivalent.

Again, this shows it to be much smaller (60 per cent less than the previous table) and a proportion of our workforce more in keeping with the European norm. The proposition that this table is a truer reflection of voluntary action is evident in the fact that well over 94 per cent of all in-kind and volunteer activity takes place in the voluntary and community categories (31,919 out of 33,690).

Dimensions: the composition of the sector
An interesting feature of the relative weight of the sectors in the Republic is provided when Salamon, Anheier and Associates (1998b) put the country in a broad international perspective. The most striking feature is the small size of the voluntary sector concerned with civic rights and advocacy. The total employment, including volunteer full-time equivalents, in civic rights and advocacy is only 0.5 per cent of the sector in the Republic, compared to 1.8 per cent in Britain, 1.9 per cent in France, 4.3.per cent in the Netherlands, 3.5 per cent in Austria, 3.4 per cent in Germany, 4.2 per cent in the European Union as a whole and a high 16.8 per cent in Finland.

Staying with the composition of the sector, Powell and Guerin (1997) provide useful information on the composition of the sector. Chapter three outlined how different parts of the voluntary sector emerged: campaigning groups, national federations and the providers of services. In their study of voluntary organisations, groups categorised themselves in ways indicated in Table 7.7.

Table 7.7. The voluntary sector in the Republic of Ireland, by composition

Umbrella body	12%
Providing services/information	49%
Self-help	11%
Promoting a cause	14%
Other	14%

Source: Adapted from Powell and Guerin (1997)

Returning to the question of employment, Powell and Guerin (1997) give figures of 2 per cent of the national population employed as salaried workers by voluntary organisations and a further 2 per cent employed on government schemes. These are crude figures based on a standard national sample, not the more reliable labour force survey, and must be treated carefully.

There have been few dedicated studies of voluntary sector employment in the Republic. Little is known of its employment patterns, career paths, remuneration, conditions or the other key features of voluntary sector employment in the broader context of the Irish labour market. Observers say that the level of interchangeability of careers between the voluntary, private and statutory sectors is generally low and much lower than Northern Ireland. O'Donovan and Varley (1993) have suggested that because of a lack of career structure, fair remuneration, job security or quality management, the Irish voluntary sector could be a secondary labour market with unfavourable terms and conditions. Having said this, it is possible that with the professionalisation of the sector, this situation may since have improved. Basini and Buckley (1999) did investigate some qualitative aspects of voluntary sector employment in the Republic showing significant differences, compared to the private sector, in the motivation, priorities, values and goals of voluntary sector workers. In order to improve standards, the Combat Poverty Agency published a guide to good employment practice in the sector (Clarke, 1995).

Dimensions: levels of participation in voluntary activities
Our knowledge of volunteering in the Republic has improved radically over the past number of years, the pioneering work having been done by Ruddle and Donoghue (1995), though their study was confined to social welfare organisations. Here we look at baseline data and trends over time, and compare the Republic to other countries. The information covers overlapping areas, making it possible to build up a cross-referenced picture.

What is our actual level of knowledge? Substantial research on volunteering in Ireland was first done in the 1990s (Ruddle and O'Connor,

1993; Ruddle and Donoghue, 1995). The main findings of the 1993 study were as follows:

- Thirty-nine per cent of people volunteered (at least one voluntary activity in the previous month), with 20 per cent engaged in current, formal volunteering through an organisation.
- The median amount of time given was 6 hours per month.
- The most frequently done activities were collecting things, visiting the elderly and helping in activities. The most time was given to helping in activities, visiting the elderly and participating on a committee.
- The principal beneficiaries of activities were neighbours, sports, the poor and the elderly, in that order.
- The principal age groups involved in volunteering were aged 41 to 50, followed by 51 to 60; the least being the under-25s and over-70s. Many people, 22 per cent, came to do the work because of a decision on their own part or because they had been invited to do so by friends or neighbours.
- The highest levels of volunteering were found among part-time workers, the least among unemployed people and the retired.

Their main finding was that volunteering in the Republic was extensive. There was a high level of informal, neighbourly volunteering that did not necessarily take place formally through voluntary organisations. Few people volunteered because they had been asked to do so by people unknown to them, suggesting that there was considerable potential for volunteering campaigns.

Their work has been supplemented by Powell and Guerin (1997). This gives a national volunteering headline figure of 32 per cent of people who had volunteered at any time and 18 per cent who described themselves as current volunteers. Although there was little gender difference in the level and nature of volunteering, there were higher rates among the higher socio-economic groups, in the 35 to 54 year age group, and in Leinster, with lower volunteering rates among the young and the lower socio-economic groups, and in Munster and Connacht/Ulster.

Donoghue (2001a) has been able to compare research from the early 1990s with the late 1990s, thus conveying a picture of changes under way. She found that the level of volunteering declined by 6 per cent over 1992-8. This was an important finding, because anecdotal information from voluntary organisations had indicated a decline in the number of volunteers coming forward and her research was confirmation of this trend. The rate of decline in volunteering was highest in the 50 to 59 year age group, where it was down 10 per cent.

Some of the key features of volunteering in the late 1990s are as follows:

- One third of the population engage in voluntary activity.
- The level of volunteering is much higher among women (42 per cent) than men (28 per cent).
- Volunteering is well spread between the age groups, the highest levels being in the 50 to 59 year age group.
- Volunteering is positively associated with educational attainment and social class (23.2 per cent for those with only a primary certificate, 48.6 per cent for those with a third level qualification).
- Regionally, the highest levels of volunteering are to be found in the south-east (55.9 per cent) and the lowest in the north-east (19.1 per cent).
- Asked why they volunteered, most volunteers give reasons of idealism (belief in the cause, 42.9 per cent), followed by altruism (a desire to help) and 'being asked' (Donoghue, 2001a).

Donoghue, Ruddle and Mulvihill (2000) studied trends in the 1990s, coming to the following further conclusions:

- There was a consolidation of volunteers in some areas, especially the elderly.
- Church-led helping had also increased.
- The proportion spent on committee work increased.
- The total amount of time volunteered was down sharply from 5,317 hours a month in 1992 to 3,674 in 1998.
- The cash value of volunteering was now quoted as £470m, or €596m (1995 figure).

Donoghue (2001b) further analysed the pattern of volunteering in the Republic according to gender, finding a universally higher disposition to volunteer by women, with differences in areas, motivations and rewards.

The National Committee on Volunteering (2002) brought together a range of data on volunteering and this provides the most up-to-date and comprehensive information available. The national committee restated the headline volunteering rate of 33.3 per cent, down from 38.9 per cent in 1992 and 35.1 per cent in 1994. Positively, the committee found that the level of volunteering among young people was probably underestimated and that there was considerable potential for involving young people, if the proper opportunities were developed and offered in an appropriate way. On the negative side, one of the themes of the representations received by the committee was that the Celtic tiger economy was seen to have diminished opportunities for community involvement, resulting from increased pressures on time, individualism, materialism, community patterns and greater pressures to earn. The national committee had a short section comparing volunteering in the Republic with Northern Ireland. Here the committee observed a similar headline rate, 35 per cent; similar patterns of volunteering in terms of areas of interest and routes into volunteering, but a better developed infrastructure. In Northern Ireland, the policy environment favoured volunteering, deriving from United Kingdom-wide initiatives such as *Community Volunteering, Make a Difference, Millennium Volunteers* and *Active Communities;* there was a well-established infrastructure with the Volunteer Development Agency, with 25 staff and a budget of £2.5m; and there were 15 local volunteer bureaux, taking part in the volunteer bureaux network, with an average funding of £25,000 each.

Finally, the National Economic and Social Forum (2003), in its study of social capital, published a new headline rate measuring the level of active involvement in unpaid voluntary activity (17.1 per cent) with, of course, higher rates in informal activity and caring (50 per cent).

Some limited sectoral information is also available. Kiernan (2000) presented information on volunteering in national and regional disability organisations. Sixty-one per cent of these organisations had volunteers. Some had up to 300 volunteers providing services, while others called on volunteers for specific activities, especially fund-raising events. Of those with volunteers, only 30 per cent had a formal volunteer policy.

It is important to set volunteering in the Republic in a European context. There are now several sources available which do so. Gaskin and Davis Smith (1995) made an extensive study of volunteering in selected European Union and accession countries, including data supplied by the researchers Donoghue and Ruddle to cover Ireland. Great Britain was also included, but the methodological note indicates that in practice this meant England, with neither Wales, Scotland nor Northern Ireland included. The following were the principal points of difference between volunteering in the Republic of Ireland and the other European countries:

- Overall volunteering in Ireland was lower than average, 25 per cent compared to 27 per cent. Overall Irish people volunteered most for sporting and recreational voluntary work (39 per cent, compared to a norm of 28 per cent) and were above the European average in volunteering for work in the areas of social services and community development. The level of volunteering was below the European average in groups dealing with adult education, culture and the arts and citizens' advocacy.
- What did the volunteers actually do? Here, Irish volunteers were overwhelmingly involved in raising money (51 per cent of activity, compared to a European norm of 27 per cent) and committee work (37 per cent compared to 26 per cent). Rates of involvement in other areas were

much below the European norm, for example administrative work, information and advice, advocacy and campaigning and visiting and befriending.

- Irish volunteers were, compared to other European countries, more likely to join because of family and friends (55 per cent, compared to 44 per cent). They were much less likely to have joined because of encouragement in their place of work (only 3 per cent, compared to 9 per cent as the European norm) or through the media, volunteer bureaux or the work of public bodies.
- Compared to other countries, Irish volunteers were more likely to have stepped forward to help themselves (46 per cent, compared to 35 per cent) and less likely to have been asked by others (45 per cent, compared to 53 per cent).
- Irish volunteers were less likely to have received training than other European countries: 22 per cent, compared to 29 per cent in Europe as a whole.
- Irish volunteers were less likely to have been offered out-of-pocket expenses, 11 per cent compared to 24 per cent in Europe as a whole.
- Voluntary organisations in the Republic of Ireland were much less likely to have a volunteer policy than in other countries (only 11 per cent had such a policy).
- Compared to other European countries, the Republic of Ireland appeared to be well represented with volunteer-involving organisations with young people, ethnic minority groups, refugees, but had lower rates of involvement in groups working with the elderly.

The researchers found much in common in volunteering between Great Britain (for which we read England) and the Republic of Ireland compared to the rest of Europe. From this, it may be fair to presume at least some similarities between the Republic and Northern Ireland. Those features were that volunteers spent much time on raising money and committee work and were likely to be involved in social services, education, religious and sports activities.

Gaskin's research is complemented by information collected by the *Eurobarometer* surveys commissioned by the European Union and the now discontinued European Community Household Panel, published in the 2000 annual social situation survey of the European Union (European Commission, 2000). Regrettably for the purpose of this study, United Kingdom data are not disaggregated between its four regions. These figures concerned not just volunteering, but broader concepts of civic participation. The social situation survey found the following:

- The overall level of active participation in voluntary activity was 7.4 per cent, with the Republic of Ireland slightly above the average at 8 per cent (the highest countries were the Netherlands and the Scandinavian countries).
- The proportion of people engaged in broad social, cultural or political activities was 46 per cent in the European Union as a whole, with the Republic of Ireland slightly above, at 51 per cent (the UK as a whole is 53 per cent).
- In the Republic, participation was unusually high in sporting activities: 29 per cent, compared to 20 per cent in the Union as a whole.

Independently, we know that the proportion of volunteering in the Irish voluntary sector concerned with advocacy work is very small, only 0.1 per cent of the sector, compared to a European Union average of 1.8 per cent and is the smallest in the EU (derived from Salamon and Anheier, 1998a).

Donoghue, Anheier and Salamon (1999) are able to give an imputed financial value of volunteering in the Republic and this is estimated as set out in Table 7.8.

Table 7.8. The imputed value of volunteering, Republic of Ireland

Field	Amount in €
Social services	272,816,460
Culture and recreation	101,083,840
Development and housing	66,030,189
Health	55,799,909
Religion	31,231,747
Education and research	30,746,707
Foundations	17,028,457
(Other)	9,488,753
Environment	4,480,906
Civic and advocacy	4,480,906
International	4,480,906
Total	**€597,669,520**

Source: Adapted from Donoghue, Anheier and Salamon (1999)

This table reflects some of the definitional problems encountered earlier, for it shows the relatively low level of volunteering in education and hospitals which otherwise account for a large portion of the sector. The high imputed levels of voluntary contribution to social services (€272 million) and sports (€101 million) are here more evident.

Funding of the voluntary sector in the Republic
Voluntary organisations in the Republic obtain funding from eight main sources:

- Statutory grants from local, regional, national and European sources
- Fund-raising, donations and other private sources
- Trusts and foundations
- Business and corporate sources
- Membership fees
- Trading
- Merchandising
- Payroll deductions.

Donoghue (1998) has detailed information on the funding of the voluntary non-profit sector in the Republic, bearing in mind the definitional caveats listed earlier. This found that funding of the voluntary sector was €3.24bn, of which 75 per cent came from governmental sources, 15 per cent from fees and 10 per cent from private sources. The figure must be qualified by the fact this study uses the broad ICNPO classification: 53.5 per cent of this amount was for schools and universities and 24.1 per cent for the health services. Table 7.9 shows the level of funding for the voluntary non-profit sector (€).

Table 7.9. Level of funding, *voluntary non-profit sector*, Republic of Ireland

	Government	Private	Fees
Education and research	1,717,407,000	18,757,840	466,486,530
Health	887,937,990	78,157,457	27,522,842
Development/housing	203,193,640	9,394,792	
Culture/recreation	96,249,955	32,656,393	56,415,732
Social services	84,014,759	73,813,683	9,185,285
Religion			146,125,260
Professional associations	1,813,186	68,238,263	
Environment	51,602,155	3,079,115	
International	11,652,386	37,715,030	
Civic and advocacy	10,617,549	5,400,000	
Foundations	1,947,778	499,007	

Source: adapted from Donoghue, Anheier and Salamon (1999)

This includes, as indicated, government funding for the education system and the health services. School and college fees are evident, as are private payments for health services.

Once we look at social services, environment, civic and advocacy categories, we get a clearer idea of the size of the core of the voluntary sector. The disaggregated data for the community and voluntary sector are set out in Table 7.10. According to Donoghue, Anheier and Salamon (1999), the financial value of the sector is €1,460,975,871.

Table 7.10. Level of funding, *community and voluntary sector*, Republic of Ireland, by category

	% government	% private	% fees	Total €
Social services	19.1	78.8	2.1	439,832,191
Culture and recreation	33.6	46.7	19.7	286,405,930
Development/housing	72.9	27.1		278,617,357
Religion		100		177,357,015
Health	16.5	82.5	1	88,173,152
Environment	87.2	12.8		59,162,176
International	21.6	78.4		53,849,592
Other	0	100		26,701,322
Civic and advocacy	51.8	48.2		20,498,652
Foundations	10	90		19,475,243
Education and research	83.9	16.1		10,903,241
Total:				€1,460,975,871
	33.1%	62.4%	4.6%	100%

Source: adapted from Donoghue, Anheier and Salamon (1999)

Powell and Guerin (1997) are not only able to give details of the funding sources of the voluntary sector by income source but also compare the situation from 1975 to 1995 (see Table 7.11).

Table 7.11. Sources of funding for the voluntary sector, Republic of Ireland, 1975-95

	1975	1995
European funding	1.3%	3.6%
Government/statutory funding*	18.0%	27.7%
Membership	22.3%	17.0%
Charges	5.8%	7.9%
Donations and other	23.5%	23.3%
Organised fund-raising	12.0%	12.0%

*Includes national lottery. Adapted from Powell and Guerin (1997)

This picture given in Table 7.11 is interesting, for it shows how European funding doubled, but is still small; the increase in government funding (understated in absolute terms, as the number of voluntary organisations looking for such funding will have grown during the period) and stability in the proportions of donations and organised fund-raising. It remains the case that only just over a quarter of income comes from government. In her study of voluntary organisations in the Eastern Regional Health Authority area, Donoghue (2002) found that these organisations derived a median of 49 per cent of their income from the regional health board.

Funding voluntary organisations
This map has looked at the financial size of voluntary organisations under broad headings. But do we know more about where the money comes from: how much and in what proportions? What do we know about what people give to voluntary organisations and how? Here we try to trace the financial picture from source, rather than point of arrival.

One of the problems here is that there is no agreed classification of funding sources for voluntary organisations, most researchers individualising their research instruments according to the tasks in hand. The four main headline funding sources are set out in Table 7.12.

Table 7.12. Annualised funding for the voluntary and community sector in the Republic of Ireland, 2001

Type of giving	Amount (€)
Private giving/fund-raising	€305 million
Government departments	€1,210 million
Corporate giving	€40 million
Trusts and foundations	€20 million
Total	**€1575 million**

Sources: Dáil Éireann, Debates; health boards; funding organisations; Donoghue, Anheier and Salamon (1999); white paper: *Supporting voluntary activity* (2000); and Harvey: *Rights and justice work in Ireland* (2002a).

Each is reviewed in order. As may be seen, fund-raising and private giving remain the principal source of income for voluntary organisations in the Republic of Ireland. Traditionally, the most common form of such fund-raising was the flag day, whereby voluntary organisations obtained a licence from the Gardaí to raise funds for their cause by street collections. This is used less now and other forms have come into vogue, such as *direct dialogue*, whereby street sellers accost pedestrians with a view to signing them up to both membership and a financial commitment to the organisation. Private fund-raising has diversified, going through a variety of phases (e.g. pub quizzes, once fashionable), and has become more sophisticated, using such forms as public events (e.g. concerts); legacies or bequests; encouragement of once-off donations; special days (e.g. daffodil day); coffee mornings/lunches; standing orders; and telephone, credit card and on-line donations

Merchandising is a little developed area and few choose to develop funding streams this way. Some voluntary organisations do recoup some of their costs through the sale of books or publications or make a profit from the holding of conferences. At least 16 voluntary organisations raise money through charity shops. The most prominent are Oxfam, Barnardos, the Royal National Lifeboat Institution and Simon. Three hundred staff and 3,000 volunteers now work in 186 shops. The number increased 17 per cent in the past two years (Worrall, 2003). Payroll deductions constitute a minor part of funds raised by voluntary organisations. Ruddle and O'Connor (1993) estimate that only 3 per cent of workers in the Republic participate in payroll-giving schemes. In 1990, United Way of Ireland operated a formalised payroll-giving scheme in a number of American-based multinationals, going to a list of selected charities.

The principal research on private giving to voluntary organisations was done by Ruddle and O'Connor (1992). The following were the principal patterns uncovered in a national sample. This remains the most detailed and comprehensive study of charitable giving in the Republic. While comprehensive and answering all the key questions, the principal drawback is that, being ten years old, it is now dated. Some methods of giving may have declined as new ones have arrived (e.g. Internet).

Key data on private giving to voluntary organisations
- Eighty-nine per cent of people gave to charities monthly.
- The most used means of donating were church door collections (50 per cent of respondents), followed by street collections (34 per cent) and raffles (30 per cent).
- The average monthly donation was £8.87 or €11.26.
- The imputed national annual value of donations was €312,394,920 (IR£246,031,000).
- The most favoured organisations for charitable giving were those concerned with specific diseases or disabilities, poverty, children and cancer research. The least favoured were those concerned with the arts and the religious. There was a general preference for domestic charity compared to the needs of developing countries. Fifty-nine per cent preferred to give to a specific organisation, the Society of St Vincent de Paul being the most frequently identified.
- The most generous age group was the 51 to 60 year group, with the lowest amounts coming from the oldest and youngest age groups. Higher occupational levels were more generous. There were no significant gender differences in giving.

- Six per cent gave through standing orders, 3 per cent gave through payroll deduction schemes and 10 per cent had made bequests in their wills.

The headline findings of the study were that most people gave to charity and that the level of giving was generous. There was 'evidence of a strong philanthropic impulse' and the Republic compared favourably with other countries. Most people gave to charity because they were asked rather than because they had a regular arrangement to do so – prompted giving rather than planned giving.

Donoghue, Ruddle and Mulvihill (2000) re-examined the level of individual giving in the late 1990s. They gave a fresh estimate on 1998 individual donations at €305m, a 13.1 per cent decline in absolute terms compared to 1992. The average prompted monthly donation was €10.55.

Some voluntary organisations use professional fund-raisers. The 2003 Yellow Pages list only five fund-raising agencies or consultants (Campaign Solutions, ChapterHouse Consulting, Cornerstone Fundraising, Pergman and Cook Enterprises, Tranaut) even though others are known to exist, such as Personal Fundraising Partnership and Caring Together (Cullen, 2002). Although there is a fund-raising institute in Ireland, it was not in a position or prepared to supply any information about the scale or nature of professional fund-raising in Ireland.

Colgan (2002) has provided some fresh data on fund-raising by the sector. In her survey of national voluntary organisations, she found that in the Republic:

- 31.5 per cent had one or more salaried fund-raisers
- 50 per cent expected their trustees to engage in fund-raising
- 52.1 per cent had other staff engaged in fund-raising
- 49.3 per cent had volunteers engaged in fund-raising.

Comparable figures were available for Northern Ireland.

Government funding

The first estimate of the level of state funding for the voluntary sector was made in 1990, when it was estimated at €253m (IR£200m) (Department of Social Welfare, 1990). The most recent estimate, commissioned by the Department of Social and Family Affairs, is €1,1557m (Goodbody, 2002).

The following is the current level of funding of NGOs by the government in the Republic of Ireland in 2001, the last full year for which information is available. The information was supplied following a series of standardised parliamentary questions (Dáil Éireann, *Debates*, 9-10 October 2002).

Information on the funding of voluntary and community organisations was sought from ten health boards. Funding is broken down under the headings of the government departments introduced in July 2002, which will enable comparisons to be made in the course of the 29th Dáil. This table has the advantage that it records the view of government as to which NGO it is funding and does so in some detail. Almost all figures are for out-turns – money actually spent – as distinct from budget allocations, not all of which have been used up. The definition of NGO is known to have caused at least one government department problems in compiling its figures. However, the figures were provided once a definition of NGO was supplied. Several figures have been eliminated from the list where clearly inappropriate (e.g. civil service staff NGOs). Several figures have been added: the funding by health boards of NGOs and the proportion of social employment estimated to supply the staffing needs of voluntary organisations and some miscellaneous headings for the sake of consistency (for example, funding of Irish voluntary organisations abroad was listed by the Department of Foreign Affairs, but not by the Department of Enterprise, Trade and Employment; the latter have been added). In the case of health boards, these figures were collected board by board. The Department of Health does not collate such information at departmental level.

Table 7.13. Funding for voluntary organisations in Republic of Ireland, 2001 (in €)

Department of Health and Children	
National lottery grants (110 organisations)	3,468,924
Health board allocations to NGOs	486,589,942
Total: Department of Health and Children	**490,058,866**
Department of Enterprise, Trade and Employment	
Grants to 11 NGOs	7,594,165
Grants for Irish voluntary organisations in Britain (Dion committee)	2,604,237
Community Employment, estimated NGO benefit	317,202,910
Total: Department of Enterprise, Trade and Employment	**327,401,312**
Department of the Environment and Local Government	
Core funding for two NGOs or groups of NGOs	271,785
14 grants for NGOs to attend conferences	15,400
24 conservation grants	593,138
28 miscellaneous grants	617,858
6 grants under the Blue Flag scheme	85,000
1 grant for national group water schemes	415,717

Table 7.13. Funding for voluntary organisations in Republic of Ireland, 2001 (in €) (contd.)

Department of the Environment and Local Government (contd.)	
179 housing grants	114,602,940
21 grants for running costs of social housing organisations	1,910,322
Total: Department of the Environment and Local Government	**118,512,160**
Department of Justice, Equality and Law Reform	
Small grants, projects against racism (290 grants)	496,723
Regular and once-off grants to 17 NGOs in justice, equality, law reform	2,847,568
Grants for refugee services (49 grants)	1,309,592
Grant for National Women's Council of Ireland	519,332
Grant in association with draft national plan for women	980,872
Equality for women measure in national development plan	800,394
Probation and welfare service (51 grants)	13,179,665
Grant aid by prison service	76,184
Childcare services – staffing	28,213,002
Childcare services – capital funding	17,087,136
Total: Department of Justice, Equality and Law Reform	**65,510,468**
Department of Community, Rural and Gaeltacht Affairs	
CAIT Community Application of Information Technology (66 projects)	3,008,532
Community development programme	16,700,000
Core funding for locally based community and family support groups	2,200,000
Grants for education, training and family support	2,800,000
Community support for older people	2,700,000
Local drugs task forces	11,320,214
Ciste na Gaeilge (25 organisations)	1,743,353
Island development	50,789
Rural farm relief	718,672
Cultural scheme/Scéimeanna Chultúrtha (9 organisations)	501,650
Total: Department of Community, Rural and Gaeltacht Affairs	**41,743,210**
Department of Family and Social Affairs	
Family and community services resource centres programme	2,654,660
Money Advice and Budgeting Services	8,267,924
Organisations providing marriage, child, bereavement counselling*	6,659,000
Development of second chance education opportunities (6 grants)	284,329
Promotion of information and welfare rights	619,418
Once-off funding for 10 organisations	142,435
School meals programme (91 organisations)	683,277

Table 7.13. Funding for voluntary organisations in Republic of Ireland, 2001 (in €) (contd.)

Department of Family and Social Affairs (contd.)	
Employment support services, special projects fund (155 organisations)	1,883,355
Total: Department of Family and Social Affairs	**21,194,398**
*Figure for 2002	

Department of Education	
Grants for 33 national or regional youth organisations	8,818,915
Grants for 300 projects under Young People's Facilities and Services Fund	13,731,273
36 local projects under drugs task forces	2,480,162
Two grants (organisations assisting children with learning difficulties)	121,894
6 NGOs for north–south co-operation projects	455,334
11 cultural and scientific organisations	1,048,041
3 projects of targeted educational responses for children at risk	57,914
5 projects Support for teenage parents	218,394
16 grants for projects for out-of-school children	379,651
The line (3 grants)	162,112
Primary disadvantaged residual fund	271,551
Total: Department of Education and Science	**27,745,241**

Department of Finance	
Economic and Social Research Institute	2,378,000
Institute of Public Administration	55,000
Irish Institute of European Affairs	25,395
Institute of Public Administration	2,472,000
Euro changeover campaign, grants to NGOs	1,634,265
Compensation for loss of revenue due to national lottery	7,618,429
Total: Department of Finance	**14,183,089**

Department of Foreign Affairs	
Development organisations	15,935,212
Royal Irish Academy	76,200
Standing committee on human rights	25,935
NGO forum on human rights	16,507
Irish groups in the United States	658,991
Irish groups in Australia	33,605
European Movement	127,000
Communicating Europe	43,578
Irish–UN association	19,046
Cultural Relations Committee	634,869
Reconciliation Fund (83 grants)	2,560,064
Total: Department of Foreign Affairs	**20,131,007**

Table 7.13. Funding for voluntary organisations in Republic of Ireland, 2001 (in €) (contd.)

Department of Communications, Marine and Natural Resources(contd.)	
8 NGOs, mainly involved in the promotion of trees	267,101
Total: Dept of Communications, Marine and Natural Resources	**267,101**
Department of Arts, Sport and Tourism	
Sports capital programme	56,179,261
GAA	19,000,000
Arts programme (20 grants)	3,013,376
Total: Department of Arts, Sport and Tourism	**78,192,637**
Department of Defence	
Irish Red Cross	773,000
Coiste an *Asgard*	640,000
Total: Department of Defence	**1,413,000**
Department of Agriculture and Food	
7 grants to NGOs for services for agricultural and rural communities	88,875
52 grants to animal welfare organisations	650,741
Total: Department of Agriculture and Food	**739,616**
Department of Transport	
Rural transport initiative*	3,000,000
Total: Department of Transport	**3,000,000**
*Figure for 2002	
Overall total	**1,210,092,105**

The level and role of government funding is reviewed in broadly descending order. The Department of Health and Children is the largest single funder of voluntary organisations. However, it is an indirect funder, since the vast bulk of this funding is distributed to the seven health boards and one regional health authority for allocation (with three area boards). The only direct funding by the Department of Health and Children for voluntary organisations is a lottery fund. However, Donoghue (2002) noted that a significant number of voluntary organisations obtained health board funding after having originally defined a funding path through the Department of Health.

The Department of Enterprise, Trade and Employment is the second largest funder of voluntary organisations. This is a reflection of the importance of community employment, of which 80 per cent of places are estimated to go to meeting the staff needs of voluntary and community organisations. Community Employment (CE) is becoming less important as a funder of voluntary and community activity. At one stage, as many as 44,000 people were employed on community employment, but this is projected to fall to about 22,000 by the end of 2003. In addition, the department provides a small amount of direct funding for eleven NGOs concerned with employment issues.

The Department of Community, Rural and Gaeltacht Affairs is a new configuration. The department was assigned a number of substantial programmes from the Department of Social, Community and Family Affairs, which functioned from 1997 to 2002. Several of these programmes could in turn be traced to the development of voluntary sector support programmes dating to the Department of Social Welfare in the late 1980s. The Department of Social and Family Affairs retains responsibility for a number of family-orientated programmes dating to the same period. The Department of Social and Family Affairs retains responsibility for Comhairle, formerly the National Social Service Board. In 2001, Comhairle provided €207,987 for three organisations to promote volunteering (Focus Ireland, Tallaght Volunteer Bureau, the Volunteer Resource Centre) and €168,804 in information and publications grants to 15 national and local organisations (Comhairle, 2003).

The Department of Foreign Affairs' budget for voluntary organisations goes primarily to voluntary organisations participating in its development aid programme. The department provides funding for north–south work under the Reconciliation Fund, which dates to 1982 (see chapter three). The department's Cultural Relations Committee supports cultural activity by individuals or organisations abroad. The Department of the Environment's budget is dominated by the allocation for social housing by voluntary organisations. However, in recent years, the department has begun to provide core funding for voluntary organisations working in the housing and environmental area, with a number of specialised schemes in the area of conservation and water quality (*Blue Flag* scheme). The Department of Arts, Sport and Tourism has two main funding streams: sports capital grants (lottery financed) and the arts programme. In addition, the GAA benefited from a once-off grant.

The Department of Education and Science is a long-standing funder of voluntary organisations. The scheme for the support of national youth organisations dates to 1969 and since then it has been supplemented by a number of specialised schemes and targeted educational initiatives, some quite small.

The Department of Finance supports a number of think-tank type bodies, like the Economic and Social Research Institute and the Institute of European Affairs. Whilst many people might regard some of these bodies as close to government, in reality they are bodies independent of government. In addition, the department provides compensatory funding for NGOs which formerly ran lotteries, but which have been adversely affected by the introduction of the national lottery. The Department of Justice, Equality and Law Reform has emerged only very recently as a significant, expanding funder of voluntary and community organisations. The department had, for some time, funded voluntary organisations working in the area of probation and criminality. In the early 1990s, the department inherited a grant from the Department of the Taoiseach for the National Women's Council and was prevailed upon, with some reluctance, to provide funding for the Free Legal Advice Centres in 1992. Now up to 17 NGOs are in receipt of regular or once-off grants. The department now funds a large childcare programme, refugee services, projects against racism and a women's programme.

The other departments are relatively small funders: the Department of Agriculture and Food (rural/agricultural and animal welfare organisations); the Department of Defence (Red Cross and the *Asgard* sail training ship), the Department of Communications, Marine and Natural Resources (voluntary organisations promoting trees and broadleaf afforestation) and the Department of Transport (rural transport initiative).

European funding for the Irish voluntary sector is focused on two programmes: EQUAL and the new Programme for Peace and Reconciliation (in shorthand called PEACE II). Twenty-two Irish projects were funded under EQUAL, averaging €36,000, covering such areas as disabilities, training and gender equality. PEACE II has five themes in the Republic: economic renewal (€13m), social inclusion (€22m), locally-based regeneration (€20m), making the area an outwards and forward-looking region (€7.5m) and cross-border co-operation (€37.5m) (total €100m). The Combat Poverty Agency jointly runs three measures in the Programme for Peace and Reconciliation – Cross-border community regeneration (measure 3.4), Developing grassroots capacity and promoting the inclusion of women (measure 4.1) and Promoting the inclusion of vulnerable groups (measure 4.4). These provide significant funding for voluntary and community groups in the border counties.

The International Fund for Ireland should also be mentioned here. Although private in appearance, it is funded by the governments of the United States, New Zealand, Australia, Canada and by the European Union. Although the main thrust of the work of the fund is for economic development, the fund has run programmes for community and social development for a number of years. The estimated spend on community projects in the Republic in 2001 is €3.6m.

Funding by trust and foundations

Now we turn to the non-governmental side, which may be divided into trusts and foundations; corporate giving; and individual giving. Colgan (2002) takes the view that there is scope for a considerable growth in the levels of organised philanthropic giving in Ireland. American rates of giving are 2 per cent of gross domestic product, which in the case of the Republic would translate at €1,700m a year – bears little comparison to the €60m estimate here (€40m for corporate donations, €20m for trusts and foundations). Donoghue (2001d) forms the view that the number of foundations in Ireland is quite small and she points out that Greece, Portugal and Spain all have a much greater number of foundations, despite being much poorer countries.

Chapter three noted the emergence in Ireland of a number of trusts and foundations. Within them were a number of sub-categories: British-based foundations, Irish foundations operating only in Ireland, Irish foundations operating in Britain and Ireland and others which did not solicit applications.

Table 7.14 attempts to assess the level of trust funding for voluntary and community organisations in the Republic (figures for 2001). Although there are known to be 25 foundations operating in the Republic Ireland, some may not fit our definition of a body grant-making for voluntary and community activity (Donoghue, 2003). Of the rest, several are not prepared to give details of the nature of their operations. The information in Table 7.14 is based on those who do meet the definition and who operate with a greater or lesser degree of openness.

These figures must be qualified in a number of ways. Some figures are broad estimates (e.g. Atlantic Philanthropies). People in Need operates on a two-year cycle, distributing money in alternate years: there would be no funding in 2002, for example, but 2001 was a distribution year. Conversely, Allen Lane has given funding every year of its operation in the Republic, but 2001 was an exception. The Community Foundation has presented figures on its funding, but they are cumulative, have not been annualised and as a result cannot be included.

Trust funding in the early 1990s was €8.5m, so the 2001 figure of more than €20m above represents an increase of 145 per cent. Chapter three gave some details of their origins and some of their present work is now reviewed briefly. The Ireland Funds raise their resources from 12 countries, principally from the United States and English-speaking countries, through a considerable fund-raising effort (events, corporate donations). The Ireland Funds not only run their own programme but work with donors to allocate a much larger proportion of donor-advised funds. Several hundred projects are assisted each year in such areas as arts, culture, community development, education and peace and reconciliation.

Atlantic Philanthropies operated in Ireland from the early 1990s, providing

Table 7.14. Annualised trust funding bodies for the voluntary sector in the Republic of Ireland, 2001

Trust	Budget	Area of interest
Ireland Funds	€9,419,953	Arts, community development, peace and reconciliation, culture, education
Atlantic Philanthropies	€1,200,000	Voluntary sector, ageing, human rights, health
People in Need	€7,750,000	Elderly, disabled, homeless, children, youth
Katharine Howard	€143,361	Children, youth, health, elderly, disadvantaged people
Co-operation Ireland	€900,000	North–south, peace and reconciliation
Allen Lane	Nil	Offenders
St Stephen's Green Trust	€120,750	Marginalised groups
Irish Youth Foundation	€447,202	Young people and children at risk
Gulbenkian Foundation	€173,954	Arts, education and social welfare
Joseph Rowntree Charitable Trust	€301,416	Rights and justice
Bewley Foundation	€420,000	Health, education and community
Total	**€20,876,636**	

Sources: Direct from organisations; Goodbody, 2002; Colgan, 2002. Figures are for 2001, financial year covering 2001, or nearest year for which information is available.

their main financial support for the universities. They operated a smaller voluntary sector programme, designed to enhance the operation of the sector itself and voluntary organisations working in the area of human rights, peace and reconciliation. In summer 2003, Atlantic Philanthropies announced that it would spend down its endowment of more than €3 billion, concentrating from 2004 on the issues of ageing, disadvantaged children and youth, reconciliation and human rights (Looney, 2003; O'Clery, 2003).

The St Stephen's Green Trust helps organisations, projects and initiatives working in the areas of vulnerable children and young people, housing and homelessness, offenders, refugees and asylum seekers, male Travellers, poverty, social exclusion, injustice and discrimination. Grants are generally small, around the €6,348 mark, but may rise to €12,697. Twenty-three grants were made, to the value of €120,750 in 2001, averaging €5,250. The Bewley Foundation provided 42 grants in the year 2001/2 to the level of €420,000 to organisations working in the health, education and community area, preferring to support capital projects to revenue funding.

People in Need, based on the telethon, provides once-off capital grants concentrated in the €1,904 to €12,697 range for organisations working with deprived and disadvantaged people such as the homeless, elderly, children and mentally and physically handicapped. The Katharine Howard Foundation focuses on supporting voluntary and community groups in the areas of young people, health care, the elderly and disadvantaged, playgroups, parents and toddlers, being especially supportive of those using community-development methods. In 2002, the foundation provided grants of €143,361 to a hundred organisations, including some in Northern Ireland. The normal bandwidth for grants is €500 to €2,500, concentrated on the €1,000 to €2,000 range.

Of the north–south funding bodies, Co-operation Ireland runs programmes for youth, education and community exchanges, business and cultural partnerships, economic co-operation, secondary schools and community development programmes, primarily provided for transport, workshops, and joint activities between north–south groups and cross-community groups within Northern Ireland, aimed at promoting mutual understanding, respect and inclusion.

The Irish Youth Foundation provides funding for projects working with children and young people in Ireland, supplemented by a programme in Britain. In 2001, 87 grants were allocated for disbursement that year to the value of €650,740, ranging in value from €634 to €63,486, an average of €7,479 in the areas of special needs, social education, volunteering, training and leadership, research and evaluation, art and cultural expression, drugs prevention, equipment and resources.

Turning to the British-based foundations, the Allen Lane Foundation came to Ireland in 1988, running an initial funding programme of UK£30,000 for three years for women's groups. In the late 1990s, the Allen Lane Foundation's programme now focused on offenders and ex-offenders, grants ranging from €6,856 to €25,394. No grants were made in 2001 and only one in 2002, €11,000 to Blanchardstown Offenders for New Directions and three more subsequently.

The Gulbenkian Foundation operates a grant programme for the UK and Republic of Ireland with the themes of arts, education and social welfare. In the Republic in 2001, Gulbenkian awarded grants of €173,954 to 12 national, region and local organisations, 5.9 per cent of its total programme.

Finally, it is important to note the Community Foundation for Ireland. The Community Foundation makes small grants in the range €500 to €1,000 for voluntary and community groups. The current priorities are in the area of lone parents; groups working with gay, lesbian, bisexual and transgendered persons; and new communities and cultures. Overall, it favours projects working for the social inclusion of communities excluded by reasons of geography, age, disability, family circumstances, poverty, gender or race. So far (autumn 2003) the Community Foundation has made 41 grants valued at €369,379 of which €88,246 was specified by donors and the rest undesignated. The smallest grant was €634, the largest €190,460 and the average €4,444 (the large grant was an exceptional investment for the Limerick Enterprise Development Partnership to regenerate a disused factory). Annualised figures are not available, as no annual report has been published.

The number of foundations operating in the Republic of Ireland appears to be quite limited. In Britain and the European Union, by contrast, voluntary organisations have a broad range of foundations to which they can turn for support. Few Irish foundations appear to be the outcome of indigenous philanthropy, the principal ones being the Katharine Howard Foundation, the People in Need telethon and the Irish Youth Foundation. The Ireland Funds rely in large measure on money raised abroad, while the Atlantic Philanthropies depend on the endowment of a successful Irish American businessman based in the United States. Several of the foundations working in Ireland are Irish outposts of British-based operations, such as Gulbenkian, Allen Lane, the St Stephen's Green Trust and the Joseph Rowntree Charitable Trust. The Community Foundation is an attempt to establish a domestic national foundation and it has made some progress. The low level of indigenous foundation development suggests that this is a weak area in voluntary sector development in the Republic. The reasons for the small number of foundations in the Republic have not been scientifically explained, but voluntary sector experts speculate that the reason may lie in the traditional lack of indigenous wealth (no longer the case), the legacy of colonialism which causes people to look outward for help and a preference for *ad hoc* rather than strategic giving. Despite this, the distinct areas funded by some of these trusts and foundations may mean that they have had a disproportionate impact.

Funding by the corporate/business sector
Information on the role of the corporate and business sector in funding voluntary and community organisations in Ireland is unsatisfactory. The business community is extremely reluctant to provide information on company funding for voluntary organisations. The first estimates of the level of corporate giving were done by the Irish Tax Reform Group (1996), which then estimated the level of corporate giving to be in the order of IR£11m (or €14m). Our current knowledge is limited to one source, Donoghue, Ruddle and Mulvihill (2000), the key points of their research being:

• Businesses, large and small, prefer to give to small, local voluntary organisations. This is true of large companies with a presence throughout the country as much as for small, single enterprises.

- Only 35.6 per cent of companies had a strategy for the support of voluntary organisations (more with larger companies, less with smaller). Businesses give in a prompted, not-planned way. There does not appear to be a national forum where businesses discuss grant-giving strategies, nor is there an interface where the business community can discuss these issues with the voluntary sector (the absence of an umbrella body for the voluntary sector may contribute to this gap). Businesses did not know about government efforts to support corporate giving to the sector.
- Most businesses and corporate donors give small grants, either in tens or hundreds of €s, rarely more. For some, the overall size of their giving programme is very small indeed compared to their turnover or profits.
- Most prefer to give to concrete, on-the-ground, charitable action projects. Some, however, will provide funding for controversial, policy-orientated work with which some statutory agencies would certainly baulk. Personal contacts, localism and the reputation of the organisation concerned were the key factors determining which organisation they would support.
- Information on funding by corporate and business organisations is exceptionally poor, making comparisons difficult. Most businesses are reluctant to give such information (the majority refuse outright) and requests for such information have very low response rates (a quarter is the norm). Others provide glossy material on their work with charities, but it can be extremely thin on detail (e.g. who got how much money to do what). Many do not have the information systems to provide data in the first place. They are secretive (Curry, 1991).

Based on returns from the 1,000 companies, the level of corporate giving is imputed at €40m a year or 0.04 per cent of company turnover of donating companies, low by international standards (Donoghue, Ruddle and Mulvihill, 2000). Corporate giving is estimated to account for much less than 10 per cent of money flowing into the voluntary sector. The research indicated that businesses might well respond better if campaigns by government to encourage corporate giving were organised and publicised and if voluntary organisations became more professional in their approaches to them.

Table 7.15 illustrates the areas of support favoured by corporate donors studied. The main areas for donations are sports, community development, education, health and social services, in that order. The main donors are the larger, more affluent companies, principally in finance, retailing and food, especially those with larger numbers of employees (e.g. over 150). Below-average giving was a feature of companies involved in transport,

Table 7.15. Level of corporate giving, Republic of Ireland

	Cash €	In kind value	Total	%
Sports	3,353,181	81,771	3,434,952	23
Community-development	2,508,907	269,882	2,778,789	19
Education	1,985,213	604,268	2,589,481	17
Other	1,477,846	102,467	1,580,313	11
Health	1,395,378	133,957	1,529,335	10
Social services	1,161,185	141,068	1,302,253	9
Arts	1,091,652	141,571	1,233,223	8
Third world	298,300	220,444	518,744	3
Total	**13,271,662**	**1,695,428**	**14,967,090**	**100**

Source: adapted from Donoghue, Ruddle and Mulvihill (2000)

communications, distribution, repairs, catering, manufacturing, chemicals, building, engineering and agriculture. The average giving per company is €69.915, though this may be spread among a large number of donees. The amount given per employee is €125.08. Non-cash support took the form of gifts, expertise, use of facilities, scholarships, training and staff secondment. When asked why they provided support, most businesses expressed a desire to support local community initiatives, public relations and a sense of social responsibility. There is a lack of strategic thinking about company giving and only 36 per cent had any formal policy at all. Donoghue's study was based on a response rate of 26 per cent, emphasising the data problems already noted.

Few businesses ever respond to routine requests for information about their charitable giving. The two exceptions are AIB Bank and Bank of Ireland, though even their information can be problematic. Compiling truly comparable, annualised figures is extremely difficult, though a picture can be built up. AIB Bank currently provides financial support for groups working with children in the areas of: education and poverty, homelessness, and drug and alcohol abuse. This takes the place of its 'Better Ireland' programme which in its last year provided support to the value of €380,992. AIB estimates suggest that the level of informal giving by its branches throughout the country may be as high as €8.57m. Bank of Ireland donates an estimated €253,992 a year, to such groups as sports clubs, schools, community organisations and local good causes, such as scanner appeals, day centres, special schools, play groups, hospices and youth clubs. In addition, staff have raised money for individual causes (e.g. Irish Cancer Society). The bank has a programme for the support of the arts, for the provision of computer training in unemployment black spots, and for the seconding of staff to voluntary organisations.

Governance

Next we map the systems of governance of the voluntary sector in the Republic. The systems of governance laid down by law were described in chapter five. Not much is known about the current systems in operation. In the face of other informational deficits, it was not a priority area for attention and lagged behind the level of knowledge in the UK. Some observers of the voluntary sector consider that many boards of voluntary organisations are ill-equipped to meet their legal and staffing responsibilities and have inadequate support or access to training. O'Ferrall (2000) noted the upsurge of interest in governance issues in Britain and elsewhere in the 1990s and sketched a useful contextual and theoretical background for developments in Ireland, but research on the question here remains limited. O'Ferrall provided a critical analysis of governance issues in the Irish hospital system, with particular reference to voluntary hospital boards. He made the point that the system of governance at work in the public voluntary hospitals, in the particular case of the Adelaide, was quite different from the command public service management system because it involved a series of layers of those working in the hospital in the decision-making process.

Our principal empirical knowledge of the governance of the voluntary sector comes from Jaffro (1998). Her principal findings were as follows:

Key governance features of the voluntary sector in the Republic
- Voluntary sector boards generally met bi-monthly.
- Boards had a overall even balance of male and female members, although the proportions varied from one sector to another.
- Fifty-seven per cent of board members were in the 35 to 55 year age group.
- Three out of four came from within the ranks of the organisation.
- Some boards included staff members. In some cases, this may be because they are 'in attendance', rather than full members (some people being unaware of this distinction). In other cases, it is possible they were unaware that the membership of paid staff on boards is illegal.
- The most common period of membership on boards was 1 to 3 years (50 per cent).
- The composition of board members was as follows: at work, 56 per cent; retired, 16 per cent; working in the home or unemployed, 24 per cent.
- Board members tended to accumulate memberships. Forty-seven per cent had been on the boards of other voluntary organisations while two-thirds currently were so.
- There was an alarmingly low level of knowledge about the responsibilities, functions and duties of board members. Very little training or factual information was actually provided for board or prospective board members.

There was a surprisingly big gap between the prescribed functions of board members and what they actually did. Many were involved in management (not necessarily a board function) while significant numbers seemed unaware of their actual legal duties (a necessary function).

- The operation of boards in the Republic was characterised by an informality which carries the danger of confusion and demotivation.

Jaffro compared the Republic of Ireland findings with similar studies in England and Wales, finding the Irish board members were younger, more female and less likely to be professional. Some governance information is also available from the study by Ruddle and Donoghue (1995) of social service voluntary organisations. This found that a management committee was the standard form of governance (93 per cent of cases), generally elected or appointed from within the organisation's membership. The median committee size was nine, holding a median of 10.5 meetings a year. It would be helpful to know much more about the profile of board members of Irish voluntary organisations, their experiences and the relationship between volunteering and changing labour market conditions.

Jaffro has also drawn attention to the governance problems arising from the legal forms taken by voluntary organisations in the Republic of Ireland. Some of these issues have already been flagged in chapter five. The most commonly used legal format, that of a company limited by guarantee and not having share capital under the Companies Act, 1963, is problematic for good governance.

- It is legalistic, requiring a knowledge of legal matters to understand and operate.
- It is inappropriate in where it locates power, placing authority in the organisation in the hands of a potentially self-perpetuating board of directors, not in the hands of the membership.
- It is a form with which most members are unlikely to be familiar. Most board members are highly unlikely to see, be presented with, or develop a working knowledge of the document, despite it being a core one for the organisation. A situation in which most board members of Irish voluntary organisations are likely to be ignorant of their governing document is not a healthy one.

Related to governance is the question of consumer issues. The role and rights of consumers of the services of voluntary organisations is a prominent issue in the discourse on the voluntary sector in other European countries, for example France. By contrast, it has been little debated or discussed in Ireland and has not been well mapped. This is a little surprising, granted the level of investment in evaluation and strategic planning in Irish voluntary organisations in recent years.

Faughnan and Kelleher (1993) found that the commitment to formally promote consumer protection was an issue that the sector must address. Almost a quarter of the organisations that they studied had indicated that the issue was not an important one, and another quarter had responded that they had given it no attention. 'Organisations needed to evaluate their own structures and the openness to involvement by consumers.' Consumer orientation has been a trend in Irish public services, but Faughnan (1997) points out that it should not be confused with consumer *empowerment*. Here, she said, the track record of voluntary organisations was not particularly encouraging. Powell and Guerin (1997) found that there was a strong and positive perception that voluntary organisations deal with those who used their services in a fair and honest way (76 per cent agreed, 13 per cent disagreed). Overall, voluntary organisations were reckoned to be fair and efficient. The organisations themselves felt that they were adequately accountable to their clients (95 per cent thought so) – but the critic would say that they were not the people to ask. Likewise, organisations felt that clients did have influence over the decision-making of the organisation (41 per cent a lot, 38 per cent some, 12 per cent a little, 9 per cent none). Within the disability movement, there has been strong criticism that voluntary organisations have been so busy pursuing organisational goals and developing services that they have failed to listen to, still less empower, people with disabilities themselves (Toolan, 1992). As a result, people with disabilities set up organisations that they alone would control on their own terms.

Further evidence of the under-developed state of governance in the voluntary sector in the Republic came in 2003 when investment managers Montgomery Oppenheim surveyed the nature of investments made by voluntary organisations. Leaving aside the fact that 17 per cent of charities had no assets at all, two-thirds put their assets into a bank account and the balance into other investments. Of these, only 29 per cent had an ethical investment policy (Slattery, 2003).

Management issues in the voluntary and community sector have received attention only in recent years. In the late 1990s, the School of Business Studies in Dublin University (Trinity College) developed the Centre for Non-Profit Management and ran a voluntary sector management research project, exploring management issues in 15 voluntary organisations. The project explored the trajectories of a number of voluntary organisations from foundation through growth to old age. It identified a number of the challenges facing managers of Irish voluntary organisations, such as addressing a state uncertain of its role and meeting greater demands on diminished resources.

They modelled Irish NGOs in three groups: emerging, established and traditional organisations (Donnelly-Cox and O'Regan, 1999).

Case studies
Chapter six considered the development of particular parts of the voluntary and community sector in Northern Ireland, namely those engaged in personal social services, housing associations and advice centres. Similar studies tracking the trajectories of different parts of the sector are not available in the Republic, at least not to the same degree. However, we do have some knowledge of some distinct parts of four sub-sectors and this is reviewed here. These are the parts that provide social welfare services, the women's movement, disability and those parts engaged in north–south co-operation.

The social welfare sub-sector is important, for it impinges on so many broad aspects of national social policy and is discussed first. Despite the secularisation of the voluntary and community sector, present-day descendants of Catholic social action of the 1930s may still be found in organisations such as Crosscare, formerly the Catholic Social Service Conference (see chapter three), which provides a range of welfare services in Dublin and in religious orders, institutions and their related services, which continue to be active in their many evolutions, forms and mutations. Nationally, much the largest voluntary organisation in the country is the Society of St Vincent de Paul, which has 9,000 volunteer members, branches in almost every parish in the country (1,000 local conferences), and a turnover of over €20m which is distributed in the form of cash and kind to needy families throughout the country. The sector was profiled by Ruddle and Donoghue (1996) (using a broader sample than Faughnan and Kelleher, 1993). The following were its principal findings:

Main features of social welfare organisations
- The average age of organisations was 17 years, so many had been established recently.
- The two main client groups were the elderly and unemployed. Compared to other European countries, young people were little targeted by social welfare organisations.
- The main services provided were information and advice, social and recreational activities and befriending/home visits. Most served a small number of clients, less than 50 a week, in small geographic areas.
- Their incomes were modest, half receiving an income of less than IR£10,000 (€12,700) a year or less. The median spending was IR£5,983.50 (€7,597). Only 52 per cent received government funding for their work.

The median government funding was IR£2,177.50 (€2,764), compared to IR£3,748.50 (€4,759) from other, non-governmental sources.
- Only one-third had full-time paid staff and these tended to be national headquarters organisations.
- Almost all the organisations (95 per cent) used volunteers. The average number of volunteers was ten. The typical amount of time given was three hours a week, very low by European standards. The main activity of volunteers (72 per cent) was fund-raising, followed by committee work (66 per cent) and administration (48 per cent). Volunteers were mainly recruited by word of mouth and personal contacts (85 per cent). Only 11 per cent of organisations had a volunteer policy.

With regard to staffing, Faughnan and Kelleher (1993) found:

- At one extreme, a fifth of the voluntary organisations studied had no staff.
- At the other end of the scale, 10 per cent employed 50 people or more.
- Two-thirds employed less than 20 people.

The picture therefore remains of a large number of small organisations, with modest incomes, only a third having staff, almost all having some voluntary input, operating to discrete groups in defined areas.

Another traditional sector of development is that of organisations working in the area of intellectual and physical disability. These date back to the institutions of the nineteenth century, with, as chapter three noted, new organisations being formed in the post-war period, and advocacy organisations in more recent times. Many disability services continue to be provided by religious orders (e.g. Brothers of Charity, St Michael's House), followed by the post-war organisations (e.g. Cork Polio, Irish Wheelchair Association) and national umbrella organisations such as the National Association for the Mentally Handicapped in Ireland and the Disability Federation of Ireland. To them may be added more recent specialised, self-help, radical and campaigning organisations such as Fighting Blindness, People With Disability Ireland and the Centre for Independent Living. Kiernan (2000) profiled the 56 member organisations affiliated to the Disability Federation of Ireland, covering the most prominent, networked organisations in the physical disability sector.

The principal findings were as follows:

- About 15 per cent were formed prior to 1959. Growth for the following two decades was slow. The main period of formation was in the 1980s, when 38 per cent were formed, with more modest growth subsequently. Generally the oldest organisations were the largest organisations.

- Almost 80 per cent were national organisations (either all of Ireland or all of the Republic), half having a branch structure.
- The range of financial turnover was wide. At one extreme, six national organisations had a turnover of less than €63,000, while one had a turnover of almost €100m. The main grouping for turnover was in the range €126,000 to €368,000.
- Although some older organisations received substantial statutory funding, newer and smaller organisations obtained little. For these groups, the norm was to raise 70 per cent to 90 per cent of their income from charitable donations.
- The principal sources of funding were European Union (23 per cent of organisations benefit from this source), community employment (54 per cent) and the Department of Health and Children (18 per cent).
- Staffing: 17 per cent had no staff while 60 per cent had staff of 5 or less.

One is left with a picture of some large, well-established organisations, but a multitude of many smaller ones with few staff and, probably, a reliance on community employment. European Union funding has played an important role here, probably because of European Social Fund support for labour market reintegration measures.

The women's sector is popularly considered a relatively young one, though, as chapter one outlined, the women's voluntary sector goes back to the end of the nineteenth century. A similar pattern of development is evident here, matching the social services and disability sectors. The oldest organisation, the Irish Countrywomen's Association, remains the largest. Specialised and campaigning organisations emerged in the 1960s and are now well established (e.g. Women's Aid, Rape Crisis Centres, National Traveller Women's Forum), with newer such groups coming to the fore in very recent times (e.g. Lesbians Organising Together). Federation has played an especially important role for the women's sector, providing cohesion and political influence much more than the sum of its individual parts. This is the National Women's Council of Ireland. Its membership expanded steadily from its foundation as the Council for the Status of Women with its original 17 members in 1972, to152 member organisations today representing 300,000 women, the council continuing to struggle for women's equality in law, politics, decision-making and the labour force. Its range of membership is diverse, from conservative to radical feminist, to trade unions, businesses and voluntary organisations.

Kelleher Associates (2001) have considerably improved our knowledge of the women's sector. They estimated that there were 2,631 women's organisations in the state, three-quarters having been established in the past ten years. The report states that 79 per cent were small, having a budget of less than €1,270 a year, and that they were badly under-funded. Only 20 per cent employed staff. The main focus of the groups (76 per cent) was women in the community, with small percentages concerned with Traveller women, lone parents and women experiencing violence. Typical locally-based groups tended to have about 19 members, and provide support and solidarity as well as training, adult education and health information. Besides community groups, women's organisations took the form of local, regional and national networks; women's resource centres and projects; lone parent groups; organisations defending women from violence; and groups representing special or sectoral interests (e.g. Traveller women, older women, minority ethnic women).

Finally, there is a small number of voluntary organisations dedicated to north–south co-operation. This sector is different from the foregoing, but despite its small size has a particular significance in this study with its north–south theme. Before looking at them, it should be mentioned that a number of voluntary organisations were established prior to 1921 and continue to operate on a north–south basis, despite the border. The principal examples are sporting bodies (e.g. rugby) and church-based groups (e.g. church-based youth organisations). In this respect, north–south working has always been a feature of the voluntary sector in both parts of the island. It may well be the case that few *new* voluntary organisations were formed on a 32-county basis after partition. After the start of 'the Troubles', a number of organisations came into existence in the Republic specifically to address north–south issues. They paralleled, to some degree, the peace and reconciliation sector in Northern Ireland. They were also, at least in the south, a concrete example of citizen initiatives attempting to address socio-political problems in a concrete, practical and constructive way. Many sought to make a specific contribution to seeking solutions to the conflict, though not all were able to last (e.g. Peace Train, New Consensus). The most enduring of these proved to be the Glencree Centre for Reconciliation and Co-operation Ireland. About twenty federated under the Platform for Peace and Reconciliation in 1997 but it has been slow to attract governmental support. The collective impact of these organisations has not yet been systematically measured.

Current level of north–south working
This leads us to a final question in this chapter, which is to make an appraisal of the current level of north–south working between the two voluntary and community sectors. It is almost certainly the case that the level of north–south working was probably very low, certainly over the period to 1969. Subsequently, it was recognised that in rebuilding relationships between the two parts of the island, voluntary organisations could provide a

practical and relatively neutral environment in which this could take place. International experts in conflict resolution term this 'track 2 diplomacy', in which civil society organisations bring organisations and people together in such a way as to underpin political co-operation between governments and the political élites (Wilson, 1999).

The major impetus to co-operation between voluntary organisations was provided by Co-operation North, then Cooperation Ireland, which provided a structured environment for exchanges, co-operation and joint working. In 1995, the Centre for Peace and Development Studies at the University of Limerick estimated that there were about 330 bodies co-operating on a north–south basis, a figure rising to 500 by 1998 (Murray, 1998). Not all of these were voluntary and community organisations (some were governmental or commercial), but they were a major element therein. Examination of these links suggests that north–south voluntary sector co-operation could be classified as follows:

- As already noted, north–south organisations pre-dating the border (e.g. Society of St Vincent de Paul, YMCA, Royal National Lifeboat Institution)
- Track 2 diplomacy organisations, as discussed
- North–south organisations formed in more recent times. These would be small in number and would tend to be coalitions of horizontal interest groups (e.g. Focus on Children). In some case, the northern or southern part might have a slightly different organisational expression (e.g. Irish National Organisation of the Unemployed/Organisation of the Unemployed NI)
- Republic-based organisations that had a defined, formal project or area of co-operation with its opposite number in Northern Ireland and *vice versa* (e.g. An Taisce with National Trust NI). Another example is Irish Rural Link with the Rural Community Network, whose co-operation emerged from the Poverty II programme. The two organisations run exchanges, share training, run a cross-border programme together and have held a joint AGM
- Republic-based organisations whose organisations took part in *ad hoc* exchanges, events or programmes but did not have a formal, organisational medium or long-term structured programme of co-operation in place (e.g. Irish Countrywomen's Association, North–South Conference on Poverty)
- Somewhere in between, many organisations that had a regular, well established, on-going but informal system of information exchange. This could take the form of exchanging newsletters, and attending each other's annual conference (e.g. Disability Federation of Ireland/Disability Action NI; NAMHI/Mencap).

Innovation and good practice

An aspiration of this research project was to identify innovation and good practice in the community and voluntary sector. This has proved to be problematical. In fact, no formal system exists to identify either, apart from some occasional programme evaluations, programmes against poverty and directories of European Union-funded projects. The voluntary sectors in both parts of the island claim to be innovative, and many umbrella bodies would express a commitment to good practice. Despite this, the literature of the voluntary section in both parts of the island affirms remarkably few examples of either innovation or good practice and those whom we consulted in the course of the research experienced a difficulty in doing so as well.

Examples of innovation and good practice as identified by project are given in Table 7.16.

Table 7.16. Examples of Innovation and Good Practice from the two jurisdictions

Northern Ireland	Republic of Ireland
Joint Government/Voluntary and Community Sector Forum	Community Development Programme
NICVA: Northern Ireland Council for Voluntary Action	Area partnerships
NIACRO: N. Ireland Association for the Care and Resettlement of Offenders/Extern	ADM
Volunteering Bureaux	Community Radio

Within the literature, one example of innovation was community radio. Community-based radio was a feature of voluntary and community-based organisation in the late 1980s, paralleling the upsurge in community radio across Europe. North Connemara Community Radio, one of the first, began broadcasting in the mid-1980s. The Broadcasting Act, 1988 introduced regulation of the sector. This was a setback, for voluntary and community stations were closed down and only two were subsequently permitted to reopen but under quite limited conditions. One of those reopening was Anna Livia FM, Dublin's first community radio, which went on the air in 1992. The station's board is drawn from community and voluntary organisations and the business community. At one stage, over 300 voluntary organisations were affiliated to the station, though that number has since fallen.

In the Republic, the Community Development Programme, established by the Minister for Social Welfare following the Poverty 2 programme, is considered a cost-effective, impactful model in delivering community development projects in disadvantaged communities. The area partnerships are considered to have pioneered good practice in local, community and voluntary action working together with statutory agencies to solve local problems within a broader framework aimed at promoting social inclusion. Area Development Management (ADM) is considered to be a model intermediary body able to deliver community and voluntary programmes in a manner sensitised to local needs, community concerns and the ethos of voluntarism.

In Northern Ireland the Joint Government/Voluntary and Community Sector forum is considered to have been innovative. It provides a regular opportunity for the exchange of information and views between representatives of the sector and of government departments and its joint secretariat enables a two-way flow of information between meetings. Furthermore, its work has enabled members drawn from each side to develop greater understanding of the issues and perspectives as perceived by the other side.

As a representative body, NICVA is an effective voice for the voluntary sector to government. It provides leadership, training, research and policy advice to organisations within the sector and is a member of Concordia, an affiliation of Third Sector organisations. NIACRO and Extern have pioneered services for disadvantaged and marginalised young people during 'the Troubles'. These organisations have developed effective work in the field of restorative justice, prevention of joyriding, and residential accommodation. Both organisations aim to help ex-prisoners and other offenders reintegrate into their communities. Fifteen volunteering bureaux throughout Northern Ireland promote volunteering and provide support for volunteers at a local level. They are supported by the Volunteer Development Agency which provides training and publications, undertakes research into volunteering in Northern Ireland and is a source of policy advice on volunteering to government.

Conclusions and observations

This chapter has provided a map of the voluntary sector in the Republic of Ireland, outlining such key features as size, employment and levels of volunteering. It is clear that there is a significant voluntary sector in the Republic, one that has built on the history outlined before the formation of the Irish state (chapter one) and its development since 1922 (chapter three). In our conclusions here, we see what can be learned about the size and key features of the sector, before making some initial comparisons with Northern Ireland in chapter eight.

A significant problem arises when we consider the size of the voluntary sector in the Republic. The defining work in the area is that of Donoghue, Anheier and Salamon (1999) which sizes the sector within a widely applied American-based instrument and classification system. On first examination, this indicates a very large voluntary sector in Ireland, indeed, by employment figures proportionately the second largest in the world (Salamon, Anheier and Associates). A theme of the work of Salamon, Anheier and Associates is that the voluntary sector is a significant economic force, implying that its economic and human values have been underestimated and undervalued.

The proposition that the Irish voluntary sector should be one of the largest in Europe, still less the world, is counter-intuitive, granted the low levels of social development in the Republic of Ireland compared to other European countries, the under-developed nature of the Irish state, and the lack of policy and other supports provided for the voluntary sector since 1922. In fact, the issue of size can be quite easily resolved if we take account of the exceptionalism of the ownership and nature of the Irish education and health systems. Donoghue, Anheier and Salamon themselves point the way to a resolution of this problem when they analyse what they describe as 'the community and voluntary sector' within the 'voluntary sector'. Here, if the exceptional Irish features are removed, we find an Irish voluntary sector that is sized, not at 8.2 per cent of GDP, and 9.3 per cent of GNP, but more realistically at 2.14 per cent of GDP and 2.4 per cent of GNP. Employment is 64,055 (FTE), rather than 159,674, giving a share of total employment not of 11.5 per cent but one closer to 5 per cent. Even these figures may be on the high side, since they include a number of categories that are questionable, such as non-altruistic associations, the religious and other foundations that give money to the voluntary sector. If we make these adjustments, then the voluntary sector in the Republic is, within the international comparative system, much closer to the middle of the international league, a position more in conformity with known levels of social development. For the purposes of this study and for the purposes of north–south comparison, the narrower 'voluntary and community sector' definition of Donoghue, Anheier and Salamon is the one preferred, rather than their broader one.

Does size actually matter? From a policy perspective, it does matter. If we take it as axiomatic that a voluntary sector is a positive attribute of modern civil society, then the level of that development poses important questions for policy-makers. If the voluntary sector is seen to be large – indeed, huge – then it would create the impression that little needs to be done by society as a whole or government in particular to sustain and develop that sector. Indeed, in the Irish case, it could perversely create the impression that a voluntary sector thrived best in the absence of policy, funding, structure, regulation, support, enablement or accountability. While such a view might be welcomed by extreme libertarians, it is not in tune with the perspective of most of those involved with the voluntary sector who have diagnosed, as problems for its development, the absence of these very frameworks. Accurately benchmarking the size, employment, funding, volunteering, regulation, policy and accountability of any country or region are important starting points for policy-makers – and essential, in this case, for useful or valid north–south comparisons.

Similar issues are echoed in the analysis of volunteering. The ICNPO-related studies indicate a healthy level of volunteering, but in-depth examinations of volunteering have put a number of reservations on the picture. Ruddle and Donoghue (1996) in their study of volunteering in the social welfare area raised serious questions about the organisation of volunteering. Their study was confined to social welfare organisations, so this caution must be borne in mind, but they found that Irish voluntary organisations spent little on recruitment, training or induction; few had a volunteer policy; support for volunteers was a low priority; most were channelled into fund-raising and administration; volunteer expenses were generally not reimbursed; and their role was poorly documented. A reinforcement of support for volunteering was clearly called for. If we put the voluntary sector in the Republic in a European context a sobering picture emerges. Gaskin and Davis Smith (1995) found that, compared to other European countries, the voluntary sector in the Republic had the following characteristics:

- Not as fast-growing as some other countries, especially those in eastern and central Europe
- Smaller. Received less government money. More dependent on public fund-raising
- Fewer paid staff
- More specialised than other countries, with smaller, distinct target groups.
- Worked little with young people
- Low level of time given by volunteers
- Gave an unusually high amount of time to fund-raising, and administration
- Low level of support for volunteers; lack of volunteer policies, lack of training, expenses not generally reimbursed.

Indeed, in the study the European country with which Ireland was most frequently compared was Slovakia. Although the voluntary sector in Slovakia has many striking and innovative features, the sector there had been retarded by the long period of communist rule (1948-89). The Republic of Ireland would have to offer a different explanation. Here, the lack of an enabling policy framework and the slowness of the state to invest in voluntary sector infrastructure may be critical.

In attempting to map the voluntary sector in the Republic, this exercise has illustrated the limited nature of the data to hand, despite the pioneering efforts of recent years. Ideally, there should be regular, comprehensive mapping of both sectors, north and south, on a comparable basis, utilising some of the frameworks developed above and setting the two sectors in their respective economic, social and political contexts.

8

Comparisons and Conclusions

Introduction
This chapter has two parts. First, we attempt to make a direct comparison of the size, dimensions and quantitative aspects of the two voluntary sectors. Second, we attempt a qualitative and comparative analysis of the evolution, current development and key features of the two sectors.

Comparing the two jurisdictions in Ireland
Now it is possible to make a direct comparison of some of the key features of the two voluntary sectors, based on the information presented above. Regrettably, direct comparisons are possible only in a limited number of fields. If we look at the 36 tables in *State of the Sector III*, only ten are matched by comparable information from the Republic and even then the match is incomplete. Table 8.1 illustrates where points of comparison exist. Data may be broken down into three categories: areas where direct comparisons exist; areas where information on both sectors is available, but where it is not comparable; and areas where information may be available in one part of the island, but not the other.

The following are areas where direct comparisons are possible:

- Number of organisations
- Financial size and spending
- Staff
- Individual giving
- Volunteering
- Methods of fund-raising.

In a further set of areas, information is available, but direct comparisons are not possible:
- The main sectors
- Main beneficiary groups
- Priorities in giving
- Sources of funding.

Here, although profiles of both sectors are available, the categories used are quite different and cannot be matched satisfactorily with one another. For example, the 'primary purpose' of voluntary organisations in Northern Ireland has 24 categories, the one in the Republic eight quite different ones. Information on the destinations of corporate giving uses different categories. Similarly, sources of income for the voluntary sector uses different classifications.

There are some areas where information exists in one jurisdiction, but not in the other. These are not listed in the table, but an example would be networks. Here, studies are available of networks in Northern Ireland, but there is no comparable research in the Republic. Northern Ireland has information on beneficiary groups, but there is no equivalent information in the Republic. The south has data on rates of civic participation, but there is no equivalent in the north.

Where direct comparisons are available, though, they are worthy of some further examination. Table 8.2 gives the comparative size of the sector.

One must be cautious with these figures, for they are based on different systems of estimates. The Republic's comes from the number of organisations with a charity number; Northern Ireland's from *State of the Sector III*. Nevertheless, they are the best likely to be available to us.

How does the density of voluntary organisations compare? Here, Northern Ireland has 3,504 organisations for 1,691,800 people and the Republic 5,106 for 3,744,700 people (1999 figures: Source: *Ireland North and South – a statistical profile*. Dublin and Belfast, NISRA and CSO). This gives us a respective figure of one voluntary organisation for every 482 people, or 0.00207 per person in the north; in the south, one voluntary organisation for every 733 people, or 0.00136 per person, a much lower density (see Table 8.3).

Next, if we look at the size of the sector by income, the following picture emerges. The exchange rate prevailing in August 2003 was used (£0.70 = €1). In the right-hand column of Table 8.4, the level of funding is adjusted for population. There are two measurements of size: one including assets and liabilities, the other based on income spending (income only in the case of the Republic). 'Size' figures give a size in Northern Ireland of £750.28m or €1,071.8m; or in the Republic €1,600m or £1,120m. Income figures give £651.7m (€931m) in Northern Ireland and €1,460m (£1,022m) in the Republic. Here we will select the income figures, since these were more precisely calculated. The proportions between the two figures are broadly similar.

Thus in Northern Ireland, £385 (€550) is spent on the voluntary sector per person while in the Republic, €389 (£272) is spent on the voluntary sector per person.

Table 8.1. Points of comparison between the voluntary sectors in Northern Ireland and the Republic of Ireland

	Northern Ireland	Republic of Ireland
Total number of organisations	4,500 to 5,000	5,106 organisations with a charity number (4,739 companies with permission not to use 'limited' on letterhead; 2,570 friendly societies)
Profile of main sectors	Education and training: 16.6 per cent; community development: 10.6 per cent; advice advocacy, information: 10.1 per cent	Social services, 30.1 per cent; religious-based services, 18.2 per cent; development and housing, 16.9 per cent; culture and recreation, 15.2 per cent
Main beneficiaries	NI by area: children and youth 18.2 per cent; older people: 12.4 per cent; disability/special needs 12.2 per cent	
Income/spending	£651.7m; spending £640.28m	Income: €1.46bn, of which €483m government, €911m private, €67m fees
Individual giving	£146.9m, or £12.17 monthly. Causes favoured: medical, 38.8 per cent, children, 16 per cent, development, 11.8 per cent; disability, 8 per cent Monthly: €6.72 (1993).	Causes favoured: disability, poverty, children, cancer research
Corporate giving	£12.41m, favouring children, 8 per cent; disability, 7.4 per cent; 6.2 per cent; older, 5.7 per cent	€40m a year (estimate), favouring sports, 23 per cent; community development, 19 per cent; education, 17 per cent.
Human resources	29,168, or 4.5 per cent of the workforce; Volunteers: 72,908 Rate of volunteering: 35 per cent	Employment: 32,136 Volunteers: 31,919 (FTE), value: €597m Rate of volunteering: 33 per cent Rate of civic participation: 52 per cent
Size/assets/ liabilities	£750.28m	€1.6bn

Table 8.2. Size of the sector, by number of voluntary organisations

Northern Ireland	Republic of Ireland
3,504	5,106

Table 8.3. Density of voluntary organisations

Northern Ireland	Republic of Ireland
0.00207	0.00136

Table 8.4. Sector size by income (left), adjusted for population to get investment level per head (right)

Financial size of sector		Annual investment per head	
Northern Ireland	Republic of Ireland	Northern Ireland	Republic of Ireland
£651.7m	£1,022m	£385	£272
€931m	€1,460m	€550	€389

Staffing is the third area where comparable information is available. This is displayed in Table 8.5.

Table 8.5. Staff employed in voluntary sector, north and south (left), adjusted for labour force (right)

Staff employed		Proportion per labour force	
Northern Ireland	Republic of Ireland	Northern Ireland	Republic of Ireland
29,168	32,136	3.99%	1.84%

Here, the numbers are comparable in absolute terms. However, if we take the different labour force sizes into account, the proportion of people employed in the voluntary sector in the Republic is much smaller: 1.84 per cent, compared to 3.99 per cent in the north. The size of the labour force is 731,000 and 1,746,000 respectively (2000 figures: Source: *Ireland North and South – a statistical profile.* Dublin and Belfast, NISRA and CSO).

If we look at corporate giving, the figure for Northern Ireland is £12.41m (€17.72m), compared to €40m (£28m) in the Republic. Adjusted for population, this gives a rate of €10.46 per head of population in Northern Ireland (£7.3) and €10.68 (£7.47) per head in the Republic: very comparable figures.

If we look at individual giving, this is £12.17 (€17.38) a month in

Northern Ireland, compared to €6.72 (£4.70) a month in the Republic. The Republic's figure is much lower, but it is an unsatisfactory figure, being much older (1993).

Finally, if we look at volunteering, a number of comparisons are possible. See Tables 8.6 and 8.7.

Table 8.6. Number of volunteers and volunteering rate

Number of Volunteers	
Northern Ireland	**Republic of Ireland**
72,908	31,919

Here, the absolute numbers in Northern Ireland are much higher, more than double the level of the Republic.

Table 8.7. Voluntary organisations and fund-raising

	Northern Ireland	Republic of Ireland
Proportion of voluntary organisations with salaried fund-raisers	36.8%	31.5%
Proportion with trustees involved in fund-raising	44.8%	50.0%
Organisations with other staff involved in fund-raising	69.8%	52.1%
Proportion with volunteers involved in fund-raising	43.7%	49.3%

Thus in those limited areas where direct comparisons are possible, the following are the main points emerging:

- The voluntary sector in Northern Ireland has twice the density of that of the Republic, 0.002 voluntary organisations per person, compared to 0.001 in the Republic.
- The financial size of the sector is larger in the Republic in absolute terms, but the annual investment in the sector in the north is larger, €550 per person a year compared to €389.
- Although more people work in the voluntary sector in the south, the proportion of the labour force employed in the sector in the north is much higher, 3.99 per cent of the labour force, compared to 1.84 per cent in the south.

- Levels of corporate giving appear to be quite similar.
- Levels of individual giving appear to be higher in the north; however, the southern figure is old and may not be a reliable guide to the present.
- Volunteering is more supported in the north.

It is regrettable that more directly comparable information is not available. An example is the composition of the sector, where the categories used to break down the different sub-sectors are so incompatible as to make meaningful comparison impossible.

The figures given above come, as noted earlier, with many caveats and qualifications. Assuming that their broad thrust is correct, they suggest a considerably higher density, investment and labour force commitment in Northern Ireland than the Republic. Suggested explanations could include:

- a policy framework for the development of the sector having been put in place in the north much sooner than in the south
- levels of voluntary sector mobilisation prompted by 'the Troubles' (albeit differential mobilisation, being higher in the nationalist areas).
- higher levels of government investment in Northern Ireland, due both to the violence and it being a deprived regional area of the UK, the voluntary sector being one of the beneficiaries.

A framework for comparison
Any attempt to establish comparisons between the two jurisdictions in Ireland using traditions in social science has to address a number of problems. The first of these is a lack of a tradition of comparative work across the Irish border in social science scholarship, the first sustained attempt being the volume of papers published by the British Academy in 1999 edited by Heath, Breen and Whelan. In his introductory essay to that volume, David Rottman notes that the comparative traditions in social science in each jurisdiction have been underdeveloped. Where they have developed, each part of Ireland tends to be compared to a range of other cases, but never with one another. Where they have occurred, comparisons have been in different directions. In the Republic of Ireland, attention has focused on state failure and late industrialisation prompting comparison with European examples of Greece and Portugal and the examples of the 'tiger economies' of the Far East. In Northern Ireland, comparative analysis has been driven by political scientists interested in communal division and politics, forcing comparisons with a wide range of cases as far apart as Burundi, Sri Lanka, Cyprus, Canada, the southern USA and the states of the former Yugoslavia.

Secondly, Rottman raises the methodological question of the choice of cases for study and the incompatibility of the two Irish cases as instances of more general theory. While the Republic of Ireland is an independent state inviting comparisons with other states, Northern Ireland is at best a quasi-state and for many purposes is more properly understood as a region (albeit with special characteristics) of the United Kingdom. This is a particular problem in comparing the voluntary sectors in the two jurisdictions, as the tools for comparison in this field of enquiry have focused on the state as the basis for selecting cases. The most important development here has been the Johns Hopkins transnational comparative research project led by Lester Salamon and Helmut Anheier. This has generated a single set of definitions and a wealth of comparative data on a wide range of jurisdictions including both the Republic of Ireland and the United Kingdom. The theoretical model developed from this project by Salamon and Anheier, the social origins theory of voluntary action, is similarly dependent on the state as the unit of analysis.

Social origins theory suggests that the disposition and form of voluntary action in any jurisdiction is a function of the political settlement of its particular welfare regime. The strength of this approach is that it puts voluntary action and the institutions of the welfare state in the same analytic category. They are both outworkings of the deal between a state and its nation as to how the state can best underpin the welfare and aspirations of its citizens.

Social origins theory built on earlier work. The first attempts to explain the existence of the voluntary sector were based on theories derived from economics and focused on ideas of market and state failure. A sophisticated variation on this theme, the idea of 'philanthropic failure', was developed also by Lester Salamon. In all these, the actions (or inactions) of the state comprised a core unit of the analysis. Similarly, there is an important literature that has attempted to develop a variety of typologies to understand the range of ways in which voluntary organisations relate to state structures. These have been criticised as being insufficiently precise and thus hard to apply in practice, but the core problem from the perspective of this work is that they offer no tools for analysis at units below that of the unitary state itself. Thus the United Kingdom may be compared to Germany or the USA, but the countries within the United Kingdom cannot be compared with the German Lander, for example, or any of the constituent states within the USA. Comparing Northern Ireland to the Republic of Ireland is thus like comparing Bavaria to France. We lack the analytical tools to do this at all easily. The lack of such a comparative tradition within any other branch of Irish social science compounds the problem, as there are no other adaptable frameworks to hand either.

As we outlined in chapter one, our solution has been to treat Ireland as a jurisdiction that was once single, but which was partitioned in 1922, and to attempt to establish a baseline at that date against which we might measure the degree of convergence or divergence. This puts Ireland into a different category to the example of Bavaria and France and makes it more typical of more recent developments in the remaking of states. The only comparisons we would have would be to wait another 70 to 80 years and examine the cases of the Czech Republic and Slovakia, East Timor and Indonesia or perhaps the constituent states of the former Yugoslavia.

This conceptual framework is based on the hypothesis that voluntary action in all its various forms can be best explained with reference to broader political processes of state-building, rather than solely by reference to the cultural and social characteristics of populations (the social origins hypothesis). The framework thus dictated the historical narrative approach that we have adopted, as without that, it would be very difficult to understand the similarities and differences evident currently in each of the two Irish jurisdictions. So before returning to the question of explanations, we shall set out in this chapter what appear the most salient similarities and differences and relate these to the historical material where this is helpful.

Different trajectories
Although at the moment just before partition, voluntary action in the island of Ireland operated under a common legal jurisdiction and political administration, it was already divided in a number of respects. Religious divisions that were to persist – even to grow – in the twentieth century had been a defining feature of voluntary action in the island from its very beginning. There were in Ireland already two distinct spheres: a Protestant one most evident in the place of its historic roots, Dublin, but also more recently in Belfast and the provincial towns; and a more universally present Catholic one. Some attempts had been made to carve out a non-affiliated voluntary sphere, but this had been done largely under the aegis of Protestant city and nation builders and few such efforts commanded more than limited acceptance. Non-affiliated voluntary organisations had almost all tended to drift into one camp or the other.

Although Irish voluntary organisations were almost entirely indigenous, the Protestant community had tended to look for models to the latest concepts of British Victorian philanthropy while the Catholic community sought inspiration from within the universal church in general and France in particular. Even if Ireland had not been partitioned, these distinct spheres would have dominated voluntary sector development in the island well into the twentieth century.

Partition inevitably accentuated these differences. The two minority communities – the Catholic community in the north and the Protestant community in the south – associated themselves closely with 'their' voluntary organisations, this being especially evident in the case of hospital services (e.g. the Mater in Belfast and the Adelaide in Dublin). Conversely, the two majority communities associated 'their' voluntary organisations with the two emergent projects of nation-building. In the Free State, independence coincided with the period when theories of Catholic social action reached their zenith. In the capable hands of John Charles McQuaid, these theories provided the foundations for an ambitious project of voluntary institution-building in Dublin that was imitated in other dioceses. In the north, a similar coincidence of objectives was evident in the formation, during a similar period, of the Northern Ireland Council for Social Services. The two sets of voluntary organisations followed similar paths, albeit for different denominational purposes.

The first area of divergence is one that can broadly be called social administration. This initially became evident in the area of industrial schools. The industrial schools that had dominated provision for children in the island since 1868 were quickly wound down in Northern Ireland. Here, the influence of more enlightened theories of child care and community welfare at work in Great Britain quickly influenced practice. The Free State, by contrast, tended to be more distant from such developments, establishing instead a practical and convenient arrangement between the Catholic caring institutions and their state funders, one that led to a peak of institutionalisation in the 1950s. This set a pattern whereby the two voluntary sectors began to follow two different sets of political, administrative and professional paths according to their different models of social administration. In Northern Ireland, this path was inspired by changes in practice across the United Kingdom, though the region had some scope to mark out distinctive local interpretation.

The political settlement that established the Free State was administratively a far from revolutionary one and, in social administration, often tended to follow the example of the former colonial master, though inevitably there was a time lag and there were distinct areas where the Free State chose not to follow, such as in more enlightened models of child care. As we have suggested, when it comes to the development of voluntary action, social administration and the sources of social administration do matter. As part of the United Kingdom, Northern Ireland experience followed the United Kingdom model, deliberately and consciously, though with local variation. The Free State and then the Republic followed this model later, more slowly, selectively and from a distance. To the degree that this was the case, then the paths of voluntary action diverged. To look forward for one moment, a concrete example of this was the efficiency scrutiny. Northern Ireland was inevitably more subjected to the types of changes around measurement, standards and performance introduced in the course of the United Kingdom public sector reforms by successive British governments. Although some of these ideas were later in evidence in the Republic, they took the form of late and often pale imitations. Lee (1989) explains the development of states very much in the context of their ability to exploit indigenous potential and their external sources of learning, both of which are at a premium for small states like Ireland. Here he was extremely critical of the failure of the Free State, and later the Republic, both to develop its indigenous potential and to learn from external example, resulting in poor economic and social performance.

Voluntary action in both parts of the island operated under social policy régimes that could be described as conservative and unadventurous. This began to change in the late 1940s, with the advent of the Welfare State in the United Kingdom, leading to the introduction of the National Health Service and much improved personal, social and care services. In the course of time these changes were to have significant effects on the role and development of voluntary organisations. In the Republic, the 1949 white paper of William Norton gave a similar commitment to follow the ideal of the British Welfare State, but it was a commitment the inter-party government was unable to deliver and one from which, in difficult economic circumstances, subsequent governments retreated.

The introduction of the Welfare State thus opened up a second path of divergence. Despite initial predictions that voluntary organisations would wither away due to the all-embracing care of the Welfare State, in reality the Welfare State found it ever more necessary to enlist voluntary organisations in the interests of effectiveness, efficiency and comprehensiveness. As chapter six showed, the Welfare State in Northern Ireland sustained and developed the voluntary sector in personal, social and care services and in the development of independent advice services.

The failure of the Republic in 1949 to follow the model of the Welfare State inevitably led to a widening developmental and resources gap between north and south. In the Republic, the Health Act, 1954 permitted the funding of voluntary organisations, but the amounts given were discretionary, small and unstrategic. The National Social Services Board (1970) was brought into being a full thirty years after its northern equivalent. The policy and structural gap widened due to the different policy-making capacities of the two states. In the United Kingdom, the first systematic efforts to define a role for the voluntary sector were evident from the issuing of the report of the Wolfenden Commission (1978). This led ultimately to a first regional strategy for Northern Ireland by 1993. In the Republic, commitments were given to define an appropriate role for the voluntary sector from 1981. This proved to be a hugely difficult challenge for the southern state, a project not brought to fruition for almost twenty years (2000). Had a fully-fledged welfare state developed in the south from 1949, with an important role for the delivery of that state through voluntary organisations, it would probably have set in train dynamics forcing a much earlier definition of that role. The introduction of the Welfare State, with consequential investment in social supports and voluntary action, may go some way to explaining the much higher density of voluntary organisations in Northern Ireland.

The third point of divergence was of course 'the Troubles'. These prompted a set of developments for the community and voluntary sector which, by definition, would not be matched in the Republic. In the first instance, they inspired the setting up of a sub-sector concerned with peace and reconciliation issues, although this was relatively small and involved not more than about a hundred voluntary organisations. More significantly, 'the Troubles' prompted an upsurge of community activity, principally in 'the nationalist and Catholic community. This marked the emergence of community development as a distinct strand of voluntary sector activity. Thus the current configuration of the voluntary sector in Northern Ireland is a product of the interactions between the institutions of the Welfare State and indigenous community-based responses to the crisis of 'the Troubles'. In the Republic, a small but important peace and reconciliation sub-sector also emerged to address the more limited southern dimension of 'the Troubles', but this was limited to a small number of organisations, about a dozen. Community development was also a distinct trend in the Republic, but emerged from more conventional and peaceful circumstances.

Difference, divergence and dissimilarity
Thus by the early twenty-first century, three distinct points of divergence were in evidence, due to differences in social administration, the Welfare State and 'the Troubles'. Moving from historical narrative to a contemporary analysis, what are the current main areas of difference, divergence and dissimilarity?

Voluntary sector representative bodies and supporting agencies
In their representative structures, there are significant differences between the two voluntary and community sectors. There is a sharp contrast between the sophisticated, highly structured system of representation evident in NICVA and the lack of a comparable body in the Republic. NICVA fits into a pattern of national voluntary sector organisation also evident in Scotland

(SCVO), Wales (WCVA) and England (NCVO). Voluntary sector commentators in Northern Ireland are often puzzled by the lack of a representative structure south of the border. Why is there no 'southern NICVA'? they often ask.

Some southern commentators and experts argue that the absence of a formal structure is less important than it seems, granted what the sector has been able to achieve in practice through such organisations as the Community Platform and, more recently, The Wheel. Despite its informality and apparent disorganisation, the sector has been able to achieve more than more formally structured systems elsewhere, so they argue. Lack of a formal structure makes the community and voluntary sector less vulnerable to capture by government. On the other hand, critics point to the lack of a formal structure as evidence for the overwhelming preoccupations of territory, immaturity and lack of trust. The voluntary sector and community sector lacks the advocacy, representational and resourcing role that an organisation like NICVA can bring and has paid a high price in policy, influence and finance as a result. Whatever the arguments, it is an important point of difference.

In a further point of comparison, the important role of the Community Foundation for Northern Ireland (CFNI), formerly the Northern Ireland Voluntary Trust, is not matched in the Republic. In the Republic, the recently established Community Foundation has so far made only a marginal impact on the voluntary sector landscape and has yet to establish a strong national profile. The type of impact made by CFNI in the north in funding and supporting the sector is unlikely to be matched by the Community Foundation in the Republic for many years.

This brings us to a second important point of contemporary difference. Governmental attitudes seem to have played an important role, both in supporting foundations and representative structures. Dealing with foundations first, NIVT was established with governmental assistance, whereas in the Republic equivalent government support was slow to come. Turning to representative structures, the United Kingdom national structures were prompted by a high level of governmental interest: NCVO was established by the Home Office, while NICSS, NICVA's predecessor, was also established by government. By contrast, the government in the Republic has taken an agnostic role, saying it will support the establishment of a representational body if the sector wants one (though not explicitly offering financial assistance), but that it is up to the sector to define its own needs. Critics point out that this is a formula likely to ensure that no such body will be set up.

Strategic development
It is in the area of strategic development that there are further divergences and dissimilarities. Long-term planning and thinking have not been features

of the voluntary sector in the Republic, partly reflecting the absence of a national representative umbrella body. That is not to say that long-term thinking has been absent: indeed, The Wheel has undertaken work to remedy some of these deficits, as have some individual organisations. However, the general absence of such thinking and the use of forecasting models means that the sector in the Republic has not been able to think far ahead, consider options, develop long-term goals or build sufficient reflective space for itself. There was no equivalent in the Republic to the millennium debate undertaken by NICVA in Northern Ireland. Partly in consequence of this, the issues flagged in *State of the Sector III* concerning citizen juries, e-democracy, a shadow youth council and e-consultation have not been echoed in the voluntary sector debate in the Republic.

Differences in the approach to strategic development are also reflected at government level. In Northern Ireland, the government has sought to mark out funding paths for the sector in response to concerns expressed about the sustainability of the sector. This took the form of the Harbison report (2000) and the current work of the task force on resourcing (due 2004). By contrast, governments in the Republic have allocated funding to the sector on an *ad hoc*, year-by-year basis, but have rarely sought to map out funding paths for the sector in a systematic way. On the contrary, the southern government replaced some three-year funding arrangements with traditional, insecure one-year contracts while the current review of optimal coherence in the Republic may have the effect of reducing funding options.

The current pattern of research echoes these different approaches to strategic development. The type of on-going research into the voluntary sector developed by NICVA and the Centre for Voluntary Action Studies has not been paralleled in the south. Individual research projects have been undertaken, notably by the National College of Ireland, Dublin University and University College Dublin, but the absence of research to match the *State of the Sector* reports is all too evident in this study. Although the government set aside money for research as part of the white paper implementation programme, this programme was cancelled two years later. The type of pressure that leads to an improvement in the self-knowledge of the sector in the north appears to be absent in the Republic. A sector that is less well informed is less likely to think or act strategically or systematically. Indeed, the anti-intellectualism of the current southern government means that this is likely to remain a point of divergence for some time.

Similarities and convergence

So far, we have itemised three historical points of divergence (social administration, the Welfare State and 'the Troubles') and two contemporary points of divergence (representative structures and strategic role). Put crudely, the infrastructure in Northern Ireland is larger, more sophisticated and better developed, reflecting a higher level of investment. Despite these different paths taken, are there points of similarity and convergence? Several may be identified.

Governmental frameworks
The voluntary and community sectors in both parts of the island are at broadly similar stages in attempting to define their relationships with government. Key documents were issued within similar time periods: in Northern Ireland, the *Compact between the Government and Voluntary Sector in Northern Ireland – Building Real Partnerships* (1998) and *Partners for Change – Government Strategy for the Support of the Voluntary and Community Sector* (2001); they straddle the key document in the Republic, *Supporting Voluntary Activity* (2000). The structures set in place to support the voluntary sector are broadly similar, the north having a Voluntary and Community Unit in the Department for Social Development, the Republic having a unit responsible for the community and voluntary sector in the Department of Community, Rural and Gaeltacht Affairs. Other commentators have contrasted the details of the governmental strategies, finding the northern one to be more practical and concrete, the one in the Republic to be more aspirational. In their detail they cover similar ground, such as relationships with government, consultation systems, standards and funding arrangements.

Where there are differences, they may lie in implementation. In the Republic, the degree to which the white paper has been implemented is questionable. It does not yet seem to have led to significant changes in the relationship between government and voluntary and community organisations, especially in the all-important funding and consultation relationships. The promised voluntary activity units in other government departments were not established, nor were departmental strategies for supporting the sector. Although the Republic has a white paper implementation body, it has a more limited brief than the Joint Government Voluntary Sector Forum in Northern Ireland. The original parent department for the white paper, the Department of Social Welfare, took an extremely limited view as to what consultation with the sector should mean, as we saw in the case of the Family Support Agency. Concrete proposals for support, training, networking and research stalled for over three years. Whether this will prove to be a temporary hiatus remains to be seen, but the loss of momentum in the implementation of the Republic's white paper seems indisputable. Pressure from the sector may yet ensure that its principles will become embedded in policy and practice.

Support for volunteering
Both parts of the island now have well-developed policies for the support of
volunteering. In Northern Ireland this may be seen in the *Compact* (1998)
and *Partners for Change* (2001). This was followed by a programme dedicated
to the region, the Northern Ireland plan for the *Active Community Initiative*
(2001). In the Republic, the concept and ideals of volunteering were
validated by the white paper *Supporting Voluntary Activity* (2000) and the
subsequent *Tipping the Balance* (2002). The two policy frameworks, north and
south, support broadly similar objectives: to encourage an awareness of and
interest in volunteering; to encourage more volunteers to come forward; to
ensure their role is recognised and systematised; and to set in place suitable
support structures. Here, the Republic had long lagged behind Northern
Ireland in its structural support for volunteers, Northern Ireland having
benefited from earlier developments in British social administration. The
impressive *Tipping the Balance* report offered the opportunity to rapidly make
good these deficits. Again, implementation in the Republic has been
problematical (indeed the government found difficulty in generating any
formal response), and the report may prove to be too ambitious for the
government. The overall point though is that the policies to support
volunteers in both parts of the island are remarkably similar.

Regulation
Whatever the differences in social administration between the two parts of
the island, their legal and regulatory frameworks strayed little from one
another. Although they were adapted over time by changes in particular areas
(e.g. lotteries, collection systems), the two frameworks are recognisably
similar and draw on the same legal basis, principles and historical case
law. Indeed, observers of the jurisdictional arrangements find them both to be
almost equally archaic and in need of modernisation. They even have a
similar pattern of peristaltic reform. In Northern Ireland, proposals put
forward in the late 1990s were withdrawn. In the Republic, the thoughtful
proposals of the Costello report were dissipated by the lack of interest of
successive ministers for justice. Cormacain, O'Halloran and Williamson
(2001) have put forward a compelling case for regulation and governance to
be updated and modernised. In the Republic, a detailed review was made by
the Law Society (2002).

   There is a widespread recognition, both within and without the sector,
that the current framework is archaic, that it is insufficiently comprehensive,
that many legal structures and forms are inappropriate and that there is
insufficient protection against fraud and abuse. A sub-text to the discussion is
the need to develop better systems of oversight and accountability,
ensuring that the operation of voluntary organisations be sufficiently open

to public scrutiny. Sensible and balanced proposals could do much to restore some dented confidence in the operation of voluntary organisations, but there is the fear, within some parts of the voluntary and community sector, that the government will deliver more regulation and control without any of the positive proposals in the area of legal form. It is interesting that the programme for government in the Republic for 2002-7 contains more references to the control and regulation of the sector, than to its support or development, in sharp contrast to Northern Ireland. The report of the Law Society (2002) outlined ways in which charity law in the Republic could be reformed, moving the Republic's law closer to the model both in England and Northern Ireland and inviting a convergence in legal frameworks.

Social partnership
Social partnership is a key theme in voluntary and community sector development in both parts of the island, although it takes different forms. The reasons that led them into social partnership seem to be quite different. In Northern Ireland, the voluntary and community sector filled some of the democratic deficit associated with direct rule, as well as offering specific expertise of benefit to government policy-making. In the Republic, economic progress in the early 1990s provided some space for the emergence of a more confident and politically influential voluntary sector to emerge.

The voluntary sector in Northern Ireland achieved a high level of consultation and recognition, most evident at the concluding period of Direct Rule when it was consulted on a series of issues, both formally and informally, and has since established channels with the new institutions of government built since 1998. In the Republic, the 'long march through the institutions' climaxed with admission to the National Economic and Social Forum in 1993 and subsequent participation in the national agreements. Here, voluntary and community sector representatives have a broad range of channels to influence government, from the plenary sessions of the agreement attended by the Taoiseach and senior ministers to its working groups where policies are hammered out in detail, as well as the range of ancillary channels developed around social partnership. The voluntary and community sector in the Republic has a point or a series of points of influence over government that is unparalleled at national level in the rest of the European Union. Having said that, the access of the voluntary and community sector to government in Northern Ireland is also close and intimate. The mechanisms are different, with the voluntary and community sector operating through the Joint Forum, the Concordia partnership, the Civic Forum and many semi-structured channels for consultation.

Nevertheless, each represents an advanced model of social partnership at government level. One difference is that the process has, in the Republic, come under fresh critical examination following the decision of a number of important voluntary organisations in the Republic not to participate in social partnership in the current national agreement *Sustaining Progress, 2003-5*. Here, dissidents argue that government has used social partnership to oblige the sector to collude in a pseudo-consultative process that actually delivers little to their constituencies. Whether this is a temporary fracture in the social partnership process, a reconfiguration, or whether it heralds its ultimate dissolution, remains to be seen. There is, however, a more critical attitude to social partnership and its benefits than may be the case in the north.

In a study that has explored trends, patterns, organisations and institutions, it is easy to overlook human factors. Social partnership was not something that happened automatically. Although it required the imagination of individual government ministers and civil servants to open their doors to a structured relationship with voluntary and community organisations, it required extraordinary leadership by individuals within those organisations to lead the march into these institutions. Indeed, one might make a further observation common to both parts of the island, concerning the role of the voluntary sector in recruitment to the political élite. In Ireland, by contrast with other countries, few voluntary sector personalities make the transition from sector leadership into politics, social partnership presumably offering higher rewards in influencing the state social and political agenda.

National social partnership has been matched by the development of local social partnership in both parts of the island. In Northern Ireland, local social partnership has developed within the local district partnerships and local strategy partnerships. In the Republic, local social partnership has developed through strategic policy committees, city and county development boards and health-board-based committees. Largely due to a clash of operational cultures, this has proved to be a difficult experience in both parts of the island, but one expected to lead to positive results in the medium to long term. In the Republic, voluntary and community organisations have established local community platforms and fora to drive such partnerships, although these have yet to attract sufficient resourcing from government. In Northern Ireland, pilot community conventions are in development.

The drawing of the two voluntary and community sectors into social partnership with government, unimaginable twenty years ago, has presented a similar set of problems. Social partnership is demanding of structures, resources and personnel. Some voluntary and community organisations have found themselves to be over-stretched in this process, suffering from a series of negative consequences from mission drift to staff burn out. 'Consultation fatigue' was the descriptive term first used in Northern Ireland and this is increasingly evident in the southern discourse on social partnership. The voluntary and community sectors have similar doubts as to the extent to which government genuinely listens to them.

Social economy, local social capital
This study started with, as its backdrop, recent frameworks of social capital and civic society. The development of the social economy and of ideas around local social capital present some recent points of convergence. The two voluntary sectors had similar experiences of labour market measures designed to integrate unemployed people into the labour force: ACE in Northern Ireland, and Community Employment in the Republic. Both schemes had important secondary impacts in providing staffing for voluntary and community organisations. These were precursors of what mutated into social economy programmes, coupled with new ideas for the development of social capital.

The National Economic and Social Forum published a report on social capital in 2003, and ideas of local social capital have been of interest to a range of voluntary and community organisations, e.g. The Wheel. In practical terms, a social economy programme was launched in the Republic in 2000, taking over some of the former community employment programme. The Local Development Social Inclusion Programme (LDSIP) run by Area Development Management has elements for the development of local social capital. In Northern Ireland, the term 'community infrastructure' emerged in the second reformed round of the structural funds (1994-9). Proposals to address weak community infrastructure were developed by the Rural Community Network and the Community Foundation for Northern Ireland. Measures to address areas of weak community infrastructure became an integral part of the PEACE II programme (2000-4). The use of intermediary funding bodies, a form of bridging social capital, is understood in both parts of the island, being evident in the PEACE II programme in Northern Ireland and the work of Area Development Management and the support structures for the Community Development Programme in the Republic. In Northern Ireland a social investment model, deriving at least some ideas from theories of social capital, is under consideration by the government Task Force for the support of the voluntary and community sector. Ideas of civic society likewise find some points of convergence. In Northern Ireland, the Civic Forum, and in the Republic, the National Economic and Social Forum, as well as the partnership structures, both show that ideals of a civic space have taken some root. In the Republic, though, the terrain is more contested, some elected representatives regarding the notion of civic society as a threat to their position rather than as complementary to democracy. The Adelaide and Tallaght Hospital saga demonstrated that some of the ideas of civil society have yet to be understood or to win acceptance.

Poverty, social exclusion, equality and diversity
The two voluntary sectors operate in relatively similar environments when it comes to poverty and social exclusion. In Northern Ireland, Targeting Social Need (TSN) was followed by New TSN, while in the Republic the National Anti-Poverty Strategy (1997) was reviewed with new targets (2002). Both governments have taken the view that poverty and social exclusion are priorities in their work and see the voluntary and community sectors as playing key roles in that process. In the Republic, the role of the voluntary and community sector is formally located within the government's brief for social inclusion (although there are administrative and departmental reasons for this). Both sectors see a commitment to working for inclusion as an important part of their work. The Northern Ireland Council for Voluntary Action has a formal commitment to working for social change and this is echoed in the language of many of the region's large and small voluntary organisations. In the Republic, a commitment to social change is emphasised in the discourse of its prominent voluntary organisations (e.g. Community Workers Co-operative, Conference of the Religious in Ireland) and is echoed, with many variations of degree, intensity and focus, among others. For both governments, the voluntary and community sectors have been willing instruments for the addressing of issues of poverty and inequality. In a sense, such recognition was a belated acknowledgment of the innovative, imaginative and professional services developed by voluntary and community organisations over decades. In the Republic the Community Development Programme became an imaginative, effective and economic way to address poverty at the local level, one area in which the Republic pioneered a model that has drawn international acclaim.

Governments in both jurisdictions have addressed issues of equality and diversity but inevitably in different ways. In Northern Ireland, the traditional focus of equality and parity policies has been around the two main political communities, an issue that does not have an echo in the Republic. Where there is a convergence is around the equality agenda. Both parts of the island have passed legislation that raises equality issues up the political agenda. In Northern Ireland, Section 75 of the 1998 Northern Ireland Act brought the sector into close contact with government agencies fulfilling their duties under the section, and in the Republic the new equality legislation led to a voluntary sector developing work around the Equality Authority. Both voluntary sectors now have sub-sectors dealing with minority communities. In Northern Ireland there is an umbrella body, the Northern Ireland Council for Ethnic Minorities (NICEM) but in the Republic there is a growing number of small and embryonic groups representing the individual new communities. It is more than likely that this will be one of the most rapidly growing parts of the voluntary sector in the

Republic over the next number of years. An umbrella body for them may in course of time emerge.

Europeanisation
Europe became a point of convergence for the voluntary sector in both parts of the island. The impact of the European Union on the funding of the voluntary and community sector has already been noted in their respective chapters. Whilst European Union funding has been important for both, the actual volume of funding may have been overstated, comprising as little as 3.5 per cent of the total funding of the sector in the south (it may be proportionately more in the north). European Union funding has undoubtedly had a discernible impact in particular sectors (e.g. community development, disability) while leaving others relatively unaffected (e.g. care of the elderly).

The real significance of European funding probably lies elsewhere. Because the pattern of European funding operates according to a broadly similar template in all states, we may presume that the effects on the voluntary sectors affected may be broadly similar. The main impacts of European funding have been as follows:

- Enabling the development of new types of services, for example childcare
- Improved standing of individual organisations, with resultant gains in statutory funding and entry into policy-making circles
- Permitting the development of new and hitherto controversial thematic areas of work, for example in the areas of poverty, inequality and discrimination
- Prioritising new areas of work, for example with women
- Driving up standards, for example in evaluation, accounting, reporting and dissemination
- Encouraging voluntary organisations to develop links with other European organisations, partner groups and networks
- Bringing the two voluntary sectors into a wider social and political discourse outside the British Isles
- Opening funding to new competitors when winners have been selected by the European institutions, rather than by local administration
- Opening doors to decision-makers through participation in the monitoring committees and, in the case of the PEACE I programme, through the consultative forum.

As a result, voluntary organisations in both parts of Ireland have converged, in some degree, toward similar standards, approaches and working methods.

New North–South institutions: a new point of convergence?

The new north–south institutions should present a point of convergence for the voluntary and community sector for both parts of the island, although there is little evidence that it has done so yet. The institution with the greatest potential for impact is the Human Rights Commission. Here, both voluntary sectors have what may be termed a rights and justice sub-sector. In the Republic, this was traditionally small but grew due to funding from the Joseph Rowntree Charitable Trust. Some of the voluntary organisations in one part of the island are mirrored in the other (e.g. Committee for the Administration of Justice/Irish Council for Civil Liberties). A big challenge for each voluntary sector will be to ensure the effective operation of the new Human Rights Commissions so that there are genuine advances in human rights protections in the next number of years. Here, there are time differences, for the Commission in Northern Ireland made an early start. In the Republic, the Commission's work was stymied and made no substantial progress for over four years. Although the Human Rights Commissions have roots common to both parts of the island (the Good Friday Agreement) and although there is co-operation between, for example, the Irish Council for Civil Liberties and the Committee on the Administration of Justice, there is as yet only limited joint working between the two voluntary sub-sectors here. Although there are new north–south bodies that open the prospect of new political relationships within the island, that part of the voluntary sector in the Republic that deals with north–south issues and reconciliation (e.g. Glencree) remains small and does not seem to be in expansion. The start of the Troubles ushered in a number of entrepreneurial voluntary organisations in the Republic devoted to improved relationships within the island. Will new groups emerge from the 1998 political settlement?

Comments and conclusions

Areas of commonality and divergence between the voluntary and community sector in both parts of the islands are apparent. They are summarised in the table.

These conclusions, qualified as they may be, are cautious and could be considered modest. Chapters six and seven, our profile of the sectors in the two jurisdictions, highlighted the degree to which our knowledge of the respective voluntary sectors is imperfect and hampered by information deficits and measurement systems that are quite unstandardised. A first step toward the better understanding of the respective sectors is for the research community to collect data along more common lines, in consultation with their colleagues in other parts of the island. This project is a first attempt to

Table 8.8. Areas of commonality and divergence

Divergent trajectories	Areas of current divergence	Areas of current convergence
• Social administration, from 1922 • Welfare state, from 1949 • 'The Troubles', from 1969	• Structures: the way in which the voluntary and community sector is represented; the role of government in encouraging such structures; foundation support • Planning, research, forecasting and strategic development	• The policy framework • Policies for volunteering • Regulation • Social partnership • Inclusion and equality • Social capital and the social economy • Europeanisation • North–south institutions • Issues of power, control and borders with the state

make a comparative study, with all the attendant risks, dangers in analysis, and limitations.

Bearing that important proviso in mind, the evidence we have presented does suggest some tentative conclusions. An overview of the development of voluntary action in the two jurisdictions shows that the narratives diverged significantly following Partition and continued to do so until the early 1990s since which time the evidence demonstrates increasing convergence.

Why? The Irish case shows that the dispositions, types of networks and institutional arrangements of communities (the forms of bonding and bridging capital available to them) do matter, but they matter much less than the processes of state and institution-building in which they are situated. The fundamental cleavage in Irish society between Catholic and Protestant was thus reflected in the development of two parallel church-based worlds of voluntary action in Ireland before Partition and which persisted in both jurisdictions for more than half a century after Partition. Its impact continued to be felt in the differential experience of communities in responding to the onset of the Troubles in the north. But the drivers of divergence we have shown to have been differing traditions in social administration and very differing approaches by the state to its role of guarantor of citizens' welfare. Even without the added dimension of the Troubles, this would have meant that there would have been considerable differences between the two jurisdictions. The participation of Northern Ireland in the political settlement of the United Kingdom Welfare State, which owed nothing to any home-grown consideration of welfare reform, fundamentally shaped the development of voluntary action. It both preserved and in the end enhanced the provision of welfare services by voluntary organisations and provided an arena for the development of new forms of secular voluntary action from the 1970s onwards.

Lacking this context, relations between voluntary organisations and the state in the south were pragmatic, governed by short-term considerations and informed by a view of the state as a residual provider of welfare, which was properly the provenance of the family and voluntary institutions such as the churches. The architects of the state in the south were thus not that interested in welfare as a means of enhancing the state's legitimacy with its citizens whereas in the north, citizens participated in a settlement in which welfare was constructed as one of the chief grounds of the state's legitimacy. Differing traditions in social administration, however, meant that the process of modernisation of the state in the south that took place from the 1960s onwards only had a marginal impact on this divergent picture. The lack of an intermediary infrastructure was both a cause and a consequence of a very unstrategic relationship between voluntary bodies and state institutions.

The convergence since the early 1990s against this background is perhaps surprising. As we have shown, the impact of the European Community and (after the Maastricht Treaty) the European Union has had a shared impact on discourse about voluntary action and the state evident in both jurisdictions that far outweighs the value of its financial contribution. This may have been because the emphasis in this discourse on social partnership has fed into similar processes in both parts of Ireland in which the state is reconfiguring its competencies and relationships with its citizens in the face of globalisation, consumerism and the attendant reconstruction of risk. In an article in which he discusses the implications of the Good Friday Agreement in Northern Ireland, Morison puts the change well:

> The general move from government to governance, with its emphasis on globalisation and the hollowing out of the nation state are well-documented. There is now not only multi-level governance but also multi-form (or multi-format) governance too where the actions of the state are augmented by interventions from elsewhere in the market or the voluntary sector. Government in a 1970s model of parliamentary institutions and departments of state who tax widely, spend high and make big choices has been replaced everywhere by notions of governance where opportunities for making significant changes are more limited and the emphasis is on 'steering' rather than 'rowing' (Morison, 2001).

At policy level such processes have been articulated in the north in *Partners for Change* setting out the basis for partnership between government and the voluntary sector. In the south, it has been articulated by the commitment expressed in the white paper on voluntary action. This expresses the government's view of the voluntary sector as a source of citizenship and social cohesion, which underpins the legitimacy of its presence in governance. It remains true that the institutional outworking of these commitments is somewhat different in each jurisdiction and will doubtless remain so, but there is a striking commonality in the discourse in both jurisdictions over the proper relationship between the voluntary action and the state. Thus the processes of globalisation, through restricting the competencies of the state to attend to the welfare of its citizens, are driving the reconfiguration of voluntary action in differing jurisdictions in a similar direction, blunting differences and enhancing similarities. In the course of time the conceptualisation and role of the voluntary sector may likewise converge through common understandings and European and wider paradigms of civil society and social capital.

The lack of good comparative data in Ireland means that our conclusions should be tentatively expressed. Furthermore we must acknowledge also that the processes in which voluntary action is structured are exceedingly complex and we have not attempted to take all possible variables into account. But the evidence we have assembled shows a pattern of divergence and subsequent convergence in the Irish experience that closely follows a broader twentieth-century story first of nation-building around the Welfare State, followed by the subsequent hollowing out of the state and the consequent need to renegotiate the social compact between a state and its citizens in an age of globalisation.

Looking to the future
In chapter one we suggested that Ireland provides a useful commentary on the disagreement between those who have argued that voluntary action underpins democracy and those who have argued that cause and effect run in the opposite direction and that the process of state and institution-building largely determines the range and types of voluntary and community organisations. Deficiencies in the comparability of the data and the unstandardised systems of measurement mean that we need to be modest in our claims. However, the Irish case we believe broadly supports the latter position. In both Irish jurisdictions the development of the voluntary sector has been closely aligned with the approaches taken to citizen welfare by government in each jurisdiction during the period of state-building in the south and institution-building in the north. These processes dragged the two apart and emphasised differences that were already evident before Partition. More latterly there has been some evidence of convergence, at least so far as the ways in which relations with the respective governments have come to be discussed.

The development of voluntary agencies as large-scale providers of certain public services (for example in the fields of mental health and the elderly) may provide opportunities for these large agencies to extend their service portfolios across the border and there is some evidence that this is beginning to happen in both directions. But in comparison with trading by private companies where the all-Ireland market is becoming increasing important, similar developments in the voluntary sector remain in their infancy. There would appear to be strong resistance factors in both jurisdictions, but it seems likely that the trend towards increased trading by voluntary organisations on an all-Ireland basis will become more pronounced as the bigger organisations look for new business opportunities.

However, there are still strong tendencies towards divergence. The interviews undertaken for this research emphasise very clearly how little contact there has been between the two Irelands at either policy or practitioner level. Until very recently the relevance of cross-border contact or work has not been at all self-evident in either jurisdiction. The differing traditions in social administration in each jurisdiction will tend to ensure that the measures taken in addressing the forces of globalisation will be different. The forces that have led to voluntary organisations in the south to look to Brussels for models of development are not so strongly replicated in the north. There, the continuing dependence on the United Kingdom exchequer to pay for welfare will mean that policy initiatives will tend to continue to address a United Kingdom context. Thus the factors that have underpinned the divergence between the two Irelands are still very much in play.

To what extent they will be modified by the factors driving convergence will depend on processes outside the specific concerns of social administration and the relations of voluntary organisations towards it. An embedding of the political settlement of the Good Friday Agreement in the north will reduce tensions and provide an institutional setting for greater co-operation with the south. Developments in United Kingdom public policy will become more flexibly applied in the context of United Kingdom devolution and may enable local politicians to diverge from models developed to meet the needs of England. A collapse of the Agreement on the other hand would be likely to lead to a modified form of Direct Rule from London with specific inputs from the government in the south. Either way, it is likely that within carefully drawn boundaries of what would be politically acceptable, aspects of social administration will continue to converge which may help shape greater convergence between the two voluntary sectors.

In the south, the partnership model of governance may come under significant strain if the economies of the euro zone go into recession; even the current retrenchment appears to have made some voluntary organisations question the value of their participation. Such a development would have knock-on effects on the way in which partnerships develop in the north and undermine developing synergies. It would also be likely to delay (perhaps indefinitely) the United Kingdom's adoption of the euro, although a common currency throughout Ireland would not in itself lead to greater convergence. Indeed there was a common currency in Ireland until 1978 and this had no impact on the rapid divergence of the two jurisdictions after Partition.

In the contemporary world where democratic governance is increasingly being developed through arms-length partnership and intermediary institutional arrangements, voluntary organisations are likely to continue to be embedded in such structures in both jurisdictions. In doing this they will continue to fulfil the two broad functions of delivering welfare services and enhancing social cohesion. How this is done may vary north and south due to differing traditions in social administration. The winners and losers in this process are likely to be similar also. There will be consolidation of service providers and there is also likely to be an inner group and an outer group of voluntary sector interests in governance structures. Organisations with a firm seat at the table that they see as delivering benefits to their constituencies are unlikely to make room for others, trying to increase their influence. The fragmentation of structures and the incommensurability of interests within the voluntary sector will inevitably play their part.

These changes in the political environment in which voluntary and community organisations in both Irish jurisdictions will have to operate in the coming years are also emphasised at a European level. The proposed European constitution commits, in article 46, the Union to open, transparent and regular dialogue with representative associations and civil society and to give citizens and representative associations the opportunity to make known, and publicly exchange, their views. The constitution sends out clear messages about civil society, consultation, dialogue and the role of non-governmental and social movements. Second, the values laid down in the new constitution speak of social progress, assisting the weakest and most deprived, equality, solidarity, pluralism, tolerance, equality between men and women, social justice and diversity. This in turn sends out messages to validate non-governmental organisations working in these areas. In the Republic of Ireland, these sentiments contrast vividly with the preamble to the 1937 constitution and the expressions of social policy contained in the main text.

A more speculative context may be found in the Scenarios 2010 exercise conducted by the European Commission's Forward Studies Unit, or *Cellule de Prospective*. This outlined how Europe might develop over the first ten years of the new century. The unit sketched five scenarios, each given a thematic name, as follows:

- *Triumphant markets*, in which European voters elected to follow the American model of economic and social development, exalting markets, increasing inequality and privatising government.

- *Hundred flowers*, in which the people of Europe lost confidence in their government, favoured the blossoming of the informal and local economy, in which big government at European and national level gave way to a patchwork of smaller states, cities and local identities.

- *Shared responsibilities*, where people elected for more participative, equal, solidaristic societies based on decentralisation, accountability and transparency, with high levels of social partnership, accompanied by welfare reform, a stronger Union and the reduction of gaps in regional and social inequality.

- *Creative societies*, where people revolted at increasing inequality in the European Union. The botched attempts of governments to respond provoked European parliamentarians to go into exile where they established a forum to voice the grievances of the marginalised. This led to widespread reform across the Union, the encouragement of the social economy, strict environmental standards and the renewal of Europe's political class.

- *Turbulent neighbourhoods*, where a dark picture emerged of rising tensions over terrorism, declining access to natural resources and immigration. Europe responded by setting up a security council, the national state using ever more repressive home affairs policies.

What is most interesting for our purposes is that the scenarios painted depend, in many ways, on critical assumptions about the role of civil society and social capital. *Triumphant markets* and *Turbulent neighbourhoods* are predicated on a relatively weak role for civil society, fragmentation and a preoccupation with individual rather than civic concerns. An important part of *Hundred flowers* is the development of small and informal organisations, local initiatives, neighbourhood solidarity and self-regulation. *Shared responsibilities* is a scenario in which there are high levels of citizen mobilisation, popular participation, social partnership and a sense of global civic society. *Creative societies* achieves not dissimilar outcomes but through a more dynamic and conflictual model of political renewal, built around voluntary social activity and the social economy (up to15 per cent of workers so engaged). One might make the political observation that whereas some American theorists of civic society associate high civic participation with the diminution of the state and the triumph of markets, the *Cellule de Prospective* makes opposite assumptions, associating the liberal *parousia* with a decline in civic activity. Civic participation and the development of the voluntary and community world is linked quite clearly with benign scenarios like *Creative societies* and *Shared responsibilities*.

This book is not an argument for, or for that matter against, convergence or divergence. It does make the point that the pattern of social administration and overall social policy can have a profound effect on how respective voluntary sectors can converge or, more probably, diverge; likewise that governments are important determinants of the size, nature and effectiveness of the voluntary sectors within their domains; and that external factors, ideas and influences can lead to convergence. The patterns that emerge, with their similarities and dissimilarities, will, we hope, serve to challenge the voluntary and community sectors of both parts of Ireland as to the best way to map their future lines of development.

References

Abbott, M. and McDonough, R. (1989). 'Changing Women: Women's Action in Northern Ireland', in E. Deane (ed.), *Lost Horizons, New Horizons: Community Development in Northern Ireland*, Workers' Educational Association, Belfast.

Acheson, N. (1989), *Voluntary Action and the State in Northern Ireland*, Northern Ireland Council for Voluntary Action, Belfast.

Acheson, N. (1995), 'A Partnership of Dilemmas and Contradictions: Unresolved Issues in Government – Voluntary Sector Relations', in N. Acheson and A.P. Williamson (eds), *Voluntary Action and Social Policy in Northern Ireland*, Avebury, Aldershot.

Acheson, N. and A.P. Williamson (1995), 'Voluntary Action in Northern Ireland: some contemporary themes and issues', in N. Acheson and A.P. Williamson (eds), *Voluntary Action and Social Policy in Northern Ireland*, Avebury, Aldershot.

Acheson, N. (2001), 'Service Delivery and Civic Engagement: Disability Organisations in Northern Ireland', *Voluntas: International Journal of Voluntary and Non-Profit Organisations*, 12, 3, 279-293.

Acheson, N. and A.P. Williamson (2001), 'The Ambiguous Role of Welfare Structures in Relation to the Emergence of Activism among Disabled People: Research Evidence from Northern Ireland', in *Disability and Society*, 16, 1, 87-102.

Acheson, N. (2003a), *Voluntary Action, Disability and Citizenship: Evidence from Northern Ireland*, unpublished PhD thesis, University of Ulster.

Acheson, N. (2003b), *Local Area Partnerships, Social Exclusion and the reform of local governance: the case of disability*, University of Ulster, Centre for Voluntary Action Studies.

Ad hoc working group (1998): 'Submission on the white paper on the relationship between the voluntary and community sector and the state to the Department of Social and Family Affairs', unpublished paper by *ad hoc* working group on sector roles, relationships and resources, numerous authors, Dublin.

Advisory Group on Charities and Fundraising Legislation (1996), *Report*, Office of the Minister of State, Dublin.

Alcorn, D. (2003), 'Taxing Times for Northern Ireland Families'. *SCOPE*, June 2003, NICVA, Belfast.

Allen, M. (1998), *The Bitter Word – Ireland's job famine and its aftermath*, Poolbeg Press, Dublin.

Armstrong, J. and A. Kilmurray (1995), 'Voluntary Action, Rural Policy and Social Development', in N. Acheson and A.P. Williamson (eds), *Voluntary Action and Social Policy in Northern Ireland*, Avebury, Aldershot.

Arthur Cox and Centre for Voluntary Action Studies (2003), 'Charity law review: report to the Department of Community, Rural and Gaeltacht Affairs', unpublished, Dublin and Coleraine.

Bacon, D. (1998), *Splendid and Disappointing: Churches, Voluntary Action and Social Capital in Northern Ireland*, Centre for Voluntary Action Studies, University of Ulster, Coleraine.

Bacon, D. (2003), *Communities, Churches and Social Capital in Northern Ireland*, Centre for Voluntary Action Studies, University of Ulster, Coleraine.

Bacon, D. (2004), *Acting in Good Faith: Churches, Change and Regeneration*, Churches' Community Work Alliance, Belfast.

Barrington, R. (1987) (reprinted 2000), *Health, Medicine and Politics in Ireland, 1900-1970*, Institute of Public Administration, Dublin.

Barritt, D.P. and C.F. Carter (1962, 1972), *The Northern Ireland Problem: a study in group relations*, Oxford, Oxford University Press.

Barry, B. (1988), *Lofty ideals, tangible results; interim report by the projects in the Republic of Ireland in the second European programme to combat poverty*, Combat Poverty Agency, Dublin.

Barry, U. (1992), 'Consensus or censorship? Community work in partnership with the state', *Cooptions, Journal of the Community Workers Co-operative*, spring 1992.

Barton, B. (1989), *The Blitz: Belfast in the War Years*, Blackstaff Press, Belfast.

Basini, S. and F. Buckley (1999), 'The meaning of work in the Irish voluntary sector', in B. Harvey and A.P. Williamson (eds): *Researching voluntary action and civil society in Ireland, north and south*, Centre for Voluntary Action Studies, University of Ulster, Coleraine.

Beck, U. (1992): *Risk Society: Towards a New Modernity*. Thousand Oaks, London; Sage Publications, CA.

Billis, D. and H. Glennerster (1998), 'Human Services and the Voluntary Sector: Towards a Theory of Comparative Advantage', *Journal of Social Policy* 27(1).

Birrell, D. and A. Murie (1980), *Policy and Government in Northern Ireland: Lessons of Devolution*, Gill and Macmillan, Dublin.

Birrell, D. and C. Wilson (1993), 'Making Belfast Work: an Evaluation of an Urban Strategy', *Administration*, 41, 1, 44.

Birrell, D. (1995), 'Government, Community Development and the Housing Association Movement', in N. Acheson and A.P. Williamson (eds), *Voluntary Action and Social Policy in Northern Ireland*, Avebury, Aldershot.

Birrell, D. and A.P. Williamson (2001), 'The Voluntary-Community Sector and Political Development in Northern Ireland since 1972', in *Voluntas: International Journal of Voluntary and Non-Profit Organisations*, 12, 3, 205-220.

Bolger, P. (1985): 'A Cooperative Faith', *New Hibernia*, 22 July 1985.

Boyle, R. and M. Butler (2003): *Autonomy vs. accountability – managing government funding of voluntary and community organisations*, Institute of Public Administration, Dublin.

Browne, N. (1986), *Against the tide*, Gill & Macmillan, Dublin.

Brudney, J. and A.P. Williamson (2000), 'Making Government Volunteering Policies More Effective: Research Evidence from Northern Ireland', in *Public Management*, 2, 1, 85-103.

Buckland, P. (1979). *The Factory of Grievances: Devolved Government in Northern Ireland 1921-39*, Gill & Macmillan, Dublin.

Burger, A. and V. Veldheer (2001), 'The Growth of the Non-Profit Sector in the Netherlands', *Non-Profit and Voluntary Sector Quarterly* 30: 2, 221-246.

Burke, C.B. (2001), 'Non-Profit History's New Numbers (and the Need for More)', *Non-Profit and Voluntary Sector Quarterly* 30: 2, 174-203.

Burns, J. (1997): *National database of voluntary sector research*, Department of Library and Information Studies, University College, Dublin.

CAFE (Creative Activity for Everyone) (2000), *Directory of funding and support for community and voluntary work in Ireland*, Dublin, CAFE, 4th edition.

Cairns, E., J. Van Til and A.P. Williamson (2003), 'Social Capital, Collectivism – Individualism and Community Background in Northern Ireland', unpublished report to the Office of the First Minister and the Deputy First Minister and the Head of the Voluntary and Community Unit, Centre for Voluntary Action Studies, University of Ulster, Coleraine.

Cameron, H. (1998), 'The Social Action of the Local Church: Five Congregations in an English City', unpublished PhD thesis, London School of Economics.

Caul, B. and S. Herron (1992), *A Service for People: Origins and Development of the Personal Social Services in Northern Ireland*, December Publications, Belfast.

Caven, N. (1982), *Evaluation Report of the Community Worker Research Project*, Department of Education for Northern Ireland, Bangor.

Cebulla, A. (2000), 'Trusting Community Developers: the Influence of the Form and Origin of Community Groups on Residents' Support in Northern Ireland', *Community Development Journal*, 35, 2, 109-119.

Clarke, J. (1995), *Guide to good employment practice in the community and voluntary sector*, Combat Poverty Agency, Dublin.

Clifford, A. (1991), *The Mater Hospital (Belfast) and the National Health Service: Past, Present and Future*, Athol Books, Belfast.

Coakley, D. (1992), *Doctor Steevens' Hospital – a brief history*, Dr Steevens' Historical Centre, Dublin.

Cochrane, F. and S. Dunn (2002): *People Power? The Role of the Voluntary and Community Sector in the Northern Ireland Conflict*, Cork University Press, Cork.

Coleman, S. (2002), 'Nano Nagle tops greatest Irish poll', *Sunday Tribune*, 22 December 2002.

Coleman, U. (1990), *It's Simon – a history of the Dublin Simon Community*, Glendale, Dublin.

Colgan, A. (2002), *Fostering fundraising in Ireland*, The Ireland Funds, Dublin.

Combat Poverty Agency (1989), *Toward a funding policy for community development*, Combat Poverty Agency, Dublin.

Combat Poverty Agency (1998), *Working for Change: a guide to influencing policy in Ireland*, Combat Poverty Agency, Dublin.

Combined European Bureau for Social Development (2000), *Putting participation at the heart of European integration – contribution to the European white paper on governance*, Combined European Bureau for Social Development, Dublin.

Comhairle (2003), *Annual report, 2001*, Comhairle, Dublin.

Comité des Sages (1996), *For a Europe of civil, social and political rights*, European Commission, Brussels.

Commission of the European Communities (1981), *Final report of the Commission to the Council on the first pilot programme to combat poverty*, European Commission, Brussels.

Commissioners of Charitable Donations & Bequests (1998), *151st annual report*, Government of Ireland, Dublin.

Committee on the Administration of Justice *et al* (1994), *Declaration on Human Rights, the Northern Ireland Conflict and the Peace Process*, Committee for the Administration of Justice, Belfast.

Committee of the Regions (2002), *Opinion on partnerships between local and regional authorities and social economy organisations – contribution to employment, local development and social cohesion*, European Union, Brussels.

Community Development Review Group (1991a), *Community Development in Northern Ireland – Perspectives for the Future*, Community Development Review Group/ Workers Educational Association, Belfast.

Community Development Review Group (1991b), *Funding for Community and Voluntary Groups in Northern Ireland*, Community Development Review Group/ Workers Educational Association, Belfast.

Community Workers Co-operative (1989), *Whose plan? Community groups and the National Development Plan*, Community Workers' Co-operative, Dublin.

Community Workers Co-operative *et al* (ed.) (1990), *Community work in Ireland – trends in the Eighties, options for the Nineties*, Combat Poverty Agency, Dublin.

Community Workers Co-operative (1990), *Participation, not representation – community groups and reformed local government*, Community Workers Co-operative, Dublin.

Community Workers Co-operative (1992), 'Consensus or censorship? Community work in partnership with the state', *Cooptions, Journal of the Community Workers Co-operative*, spring 1992.

Community Workers Co-operative (1996), *The role of community development and partnership in Ireland*, Community Workers Co-operative, Galway.

Conference of Major Religious Superiors (1992), *Power, participation and exclusion*, Conference of Major Religious Superiors, Dublin.

CORI [Conference of Religious in Ireland] (2000), *Prosperity and exclusion – toward a new social contract: Socio-economic review, 2001*, CORI, Dublin.

Conroy, P. and M. McDermott (2001), Volunteering and the organisation, Ralaheen Ltd, for National Committee on Volunteering, Dublin.

Conroy, P. and M. Pierce (2001), *Final report to Dublin inner city partnership on voluntary activity and services for senior citizens in Dublin's North West inner city*, Ralaheen Consultants, Dublin.

Cooney, J. (1999), *John Charles McQuaid – Ruler of Catholic Ireland*, O'Brien Press, Dublin.

Cormacain, R., K. O'Halloran and A.P. Williamson (2001), *Charity Law Matters*, University of Ulster Centre for Voluntary Action Studies, Coleraine.

Cosgrove, S. and N. Ryder (2001), *Community and voluntary involvement in the new local authority structures – survey report for the Local Government Anti-Poverty Learning Network*. Dublin, Combat Poverty Agency.

Costello, Mr Justice D. (1990), *Report of the committee on fundraising activities for charitable and other purposes*, Stationery Office, Dublin.

Courtney, R. (2001), *A Guide for the Journey. A Research Study into Mentoring in Northern Ireland*, Volunteer Development Agency, Belfast.

Cousins, M. (1994), *A guide to legal structures for voluntary and community organisations*, Combat Poverty Agency, Dublin.

Couto, R.A. (2001), 'The Third Sector and Civil Society: The Case of the 'YES' Campaign in Northern Ireland', *Voluntas: International Journal of Voluntary and Non-Profit Organisations*, 12, 3, 221-238.

Craig, S. and K. McKeown (1994), *Progress through partnership – final evaluation report on the PESP pilot initiative on long-term unemployment*, Combat Poverty Agency, Dublin.

Craig, G. and M. Taylor (2002), 'Dangerous Liaisons: Local Government and the Voluntary and Community Sectors', in C. Glendinning, M. Powell and K.

Rummery (eds), *Partnerships, New Labour and the Governance of Welfare*, The Policy Press, Bristol.

Cullen, B. (1990), *Overview of community development initiatives in Ireland*, Howard Foundation.

Cullen, B. (1994), *A programme in the making – a review of the Community Development Programme*, Combat Poverty Agency, Dublin.

Cullen, P. (2002), 'A time bomb for charities', *Irish Times*, 19 July 2002.

Curry, J. ([n.d.]1990), 'Company giving in the Republic of Ireland – an overview', unpublished paper, Dublin.

Curry, J. (1991), 'Company giving in the Republic of Ireland – an overview', in B. Dabson (ed.), *Company giving in Europe*, Directory of Social Change, London.

Curry, J. (2nd edition 1993), *Irish social services*, Institute of Public Administration, Dublin.

Daly, M.E. (1984), *Dublin, the deposed capital – a social and economic history, 1860-1914*, Cork University Press, Cork.

Daly, M.E. (1997), *The buffer state – the historical roots of the Department of the Environment*, Institute of Public Administration, Dublin.

Darby, J. and A.P. Williamson (1978), *Violence and the Social Services in Northern Ireland*, Heinemann, London.

Deakin, N. (1996), *Meeting the challenge of change – voluntary action into the 21st century. Report on the Commission on the Voluntary Sector*, National Council for Voluntary Organisations, London.

Delany, H. (1996), *Equity and the law of trusts in Ireland*, Roundhall, Sweet & Maxwell, Dublin.

Department for Social Development (2003), *Northern Ireland Grants Programme: Funding of the Voluntary Sector, Research Paper 1*, Department for Social Development, Belfast.

Department of Arts, Culture and the Gaeltacht (1997), *Treo 2000 – the Commission to examine the role of the Irish language voluntary organisations*, The Stationery Office, Dublin.

Department of Health (undated), *Enhancing the relationship*, author, Dublin.

Department of Health (undated), *Widening the relationship*, author, Dublin.

Department of Health and Social Services (1993), *Strategy for the Support of the Voluntary Sector and for Community Development in Northern Ireland*, HMSO, Belfast.

Department of Health and Social Services (1998), *Compact Between Government and the Voluntary and Community Sector in Northern Ireland*, DHSS, Belfast.

Department of Health, Social Services and Public Safety (2003), *A Better Future: 50 Years of Child Care in Northern Ireland 1950-2000*, Belfast.

Department of Justice, Equality and Law Reform (2000), *Review of the Gaming and Lotteries Acts, 1956-86, a report of the interdepartmental group*, The Stationery Office, Dublin.

Department of Social Welfare (1991), *Charter for voluntary social services*, unpublished note.

Department of Social Welfare (1997), *Supporting voluntary activity* [green paper], Stationery Office, Dublin.

Department of Social Welfare (2000), *Supporting voluntary activity* [white paper], Stationery Office, Dublin.

Devereux, E. (1992), 'Community development – problems in practice: the Muintir na Tíre experience, 1931-1958', *Administration*, 39, 4.

Dolan, J. (2000), 'General position paper on funding for voluntary physical and sensory disability organisations providing health and personal social services', unpublished paper, Disability Federation of Ireland, Dublin.

Donnelly-Cox, G. (1998), 'A white paper for the Irish voluntary sector – linkages between policy and third sector organisations', paper presented to the CVO 20th anniversary conference, London School of Economics, 17-18 September 1998.

Donnelly-Cox, G. and G. Jaffro (1999), 'The voluntary sector in the Republic of Ireland – into the 21st century', in B. Harvey and A.P. Williamson (eds), *Researching voluntary action and civil society in Ireland, north and south*, Centre for Voluntary Action Studies, University of Ulster, Coleraine.

Donnelly-Cox, G. and A. O'Regan (1999), 'Resourcing organisational growth and development – a typology of third sector service delivery organisations', paper presented to the Third International Research Symposium on Public Management, III, 25 March.

Donnelly-Cox, G., F. Donoghue and R. Taylor (eds) (2001), 'The Third Sector in Ireland', special edition of *Voluntas, International Journal of Voluntary and Non-Profit Organisations*, 12, 3, September.

Donnelly-Cox, G., F. Donoghue and T. Hayes, 'Conceptualising the Third Sector in Ireland, North and South', in *Voluntas, International Journal of Voluntary and Non-Profit Organisations*, 12, 3, 195-204.

Donnelly-Cox, G. (undated), 'The National Action Learning Programme – assessing its value for managers of voluntary organisations', unpublished paper, Dublin.

Donoghue, F. (1998), *Defining the non-profit sector: Ireland*, Working paper 28, National College of Ireland, Dublin and Johns Hopkins University, Baltimore.

Donoghue, F., H. Anheier and L. Salamon (1999), *Uncovering the non-profit sector in Ireland – its economic value and significance*, National College of Ireland, Dublin and Johns Hopkins University, Baltimore.

Donoghue, F., H. Ruddle and R. Mulvihill (2000), 'Warm glow in a cool climate? Philanthropy in Ireland', paper presented to the International Society for Third Sector Research, Dublin University (Trinity College), July 2000.

Donoghue, F. (2001a), 'Volunteering in the Republic of Ireland – history, socio-economic context and meaning', paper presented at *Tipping the Balance* conference held in Cavan, 26-7 November.

Donoghue, F. (2001b), 'Women and volunteering – a feminized space?' paper presented at *The bigger picture – a reflection on volunteering in Ireland in 2001*, International Year of the Volunteer, National University of Ireland, Galway, 7 July.

Donoghue, F. (2001c), 'Changing patterns of civic engagement and community ties in Ireland', paper presented at the conference *The importance of social capital. International lessons for community volunteering in Ireland*, Dublin, 29 March.

Donoghue, F. (2001d), 'Ireland', in *Foundations in Europe*, Directory of Social Change and Charities Aid Foundation, London.

Donoghue, F. (2001e), *Volunteering in Ireland, the 1990s and beyond*, National College of Ireland, Dublin.

Donoghue, F. (2002), *Reflecting the relationship – an exploration of relationships between the former Eastern Health Board and voluntary organisations in the eastern region*, The East Coast, Northern, and South Western Area Health Boards, Dublin.

Donoghue, F. (2003), 'Foundations in Ireland – identity and role', paper presented to the Centre for Non-Profit Management, Dublin University, Trinity College, 5 February.

Donoghue, F. (undated), 'Non-profit organisations as builders of social capital and channels of expression – the case of Ireland', paper presented at the conference *Non profit impact: evidence from around the globe*.

Drucker, P. (1994), 'The Age of Social Transformation, *The Atlantic Monthly*, 274, (5).

Duffy, M.J. (1993), 'The voluntary sector and personal social services', *Administration*, 41, 3.

Duggan, C. and T. Ronayne (1991), *Working partners? The state and the community sector*, Work Research Centre, Dublin.

ECOTEC (2001), *Evaluation of the third system and employment pilot action – final report.* Brussels, European Commission.

Edwards, B., M.W. Foley and M. Diani (eds) (2001), *Beyond Tocqueville: Civil Society and the Social Capital Debate in Comparative Perspective*, University Press of New England, Hanover and London.

Elliott, F.A. (1998), *Curing and Caring: Reflections on fifty years of health and personal social services in Northern Ireland prepared for the fiftieth anniversary of the services by Alan Elliott*, Stationery Office Ltd, Belfast.

Elliott M. (2001), *The Catholics of Ulster*, Allen Lane Press, London.

Enright, S. (2000), 'Women and Catholic life in Dublin, 1766–1852', in J. Kelly and D. Keogh (eds), *History of the Catholic Diocese of Dublin*, Four Courts Press, Dublin.

Etzioni, A. (1993), *The Spirit of Community: Rights, Responsibilities and the Communitarian Agenda*, The Fontana Press, London.

European Commission (2000), *The social situation in the European Union, 2000*, Office of Official Publications, Luxembourg.

European Commission (2001), *European governance – a white paper*, Office of Official Publications, Luxembourg.

Evason, E., J. Darby and M. Pearson (1976), *Social need and social provision in Northern Ireland*, University of Ulster, Coleraine.

Everett, J. (1998), *Community foundations – an introductory report on international experience and Irish potential*, Combat Poverty Agency and Smith Everett & Associates, Dublin.

Fagan, P. (1986), *The second city – a portrait of Dublin, 1700-60*, Branar, Dublin.

Faughnan, P. (1990), 'Voluntary organisations in the social service field', paper presented to the conference *Partners in progress*, Department of Social Welfare, Dublin.

Faughnan, P. and P. Kelleher [n.d. 1993], *The voluntary sector and the state – a study of organisations in one region*, Conference of Major Religious Superiors, Dublin.

Faughnan, P. (1997), 'A healthy voluntary sector – rhetoric or reality?', in J.Robbins (ed.), *Reflections on health – commemorating 50 years of the Department of Health*, Department of Health and Institute of Public Administration, Dublin.

Faughnan, P. and A. O'Donovan (2002), *A changing voluntary sector – working with new minority communities in 2001*, Social Science Research Centre, University College Dublin.

Fay, M.T., M. Morrissey and M. Smyth (1999), *Northern Ireland's Troubles: the Human Costs*, Pluto Press, London.

Fay, R. and N. Crowley (1990), 'Travellers and community work', Community Workers Co-operative *et al* (ed.) (1990), *Community work in Ireland – trends in the Eighties, options for the Nineties*, Combat Poverty Agency, Dublin.

Fitzduff, M. (1995), 'Managing Community Relations and Conflict: Voluntary Organisations and Government and the Search for Peace', in N. Acheson and A.P. Williamson (eds), *Voluntary Action and Social Policy in Northern Ireland*, Avebury, Aldershot.

FLAC (2002), 'Ballymun Law Service – progress made', *FLAC News*, 12, 1.

Flynn, S. and J. O'Connell (1990), 'The Catholic Church and Community Work', in Community Workers Co-operative *et al* (ed.) (1990), *Community work in Ireland – trends in the Eighties, options for the Nineties*, Combat Poverty Agency, Dublin.

Forrest, R. and A. Kearns (2001), 'Social cohesion, social capital and the neighbourhood', *Urban Studies*, November, Vol. 38, No. 12.

Fraser, M. (1993), *John Bull's Other Homes: State Housing and British Policy in Ireland, 1883-1922*, Liverpool University Press, Liverpool.

Gaffikin, F. and M. Morrissey (1990), 'Dependency, Decline and Development: the case of West Belfast, in *Policy and Politics*, 18, 2, 105-117.

Gaffikin, F. and M. Morrissey (1994), *Brownlow Community Trust, Evaluation Report*, Craigavon: Brownlow Community Trust.

Gaskin, G. and J. Davis Smith (1995), *A new civic Europe? The extent and role of volunteering in Europe*, Volunteer Centre, London.

Giddens, A. (1998), *The Third Way: The Renewal of Social Democracy*, Cambridge University Press, Cambridge.

Gidron, B., R. Kramer and L. Salamon (eds) (1992), *Government and the Third Sector: Emerging Relations in Welfare States*, Jossey-Bass, San Francisco.

Goodbody, Economic Consultants (2002), *Mapping state support for the community and voluntary sector*, author, Dublin.

Gormley, J. (1990), *The Green Guide for Ireland*, Wolfhound Press, Dublin.

Gray, A.M. (1993), 'Government and the Administration of Hospital Services in Northern Ireland, 1948-1973: The Northern Ireland Hospitals Authority', unpublished PhD thesis, University of Ulster.

Greeley, A. (1997), 'Coleman Revisited: Religious Structures as a Source of Social Capital', in *American Behavioral Scientist*, 40, 5.

Greer, J. and M. Murray (1999), 'Changing Patterns of Rural Planning and Development in Northern Ireland', in J. Davis (ed.), *Rural Change in Ireland*, Institute of Irish Studies, Queen's University of Belfast, Belfast.

Griffiths, H. (1978), 'Community reaction and voluntary involvement', in J. Darby and A.P. Williamson (eds), *Violence and the Social Services in Northern Ireland*, Heinemann, London.

Griffiths, H., T. Nic Giolla Choille and J. Robinson (1978) *Yesterday's Heritage, Tomorrow's Resource*, New University of Ulster, Coleraine.

Guelke, A. (2003), 'Civil Society in the Northern Ireland Peace Process,' *Voluntas* 14, (1), March, 61-78.

Hall, P.D. (1992), *Essays on Philanthropy, Voluntarism, and Nonprofit Organizations*, Baltimore, Johns Hopkins University Press.

Hamilton, N. (2002), *Church and Community in North Belfast*, available at: http://www.ulst.ac.uk/cvas/pdf/hamilton_book.pdf

Hanon, R. (2003), *First draft comments on the National Action Plan for Social Inclusion, 2003-2005*, European Anti-Poverty Network, Dublin.

Harris, M. (1998), *Organising God's Work: Challenges for Churches and Synagogues*, Macmillan, London.

Harris, M. (1993), *The Catholic Church and the Foundation of the Northern Irish State*, Cork University Press, Cork.

Hardt, M. and A. Negri (2001), *Empire*, Harvard University Press, Cambridge, Mass.

Harvey, B. (1986), 'The emergence of the western problem in the Irish economy in the latter part of the 19th century and its persistence into the 20th century with special reference to the work of the Congested Districts Board for Ireland between 1891 and 1923', unpublished MA thesis, University College, Dublin.

Harvey, B. (1989), *Homelessness in Ireland*, National Campaign for the Homeless, Dublin & Labos Institute, Rome, Italy.

Harvey, B. (1990), *Resource centres in Ireland*, Combat Poverty Agency, Dublin.

Harvey, B. (1992), 'Report to the National Federation of ARCH clubs into problems concerning the recruitment and retaining of helpers', unpublished report, Dublin.

Harvey, B. (1993), *Rights and justice work in Ireland*, Joseph Rowntree Charitable Trust, York.

Harvey, B. and J. Kiernan (1993), *Report on the perceptions of voluntary organisations in Ireland on the impact on funding by the Irish national lottery*, National Council for Voluntary Organisations, London.

Harvey, B. (1994a), *Children and young people in Ireland – a background report*, International Youth Foundation, Battle Creek, Michigan.

Harvey, B. (1994b), *Combating exclusion – lessons from the third EU poverty programme in Ireland*, Combat Poverty Agency, Dublin.

Harvey, B. (1997a), *The Programme for Peace and Reconciliation*, Joseph Rowntree Charitable Trust, York.

Harvey, B. (1997b), *Feasibility study of a newsletter for the voluntary sector in Ireland*, Dublin City University, Dublin.

Harvey, B. (1998), *Working for change – a guide to influencing policy in Ireland*, Combat Poverty Agency, Dublin.

Harvey, B. (1999a), *European manual on the management of the structural funds*, European Anti-Poverty Movement, Brussels.

Harvey, B. (1999b), *Emigration and services for Irish emigrants: toward a new strategic plan*, Irish Episcopal Commission for Emigrants, Dublin.

Harvey, B. (2000), *Policy issues in the work of the Carmichael Centre*, author, Dublin.

Harvey, B. (2002a), *Rights and justice work in Ireland – a new base line*, Joseph Rowntree Charitable Trust, York.

Harvey, B. (2002b), The *role of the community sector in local social partnership*, Area Development Management Ltd, Dublin.

Harvey, B. (2003), *Report on the Programme for Peace and Reconciliation*, Joseph Rowntree Charitable Trust, York, 1997.

Hayes, Á. (2000), 'Housing Co-Operatives in Ireland; the impact of government policy on the development of Irish housing co-operatives and on their contribution to the provision of housing', unpublished thesis, National University of Ireland, Cork.

Hayes, Á., K. O'Halloran and A.P. Williamson (1999), *The Involvement of Volunteers in Two Health and Social Services Trusts in Northern Ireland*, Centre for Voluntary

Action Studies, University of Ulster, Coleraine.

Hayes, M. (1995) *Minority Verdict: Experiences of a Catholic Public Servant*, Blackstaff Press, Belfast.

Hayes, T. (1999), 'Government and the voluntary sector in the Republic of Ireland', in B. Harvey and A.P. Williamson (eds), *Researching voluntary action and civil society in Ireland, north and south*, Centre for Voluntary Action Studies, University of Ulster, Coleraine.

Healy, A. (2002), 'Anti-poverty and equality groups walk out of social partnership meeting', *Irish Times*, 30 April 2002.

Healy, T. (2001), 'Social capital and lifelong learning – some practical issues for public policy', paper presented to Economic and Social Research Council, author, Dublin.

Heath, A.F., R. Breen and C.T. Whelan (eds), (1999), *Ireland, North and South: Perspectives from Social Science*, Proceedings of the British Academy 1998, Oxford University Press, Oxford.

Hedley, R. and J. Davis Smith (eds) (1992), *Volunteering and society – principles and practice*, National Council for Voluntary Organisations, London.

Hennessy, M. (2003), 'Inadequate staffing means a resort to locks and straightjackets', *Irish Times*, 27 January 2003.

Hewitt, C. (1985), 'Leisure and the mentally handicapped – a study of ARCH clubs in Dublin', unpublished MSc thesis, Dublin University, Dublin.

Hinton, N. (1976), *Voluntary Organisations for Offenders in Northern Ireland, a report commissioned by the Northern Ireland Office*, Northern Ireland Office, Belfast.

Hodgett, S.L. (1996), 'The Development of a European Policy Network: A case study of the Northern Ireland Voluntary Sector', unpublished MSSc thesis, Queen's University, Belfast.

Hodgett, S.L. and D. Johnson (2001), 'Troubles, partnerships and possibilities: a study of the Making Belfast Work development initiative in Northern Ireland', *Public Administration and Development*, 21, 4, 321-332.

Holloway, T. and S. Mawhinney (2002), *Providing support, reducing exclusion: the extent, nature and value of volunteer befriending in Northern Ireland*, Praxis Care Group, Belfast.

Holmes, E. (1995), *Housing Associations Accommodating Differences: 25 Years/25 Schemes, 1975-1995*, Northern Ireland Federation of Housing Associations, Belfast.

Home Office (1978), *The Government and the Voluntary Sector: A Consultative Document*, Voluntary Services Unit, London.

Home Office (1990), *Efficiency Scrutiny of Government Funding of the Voluntary Sector: Profiting from Partnership*, HMSO, London.

Home Office (2003), *Charities and Not-for-Profit. A Modern Legal Framework*, HMSO, London.

Hughes, J., C. Knox, M. Murray and J. Greer (1998), *Partnership Governance in Northern Ireland: The Path to Peace*, Oak Tree Press, Dublin.

Hughes, J. and P. Carmichael (1998), 'Building Partnerships in Urban Regeneration: A Case Study from Belfast', *Community Development Journal* 33, 3, 205-225.

Hurd, D. (1985), House of Commons, written parliamentary answer to Mr John Taylor concerning the intention to withdraw government funding from community groups with connections with paramilitary organisations. Hansard, 27 June.

Independent Poverty Action Movement (IPAM) (1987), *To scheme or not to scheme?* author, Dublin.

Irish Marketing Survey (IMS)(1987), *Young Ireland 1987 survey*, IMS and Irish Youth Foundation, Dublin.

Irish Tax Reform Group (1996), *Taxation of corporate charitable donations*, author, Dublin.

Jaffro, G. (1998), 'Insights into the boards of Irish voluntary agencies', *Administration*, 46, 3.

Johnston, S. (1995), 'The European Union and the Development of Supra-National Policy Toward the Voluntary Sector', in N. Acheson and A.P. Williamson (eds), *Voluntary Action and Social Policy in Northern Ireland*, Avebury, Aldershot.

Jordan, A.(1989), 'Voluntary Societies in Victorian and Edwardian Belfast', unpublished PhD thesis, Queen's University, Belfast.

Kearney, J.R. (1995), 'The Development of Government Policy and its Strategy towards the Voluntary and Community Sectors', in N. Acheson and A.P. Williamson (eds), *Voluntary Action and Social Policy in Northern Ireland*, Avebury, Aldershot.

Kearney, J.R. and A.P. Williamson (2001), 'The Voluntary and Community Sector in Northern Ireland: developments since 1995/96', in *Next Steps in Voluntary Action: An analysis of five years of developments in the voluntary sector in England, Northern Ireland, Scotland and Wales*. Centre for Civil Society, London School of Economics and National Council of Voluntary Organisations, London.

Kearney, J.R. (2001a), 'The values and basic principles of volunteering: complacency or caution?' *Voluntary Action*, 3, 3, autumn, Institute for Volunteering Research, London.

Kearney, J.R. (2001b), 'Youth Empowerment through Volunteering: A Case Study of Voluntary Service Belfast's Young Citizens in Action Programme', *Scottish Youth Issues Journal*, 3, University of Strathclyde and Community Learning Scotland, Glasgow.

Kearney, J.R. and W. Osborne (2003), 'Time changes lives – trust changes everything: volunteer work for conflict resolution and reconciliation in Northern Ireland', opening Plenary Paper at the 17th IAVE World Volunteer Conference, Seoul, South Korea. *Voluntary Action*, 5, 2, spring, Institute for Volunteering Research, London.

Kearney, J.R. (2003), 'Bowling along together', *Scope*, April. NICVA, Belfast.

Kelleher, P. and M. Whelan (1992), *Dublin Communities in Action*, Combat Poverty Agency, Dublin.

Kelleher Associates, *Framing the future* (2001), National Women's Council of Ireland, Dublin.

Kelly, J. and D. Keogh (eds) (2000), *History of the Catholic Archdiocese of Dublin*, Four Courts Press, Dublin.

Kelly, S. (2002), 'One in three have got the message', *Irish Times supplement*, 23 February 2002.

Kendall, J. and M. Knapp (1996), *The Voluntary Sector in the United Kingdom*, Manchester University Press, Manchester.

Kenna, P. (2000), 'Which way for voluntary housing associations in Ireland?' *Administration*, 48, 3, autumn.

Kerins, A. (1991), 'The jobs forum – its eventual arrival?' *Administration*, 39, 3.

Kerr, D. (2000), *Dublin's forgotten archbishop – Daniel Murray, 1768-1852*, in J. Kelly and D. Keogh (eds), *History of the Catholic Archdiocese of Dublin*, Four Courts Press, Dublin.

Kiernan, J. and B. Harvey (1996), *Funding Europe's solidarity*, L.P. Doyle & Associates.

Kiernan, J. (2000), *Painting our picture – a guide to the Disability Federation of Ireland affiliated organisations for people with physical or sensory disabilities or with mental health problems*, Disability Federation of Ireland, Dublin.

Kilmurray, A. (2000), 'The Seventies', in *The Times that Were In It*, Northern Ireland Council for Voluntary Action, Belfast.

Kilmurray, E. (1989), *Fight, starve or emigrate*, The Larkin Centre for the Unemployed, Dublin.

Knox, C., 'The emergence of power sharing in Northern Ireland: lessons from local government', *Journal of Conflict Studies*, 16, 1, 7-29.

Knox, C., 'The European model of service delivery: a partnership approach in Northern Ireland', *Public Administration and Development*, 18, 2, 151-168.

Knox, C., 'Northern Ireland: at the crossroads of political and administrative reform', *Governance: An International Journal of Policy and Administration*, 12, 3, 311-328.

Knox, C. (2003), *Resourcing the Voluntary and Community Sector*. Infrastructure Working Group. A Scoping Paper, 30 June 2003 on www.taskforcevcsni.gov.uk

Langhammer M. (2003), 'Cutting with the grain: policy and the Protestant community: What is to be done?' paper to the Secretary of State for Northern Ireland, Mr Paul Murphy and the Northern Ireland Office team.

Larragy, J. (2001), *International approaches to volunteering*, Centre for Applied Social Studies, Maynooth.

Law Society (2002), *Charity law – the case for reform*, The Law Society of Ireland, Dublin.

Lawrence, R.J. (1965), *The Government of Northern Ireland: Public Finance and Public Services, 1921-1964*, Oxford University Press, Oxford.

Leadbetter, C. (1997), *The Rise of the Social Entrepreneur*, Demos, London.

Lee, J.J., (1989), *Ireland 1912-85 – Politics and Society*, Cambridge University Press, Cambridge.

Leonard, L. (1992), 'Voluntary-statutory partnership in the housing area – the experience of the Simon Community', Community Workers Co-operative (1992), *Cooptions, Journal of the Community Workers Co-operative*, spring 1992.

Leong, Fee Ching (2001), *A unique way of sharing: the participation of black and minority ethnic people in volunteering and community activity in Northern Ireland*, Department for Social Development & Volunteer Development Agency, Belfast.

Lewis, J. (1995), *The Voluntary Sector, the State and Social Work in Britain: the Charity Organisation Society/ Family Welfare Association since 1869*, Edward Elgar Publishing, Aldershot.

Lewis, J. (1996), 'What does Contracting do to Voluntary Agencies?' in D. Billis and M. Harris (eds), *Voluntary Agencies: Challenges of Organisation and Management*, Macmillan Press, Basingstoke and London.

Lewis, J. (1999), 'Reviewing the Relationship between the Voluntary Sector and the State in Britain in the 1990s', *Voluntas* 10, 3, 255-270.

Linehan, D. (1984), *Community Involvement in Mayfield*, Turoe Press, Dublin.

Local and Regional Development Partnership (LRDP) (2002), *Evaluation of local social capital project*, European Commission, Brussels.

Looney, F. (2003), 'Working-Class Hero', *Sunday Tribune*, 3 August.

LRDP (1999), *Evaluation of the International Fund for Ireland's Communities in Action Programme*, Local and Regional Development Partnership, London and Armagh.

Luddy, M. (1995), *Women and Philanthropy in Nineteenth-Century Ireland*, Cambridge University Press, Cambridge.

Luddy, M. (1996), 'Women and Philanthropy in Nineteenth-Century Ireland', *Voluntas: International Journal of Voluntary and Non-Profit Organisations*, 7, 4, 350-364.

Lundy, L. and R. Glenn (1999), *Advice Services in Northern Ireland*, Research Report to the Lord Chancellor's Department, Belfast.

Lyner, O. (2003), 'Are core costs on Taskforce agenda?' *SCOPE*, May 2003, NICVA, Belfast.

McCall, C. and A.P. Williamson (2000), 'Fledging Social Partnership in the Irish Border Region: European Union 'Community Initiatives' and the voluntary sector', *Policy and Politics* 28, 3, 397-410.

McCall, C. and A.P. Williamson (2001), 'Governance and Democracy in Northern Ireland: The Role of the Voluntary and Community Sector after the Agreement', *Governance*, 14, 3, 363-385.

McCann, E. (1974), *War in an Irish Town*, Penguin, Harmondsworth.

McCarron, J.J. (2003), *Squaring the Circle: Defining Networks in the Voluntary and Community Sector*, Northern Ireland Council for Voluntary Action, Belfast.

McCashin, A., E. O'Sullivan and C. Brennan (2002), 'The National Economic and Social Forum – social partnership and social policy formulation in the Republic of Ireland', *Policy & Politics*, 30, 2.

McConkey, R. and N. Donlon [n.d.], 'Volunteers and mental handicap', *St Michael's House Research Bulletin*.

McCready, S. (2001), *Empowering people – community development and conflict, 1969-1999*, Centre for Voluntary Action Studies, University of Ulster and The Stationery Office, Belfast.

McCreary, A. (1999), *Making a Difference: The Story of Ulster Garden Villages, Ltd*, Ulster Garden Villages, Belfast.

McDonough, R. (1995), 'Europe's Third Anti-Poverty Programme in Northern Ireland: the Experience of Brownlow Community Trust', in J. Kiernan and B. Harvey (eds), *Putting Poverty 3 into Policy: Conference Proceedings on the European Union Programme to Foster the Social and Economic Integration of the Least Privileged Groups*, Department of Social Welfare, Dublin, and the European Commission, Brussels.

McDowell, E. (2002), 'Acting in Good Faith', in *SCOPE*, November, Northern Ireland Council for Voluntary Action, Belfast.

McGarry, J. (ed.) (2001), *Northern Ireland and the Divided World: Post-Agreement Northern Ireland in Comparative Perspective*, Oxford University Press, Oxford.

McGinley, A. (1988), 'District councils and community services: who really cares?' in A. Kilmurray, F. McCartney, N. Fitzduff and S. Burnside (eds), *Lost Horizons, New Horizons*, Workers' Educational Association, Belfast.

Mackay, C., H. Dawson and A.P. Williamson (1998), *Training and Development Needs of Board Members of Housing Associations*, Centre for Voluntary Action Studies, University of Ulster.

McKevitt, D. (1999), 'Position paper on learning disability strategy for Mid-Western Health Board,' unpublished paper, Mid-Western Health Board, Limerick.

McKevitt, D. [n.d.], *Mid-Western Health Board – stakeholder analysis*, unpublished paper, Mid-Western Health Board, Limerick.

McLachlan, P. (1997), 'The 1974 Corrymeela Conference and its Origins', in *Celebrating 21 Years of Voluntary Housing in Northern Ireland, 1976-1997*, Northern Ireland Federation of Housing Associations, Belfast.

McMahon, D. (2000), 'John Charles McQuaid, Archbishop of Dublin, 1940-72', in J. Kelly and D. Keogh (eds), *History of the Catholic Diocese of Dublin*, Four Courts Press, Dublin.

McManus, R. (1996): 'Public Utility Societies, Dublin Corporation and the Development of Dublin, 1920-1940', *Irish Geography*, 29, 1, 27-37.

McManus, R. (1998), 'The Dundalk Premier Public Utility Society', *Irish Geography*, 31, 2, 75-87.

McManus, R. (1999), 'The "Building Parson". The role of Rev. David Hall in the solution of Ireland's early twentieth-century housing problems', *Irish Geography*, 32, 2, 87-98.

McNeill M. (1960 and 1988), *The Life and Times of Mary Ann McCracken 1770-1866: A Belfast Panorama*, The Blackstaff Press, Belfast.

Mageean, P. and M. O'Brien (1999), 'From the Margins to the Mainstream: Human Rights and the Good Friday Agreement', *Fordham International Law Journal*, 22, 1499-1538.

Manley, D. (1991), 'Corporate survey on Charitable Donations', D. Manley and Associates for Prospective United Way of Ireland, unpublished paper.

Miley, J. (1994), *A Voice for the country: Fifty years of Macra na Feirme*, Macra na Feirme, Dublin.

Mjoset, L. (1992), *The Irish economy in comparative institutional perspective*, National Economic and Social Council, report 93, Dublin.

Morison, J. (2001), 'Democracy, Governance and Governability: The Role of the Voluntary Sector in the Democratic Renewal of Northern Ireland', in C.J. Harvey (ed.) *Human Rights, Equality and Democratic Renewal in Northern Ireland*, Hart Publishing, Oxford.

Morrissey, M. (2003), Briefing Paper 3 prepared for the Task Force on Resourcing the Voluntary and Community Sector's Working Group on Sustainability, available on Task Force's website: www.taskforcevcsni.gov.uk

Morrow, D. (1995), 'The Protestant Churches and Social Welfare: Voluntary Action and Government Support', in N. Acheson and A.P. Williamson (eds), *Voluntary Action and Social Policy in Northern Ireland*, Avebury, Aldershot.

Mullins, D., M. Lee Rhodes and A.P. Williamson (2003), *Non-Profit Housing Organisations in Ireland, North and South: Changing Forms and Challenging Futures*, Northern Ireland Housing Executive, Belfast.

Mullins D., M. Lee Rhodes and A.P. Williamson (2001), 'Organizational Fields and Third Sector Housing in Ireland, North and South', in *Voluntas: International Journal of Voluntary and Non-Profit Organisations*, 12,3, 257-278.

Mulvey, C. (1992), *Changing the View*, Allen Lane Foundation, London.

Mulvihill, R. (1993), *Voluntary statutory partnership in community care for the elderly*, National Council for the Elderly, report 25, Dublin.

Murray, D. (1998), *A Register of Cross-Border Links in Ireland*, Centre for Peace and Development Studies, University of Limerick.

Murray, M.R and J.V. Greer (1992), 'Rural Development in Northern Ireland', *Journal of Rural Studies*, 8, 2, 173-184.

National Committee on Volunteering (2002), *Tipping the balance – report and recommendations to government on supporting and developing volunteering in Ireland*, author, Dublin.

National Economic and Social Council (NESF) (2003), *The Policy Implications of Social Capital*, NECS, Dublin.

National Youth Council of Ireland (2001), *Young people and volunteering*, National Committee on Volunteering, Dublin.

Nic Giolla Choille, T. (1982), *Wexford Family Centre*, Irish Society for the Prevention of Cruelty to Children, Dublin.

Nic Giolla Choille, T. (2002), 'Update – the White Paper on Voluntary Activity', *News & Views*, Community Workers Co-operative, Galway.

NICVA (Northern Ireland Council for Voluntary Action)(2002), *State of the Sector III*, Northern Ireland Council for Voluntary Action, Belfast.

O'Carroll, C. (2000), 'The pastoral politics of Paul Cullen', in J. Kelly and D. Keogh (eds), *History of the Catholic Archdiocese of Dublin*, Four Courts Press, Dublin.

Ó Cinnéide, S. (1999), 'Local development agencies, in T. Fahey (ed.), *Social housing in Ireland – a study of success, failure and lessons learned*, Combat Poverty Agency, Katharine Howard Foundation and Oak Tree Press, Dublin.

Ó Cinnéide, S. (2000), 'The 1949 white paper and the foundations of social welfare', in A. Lavan (ed.), *Fifty Years of Social Welfare Policy*, Department of Social, Community and Family Affairs, Dublin.

O'Clery, C. (2003), 'The Silent Giver', *Irish Times*, 4 October.

O'Connor, J. and H. Ruddle (1993), *Reaching out – volunteering and charitable giving in Ireland*, National College of Industrial Relations, Dublin.

O'Donnell, R. and D. Thomas (1998), 'Partnership and policy-making', in S. Healy and B. Reynolds (eds), *Social policy in Ireland – principles, practice and problems*, Oak Tree Press, Dublin.

O'Donnell, S., B. Trench and K. Ennals (1998), *Weak connections – final report of the research project 'the voluntary sector in the information age'*, Dublin City University, Dublin.

O'Donnell, S. and B. Trench (1999), 'Voluntary and community organisations in Ireland's Information Society', in B. Harvey and A.P. Williamson (eds), *Researching voluntary action and civil society in Ireland, North and South*, Centre for Voluntary Action Studies, University of Ulster, Coleraine.

O'Donnell, S. (2002), *Toward an Inclusive Information Society in Europe*, Models Research, Dublin.

O'Donovan, O. and T. Varley (1992), *Paid employment in the voluntary sector*, Combat Poverty Agency, Dublin.

Offer, J. (1995), 'Voluntary Action and Community Care', in N. Acheson and A.P. Williamson (eds), *Social Policy and Voluntary Action in Northern Ireland*, Avebury, Aldershot.

O'Ferrall, F. (2000), *Citizenship and Public Service: Voluntary and Statutory Relationships in Irish Healthcare*, The Adelaide Hospital Society, Dublin, in association with Dundalgan Press, Dundalk.

O'Ferrall, F. (2001), 'Civic Republicanism, citizenship and voluntary action', *The Republic, a journal of contemporary and historical debate*, 2 (spring/summer).

O'Ferrall, F. (2003), 'People Centredness: the contribution of community and voluntary organisations to healthcare', *Studies*, 92, 367, 366-376.

O'Halloran, K. (2000), *Charity Law*, Round Hall Sweet & Maxwell, Dublin.

O'Halloran, K. and R. Cormacain (2001), *Charity Law in Northern Ireland*, Round Hall Sweet & Maxwell, Dublin.

O'Halloran, K. (2002a), 'Charity Law Review and Civil Society: Paving the Way from Alienation to Social Inclusion in Northern Ireland; the resonance with experience in Australia', The Centre of Philanthropy and Non-Profit Studies, QUT, working papers series, No. 11, Brisbane, Australia.

O'Halloran, K. (2002b), 'Charity Law Review as an Opportunity to Consolidate Civil Society: A Case Study of Charity Law and the Social Inclusion Agenda in the Two Jurisdictions of Ireland', *Third Sector Review (Australia & New Zealand)*, 8, 1, 133-152.

Oliver, Q. (2000), 'For Richer or Poorer: the Social Impact [of the European Union]', in D. Kennedy, *Living with the European Union: the Northern Ireland Experience*, Macmillan, London.

O'Mahony, A. (1985), *Social need and the provision of services in rural Ireland*, An Foras Talúntais, Dublin.

O'Regan, A. (2001), 'Contexts and Constraints for NPOs: The Case of Co-operation Ireland', *Voluntas: International Journal of Voluntary and Non-Profit Organisations*, 12, 3, 239-256.

Osborne, S.P., R.S. Beattie and A.P. Williamson (2002), *Community Involvement in Rural Regeneration Partnerships in the United Kingdom: Evidence from England, Northern Ireland and Scotland*, The Policy Press, London.

O'Sullivan, E. (1996), 'Homelessness and social policy in the Republic of Ireland', Occasional paper, 5, Department of Social Studies, University of Dublin (Trinity College), Dublin.

O'Sullivan, E. (1999), *European observatory – national report for Ireland*, FEANTSA, Brussels.

O'Sullivan, E. (1999/2000), 'Voluntary agencies in Ireland – what future role? *Administration*, 47, 4.

O'Sullivan, T. (1994), 'The voluntary-statutory relationship in the health services', *Administration*, 42, 1.

Pearson, I. (2003), Speech by Ian Pearson MP at the Social Economy Conference, 22 January 2003, Belfast.

Peillon, M. (2001), *Welfare in Ireland – actors, resources and strategies*, Praeger, Connecticut and London.

Plowden, W. (2001), *Next Steps in Voluntary Action*, National Council for Voluntary Organisations and Centre for Civil Society, London School of Economics, London.

Policy Research Centre, *Volunteering in Ireland – 1990s and beyond*, National Committee on Volunteering, Dublin.

Powell, F. (1992), *The Politics of Irish Social Policy, 1600-1990*, Edwin Mellen Press, Lampeter.

Powell, F. and D. Guerin (1997), *Civil society and social policy*, A&A Farmar, Dublin.

Powell, F. and D. Guerin (1999), 'Civil society and active citizenship – the role of the voluntary sector', in B. Harvey and A.P. Williamson (eds), *Researching voluntary action and civil society in Ireland, north and south*, Centre for Voluntary Action Studies, University of Ulster, Coleraine.

Powell, F. (2001), *The Politics of Social Work*, Sage, London and New Delhi.

Powell, F. and M. Geoghegan (2004), *The Politics of Community Development*, A. & A. Farmar, Dublin.

Praxis Care Group (2002), *Providing Support, Reducing Exclusion: The Extent, Nature and Volunteer Befriending in Northern Ireland*, Praxis Care Group, Belfast.

Prochaska, F. (1999), 'Swimming into the mouth of the leviathan – the King's Fund and the Voluntary Tradition', in R. Whelan (1999), *Involuntary action – how voluntary is the voluntary sector?* Institute of Economic Affairs, London.

Purcell, M. (1991), *The Catholic Social Service Conference – 50 years targeting care and justice*, author, Dublin.

Putnam, R.D. with R. Leonardi and R. Nanetti (1993), *Making Democracy Work: Civic Traditions in Modern Italy*, Princeton University Press, Princeton.

Putnam, R.D. (2001), *Bowling Alone: The Collapse and Revival of American Community*, Simon & Schuster, New York and London.

Rafferty, M. (1992), 'The colour of the cat', in Community Workers Co-operative *Co-options, Journal of the Community Workers Co-operative*, spring.

Rafter, K. (1992), *Charitable organisations and value added tax – a study of the charitable sector in Ireland with emphasis on value added tax*, Irish Charities Tax Reform Group, Dublin.

Raftery, M. and E. O'Sullivan (1999), *Suffer the little children*, New Island Books, Dublin.

Raftery, M. (2003), 'Restoring dignity to the Magdalens', *Irish Times*, 21 August.

Ralaheen Research & Design, *Volunteering and the organisation*, National Committee on Volunteering, Dublin.

Randon, A. and 6, Perri (1992), *Liberty, charity and politics – cross-national research on campaigning/policy advocacy by non-profit organisations: findings from 24 countries*, National Council for Voluntary Organisations, London.

Registrar of Friendly Societies (1999), *Report, 1999*, Stationery Office, Dublin.

Ronayne, T. (1992), *Participation in youth service provision during the transition from school to the labour market – gaps in provision and policy issues arising*, Work Research Centre, Dublin.

Rottman, D.B. (1999), 'Problems of, and Prospects for: Comparing the Two Irelands', in A.F. Heath, R. Breen and C.T. Whelan (eds) (1999), *Ireland, North and South: Perspectives from Social Science*, Proceedings of the British Academy 1998, Oxford University Press, Oxford.

Rourke, S. (1989), 'Funding options and opportunities in the Republic of Ireland', unpublished report for the Calouste Gulbenkian Foundation.

Ruane, J. and J. Todd (1996), *The Dynamics of Conflict in Northern Ireland: Power, Conflict and Emancipation*, Cambridge University Press, Cambridge.

Ruddle, H. and J. O'Connor (1992), *A model of managed co-operation*, Co-operation Ireland, Belfast and Irish Peace Institute, Limerick.

Ruddle, H. and J. O'Connor (1992), *Reaching Out: Charitable Giving and Volunteering in the Republic of Ireland*, Policy Research Centre, National College of Ireland, Dublin.

Ruddle, H. and F. Donoghue (1995), *The organisation of volunteering – a study of Irish voluntary organisations in the social welfare area*, Policy Research Centre, National College of Ireland, Dublin.

Ruddle, H. and R. Mulvihill (1999), *Reaching Out: Charitable Giving and Volunteering in the Republic of Ireland, the 1997/98 survey*, Policy Research Centre, National College of Ireland, Dublin.

Sabel, C. (1996), *Ireland – local partnerships and social innovation*, Organisation for Economic Co-operation & Development, Paris.

Salamon, L. (1987), 'Partners in Public Service: The Scope and Theory of Government Non-Profit Relations', in W.W. Powell (ed.), *The Non-Profit Sector: A Research Handbook*, Yale University Press, New Haven and London.

Salamon, L. and H. Anheier (1994), *The emerging sector revisited – an overview*, Johns Hopkins University Press, Baltimore.

Salamon, L. and H. Anheier (1998a), *The emerging sector revisited – initial estimates*, Johns Hopkins University Press, Baltimore.

Salamon, L., H. Anheier and Associates (1998b), 'Social Origins of Civil Society: Explaining the Non-Profit Sector Cross-Nationally', in *Voluntas*, 9, 3, 213-248.

Sarkis, A. (2001), 'Volunteering Matters – or Does It? The Role of Voluntary Action in the Twenty-First Century', a paper presented to the Church Urban Fund, January.

Scottish Council for Voluntary Organisations (1997), *[The Kemp] Commission on the Future of the Voluntary Sector in Scotland*, SCVO.

Sheriff, A. (1999), 'International aid agencies and complex humanitarian emergencies', in B. Harvey and A.P. Williamson (eds), *Researching voluntary action and civil society in Ireland, North and South*, Centre for Voluntary Action Studies, University of Ulster, Coleraine.

Simon Community (2003), 'Social partnership delivers nothing on homelessness', *Simon News*, 5, March.

Simpson, J. (1995), 'Government Financial Support for Voluntary Organisations: a preliminary analysis and discussion', in N. Acheson and A.P. Williamson (eds), *Social Policy and Voluntary Action in Northern Ireland*, Avebury, Aldershot.

Slattery, L. (2003), 'Charities lack investment policy', *Irish Times*, 7 August.

Smyth, M. (1995), 'Women, Peace, Community Relations and Voluntary Action', in N. Acheson and A.P. Williamson (eds), *Social Policy and Voluntary Action in Northern Ireland*, Avebury, Aldershot.

Social Services Inspectorate (1998), *Adding Value: The Contribution of Voluntary Organisations to Health and Social Welfare*, Department of Health and Social Services, Belfast.

Society of Friends (1852), Transactions of the Central Relief Committee of the Society of Friends during the Famine in Ireland, in 1846 and 1847, Dublin, Hodges and Smith. (Available at: http://www.quinnipiac.edu/other/abl/etext/irish/transactions/transactions.html)

Spence, R.B. (1995), 'The Northern Ireland Approach to Partnership and Local Community Development', in J. Kiernan and B. Harvey (eds), *Putting Poverty 3 into Policy: Conference Proceedings on the European Union Programme to Foster the Social and Economic Integration of the least Privileged Groups*, Department of Social Welfare, Dublin, and the European Commission, Brussels.

Sproule, J. (2001), 'Voluntary Action, Health & Social Well-Being in the Derry City Council Area', unpublished PhD thesis, University of Ulster.

Stoker, G. (2000), Introduction, in G. Stoker (ed.) *The New Politics of British Governance*, Macmillan, Basingstoke.

Strain, R.W.M. (1961), *Belfast and its Charitable Society*, Oxford, Oxford University Press.

Stutt, C., B. Murtagh and M. Campbell (2001), *The Social Economy in Northern Ireland*, Colin Stutt Consulting, Helen's Bay.

Taylor, M., P. Hoggett and J. Langon (1994), 'Independent Organisations in Community Care', in S. Saxon-Harrold and J. Kendall (eds), *Researching the Voluntary Sector (2nd edition)*, Charities Aid Foundation, London.

Taylor, M. and P. Hoggett (1994), 'Quasi-Markets and the Transformation of the Independent Sector', in W. Bartlett, C. Propper, D. Wilson and J. Le Grand (eds), *Quasi-Markets and the Welfare State*, SAUS Publications, Bristol.

Taylor, M. (2000), *Changing political culture – first thoughts on political exclusion*, Local Government Association, London.

Tarrow, S. (1996), 'Making Social Science Work Across Time and Space: A Critical Reflection on Robert Putnam's *Making Democracy Work*', *American Political Science Review* 90, 389-397.

Tobin, P. (1990), 'Women in community work', Community Workers Co-operative *et al* (ed.), *Community work in Ireland – Trends in the Eighties, Options for the Nineties*, Combat Poverty Agency, Dublin.

Toolan, D. (1992), 'Divide and conquer – the state, voluntary organisations and people with disabilities', in Community Workers Co-operative, *Co-options, Journal of the Community Workers Co-operative*, spring.

Tubridy, J. and A. Colgan (1999), *White paper on voluntary activity – summary of submissions*, Department of Social, Community and Family Affairs, Dublin.

Tucker, V. (1982), *Co-operative Housing in Ireland*, Bank of Ireland, Centre for Co-operative Studies, National University of Ireland, Cork.

Tweedy, H. (1992), *A link in the chain*, Attic Press, Dublin.

Unique Perspectives (2002), *Case studies of the experiences of voluntary groups of developing accredited training for volunteers*, Dublin, National Committee on Volunteering/Comhairle.

Van Til, J. and A.P. Williamson (2001), 'Voluntary Action', *International Encyclopaedia of Social and Behavioural Sciences*, Elsevier Science/ Pergamon Press.

Varshney, A. (1998), *Civic life and ethnic conflict: Hindus and Muslims in India*. Yale University Press.

Volunteer Development Agency (1995), *Volunteering in Northern Ireland*, Volunteer Development Agency, Belfast.

Volunteer Development Agency (2001), *Volunteering in Northern Ireland 2001*, Volunteer Development Agency, Belfast.

Volunteer Development Agency (2003), *Committee Matters: An assessment of the characteristics, training needs and governance role of voluntary management committees in Northern Ireland*. Volunteer Development Agency, Belfast.

Walsh, J., S. Craig and D. McCafferty (1998), *Local partnerships for social inclusion?* Combat Poverty Agency and Oak Tree Press, Dublin.

Whelan, R. (1999), *Involuntary action – how voluntary is the voluntary sector?* Institute of Economic Affairs, London.

Whyte, J.H. (1971), *Church and state in modern Ireland*. Dublin.

Whyte, G. (2002), *Social inclusion and the legal system – public interest law in Ireland*, Institute of Public Administration, Dublin.

Williams, G.D. (1902), *Dublin charities: a handbook including organisations in, or applicable to, Ireland*, with introduction by G.D. Williams, compiled and published by the Association of Charities, Dublin.

Williams, J. (1999), *Volunteering in Museums in Northern Ireland: Practice and Potential*, Centre for Voluntary Action Studies, University of Ulster, Coleraine.

Williamson, A.P. (1992a), 'Enterprise, Industrial Development and Social Planning: Quakers and the emergence of the textile industry in Ireland', in *Planning Perspectives*, 7, 303-328.

Williamson, A.P. (1992b), 'The voluntary sector's central role in managing societal instability in Northern Ireland', in L. Salamon, R. Kramer and B. Gidron, *Government and the Non-Profit Sector: Emerging Relationships in Welfare States*, Jossey Bass Publishers, San Francisco.

Williamson, A.P. (ed.) (1995), *Beyond Violence: the capacity of voluntary action to contribute to rebuilding civil society in Northern Ireland*, Community Relations Commission, Belfast.

Williamson, A.P. (1995), 'The Origins of Voluntary Action in Belfast', in N. Acheson and A.P. Williamson (eds), *Social Policy and Voluntary Action in Northern Ireland*, Aldershot, Avebury.

Williamson, A.P. (1998), 'The Third Sector in Ireland's Two Jurisdictions: toward a policy analysis', paper given at the Third International Conference of the International Society for Third Sector Research, University of Geneva, Switzerland, July.

Williamson, A.P. (1999a), 'Development partnerships in Ireland, north and south – the European Union's role in shaping policy in Ireland's two jurisdictions', in B. Harvey and A.P. Williamson (eds), *Researching voluntary action and civil society in Ireland, North and South*, Centre for Voluntary Action Studies, University of Ulster, Coleraine.

Williamson, A.P. (1999b), 'New Models of Governance in Ireland: the European Union and the Involvement of the Voluntary and Community Sector in Multi-Level Development Partnerships in the 1990s', in D. Robinson (ed.), *Partnership: From Practice to Theory*, No.2, Institute of Policy Studies, Victoria University, Wellington, New Zealand.

Williamson, A.P. (2000), 'Housing Associations in the Republic of Ireland: Can they respond to the government's challenge for major expansion? *Housing Studies*, 15, 4, July, 639-650.

Williamson, A.P. and C. McCall (2000), 'Voluntary Action and European Union Social Partnership in Ireland, North and South', *International Journal of Public-Private Partnerships* 2, 3, 417-434.

Williamson, A.P., D. Scott and P. Halfpenny (2000), 'Rebuilding Civil Society in Northern Ireland: The community and voluntary sector's contribution to the European Union Peace and Reconciliation District Partnership Programme', *Policy and Politics*, 28, 1, 49-66.

Williamson, A.P. (2003), 'The co-operative housing movement in Ireland', paper presented at the International Congress of the Research Committee of the International Co-operative Alliance, Mapping co-operative studies in the new millennium, University of Victoria, British Columbia, 29 May 2003.

Wilson, Robin (ed.) (1999), *No frontiers – north-south integration in Ireland* (report 11), Democratic Dialogue, Belfast. Wolfenden, J., Baron (1978), *The Future of Voluntary Organisations: the Report of the Wolfenden Committee*, Croom Helm, London.

Worrall, J. (2003), 'Second hand, first choice', *Consumer Choice*, April.

Index